Computational Legal Studies

ELGAR STUDIES IN LEGAL RESEARCH METHODS

This highly topical series provides a focus on the role of research methods in current legal scholarship. It explores the diverse range of approaches from within the legal discipline as well as the growing role of interdisciplinary methods, and highlights the impact of different research methods on our understanding of the law. The series offers a place both for studies which are defined by their choice of method, and also for discursive work analysing the nuanced insights brought to light by different methodological approaches.

Computational Legal Studies

The Promise and Challenge of Data-Driven Research

Edited by

Ryan Whalen

Faculty of Law, National University of Singapore

ELGAR STUDIES IN LEGAL RESEARCH METHODS

 Edward Elgar PUBLISHING

Cheltenham, UK • Northampton, MA, USA

Published by
Edward Elgar Publishing Limited
The Lypiatts
15 Lansdown Road
Cheltenham
Glos GL50 2JA
UK

Edward Elgar Publishing, Inc.
William Pratt House
9 Dewey Court
Northampton
Massachusetts 01060
USA

A catalogue record for this book
is available from the British Library

Library of Congress Control Number: 2020942939

This book is available electronically in the **Elgar**online
Law subject collection
http://dx.doi.org/10.4337/9781788977456

ISBN 978 1 78897 744 9 (cased)
ISBN 978 1 78897 745 6 (eBook)

Typeset by Servis Filmsetting Ltd, Stockport, Cheshire

Printed and bound in Great Britain by TJ International Ltd, Padstow, Cornwall

Contents

Contributors

Charlotte S. Alexander, Connie D. and Ken McDaniel WomenLead Chair, Associate Professor of Law and Analytics, Institute for Insight, J. Mack Robinson College of Business, Georgia State University and Director, Legal Analytics Lab, USA.

Wolfgang Alschner, Associate Professor, Common Law Section, University of Ottawa, Canada.

Elliott Ash, ETH Zurich, Switzerland.

Kevin D. Ashley, Professor of Law and Intelligent Systems, University of Pittsburgh, USA.

Janis Beckedorf, Bucerius Law School, Hamburg, Germany and Faculty of Law, Heidelberg University, Germany.

Daniel Behn, Senior Lecturer in Law, Queen Mary University of London and Associate Professor, PluriCourts Centre of Excellence, Faculty of Law, University of Oslo, Norway.

Daniel L. Chen, Toulouse School of Economics, France.

Magnus Esmark, PhD Fellow, iCourts – Centre of Excellence for International Courts, Faculty of Law, University of Copenhagen, Denmark.

Mohammad Javad Feizollahi, Assistant Professor of Business Analytics, Institute for Insight, J. Mack Robinson College of Business, Georgia State University and Faculty Affiliate, Legal Analytics Lab, USA.

Paul Gowder, Professor of Law, Northwestern University, Chicago, USA.

Dirk Hartung, Bucerius Law School, Hamburg, Germany.

Malcolm Langford, Professor, Faculty of Law, University of Oslo and Co-Director, Centre on Law and Social Transformation, University of Bergen, Norway and CMI.

Runar Lie, Doctoral Research Fellow, PluriCourts Centre of Excellence and Forum for Law and Social Science, Faculty of Law, University of Oslo, Norway.

John Zhuang Liu, Assistant Professor, School of Management and Economics, Chinese University of Hong Kong, Shenzhen, People's Republic of China.

Michael A. Livermore, Professor of Law, University of Virginia School of Law, USA.

Nischal Mainali, NYU Abu Dhabi, United Arab Emirates.

Liam Meier, NYU Abu Dhabi, United Arab Emirates.

Henrik Palmer Olsen, Professor, iCourts – Centre of Excellence for International Courts, Faculty of Law, University of Copenhagen, Denmark.

Jonathon W. Penney, Visiting Scholar, Harvard Law School; Senior Research Fellow, Technology and Social Change Project, Shorenstein Center on Media, Politics, and Public Policy, Harvard Kennedy School; and Research Affiliate, Berkman Klein Center for Internet & Society, Harvard University, USA.

Marcel Schaper, Associate Professor of Law, Maastricht University, Netherlands.

Alex Schwartz, Faculty of Law, The University of Hong Kong.

Phillip Sittig, Department of Informatics, University of Hamburg, Germany.

Nicolas Suzor, QUT School of Law and Digital Media Research Centre, Australia.

Yingmao Tang, Associate Professor, Law School of Peking University, People's Republic of China.

Gijs van Dijck, Professor of Law, Maastricht University, Netherlands.

Dafne van Kuppevelt, Netherlands eScience Center, Netherlands.

Nina Varsava, Assistant Professor of Law, University of Wisconsin–Madison, USA.

Ryan Whalen, Faculty of Law, National University of Singapore.

The emergence of computational legal studies: an introduction

Ryan Whalen

This volume arrives at an important inflection point in the relationship between law and computation. Technological, scientific, and methodological developments are increasingly allowing computation to provide not just efficiencies in the traditional ways we practice or study the law, but new perspectives on the law and potential paradigmatic shifts in how we think about and understand it. These developments have already been major factors in the recent evolution of many other academic fields, as evidenced for example by the rise of computational social science, computational biology, the digital humanities, and many more emerged and still-emerging subdisciplines. Although law has perhaps lagged somewhat behind its peer disciplines in adopting and adapting computational research methods, that has begun to change in recent years as more and more legal scholars have begun applying computational methods in the course of their research. This volume explores this emergence of computational legal studies by presenting a variety of research that is either representative of, or in conversation with, the field.

Before setting out to explore the state of computational legal studies, it is important first to provide at least a general delineation of what it might include and exclude. Computers and the law intersect in a variety of ways, none of which is entirely independent of one another, but all of which benefit from being independently identified in a discussion about computational legal studies. Perhaps the most common association between computers and the law is the substantive law that is increasingly faced with questions that arise as society becomes more and more digitally mediated. This area of study and practice is sometimes referred to as *cyberlaw*, and extends to a diverse set of legal areas including free expression, cybersecurity, privacy, and more. Although cyberlaw is broad in the legal areas it extends to, its scholarship is united by the central relevance of technology and technologically mediated social behavior to the questions it explores.

The application of technology to the practice of law is a second intersection between computation and law. This area, frequently referred to as *legal tech*, encompasses a variety of increasingly diverse and capable technologies that make the work of those engaging with the legal system—including, but not limited to lawyers—more efficient. In recent years, there has been substantial growth in the world of legal tech both in the market as developers and firms develop and deploy new legal technologies, and in the academy as both applied and theoretical research and training in legal tech have become more common in law schools. These developments are important not only because they promise to help train more technologically capable practitioners, but also because they increase the exposure of future researchers to methods and technologies that they might not otherwise have been exposed to.

The third intersection between computation and the law occurs when computational research methods are applied to the law as a subject of study. This area—sometimes referred to as *computational legal studies*—is related both to the long tradition of empirical legal studies and the burgeoning field of computational social science. Computational legal studies includes a wide variety of research and can focus on any substantive area of law. Some projects may use computational techniques to gather data—for instance, by writing a custom web scraper or by downloading and parsing data from open data sources—others might use machine learning or natural language processing techniques to analyze legal data. What unites computational legal research is the fact that it would not be possible without the power of computation—that is, the power to make easy otherwise difficult calculations, or to make trivial otherwise burdensome tasks.

These three intersections are not distinct, and indeed at times intersect with one another. For instance, one might imagine a piece of empirical cyberlaw scholarship that relies on computational techniques for data gathering and analysis (intersecting cyber law with computational legal studies). Similarly, one might study the substantive legal implications of an emerging legal technology such as smart contracts (intersecting cyberlaw with legal tech). Or alternately a computational legal studies approach to understanding a legal technology (intersecting each of cyberlaw, legal tech, and computational legal studies). Although this volume focuses largely on the third of these intersections—the use of computational techniques to study the law—it also touches on issues related to both legal technology, and substantive questions of how the law affects, and is affected by, technology. The complex ways these various intersections between law and technology are intertwined lead any volume such as this to at times touch on each.

The contributions to this volume are diverse both in substantive content, and in methodological focus. They draw on distinct bodies of literature, some growing out of the relatively long tradition of Artificial Intelligence (AI) and Law scholarship, others drawing more inspiration from the burgeoning field of computational social science, while still others evolve out of the legal academy's own response to the demand for innovation in law schools. Despite their diversity, these varied contributions can be roughly grouped into four topical categories: text, data, artificial intelligence, and methods and training.

Text has long been central to the law. Indeed, many of humanity's oldest and most famous texts are legal documents, describing contractual relations or legal codes. Because of the central importance of text to the law, the capacity for computational techniques to provide new perspectives and insight into textual data is of particular interest to computational legal scholars. In his chapter on automating legal text comparisons, Alschner details how technological developments have enabled new perspectives on legal documents. Lawyers, policymakers, and law scholars have long been trained to read documents closely and largely in isolation from other related documents. Alschner shows that "distant reading" can also provide useful insight, and goes on to demonstrate methods for doing so by analyzing many subsequent versions of a large body of regulations. In doing so, the chapter helps demonstrate the utility of automated text comparison techniques to those interested in the law and particularly legal change, while also discussing how those applying these techniques must also be cognizant of their particular strengths and weaknesses.

The law is not the only discipline with a special relationship with text. The humanities, with its own special relationship to text, has responded to the computational turn by developing a robust and active subdiscipline often referred to as the digital humanities. In her chapter on textual analyses Varsava provides an overview of textual analytic techniques that have evolved in the digital humanities, and provides insight into the utility these approaches can bring for legal scholars. Digital humanists have developed a robust toolkit, informed by the questions of interest within the humanities and the sources—often texts—that serve as research subjects. As Varsava points out, much of the computationally enabled research done by computational legal scholars can be thought of as an extension of computational social science. Law, however, shares many aspects in common with the humanities, and thus looking to the digital humanities for inspiration and guidance will be fruitful for many computational legal scholars. Varsava leverages these approaches to demonstrate how using computational techniques to measure and compare writing styles can provide insight into judges and the way they write, reason, and work.

Langford, Behn, and Lie also focus on legal texts in their chapter applying stylometric analyses to the text of international investment arbitration decisions. The majority of the work on legal writing styles has focused on the work product of judges, and to a lesser extent lawyers. By demonstrating how stylometric techniques show promise in identifying authorship of arbitral award decisions, Langford et al. provide an important methodological contribution that offers promising perspective into an area of law that has long been notoriously opaque. This chapter also offers an example of how legal text extends well beyond judicial opinions, which have tended to be the dominant subject of study especially for those in common law jurisdictions. Legal texts include not just opinions drafted by judges and their clerks, but also arbitral agreements, patents, treaties, statutes, and many other types of documents that are themselves amenable to computational text analyses.

Mainali, Meier, Ash, and Chen also take a language-centric approach to the study of law. However, their approach focuses not on the style of judicial writing, but rather on the degree to which the author's style of reasoning can be detected via machine learning. This approach highlights the potential for semi-supervised classification techniques to aid in the sorts of legal research that requires analyzing many hundreds, thousands, or even millions of documents. These techniques enable research at a scale not feasible for researchers unassisted by automated classification methods. The emergence and popularization of these methods—along with the rapid growth in the availability of machine-readable judicial opinions—is in the midst of generating a new style of empirical judicial behavior research.

The importance of textual data to computational legal studies has turned many scholars' attention to questions about access to legal texts and the quality and coverage of existing databases. In their chapter demonstrating the data-collection efforts underpinning a research project examining labor law decisions, Alexander and Feizollahi explore these questions about data access and coverage and the implications for computational legal scholars. Data-driven research quite naturally requires data, and if it is to make statistical extrapolations it requires not only access to data, but an understanding of potential sampling biases. Alexander and Feizollahi show that the traditional sources of American judicial opinion data can have dramatically different levels of coverage. As a partial solution, they advocate for courts to produce easily accessible and machine-readable data. Doing so would improve scholars' ability to engage in large-scale data-driven research and help ensure that American courts do not fall too far behind their international peers in this regard.

Much of the existing legal academic research that uses computational research methods is either performed in Western jurisdictions or focuses on Western legal systems. However, the evolution of the Chinese legal system, and especially its adoption of data-driven decisionmaking, offers rich ground for computationally enabled empirical legal studies. In their chapter on the role of computational legal studies within China, Tang and Liu chart the rise of Chinese empirical legal studies, and discuss both the potential for computational approaches to contribute to the development of the Chinese legal academy as well as some of the challenges they foresee along the way. Many of these challenges mirror those facing the emergence of computational legal studies globally, but some are challenges with Chinese characteristics. Regardless of precisely how computationally enabled legal scholarship evolves in China, it is almost certain to become a more important element of that country's academy, and Tang and Liu's contribution offers a valuable overview and discussion of the field for those who would like to better appreciate its current state and future prospects.

The data access revolution is not limited to the increasing availability of legal documents such as judicial opinions. Indeed, as more and more social behavior becomes digitally mediated, the digital traces of that behavior leave more and more data of interest to legal scholars. In his chapter on measuring regulatory impact at scale, Penney demonstrates the implications that the increase in computer mediated social interaction has for empirical legal scholars. As regulation increasingly affects digitally mediated activity, legal scholars are left with an obligation to better understand how these regulations may alter behavior, and are also left with a rich body of data with which to do so. Penney capitalizes on a natural experiment arising from policy disclosure and uses the digital trace data left by Wikipedia editors to convincingly demonstrate the power of his approach in furthering our empirical understanding of how regulation affects behavior. In doing so, he shows how the legal issues, such as the disclosure of US Government surveillance activities, can manifest in changed online activity that can be detected and measured with the use of computational techniques.

Suzor's chapter on understanding content moderation systems likewise engages with the shift towards increasing digitally mediated social behavior. As this has occurred, individuals have not only become more likely to have their online behavior affected by official regulations and policies—as evidenced in Penney's contribution—but also to be subject to regulation by online platforms themselves. The regulation by platform is potentially just as important as state-sponsored laws and regulations in affecting social behavior. As such, understanding how it manifests is a crucially important task for contemporary legal scholars. However, as private enterprises, online platforms are not bound by the same expectations of transparency as public actors are. Suzor's contribution is to detail a sophisticated data gathering project that allows researchers to track and better understand content moderation at scale. This is an example of what one might call a "data infrastructure" project that facilitates future work and improves the capacity of computational legal studies to contribute to emerging policy debates.

Following the contributions focused on text analysis and data, the volume then turns to one of the highest visibility areas of contemporary computational legal studies—artificial intelligence and machine learning. As access to data has increased, and computational methods have become more sophisticated and capable, the capacity for machine-learning models to mimic human intelligence has improved. This has raised the profile of legal artificial intelligence, with increased focus both on practical aspects of how to develop and deploy these technologies as well as more theoretical questions about what AI may mean for the practice of law and whether indeed there are some elements of legal systems that are so human-centric that they are not amenable to automated decisionmaking.

In a chapter discussing whether artificial intelligence can be designed to account for complexity, Ashley demonstrates how AI models can be specified to consider not just questions of law and fact, but to also account for social values. Doing so provides an empirical perspective on values-based reasoning that will be of interest not only to designers and consumers of legal AI models, but also to those interested in the role that values play in legal reasoning. In doing so, Ashley's contribution demonstrates the capacity for computational legal studies to engage simultaneously with practical questions facing the development of legal AI and more fundamental questions of jurisprudence.

These fundamental questions include those that computation and computational research methods raise about how technological development might affect legal decisionmaking and ultimately the law itself. Gowder takes up this line of questioning at the intersection between computation and law by asking whether legal cognition is computational. Using a classic legal classification problem to demonstrate, Gowder shows how modern machine-learning methods could be used as decisionmaking aides to help answer a subset of legal questions. By demonstrating the potential for computation as a judicial aide, Gowder's contribution shows how computational approaches could conceivably influence the future development of how courts function, while also reminding us of their limitations.

Livermore also takes up questions at the very heart of law and computation by exploring the implications of a legal system adopting machine-learning decisionmaking tools. In doing so, Livermore highlights both the potential strengths and weaknesses of computational decisionmaking technologies, while also raising important questions about the degree to which getting the right answer is as important as legal process, and whether or not machines can be meaningful participants in legitimate legal systems. These questions that Livermore tackles are of fundamental importance to those who foresee or advocate for an increasing reliance on technology in legal systems. As those technologies become more capable, and more widely adopted, better understanding the degree to which law-as-computation risks impinging upon law's essential humanity and its ability to evolve in step with the societies it rules is imperative.

Following its exploration of the intersection of computational law and jurisprudence, the volume's final section turns to specific computational legal studies methods, applications, and education. Among the varied methods at the disposal of computational legal scholars, network analysis has shown promise in providing a structural and system-level perspective that is quite distinct from traditional legal scholarship methods. In their chapter on citation network analyses of case law, van Kuppevelt, van Dijck, and Schaper provide an overview of this increasingly popular area of research. In doing so, they detail methodological developments required to ensure that legal citation network analyses are sufficiently rigorous, reproducible, and interpretable. As a relatively new area of inquiry, this detailed overview and comparison of various network analysis methods and sampling strategies provides an important cautionary tale to researchers, demonstrating the importance of the research design decisions they make.

Following van Kuppevelt et al.'s overview of legal network analyses, Olsen and Esmark provide an applied demonstration of the utility that a network perspective can provide. After mapping citations to case law from the European Court of Human Rights, they use centrality measures to identify those cases containing general principles of law, as opposed to those related to more narrow or specific legal questions. Doing so demonstrates the potential of a network-driven approach to make sense of case law in ways that traditional legal scholarship would not, and thereby exemplifies the way a computational perspective can provide a unique quality of insight into the law.

Network analysis is just one of a wide variety of techniques at the disposal of computational legal scholars. Schwartz introduces another in his chapter where he provides an overview of agent-based simulations, and subsequently a demonstration of how they can be applied to questions of interest to legal scholars. Schwartz shows how agent-based models can be used to provide insight into aspects of legal systems that are otherwise difficult to study. By simulating the behavior of legal actors—in this chapter's case, the actions of courts and government agents—agent-based models are able to play out various scenarios and demonstrate how system-level effects like the emergence of a stable high court, or the failure of the rule of law, can be affected by agent-level behavior. Social simulations have proven very insightful throughout the social sciences, and Schwartz shows in his research that this utility also extends to the study of the law.

In the volume's final chapter Beckedorf, Hartung, and Sittig discuss an area of central importance to the emergence of computational legal studies—that is, integrating computational training into the law school curriculum. Their chapter demonstrates the potential of hands-on inter-disciplinary training to empower teams of law and computer science students to engage in meaningful computationally enabled legal research. In doing so, they highlight how their educational program, and others like it, are facilitating the emergence of computational legal studies. Training programs are central to the development of academic subfields and meth-odological camps. Traditional legal training models have perhaps lagged behind others in providing avenues through which their graduates can become proficient in empirical and computational research techniques. Programs such as that highlighted by Beckedorf et al. will not only help train computationally literate practitioners but also researchers and academics.

Taken together the contributions in this volume sketch out many of the promises of computational legal studies in furthering our understanding of the law and sociolegal systems. Meanwhile, this collection also helps identify the challenges facing computational legal scholars and students as they seek to further establish the field, its methods, and how it engages with a wider community of scholars, policymakers, and practitioners. Although these challenges are substantial, the field's promise—coupled with the rapid growth in computing power, data access, research methods, and trained researchers—suggests that computational legal studies will thrive as it continues to provide its unique perspective on the law.

1. Sense and similarity: automating legal text comparison*

Wolfgang Alschner

1. INTRODUCTION

As lawyers we often compare legal documents. We want to know which case is similar to the one we are currently litigating; we want to know where a contract deviates from an industry template; we want to know which part of a regulation was amended following a public comment procedure or how the commercial code in Canada differs from the commercial code in the United States. In short, a wide range of legal tasks involves a comparison between two or more legal texts. Improvements in technology now allow us to rethink and to scale up such legal document comparisons. Whereas human lawyers struggle to compare more than a few dozen contracts, statutes or cases in a day, computers can relate thousands of legal texts to each other in a few seconds. This creates a host of new opportunities for lawyers and legal researchers engaged in comparative legal analysis.

In this chapter, I will outline the technological underpinnings of automated legal text comparison and discuss the practical implications, applications and limitations arising from its increasing use. Automated legal text comparisons change comparative legal work in two ways. First, existing comparative tasks can be performed more efficiently through technology. Second, novel tools are added to the repertoire of legal scholars and lawyers to automatically identify patterns of similarities and differences in large legal corpora. Comparative text analysis of big legal data can thus reveal insights that were impossible to detect for human researchers using traditional methods. Automated text comparison is thus becoming a powerful and versatile tool in a range of legal research

* I gratefully acknowledge the research assistance of Samantha Lo and the financial support of the Ontario Early Researcher Award "Equipping Tomorrow's Lawyers: Using Artificial Intelligence for Automatic Legal Document Production and Analysis".

and technology applications. At the same time, these new tools primarily complement rather than substitute traditional comparative analysis, since they focus on comparing text tokens rather than their underlying meaning, interpretation and significance.

This chapter is structured as follows. First, I introduce the technology of modern automated text comparison and discuss its promises and limitations. In that context, I highlight the important distinction between similarity of text and similarity of meaning. I then explore how automated text comparison scales and improves the performance of existing legal work and introduces new tools to lawyers to carry out analyses on big legal data. Specifically, I discuss applications of automated legal text comparison for the study of (1) specific legal documents, (2) legal processes and (3) large legal corpora. The final section of the chapter concludes on how scholars and lawyers can acquire the skills to leverage automated legal text comparisons in their own work.

2. THE TECHNOLOGY OF AUTOMATING TEXT COMPARISON

To automate and scale legal document comparison, we have to re-conceptualize how we deal with legal texts. Lawyers and legal researchers compare legal texts through *close reading*. As humans, we carefully scan documents and can pick up a wide variety of commonalities between texts in the process, from similarity in content to related underlying legal concepts or parallels in writing style. Moreover, we can read between the lines, detect subtle irony and interpret words drawing from our legal background knowledge. What we cannot do, however, is to conduct legal document comparison at scale. For that we need what Franco Moretti termed *distant reading* (Moretti, 2013). In essence, we need to treat text as data to analyze more of it in less time. While we will lose some of the benefits associated with close reading in the process, distant reading not only offers efficiency gains but also an entirely new perspective on the law.

In this section, I explain how to transform text to data, how to compare the resulting text representations and how to visualize and interpret the results. Finally, I offer some reflection on the limitations and promises of automated text comparison.

In order to make the sometimes-technical discussion more tangible, I will lead with an example. Say you are a young associate in a tax law boutique in Toronto. One of the partners asks you to draft a memo on the evolution of the Canadian Federal Income Tax Regulation (C.R.C.,

c. 945) since the early 2000s.[1] The partner knows that the Regulation has been revised many times during that period but also knows that some revisions have been more important than others. For a report the firm is now working on, they specifically want to focus on major revisions to that Regulation, which you are tasked to identify. You quickly realize that the Regulation is extremely long, containing more than 360,000 words on 1217 pages in its current version. Moreover, the Regulation has been revised 72 times since 2004. In short, an impossible task for close reading. But, as we will see, not for distant reading.

1) Transforming Legal Text to Data

There are many methods to transform text to data, that is, to represent or model text quantitatively, to make it amenable for distant reading.[2] What these methods have in common is that, as Grimmer and Stewart put it, "all quantitative models of language are wrong" (Grimmer and Stewart, 2013, p. 4). That is because a text is partially constructed through information outside of the text. We understand the semantics of a text – the sense of words, legal concepts, connotations, irony or puns – because we can tap into a wider pool of knowledge that computers (currently) do not have access to. As a result, any conversion from text to data will lead to some of that semantic information, which would be accessible to human readers, to be lost in translation. This is not necessarily a problem, though. As Grimmer and Stewart stress, quantitative models of language can be useful even if they are "wrong" (Grimmer and Stewart, 2013, p. 4). The benchmark of any text-as-data representation is not how accurately it can represent meaning, but how useful it is in relation to the performance of a specific task.

We can think about available methods to convert text to data as a spectrum between model simplicity and complexity. From that spectrum, users can select the text-as-data model that corresponds most closely to their research needs. On one end of the spectrum are simple language models that entail a greater loss of semantic information, but that are easy and quick to implement. They include so-called bag-of-words approaches, which treat words as tokens whose frequency in a text is counted without regard to word order (Manning et al., 2008). Unigram language models,

---

[1]   The Regulation is available at http://laws.justice.gc.ca/eng/regulations/C.R. C.,_c._945/index.html (retrieved 12 March 2019). The subsequent analysis uses point-in-time versions of that Regulation available at ftp://205.193.86.89/PITXML/ regulations/C.R.C.,_c._945/ (retrieved 12 March 2019).

[2]   For an introduction to natural language processing and text-as-data analysis, see Arnold and Tilton, 2015, ch. 9; Manning et al., 2008, ch. 12.

for instance, count the frequency of individual words, bigram models count the frequency of word pairs, trigrams consider three consecutive words, and so on. A step closer towards greater complexity are character-gram models, which split text into chunks of consecutive characters, for example of five, six, seven or more character length, and thereby incorporate word order (see e.g. Spirling, 2012). This can be particularly important in law where the phrase "guilty not to" shares a word frequency with "not guilty to", but they differ in their character sequence. Character-gram models, however, take longer to compute as they segment text into more fine-grained components.

As we advance on the spectrum towards greater complexity, models incorporate syntactical elements through so-called part-of-speech tagging to tell verbs from nouns and identify word dependencies in text (Arnold and Tilton, 2015, pp. 134–43). The currently most sophisticated data-driven language models treat words as vectors. These *word2vec* representations of language deploy neural networks to learn the contexts in which words appear. Words that are textually unrelated, such as "cat" and "dog" or "father" and "son", but that are semantically related given their shared word context are then placed closer together in a vector space (Mikolov et al., 2013). But even the most complex procedures currently remain approximations of the deeper semantic connections between words that a lawyer would be able to detect. Those engaged in text-as-data conversion thus face a trade-off: the closer one gets towards model complexity the more contextual information is incorporated reducing the information lost in the text-to-data translation, but at the same time parsimony declines and computational costs increase.

The above description is only a cursory overview. Moreover, each text-as-data method comes with a set of additional methodological choices (Denny and Spirling, 2018; Grimmer and Stewart, 2013). These choices include whether to disregard punctuation, whether to eliminate certain words (such as "and", "is", "or") or to focus on certain words (e.g. only nouns), whether to reduce words to their stems to limit variation (e.g. "gone" and "going" become "go") and so forth. As a result, there is no single or "true" representation of text as data.

The choice among different language representations will instead depend on the task at hand. Surprisingly to most lawyers who are trained to see significance in the placement of a comma (and sometimes rightfully so), many automated text-processing applications do not rely on sophisti-cated models of language to add value (Manning et al., 2008). In order to classify 1000 cases on whether they deal with a contract breach or a tort claim, for instance, we do not need to worry about commas and can rely on a simple unigram model. Similarly, if we want to detect which contracts from a pool of 1000 contracts follow a specific template, a relatively simple character-gram model that incorporates word order will work just fine. In contrast, where we want to identify semantically related but textually distinct legal concepts such as good faith, the clean hands doctrine and abuse of rights, a more complex, semantically informed conversion model is necessary. In short, the task dictates how simple a language model can be to still be useful. But in most cases, simple models work surprisingly well.

Following this brief introduction into text-as-data approaches, we can now apply these techniques to the task of the young associate who is to investigate the evolution of the Canadian Federal Income Tax Regulation. Since the objective is to identify major revisions of that Regulation, there is no need, at this initial stage, to employ a sophisticated, semantically aware language model. As long as that model can represent changes to a text, it will suffice. Given the significant length of the Regulation and the ensuing computational costs, the young associate can settle on the simple model of a unigram representation of text that counts the frequency of each word for each document and stores results in what is called a document-term matrix where every row represents one version of the 72 iterations of the Income Tax Regulation since 2004 and every column represents a word and its frequency in each of these versions. This representation will then allow the young associate to compare the different iterations of the Income Tax Regulation texts.

2) Comparing Texts Computationally through Distance Measures

When lawyers compare texts, they assess qualitatively what two documents have in common. In order to automate that process, however, we need to express the commonality between texts quantitatively. In other words, we need to find a way to compute how different or similar two texts are. In mathematics the notion of similarity or difference can be expressed as the *distance* between two objects. The intuition is that in a virtual space two identical texts will occupy the same spot, whereas two very different texts will be located far apart.

Having represented text as data, we can calculate the distance between two texts relatively easily. A range of different metrics exists that require different data formats and use different techniques to perform this calculation. The most intuitive of them is the *Jaccard* distance. It simply counts the share of textual elements that a text pair has in common in relation to all text elements present in the pair. Subtracted from 1 this number yields the Jaccard distance, otherwise it indicates Jaccard similarity (Alschner and Skougarevskiy, 2016). A useful property of the Jaccard measure is that it is bounded between 0 and 1. Other distance metrics include

Euclidean, or more popular for text data, *Cosine* distances that measure the distance between documents, typically represented as word frequency vectors in a document-term-matrix, in a vector space.[3]

Given that textual similarity can vary starkly from one text corpus to another and that some of the distance measures (such as Euclidean) are not bounded, it is useful to interpret distance measures through intra-corpus benchmarking. How similar are the two most similar documents in the corpus? How different are the two most different documents? What is the average similarity and standard deviation in the corpus? On that basis, texts can be compared and their commonality assessed relative to other texts in the same corpus.

Going back to our example, the young associate can now compute the textual distance between the 72 versions of the Income Tax Regulation. To keep things simple, the young associate will calculate the Jaccard distance between versions of the Regulation. He thus essentially computes to what extent the same words are contained in a pair of regulations that is being compared. Given that we are dealing with the same Regulation over time, that distance should be comparatively low. After running the analysis, the young associate finds that the average distance between all 72 regulations is 0.12 with a standard deviation of 0.08. Recall that the Jaccard distance is bounded between 0 and 1, with 0 indicating perfect similarity. The minimum similarity in our corpus is 0, that is, at least two versions of the Regulation are essentially identical when it comes to words used and the maximum distance is 0.30, which means that 30 percent of unique words are different in two versions of the same Regulation. As we would expect, this latter, maximum distance is between the first (2004) and the last version (2018) of the Regulation in our dataset highlighting an incremental change of the text over time.

3) Visualizing Text Comparisons

Comparing raw similarities scores can be sufficient for some legal tasks. If the goal is to find the most similar case to the case at hand, for instance, raw scores are enough to identify the match. If the goal is to compare a large number of texts based on their similarity, to identify structural breaks where small changes give way to more drastic ones or if the analysis is to prepare a subsequent targeted close reading of texts, further visualizations

---

[3] For an informative comparison of different distance measures, see the blog post Chris Emmery, Euclidean vs. Cosine Distance, 25 March 2017, retrieved 12 March 2019 from https://cmry.github.io/notes/euclidean-v-cosine.

are helpful. Through past research, I have come to appreciate the use of so-called heat maps to visualize textual similarity across a large corpus of texts.

The output resulting from applying distance measures to text-as-data representations is a distance matrix. Each cell in that matrix is a pairwise comparison of the similarity of two texts. What a heat map does is to overlay the raw distance scores with a color-coding that makes it easy to differentiate low and high scores. Pairs of similar texts can thus be easily spotted. Moreover, as I will further explain below in the section on corpora analysis, heat maps can also facilitate the identifications of groupings of similarly worded documents when combined with clustering algorithms. Heat maps can therefore reveal patterns as well as candidates for further manual inspection (e.g. to identify remaining differences between the most similar pair of texts).[4]

Going back to the Income Tax Regulation example, the young associate can plot the distance matrix calculated as a heat map. The results are displayed in Figure 1.1. The heat map's axes are identical and list the versions of regulations chronologically by their enactment date. The map (and distance matrix) is symmetrical, meaning that in the diagonal line from top-left to bottom-right the same version of the Regulation is always compared to itself. The segments of the heat map above and below that diagonal are mirror images of each other. Where two versions of the Regulation are identical or very similar, the heat map will color-code them dark, where two versions are different, they will be color-coded bright.

The heat map visualizes the incremental evolution of the Regulation's text over time where small changes to each new version slowly change the Regulation, creating the greatest deviation between the first and the last version. The heat map, however, also allows us to spot a significant structural break between the February 2013 and June 2013 versions of the Regulation, where rather than small, incremental change, we see an abrupt and significant change corresponding to an 8 percent textual difference between the two versions.

The young associate has thus fulfilled part of the task. Canada's Federal Income Tax Regulation changed incrementally between 2004 and 2018. Over that period, 30 percent of the Regulation was gradually revised. Only one major revision occurred changing 8 percent of the Regulation between February and June 2013. The associate can subsequently focus

---

[4]   Such further inspection can also be facilitated by technology. Diff algorithms, for instance, are programs that display text side-by-side, color-coding differences between texts. There are free diff websites, which can be useful to quickly assess textual differences between two documents. See e.g. https://www.diffchecker.com.

Figure 1.1   Comparison of successive versions of the Canadian Federal Income Tax Regulation (2004–18)

on that specific revision and explore the legal changes brought about by it. Without going into too much detail, the 2013 major revision of the Canadian Federal Income Tax Regulation implemented changes resulting from the 2012 Technical Tax Amendments Act (S.C. 2013, c. 34). Among other things, the Regulation introduced a new regime relating to the taxation of Canadian multinational corporations with foreign affiliates (Section 5907) and changed taxation rules for taxpayers with interests in offshore investment fund property (Section 202(6.1)).[5]

4) Promises and Limitations of Automated Text Comparisons

The automated comparison of legal texts provides a scalable means to efficiently assess the similarity of large corpora of legal documents. But it also comes with limitations that stem from the fact that such analysis is rooted in the comparison of text tokens and not meaning. As a result, where similarity in meaning is not accompanied by similarity in text, the findings of automated text comparisons can be misleading. This is most obvious when comparing identical texts in different languages: an automated text comparison will then classify the same texts as very different. This limits the applicability of automated text comparisons across languages without intervening translation. Similarly, even within a language, different words can often express similar meaning. While more sophisticated word2vec approaches can pick up the underlying semantic similarity, the more common bag-of-words models cannot.

The above example of the Income Tax Regulation highlights some of these limitations. While we now know that a significant revision of the Canadian Federal Income Tax Regulation occurred between February and June 2013, we do not yet know what specific legal changes it entailed. Furthermore, we only looked for the magnitude of textual changes. Other amendments of the same Regulation may have brought about equally or even more significant *legal* changes, but they did not lead to major *textual* changes and were thus not uncovered using the approach adopted. In part, these limitations can be overcome through a second iteration of the analysis using a more sophisticated language model or by computationally identifying what sections and what words were changed.

More generally, however, these limitations point to the *complementarity*

---

[5]   See Technical Tax Amendments Act, 2012, S.C. 2013, c 34, Summary, and Department of Finance, *Explanatory Notes Relating to the Income Tax Act, the Excise Tax Act and Related Legislation*, October 2012, retrieved 12 March 2019 from https://www.fin.gc.ca/drleg-apl/nwmm-amvm-1012n-05-eng.asp.

of close reading and distant reading. The latter can provide insights that traditional analysis could not have delivered (such as the structural break in the Tax Regulation of 2013), while the former allows one to interpret the textual changes and evaluate their legal significance. Distant reading is therefore no substitute for close reading.

Another way of looking at this is that automated text comparison is most useful when it plays to its inherent strengths. Automated text comparison works especially well when the task involves comparing text rather than interpreting content. Diverse applications in law, which I will discuss below, actually look for common text rather than common meaning, making automated text comparison useful. Moreover, such comparisons work particularly well with transactional or statutory documents, where text and normative content is typically closely intertwined. That is because contracts and statutes are written in a stylized, standardized legal language that does not normally vary for stylistic reasons alone. In contrast, judicial decisions are written in natural language and, as a result, normative content and text are more loosely connected making semantically agnostic textual similarity analysis somewhat less insightful. Ultimately, however, it depends on the specific task and choice of technique that determines what contributions automatic text analysis can make and what limitations remain.

In the remainder of this chapter, I will therefore showcase some useful applications for automatic text comparisons in law differentiating between the analysis of (1) targeted documents, (2) legal processes and (3) large legal corpora.

3. APPLICATIONS I: SUPPORTING LEGAL DOCUMENT ANALYSIS

In this section, I begin with a review of applications for automated text comparison in (1) legal search, (2) authorship identification, (3) legislative implementation and influence detection and (4) template deviation assessment. This list is not exhaustive, but it highlights the contribution automated legal text comparisons can make to support targeted document analysis.

1)   Similarity Analysis in Legal Search and Recommender Systems

Say you found a judicial decision and want to know whether there are other cases like it. In the past, legal search engines sought to address such queries by relying primarily on metadata. A human extracted key information from a judgment and this information was then linked to the decision in a database as metadata. Similarity of cases is then expressed as the similarity of metadata. The efficacy of this approach is dependent on the quality of the metadata, but since cases can be similar across many dimensions, for example they share the same legal principle, same facts, same parties, same location, and so on, there is a risk that metadata entries do not capture all potentially useful information.

Automatically comparing the full text of legal documents has therefore become a useful tool for legal search applications and legal recommender systems (Winkels et al., 2014). One way to think about a search operation is to imagine that legal documents form a network that contains both formal links, such as cross-references and shared metadata, but also informal links, such as similar text content, which can be revealed through full text comparisons (Landthaler et al., 2016). Textual similarity metrics can then find close neighbors of the target case in the network by comparing its text to all other decisions in the database. Furthermore, similarity measures can be incorporated into legal recommender systems to suggest documents similar to the one returned through the initial search query. Thereby users can gain access to pertinent cases, which they would not have found through curated metadata connections.

Challenges for these types of applications include the above-discussed text versus meaning distinction. Users are typically interested in finding semantically or legally similar cases, whereas most computational approaches can only provide textually similar ones. Cases may thus be similar because the same judge wrote them, not because they cover identical issues. At the same time, this type of similarity may also be useful to litigants. A second challenge relates to the choice of a threshold. Similarity is a continuum between the extreme dissimilar and the extreme similar. On what point of that spectrum do two documents become similar enough for a legal search or recommender algorithm to consider them linked? Commercial legal search and recommender systems typically do not disclose their specific matching algorithm, but research suggests that a combination of textual similarity metrics with other information such as ontologies and manual annotation provides the most promising results to leverage both formal and informal connections between documents (Geist, 2008; Landthaler et al., 2016; Schweighofer and Geist, 2007).

2)   Similarity and Authorship Detection

The detection of document authorship through text comparison is popular in the field of linguistic forensics, and has applications in law. In contrast to legal search applications discussed above, similarity here is not primarily used to detect content links but stylistic ties between two documents, which is why the field is also known as stylometry. In the process, the text of a document of unknown authorship is automatically compared to texts of known authors to identify the writer among the group of potential candidates. Such stylometry is used in law to produce evidence in litigation as part of the larger field of legal forensics (Coulthard and Johnson, 2010). For instance, in the *Yukos v Russia* arbitration, which yielded the biggest investment arbitration award to date of USD 50 billion, Russia sought to set aside the arbitral award in Dutch courts on the grounds that a linguistic analysis had revealed that, illegitimately, the tribunal's secretary and not the three arbitrators had written large portions of the award.[6]

3)   Legislative Drafting

Another application of automated text comparison lies in legislative drafting to assess whether one document influences the text of another. On the one hand, such influence may be explicit. For instance, where states implement an international treaty in domestic law, international law provides the normative content that is to be translated into municipal law. Such national implementation of international law is particularly common in Europe where directives of the supranational European Union (EU) are being implemented through national measures within the organization's member states. While the EU currently tasks specialized consulting companies to manually monitor the faithful implementation of such directives, researchers have shown that text-based similarity measures can identify national implementing statutes with reasonable accuracy across different EU member states (Nanda et al., 2018).

On the other hand, textual similarity may also reveal less explicit textual sources that leave traces in national legislation. Scholars at the University of Chicago, for instance, have used textual similarity to build a "Legislative Influence Detector" that compares how statutes in one US state are influenced by those of another state (Burgess et al., 2016). The project also investigated whether proposals submitted by lobby groups made their way into final legislation. Other scholars have tracked text reuse to trace where policy ideas that end up in US or EU legislation first originated (Cross and Hermansson, 2017; Wilkerson et al., 2015). When it comes to international law, political scientists have compared

---

[6]   Jarrod Hepburn, Battling $50 Billion Yukos Awards on Two Fronts, Russia Focuses on Claimants' Alleged Fraud and Linguistic Analysis of Tribunal Assistant's Alleged Role in Drafting Awards, INV. ARB. Rep. (3 November 2015).

text of model bilateral investment with negotiated agreements to detect what party had greater say over the final outcome (Berge and Stiansen, 2016).

These approaches employ the same intuition as plagiarism detection software, which uses exact or near textual matches to detect academic fraud. The low probability of exact textual matches by chance suggests that two otherwise distinct documents with identical or highly similar language share a common author or, at least, are linked through a third factor. While such similarity-based analysis yields robust results when actual copy-and-pasting has taken place, it is unable, for the reasons discussed above, to detect legislative influence when it is manifested in the underlying policy ideas but not the actual texts.

4) Similarity, Boilerplate and Novelty

A fourth use of similarity compares targeted legal texts, typically con-tracts, statutes or treaties, to benchmark texts to assess to what extent they follow boilerplate language or deviate from established practice. The same technique can also be used to detect legal innovations or idiosyncrasies in texts that display passages not found in other texts of the same domain. This is particularly fruitful in relation to transactional and statutory docu-ments, which tend to recycle legal language to benefit from established meaning of legal concepts, terms of trade and other industry terminology, making deviations from established wording noteworthy.

In the domain of international law, for instance, political scientists have compared the text of the Transpacific Partnership Agreement negotiated in 2016 to other trade agreements, to verify claims by the US administra-tion that the agreement set new standards, finding instead that the text of the agreement had been taken in large parts from earlier agreements (Allee and Lugg, 2016). The same technique, however, also allows the research-ers to identify those areas that were truly novel with no textual precedent in prior practice.

4. APPLICATIONS II: TRACKING LEGAL PROCESSES

A different type of legal application leverages automated text comparisons not to analyze individual documents but to track legal processes. The evo-lution of Canadian Federal Income Tax Regulations described above is an example of a process-oriented text comparison. These applications trace textual similarity patterns over time across large sets of comparators to better understand, among others, negotiation dynamics as well as policy evolution and diffusion.

1) Dissecting Negotiation Processes

When distinct parties come to the bargaining table, their preferences and objectives initially diverge, but as negotiations unfold, the positions converge as each side gives and takes until they agree on a joint text. This convergence of views often leaves textual traces as parties table proposals, accept revisions and work towards the final document. Negotiations can thus be tracked through the lens of automated document comparison as a process, in which distinct texts are merged into a common document.

The negotiations of the North American Free Trade Agreement (NAFTA) in the early 1990s is a case in point. The 42 negotiation drafts of one of its chapters – Chapter 11 on investment protection – have been made public and allow researchers to track how the negotiations unfolded from the original proposal submitted by each party to the convergence in the final text. The comparison of these drafts suggests that no country dominated that negotiation as each had to compromise significantly based on their initial submission to reach a final outcome. Such text comparison also helps identify particularly contentious areas in negotiations. In the NAFTA talks consensus was reached quickly on many of the substantive protection provisions, but it took longer to find common ground on the role of escape clauses and dispute settlement (Alschner et al., 2018a).

Similarity analysis can thus cast new light on negotiating processes by comparing the language of drafts over time. But it also has shortcomings that again go back to the distinction between text and semantics. For the United States the inclusion of investor-state arbitration was the primary negotiation objective, while Canada and Mexico initially opposed it. In the end, the US got what it wanted, the inclusion of arbitration, even though it had to strongly compromise on the surrounding text. So by what metric should we evaluate whether the US lost or won that negotiation? Textual similarity can quantify the give-and-take in negotiations, but cannot discern what textual concession mattered more in legal or policy terms.

2) Policy Evolution and Diffusion

Another way automated document comparison can help understand legal processes is by tracking how policies evolve through the changing language in legal texts. Staying with the example of international treaties, NAFTA

Chapter 11 marked a clear departure from US bilateral investment treaty (BIT) practice (Alschner et al., 2017b). Prior and subsequent to NAFTA, the US concluded BITs that closely mirrored a common template. The NAFTA text remained an outlier and deviation from that template. Yet, after the US was sued by foreign investors based on NAFTA Chapter 11 and won a string of cases in the late 1990s, the country not only started to conclude other free trade agreements with investment chapters, but also changed its BIT practice to align it closer with the tried and tested NAFTA text (Alschner et al., 2017b).

While this US policy shift is anecdotally well known, automatic text comparison can also inductively reveal otherwise undocumented policy changes. An analysis of the investment treaty practice of Japan, for instance, reveals that the country undertook a major overhaul of its investment treaty practice in 2001 or that Spain and Finland introduced new template texts in 1996 and 1999 respectively. Hence, similarity analysis can reveal latent policy changes over time identifying periods of consistency and breaks of innovation. Moreover, the same type of analysis can help track policy diffusion patterns. By comparing treaty texts across countries, it is possible to identify when one country borrowed treaty language from another country and how new policies thereby spread from one state to the next (Alschner and Skougarevskiy, 2016).

A downside of focusing purely on similarity, however, is that it can tell us little about the direction of the policy change or the driver of diffusion. Strictly speaking, all we know is that texts at time 1 look different than those concluded at time 2 and that in the intervening period a change occurred. Automated text comparison tools therefore need to be combined with other social science research methods such as interview-based or archival research to understand the causal forces and direction behind patterns made visible through the text comparison.

5. APPLICATIONS III: PATTERN RECOGNITION IN LARGE TEXT CORPORA

Finally, automated text comparison can be used to reveal patterns in large legal corpora. On the one hand, such analysis can follow a deductive approach where we expect documents to vary systematically in similarity and difference as a function of some other variable, such as the underlying bargaining power of parties. On the other hand, the analysis can also be fully inductive letting the data speak for itself to reveal patterns that we did not know to exist (Alschner et al., 2017a). In each case, automated text comparison can confirm or reveal clusters and ordering in large legal corpora.

1) Deductive Pattern Recognition

A classic empirical research design can use automated text comparison deductively to test hypotheses on a given legal text corpus. For instance, we may hypothesize that bargaining outcomes in treaty negotiations are a function of power asymmetries. Where two parties each equipped with a treaty proposal enter negotiations, the hypothesis would suggest that the final text would be more similar to the more powerful party's proposal than to the weaker party's one. In previous research, Dmitriy Skougarevskiy and I tested that hypothesis with respect to the negotiation of bilateral investment treaties. We found that developed countries tended to be the system's rule-makers, while developing countries were the system's rule-takers. Bargaining dynamics thus helped to explain the patterns of textual similarity and difference that we observed in the universe of investment agreements (Alschner and Skougarevskiy, 2016).

In the above example, the similarity or dissimilarity of texts in a legal corpus is the phenomenon to be explained. Similarity patterns can, however, also be used as explanatory variables on the right side of the equation to describe or explain a certain outcome. Ryan Whalen, for instance, has used the textual similarity of the corpus of patent applications to describe change in innovation styles (Whalen, 2018). By using textual distance to weigh citations between patent applications, he found that recent patents increasingly cite inventions from textually different domains indicating a shift in how creative recombination contributes to innovation (Whalen, 2018). Hence, automated text comparisons of large legal corpora can yield new, insightful weights and variables for deductive research design.

2) Inductive Pattern Recognition

Often we do not have a good intuition about whether texts in a legal domain are converging or diverging or what patterns characterize large legal text collections. After all, as lawyers we seldom engage with the big data environment of large legal corpora and instead traditionally prefer the small data environment of the close reading of selected texts. But by applying big data approaches to "let data speak for itself", we can detect patterns that enhance our understanding of these corpora (Mayer-Schönberger and Cukier, 2014, p. 14).

For instance, when colleagues and I investigated a corpus of 450 free trade agreements (FTAs), we first thought that it would behave like bilateral investment treaties clustering in groups along developed/

a) FTA universe ordered alphabetically
and chronologically by richer treaty party

b) FTA universe ordered automatically
by hierarchical clustering algorithm

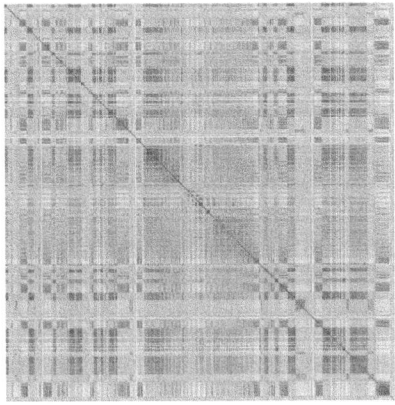 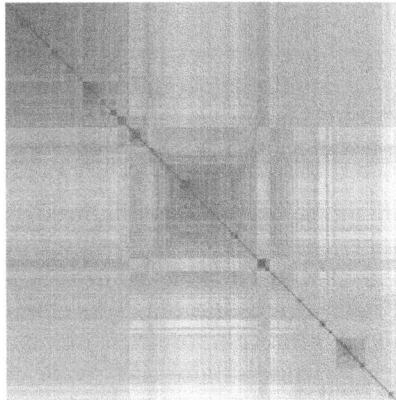

*Figure 1.2   Deductive and inductive ordering of similarity groupings in
large corpora*

developing country boundaries. We thus visualized treaty similarity scores
through a heat map ordered alphabetically by the richer party in each
treaty (Figure 1.2a). While the figure suggests that there are groupings
of similarly worded agreements, the map remained patchy. The FTA
corpus unlike the investment treaty corpus could thus not be meaningfully
described through a rule-maker/rule-taker pattern. Instead of testing
another hypothesis, however, we decided to follow an inductive approach
of letting the data speak for itself. We used a hierarchical clustering
algorithm to reorder the same heat map. After interpreting the resulting
structure depicted in Figure 1.2b we realized that regional clusters of
similarly worded treaties characterized the FTA corpus: European states
were concluding one type of agreement, while states in America and East
Asia were following a different treaty template. This regionalization of
FTA language was a structure we "discovered" inductively (Alschner et al.,
2018b).

Using automated legal text comparison to understand how legal documents group together in large corpora then prepares the ground for new
questions and theories. What makes investment treaties behave differently
from FTAs? Why are some regions concluding more homogenous agreements than others? Inductive analysis can thus lead to questions that we
did not conceive of before because we lacked a grasp of the underlying
data structure. This, in turn, can give rise to new theories that formalize
the explanations for the patterns we observe.

6.   ACQUIRING THE SKILLS TO CONDUCT AUTOMATED TEXT COMPARISONS

The above overview has shown that automated text comparison enjoys a wide range of applications in the legal field. So how can lawyers and legal researchers not yet in possession of the necessary skills to conduct such analysis acquire them?

First, a growing number of online applications allow users to engage in simple corpus analytics and basic text comparisons. One of these tools is *Voyant*.[7] It allows users to explore texts through an appealing interface and a wide range of analytics that draw on word frequency counts and collocations. As computational linguistics and natural language processing touches ever more aspects of the human, social and legal sciences, more such tools will become available that provide an entry point into corpus analytics without requiring any programming background.

Those thinking more seriously about applying automated text comparisons to legal questions should consider acquiring basic programming skills. Programming environments such as R allow users to webscrape, analyze and visualize legal texts. They allow a degree of customization that existing introductory websites do not offer and can thus be tailored to the specific task and research needs at hand. In addition, a growing body of resources including online materials, textbooks and a computational legal community with annual conferences allows all those interested in computational legal analysis to learn more about the field and to acquire the necessary skillset.[8]

As more legal texts become digitized, the corpus of machine-readable law is growing. Traditional legal tools of relying on close reading cannot be scaled and can thus not keep up with the growth of legal text information available. Particularly young lawyers and law students should therefore invest in acquiring distant reading skills to complement their close reading abilities in order to seize the many opportunities that increased use of automated text comparison creates in the legal domain.

---

[7]   http://docs.voyant-tools.org/.
[8]   See e.g. www.datascienceforlawyers.org, https://www.computationallegal studies.com. International conferences include JURIX and ICAIL.

BIBLIOGRAPHY

Allee, T., and Lugg, A. (2016). Who Wrote the Rules for the Trans-Pacific Partnership? *Research & Politics*, *3*(3), 1–9, 2053168016658919. https://doi.org/10. 1177/2053168016658919.

Alschner, W., and Skougarevskiy, D. (2016). Mapping the Universe of International Investment Agreements. *Journal of International Economic Law*, *19*(8), 561–88.

Alschner, W., Panford-Walsh, R., and Skougarevskiy, D. (2018a). *What Can the Negotiations of NAFTA 1.0 Teach Us about the Fate of NAFTA 2.0?* Ottawa Faculty of Law Working Paper No. 2018-05.

Alschner, W., Pauwelyn, J., and Puig, S. (2017a). The Data-Driven Future of International Economic Law. *Journal of International Economic Law*, *20*(2), 217–31. https://doi.org/10.1093/jiel/jgx020.

Alschner, W., Seiermann, J., and Skougarevskiy, D. (2017b). Text-as-Data Analysis of Preferential Trade Agreements: Mapping the PTA Landscape. UNCTAD Research Paper, UNCTAD/SER.RP/2017/5.

Alschner, W., Seiermann, J., and Skougarevskiy, D. (2018b). Text of Trade Agreements (ToTA): A Structured Corpus for the Text-as-Data Analysis of Preferential Trade Agreements. *Journal of Empirical Legal Studies*, *15*(3), 648–66. https://doi.org/10.1111/jels.12189.

Arnold, T., and Tilton, L. (2015). *Humanities Data in R: Exploring Networks, Geospatial Data, Images, and Text* (1st ed.). Cham: Springer.

Berge, T.L., and Stiansen, Ø. (2016). Negotiating BITs with Models: The Power of Expertise. Retrieved 12 March 2019 from https://papers.ssrn.com/sol3/papers. cfm?abstract_id=2851454.

Burgess, M., Giraudy, E., Katz-Samuels, J., Walsh, J., Willis, D., Haynes, L., and Ghani, R. (2016). The Legislative Influence Detector: Finding Text Reuse in State Legislation. In *Proceedings of the 22nd ACM SIGKDD International Conference on Knowledge Discovery and Data Mining* (pp. 57–66). New York, NY: ACM Press, https://doi.org/10.1145/2939672.2939697.

Coulthard, M., and Johnson, A. (eds). (2010). *The Routledge Handbook of Forensic Linguistics*. Milton Park, Abingdon, Oxon; New York, NY: Routledge.

Cross, J.P., and Hermansson, H. (2017). Legislative Amendments and Informal Politics in the European Union: A Text Reuse Approach. *European Union Politics*, *18*(4), 581–602. https://doi.org/10.1177/1465116517717071.

Denny, M.J., and Spirling, A. (2018). Text Preprocessing for Unsupervised Learning: Why It Matters, When It Misleads, and What to Do about It. *Political Analysis*, *26*(2), 168–89. https://doi.org/10.1017/pan.2017.44.

Geist, A. (2008). The Open Revolution: Using Citation Analysis to Improve Legal Text Retrieval. *European Journal of Legal Studies*, *2*(3), 137–45. Retrieved 12 March 2019 from http://cadmus.eui.eu//handle/1814/15121.

Grimmer, J., and Stewart, B.M. (2013). Text as Data: The Promise and Pitfalls of Automatic Content Analysis Methods for Political Texts. *Political Analysis*, *21*(3), 267–97. https://doi.org/10.1093/pan/mps028.

Landthaler, J., Waltl, B., and Matthes, F. (2016). Unveiling References in Legal Texts: Implicit versus Explicit Network Structures. *IRIS: Internationales Rechtsinformatik Symposium*, *8*, 71–8.

Manning, C.D., Raghavan, P., and Schütze, H. (2008). *Introduction to Information Retrieval* (1st ed.). New York: Cambridge University Press.

Mayer-Schönberger, V., and Cukier, K. (2014). *Big Data: A Revolution That Will Transform How We Live, Work, and Think* (reprint edition). Boston: Eamon Dolan/Mariner Books.

Mikolov, T., Chen, K., Corrado, G., and Dean, J. (2013). Efficient Estimation of Word Representations in Vector Space. *ArXiv Preprint ArXiv:1301.3781*. Retrieved 12 March 2019 from http://arxiv.org/abs/1301.3781.

Moretti, F. (2013). *Distant Reading*. London New York: Verso.

Nanda, R., Siragusa, G., Di Caro, L., Boella, G., Grossio, L., Gerbaudo, M., and Costamagna, F. (2018). Unsupervised and Supervised Text Similarity Systems for Automated Identification of National Implementing Measures of European Directives. *Artificial Intelligence and Law*, *27*(1), 199–225 https://doi.org/10.1007/s10506-018-9236-y.

Schweighofer, E., and Geist, A. (2007). Legal Query Expansion Using Ontologies and Relevance Feedback. In Casanovas, P., Biasiotti, M., Francesconi, E., and Sagri, M. (eds), *Proceedings of the 2nd Workshop on Legal Ontologies and Artificial Intelligence Techniques June 4th, 2007, Stanford University, Stanford, CA, USA* (pp. 149–60), available at: http://ceur-ws.org/Vol-321/LOAIT07-Proceedings.pdf.

Spirling, A. (2012). U.S. Treaty Making with American Indians: Institutional Change and Relative Power, 1784–1911. *American Journal of Political Science*, *56*(1), 84–97. https://doi.org/10.1111/j.1540-5907.2011.00558.x.

Whalen, R. (2018). Boundary Spanning Innovation and the Patent System: Interdisciplinary Challenges for a Specialized Examination System. *Research Policy*, *47*(7), 1334–43. https://doi.org/10.1016/j.respol.2018.04.017.

Wilkerson, J., Smith, D., and Stramp, N. (2015). Tracing the Flow of Policy Ideas in Legislatures: A Text Reuse Approach. *American Journal of Political Science*, *59*(4), 943–56. https://doi.org/10.1111/ajps.12175.

Winkels, A.R., Boer, A., Vredebregt, B., and Someren, A.V. (2014). Towards a Legal Recommender System. In Hoekstra R. (ed.), *JURIX 2014: International Conference on Legal Knowledge and Information Systems* (pp. 169–78). Amsterdam: IOS Press.

2. Computational legal studies, digital humanities, and textual analysis*

Nina Varsava

INTRODUCTION

Scholars in the humanities are increasingly turning to computer-assisted methods of analyzing both the form and substance of textual data. Legal scholars, too, increasingly use computational approaches to analyze texts—judicial opinions, litigant briefs, and statutes, for example. But these two fields of computational inquiry have been developing in parallel, and not so much in conversation with one another.

Digital humanities tools, designed to dissect and measure formal and topical elements of texts in digital form, are well-suited to legal textual data. Computational legal studies can benefit not only from digital humanities tools, but also from the humanist sensibilities that inform these tools. Humanists are highly attuned to the importance of formal and stylistic elements of texts, and to the relationship between form and other variables of interest.

In my own computational work, I have been most concerned with the form and style of judicial opinions. A judge's writing style might tell us something about her philosophy or personality.[1] Trends in writing style might also reflect and alert us to jurisprudential trends. And we might be able to trace lines of influence through stylistic similarities and differences among judges, courts, and jurisdictions. More generally, "[b]ecause '[t]he design of legal doctrine (the words, the syntax, and structure of the written opinions) may have serious implications' for the functioning of the judiciary[,] any insight into the ways in which judges choose the form of their language offers insight into the functioning of our judicial system" (Tiller

---

*   I am grateful to Doug Duhaime and the Digital Humanities Lab at Yale, as well as Ryan Heuser, for computational support.

[1]   See Carlson et al., 2016, p. 1470: "[s]tyle may serve as an indicator of judicial temperament or disposition"; Cross and Pennebaker, 2014, p. 893: "The opinion language chosen by a judge also provides insight into that judge's personality."

and Cross as cited in Hinkle et al., 2012, p. 408). And, as Keith Carlson and coauthors (2016, p. 1470) assert, judicial opinion style "may be deserving of study simply as an empirical feature of an important cultural artifact." Separating form from substance is a tricky business, however, and my analyses often implicate semantics as well as style.

This chapter begins with a discussion of computational textual analysis in the humanities, with a focus on stylometry, and elaborates the promise of these methods for legal studies. Part two presents an example—a quantitative analysis of now-Justice Kavanaugh's opinion writing. And part three delineates some of the challenges and limitations of computational textual analysis. Computational legal scholars often come from political science or economics, and rarely, it seems, from the humanities. Overall, this chapter seeks to initiate and encourage conversation between digital humanities and computational legal studies.

1. DIGITAL HUMANITIES AND COMPUTATIONAL TEXTUAL ANALYSIS

Scholars in the humanities, especially in history and literary studies, are increasingly dealing with digital texts and embracing computational methods of textual analysis. These methods have enabled a shift in scale and vantage point. Traditionally, both historians and literary scholars would read texts for themselves, engaging in close, and typically linear, reading to discover patterns and draw out themes.

The move to computer-assisted analysis enables researchers to process far more textual data than traditional methods would permit. Moreover, computational methods facilitate a bird's-eye or macroscopic view of textual data, enabling researchers to perceive a text or body of texts all at once. We can now visualize, by way of graphs, patterns and trends in style and content across vast swaths of textual data. As some digital humanists observe, it is "like having a telescope that makes you see entirely new galaxies" (Algee-Hewitt et al., 2016, p. 1).[2] Digital humanists have explored, for example, the systematic differences in descriptions of men and women characters in fic-

---

[2]   As Wolfgang Alschner explains in his chapter in this volume, human readers cannot "conduct legal document comparison at scale"; "[f]or that we need . . . *distant reading*," which "not only offers efficiency gains but also an entirely new perspective on the law" (p. 10). And, as Jonathon Penney observes in his chapter, relationships among variables of interest and especially subtle effects "may not always be clear or obvious on an individual or group-level basis," but "may be far easier to detect, measure, and document at larger scales" (p. 151).

tion; whether and how writing style correlates with an author's demographic features, such as gender, race, and nationality; and the textual features that set novelistic genres, such as the bildungsroman and gothic, apart.[3]

In a parallel universe, legal scholars are increasingly turning to computational methods to facilitate the analysis and interpretation of legal texts. In the realm of statutory and constitutional interpretation, some scholars and judges of the originalist and textualist persuasion have turned to corpora of digitized texts to help determine the original public meaning of constitutional or statutory language. For example, in a case concerning a contemporary statutory provision (*State v. Rasabout*, 2015), Justice Thomas Lee of the Utah Supreme Court used Google news search results as well as an online corpus of contemporary U.S. English-language texts to ascertain the most common public meaning of a key phrase ("discharge a firearm"). And Brigham Young University Law School is creating a corpus of Founding-Era English-language texts (Brigham Young University Law School, 2019), which will facilitate originalist constitutional interpretation.

Although the field of corpus linguistics and law has been associated with originalism, there is nothing inherently originalist about the intersection of corpus linguistics and legal studies. Corpus linguistics refers simply to the study of language based on (usually large) textual datasets, where the text data is "natural" as opposed to experimentally generated.[4] As corpus linguist Stefan Gries (2009, p. 1226) explains, "linguists of every theoretical persuasion can use corpus data." I believe that the same is true of legal scholars: they can take advantage of corpus data no matter their theoretical commitments. For example, a living constitutionalist might be interested in tracking the changing meaning of morally loaded

---

[3] See, e.g., Underwood et al., 2018: finding that, beginning in the mid-nineteenth century, "characters are less and less clearly sorted along a masculine-feminine axis"; Koppel et al., 2002, pp. 403–4: using a "set of lexical and quasi-syntactic features" to predict author gender of a corpus of fiction and non-fiction texts, and achieving an 80 percent accuracy rate; Weidman and O'Sullivan, 2017, p. 383: finding greater stylistic differences between men and women authors today than in the Victorian period, and that "[f]emales generally tend toward the language of place in the private or micro-sense—'home', 'kitchen', 'church', 'hallway', and 'school'—whereas males throughout all periods tend toward greater spaces— 'country', 'earth', 'city', 'town', and 'world'"; Allison et al., 2011: uncovering systematic differences in part-of-speech frequencies, vocabulary, and tense among novel genres. And see generally Jockers, 2013.

[4] See Gries, 2009, p. 1232: explaining that "[t]he texts that make up the corpus must have been produced in a natural communicative setting[, which] means that the texts were spoken or written for some authentic communicative purpose [and] not for the purpose of putting them into a corpus."

constitutional terms, such as "cruel and unusual," over time (which would require a diachronic corpus rather than the synchronic or time-slice corpora that suit originalists).

Moreover, corpus-based studies need not be concerned with meaning at all, but might be concerned rather with the form or style of texts. "Stylometry" refers to the quantitative study of style, and most contemporary stylometric work relies on digital corpora and computational methods of analysis. Despite the massive amount of digital textual data available for legal scholars to study, stylometry of legal texts is still relatively rare. Some scholars, however, have pursued stylometric studies in the context of law—in particular of lawyers' briefs and judicial opinions. For example, one study explores the relationship between expressions of certainty in briefs and litigant success rates, finding that certainty terms are negatively associated with success (Long and Christensen, 2008, p. 185). Another study found that the reading ease of briefs is positively associated with litigant success (Spencer and Feldman, 2018).

Previous stylometric studies of judicial opinion style have focused largely on rudimentary formal features—for example, opinion length, quantity of block quotations, and "function words" (which are words that carry little or no semantic value, such as articles and prepositions).[5] Moreover, much of the existing stylometric research on judicial opinions revolves around ideological and political concerns. For example, Rachael Hinkle and coauthors (2012) examined the effect of ideology on federal district court opinions, finding that, at least in some contexts, the ideological distance between a district court judge and the overseeing appellate court judge affects the style of the district court's opinions.

Law and humanities scholars, especially in the law and literature tradition, have long been interested in legal style and rhetoric, in particular in the context of judicial writing. And they have carried out detailed studies of opinion style, often focusing on sophisticated aspects such as narrative and suspense.[6] These studies focus on individual cases, however, and

---

[5] See, e.g., Black and Spriggs, 2008: analyzing opinion length; Bodwin et al., 2013, p. 162: "measuring writing variability through the use of common function words"; Carlson et al., 2016: measuring stylistic change across time through analysis of function words; Hume, 2009, p. 138: analyzing block quotations; McCormick, 2016: using function-word analysis to detect likely authors of Canadian judgments that are signed "By the Court."

[6] See, e.g., Nussbaum, 1995: discussing Richard Posner's narrative style of writing through an analysis of a single opinion; Posner, 1995, pp. 1442–4: contrasting an opinion by the late Judge Patricia Wald with a Justice Holmes opinion to illustrate the stylistic camps of "pure" and "impure" writing; Stern, 2011, p. 342: discussing the use of plot and suspense in judicial opinions.

employ qualitative rather than quantitative methods of analysis.[7] The traditional, qualitative approach to rhetoric has yielded rich insights about particular judicial opinions, and is particularly well-suited to the study of exceptional cases. But close reading is not cut out for large-scale analysis. Stylometric methods can complement traditional approaches to the study of style by enabling us to quantify the prevalence of stylistic features across many cases, detect patterns among these features, and ascertain relationships between them and other variables of interest.

Stylometry also enables us to test judgments about judicial writing style and to get a better grasp of how jurists achieve particular rhetorical effects. For example, in the months leading up to and following his confirmation hearing, now-Justice Neil Gorsuch's writing received a great deal of attention from the media and legal community. Commentators focused on individual opinions to support conclusions about Gorsuch's writing generally—for example, that it is lively, accessible, and non-technical (CBS News, 2017; Johnson, 2017; Palazzolo, 2017; Savage, 2017; Schiess, 2017; Stern, 2018). Ross Guberman (2017a) stated that, "[u]nlike, say, Judge Merrick Garland, whose writing is excellent but rather ordinary, . . . Gorsuch appears to strive to be a Great Writer, not just a great opinion writer." The particular opinions that commentators focus on in their qualitative analyses, however, might not be representative of a judge's corpus of writing as a whole. Moreover, the human eye might be insensitive to certain stylistic details and patterns that contribute to the rhetorical effect of a text.

In a previous study, I analyzed the corpus of published, majority opinions that Gorsuch wrote for the Tenth Circuit Court of Appeals; I compared his opinions stylistically to those of his Tenth Circuit peers, to see whether and how his writing style differs systematically from other judges (Varsava, 2018a).[8] My findings suggest that, for better or worse, Gorsuch really is an exceptional writer. For example, his opinions are highly informal and have grown increasingly so over time (Varsava, 2018a, pp. 113–15). Moreover, and as commentators who have criticized Gorsuch's tone as condescending and arrogant might expect,[9] he uses

---

[7] See Meyler, 2016, p. 89: explaining that "rhetorical accounts of law [have] placed priority on interpretation of the individual case," and encouraging scholars interested in the style and rhetoric of legal texts to consider computational methods of analysis.

[8] Digital humanities scholars have done the same with literary authors. See, e.g., Rice, 2018.

[9] See, e.g., Greenhouse, 2017; Stern, 2018: "Gorsuch has a habit of lecturing his colleagues in the most condescending tone possible."

language expressing certainty, such as "obviously" and "surely," much more than average. However, I found that he also uses terms expressing hesitancy, such as "possibly" and "maybe" a lot more than normal—a rhetorical tendency that has been overlooked by commentators, fans, and critics alike. Some commentators have associated Gorsuch's opinion-writing style with Scalia's (Citron, 2017; Liptak, 2017);[10] this is another claim that we could test using stylometric methods.

Many books and articles are devoted to advising lawyers and judges about writing style. But the prescriptions this literature supplies are based largely on individual critics' subjective assessments of what makes for strong legal writing. For example, commentators urge judges to avoid legalese, especially legal Latin, and to embrace informality.[11] The Federal Judicial Center produces a writing manual that instructs judges to use the real names of litigants in their opinions, rather than technical terms such as "plaintiff" and "appellee," since the latter "tend to be confusing" (2013, p. 14).[12] And commentators often imply that judicial influence depends on writing style. Bryan Garner (2013, p. 57), for example, observes that "some of the most influential judicial stylists [use contractions] routinely."[13]

In work-in-progress based on a corpus of federal appellate decisions, I am testing the relationship between, on the one hand, stylistic variables such as use of contractions and, on the other, a decision's legal importance

---

[10]   "In turn, commentators suggest that Scalia's style resembles that of jurists such as Robert Jackson and Oliver Wendell Holmes. See, e.g., Pusey, 2008: noting that Cass Sunstein "has likened [Scalia's] writings to those of Justices Robert H. Jackson and Oliver Wendell Holmes" (fn 10).

[11]   See, e.g., Aldisert, 2009, p. 7: asserting that judges should write opinions in a "plain English" style; George, 2000, p. 162: asserting that opinions "should be easy to read," with simple sentences and without legal jargon; Guberman, 2015, p. 162: suggesting that opinions are "too stuffy and formal."

[12]   See also Aldisert, 2009, p. 223: encouraging judges to write in plain language; George, 2000, p. 29: urging judges to avoid "Latin words or phrases unless they are unavoidable"; Guberman, 2017b: suggesting that lawyers should avoid legal Latin in their briefs; Lebovits et al., 2008, p. 259: "Legalese has no place in judicial opinions."

[13]   See also Posner, 1990, p. 143: suggesting that great rhetoricians, by his own standards, have the greatest long-term impact on the law; Posner, 1995, p. 1425: "The sparkling, vivid, memorable opinion is not so chained to the immediate context of its creation"; Posner, 2009, p. 334: discussing "the effect of style on portability" and asserting that "[t]he vivid and therefore memorable opinion is not chained to the immediate context of its creation[, and] can be pulled out and made to exemplify law's abiding concerns"; CBS News, 2017: "Justices who write poorly tend to have little lasting influence and can be easily forgotten" (paraphrasing Bryan Garner).

or impact, measured by the number of subsequent cases that cite it. Based on preliminary tests, stylistic variables appear to be strongly associated with citations. However, the relationships run largely in the opposite direction from what we might expect based on the judicial writing litera-ture. For example, signifiers of formality, such as legal Latin and technical terms for litigants, seem to be positively associated with citations, whereas signifiers of informality, such as contractions, are negatively associated with citations.[14] I am also testing for relationships between judge gender and judicial opinions, as I suspect that there are systematic gender differ-ences in opinion-writing practices.

Some commentators have speculated on the relationship between writing style and judicial philosophy. For example, Posner (1995, p. 1432) claims that judges who write in an "impure" style—which is "direct, forth-right, 'man to man,' colloquial, [and] informal"—are more likely to be pragmatists, whereas judges who write in a "pure" style—which is "lofty, formal, imperious, impersonal, [and] 'refined'"—are more likely to be for-malists.[15] With a corpus of opinions and computer algorithms, we could test claims about the relationship between stylistic tendencies and all kinds of other variables of interest, including jurisprudence,[16] citations, quality of reasoning,[17] and judge demographics. Moreover, following digital humanists who have studied differences in language used to describe male and female fiction characters, we could study whether and how judicial descriptions of litigants differ systematically according to litigant gender, race, class, and other dimensions of interest.

Some commentators suggest that opinions can and should take on a narrative structure. For example, Guberman (2015, p. 162) says that an opinion should have a "strong dramatic arc." Using sentiment analysis, we could explore whether opinions have plots and what shape those plots

---

[14]   Moreover, if machine-detectable stylistic features are systematically associ-ated with citations, then we should be able to use computer-assisted stylometrics to predict legal impact, measured by citation counts. Digital humanists have already shown that we can use computational methods of textual analysis to predict whether a novel will be a bestseller (Archer and Jockers, 2016).

[15]   See also Domnarski, 1996, p. 61: based on a qualitative review of opinions, observing "a connection between a Justice's effective writing style and his contri-bution to constitutional jurisprudence."

[16]   In their chapter in this volume, Nischal Mainali and coauthors use compu-tational techniques to identify linguistic differences between consequentialist and deontological philosophical papers. They then use those linguistic differences to classify judicial opinions by moral reasoning type.

[17]   Some commentators have suggested that the style of an opinion affects its substantive merit (see, e.g., George, 2000, p. 385).

take.[18] Computational methods can also enable us to track stylistic trends across time, as well as stylistic networks of influence among judges, courts, and jurisdictions.[19]

Moreover, several scholars have suggested that perceptions of the fairness and legitimacy of the legal system depend on the extent to which participants in the system feel that legal authorities take their concerns seriously. Chad Oldfather (2007, p. 1338) suggests that "[p]arties want to feel that they have had a meaningful opportunity to present their position to the decisionmaker," and that "[a]n opinion, simply by engaging with the parties' arguments, can provide such assurance." Legal scholars and social scientists claim that legal procedures come across as legitimate when they make people "feel that legal authorities listen to and consider their concerns" (Tyler and Mitchell, 1994, p. 751). Using computational methods, we could test the force of this claim in the context of judicial opinions. Tools designed to measure the similarity or distance between texts would enable us to ascertain the extent to which judicial opinions reflect litigant briefs.[20] We could then explore the relationship between an opinion's engagement with litigant briefs and whether the losing party filed an appeal. We could also measure the relationship between judicial uptake of litigant material and litigant satisfaction rates or perceptions of legitimacy, although such an inquiry would require some kind of methodological intervention in addition to computational analysis, such as a survey study.

More generally, using a computational approach we can gain insight into the opinion-writing process—an unregulated activity that varies by court and judge, and that unfolds behind closed doors. For example, computational methods can help us identify whether and to what extent judges collaborate in the opinion-writing process, and how much influence clerks have over the final product. Some judges have suggested that the role of clerks in the researching and drafting process ultimately does not affect the style of opinions.[21] However, computational textual studies have revealed

---

[18]   Sentiment analysis is based on sentiment "dictionaries"—lists of words expressing different types of sentiment or emotion. Sentiment analysis can help to identify the emotional valence of passages of text as well as points of shifting sentiment. Researchers have conducted large-scale studies of plot structure in novels using sentiment analysis. See, e.g., Reagan et al., 2016: using sentiment analysis to examine the emotional arcs of 1327 works of fiction.

[19]   As digital humanists observe, "[t]o chart influence empirically, we need to go beyond the individual cases and look to the aggregate" (Jockers, 2013, p. 156). Computational methods make this kind of aggregate view possible.

[20]   For example, the R package "text2vec," and the Python packages Gensim and scikit-learn, include functions for measuring the degree of similarity between texts.

[21]   See Wilson, 2002, p. 265: "I do not believe that [the] role [of clerks] in this

notable clerk effects on opinion style (Carlson et al., 2016, p. 1505; Choi and Gulati, 2005, p. 1105; Peppers and Zorn, 2008, p. 53; Rosenthal and Yoon, 2011, p. 287; Wahlbeck et al., 2002).

Now that we have a sense of the multifarious questions that methods of computational textual analysis might help us to answer, let us turn to an example. In the next section, I present results from a computational study of now-Justice Brett Kavanaugh's opinion writing, and I introduce some natural language processing tools along the way.

2. WHAT KIND OF WRITER IS JUSTICE KAVANAUGH?

I conducted a computational study of D.C. Circuit of Appeals opinions during Kavanaugh's time on that court. My results suggest that, unlike Gorsuch, whose opinions on average stand out from the pack stylistically, Kavanaugh's opinions, on average at least, are unexceptional. I did find that Kavanaugh's writing is highly stylistically variable from opinion to opinion, compared to that of his peers. Kavanaugh's style also oscillates considerably from year to year, with few discernable trends across time.

A. Corpus

My corpus or dataset includes almost all published majority opinions issued by the D.C. Circuit Court of Appeals between June 2006 and August 2018. I omitted opinions with fewer than 200 words and included only judges who authored at least 20 published opinions during Kavanaugh's tenure on the court. With these filters, my corpus contains 2684 opinions—190 by Kavanaugh, 172 per curiam, and the rest divided among 16 other judges. Women judges are responsible for 29.8 percent of the opinions, and judges appointed by Republican presidents are responsible for 47.6 percent.

B. Methods

Using the Python programming language, I detected stylistic features and measured their density or frequency in each opinion. I used the natural language processing package SpaCy for part-of-speech and

---

process affects my style, because I am responsible for each opinion, and I edit each opinion to ensure that the final draft reflects my thoughts and analysis."

dependency parsing, and named entity recognition. Part-of-speech parsers are "trained" on sets of texts that humans tagged for parts of speech such as "noun" and "verb." Based on its training set, the parser predicts parts of speech in new texts. Dependency parsing and named entity recognition work much the same way. Dependency parsers analyze relationships among parts of a sentence and can thereby detect, for example, instances of active and passive voice. Named entities are objects that have been assigned a name in natural language—countries and persons, for example. If we want to detect how many times a text refers to certain types of named entities, then named entity recognition comes in handy. To calculate the Flesch-Kincaid grade level for the opinions, I used the Textacy package, which is a companion to SpaCy. Textacy has built-in functions for multiple natural language processing tasks.

To find specific terms and phrases in the opinions, I used regular expressions—a method of natural language processing that is compatible with various programming languages. Regular expressions enable us to detect specific character patterns of interest. By way of regular expressions, I searched for and flagged contractions, sentences starting with conjunctions (such as "or" and "so"), legal citations, references to litigants by technical term (such as plaintiff and appellee), and expressions of certainty and hesitancy.[22]

To count words and unique words, I turned each opinion into a "bag of words" and then performed operations on the contents of the bags. I first used regular expressions to clean the opinions of extraneous material such as punctuation and parentheses. Then I split the text on white space and made a list of words corresponding to each opinion. This process is called "tokenizing." From there, I simply ran a count function on the list to get word count, and then counted the number of unique words in the list (by first turning the list into a mathematical set, and then counting the items in the set). I calculated the lexical diversity or range of vocabulary for each opinion using the type-token ratio: this is the ratio of unique to total words. I also used a bag-of-words approach to search for instances of legal Latin: I developed a list of legal Latin terms and then searched for matches among the bag-of-words associated with each opinion.[23]

To detect whether an opinion takes a "suspenseful" structure, saving

---

[22] Regular expressions are an almost inevitably over- and under-inclusive means of capturing features of interest. Determining which character strings to capture often requires debatable judgment calls. See *infra* footnote 27 for an elaboration of some of these judgments. The Python code used for all the analyses discussed here is on file with the author.

[23] My legal Latin list is based on Wikipedia's "List of Latin legal terms."

the conclusion for the end rather than revealing it up front, I searched for judgment or outcome keywords such as "affirm" and "reverse" in the opening (first 400 words) of each opinion.[24] My suspense algorithm marks an opinion as suspenseful if a judgment keyword does not appear in the opening; otherwise, the opinion is marked as non-suspenseful.

Finally, I wrote Python scripts to connect key pieces of metadata, such as authoring judge and whether the decision has a dissent or concurrence, with the majority opinion text data. I compiled a dataframe that includes each piece of metadata as well as each style variable, and ultimately ran my statistical analyses, using SPSS,[25] on this dataframe.

C. Results

I found that, on many of my measures—certainty, lexical diversity, technical terms for litigants, references to people, and suspense—Kavanaugh's opinions fall roughly in the middle of the pack.[26] This is in sharp contrast to Gorsuch, whose federal appellate opinion writing stands out from his peers on most measures. Accordingly, Kavanaugh's writing style is more difficult to characterize than Gorsuch's. Whereas a quantitative analysis showed Gorsuch's writing to be, for the most part, distinctive, the same kind of analysis shows Kavanaugh's writing to be unexceptional.

Kavanaugh's opinions are relatively high in hesitancy, and low on length, reading grade level, and passive voice. On some indicators of informality, Kavanaugh's opinions fall on the high end, but not on others. Overall, Kavanaugh uses fewer contractions than average, but he also uses less legal Latin, and he starts more of his sentences with short conjunctions.

Kavanaugh's opinions display some notable patterns in terms of citations to legal authority.[27] He cites cases relatively infrequently (on average,

---

[24]   The total list of search terms I used is as follows: "dismiss(es)," "reverse(s)," "affirm(s)," "remand(s)," "vacate(s)," "grant(s)," "deny(ies)," "agree," and "disagree." I included the latter two terms because I noticed from reading D.C. Circuit Court of Appeals decisions that judges often communicate the case outcome by stating "we agree" or "disagree [with the district court]." My suspense algorithm inaccurately marks as suspenseful opinions that reveal the outcome in unconventional ways, and incorrectly marks as non-suspenseful opinions that use one or more of my search terms for purposes other than to state the outcome of the case.

[25]   SPSS is a statistical software program commonly used for statistical analysis in the social sciences.

[26]   See Appendix Table 2A.1 for judge means and standard deviations on the style variables.

[27]   As noted above, I used regular expressions to detect legal citations, which

less than all except one of his D.C. Circuit peers) (see Figure 2.1). But he cites statutory and constitutional provisions relatively frequently (more than all but one of his peers) (see Figure 2.2).[28] And, the results regarding citations to cases and statutes are distinct in that we can discern something of a Kavanaugh trend on these variables across time, whereas his opinions oscillate substantially from year to year on the other variables. During his time on the D.C. Circuit, his citations to cases decreased, particularly if we look at his later years on the court, but his citations to statutory and constitutional provisions increased (see Figures 2.3 and 2.4).[29] These findings may be indicative of a decreasing concern for precedent and a growing concern for legislation and the Constitution.[30]

On most of the textual variables I measured, Kavanaugh's opinion

---

means that I manually constructed a list of text strings that correspond to case citations and statutory citations. My regular expressions seem to do a relatively good job at capturing and disambiguating citations, but they are both under- and over-inclusive. For examples of under-inclusivity, my code did not count instances of "Id.," since that abbreviation can signify a citation to any type of source; accordingly, the code missed back-to-back citations to both statutes and cases. And the code catches references to an "Act," but does not detect abbreviations for specific Acts, such as "FERPA." It does catch references to "U.S.C." For examples of over-inclusivity, the code counts instances of the capitalized word "Article" as a constitutional citation, but sometimes part of a contract is referenced as an "Article." And, in some instances the code double counts references to statutory and constitutional provisions. For example, the regular expressions count instances of both "Act" and "U.S.C.," but sometimes both terms are used in a single reference to a piece of legislation. All of this is to say that the regular expression method of detecting citations is highly imperfect, and different researchers might reasonably make different judgment calls as to which text patterns to include and exclude. In any event, though, my trend analyses and judge comparisons should still be informative, since the same code was used across all years and judges, and I have no reason to believe that different D.C. Court of Appeals judges use different citation conventions in their opinions.

[28] My code for capturing statutory and constitutional references also captures citations to federal regulations and rules issued by the Supreme Court, such as the Federal Rules of Civil Procedure, but it does not capture local regulations such as the D.C. Municipal Regulations.

[29] For the trend figures, I removed the years that bookend Kavanaugh's D.C. Circuit career (2006 and 2018), since he wrote relatively few published majority opinions in those years.

[30] In another computational study of Kavanaugh's D.C. Circuit opinions, Elliott Ash and Daniel Chen suggest that Kavanaugh's citations to the Constitution, and in particular his more frequent citations to Articles II (concerning the powers of the president) and III (concerning the judicial powers) than other judges, indicate that Kavanaugh's opinions are relatively conservative and Originalist in reasoning (Ash and Chen, 2018, pp. 92–3).

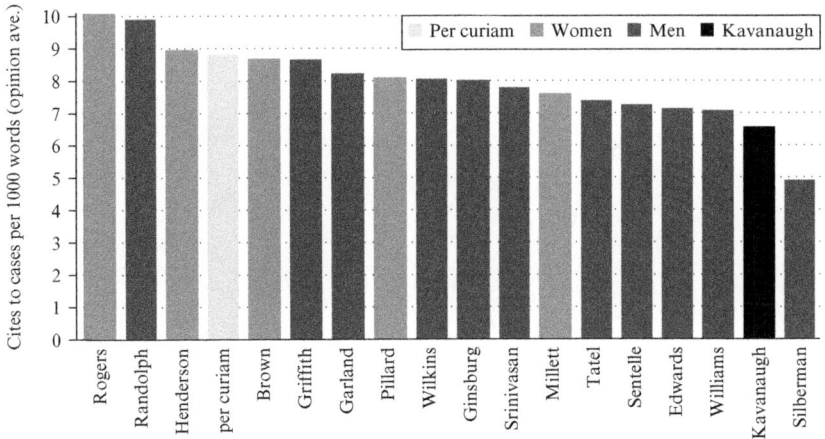

Figure 2.1   Average citations to cases on the D.C. Circuit Court of Appeals by judge

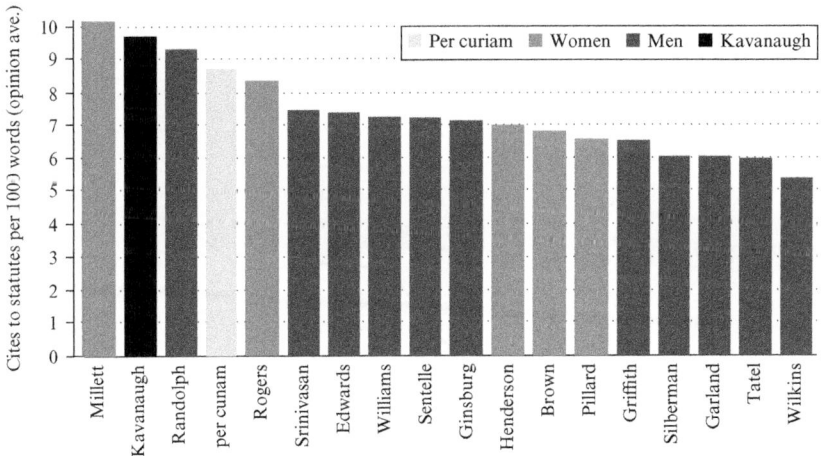

Figure 2.2   Average citations to statutes and the Constitution on the D.C. Circuit Court of Appeals by judge

means do not stand out from his D.C. Circuit peers. His opinion standard deviations, however, do stand out on most variables. On citations to statutes, expressions of certainty and hesitancy, lexical diversity, passive voice, and references to people, Kavanaugh's opinions have the highest standard deviation of all the judges in my set; on references to litigants by technical

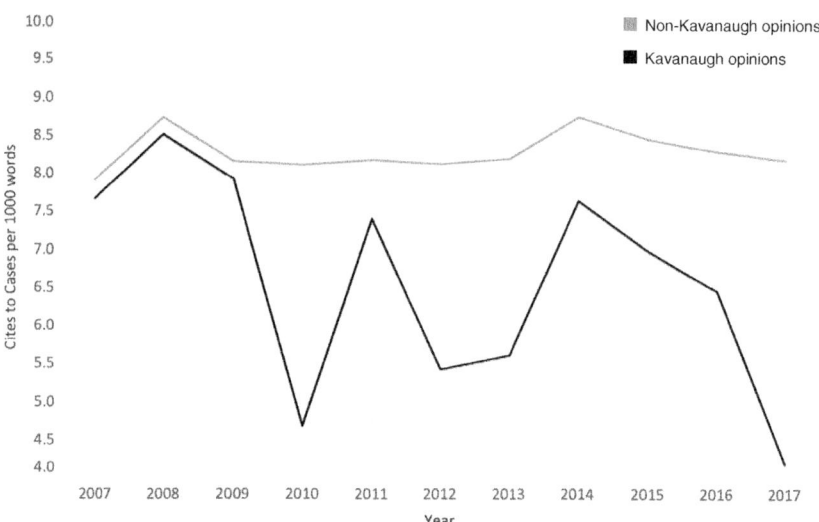

Figure 2.3   Trends in average citations to cases on the D.C. Circuit Court of Appeals

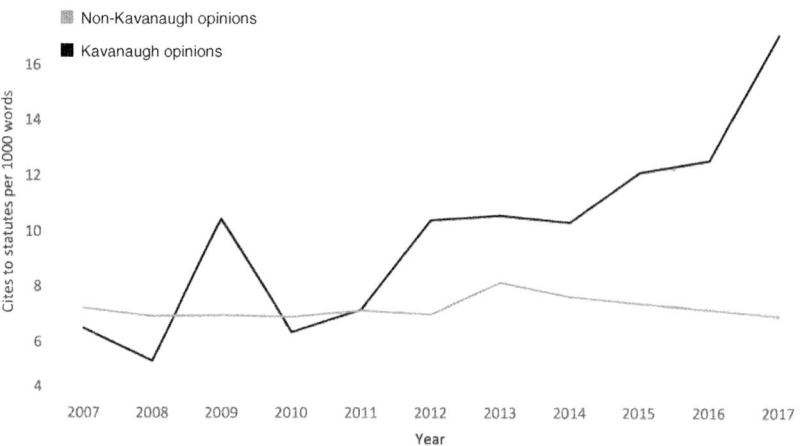

Figure 2.4   Trends in average citations to statutes and the Constitution on the D.C. Circuit Court of Appeals

term and sentences starting with short conjunctions, his opinions have the second highest standard deviation; and on legal Latin and citations to cases they have the third highest standard deviation.

My empirical results suggest that, from case to case, Kavanaugh's writing exhibits relatively little stylistic consistency. The most plausible explanation for this finding may be that his law clerks have an outsized degree of influence on his opinions—so that the style of a given opinion depends heavily on which clerk worked on it. Even setting aside the possibility of substantial clerk influence, though, Kavanaugh may care less than other judges about creating and maintaining a consistent personal style, which would also help to explain the substantial variation we see across his opinions.

Kavanaugh's opinions also stand out in terms of their tendency to inspire dissent. Dissenting opinions accompanied 11.6 percent of his majority opinions, whereas the average among the other judges was 7.9 percent. Judge Merrick Garland (Chief Judge since 2013) is a major outlier on the other end of the spectrum. Only 0.6 percent of Garland's opinions generated dissents. The women judges cluster at the high end for percent of majority opinions generating dissent (see Figure 2.5).[31] Whether this gender pattern is generalizable—and, if so, why judges are more likely to dissent against opinions authored by women—are questions I am addressing in ongoing research.

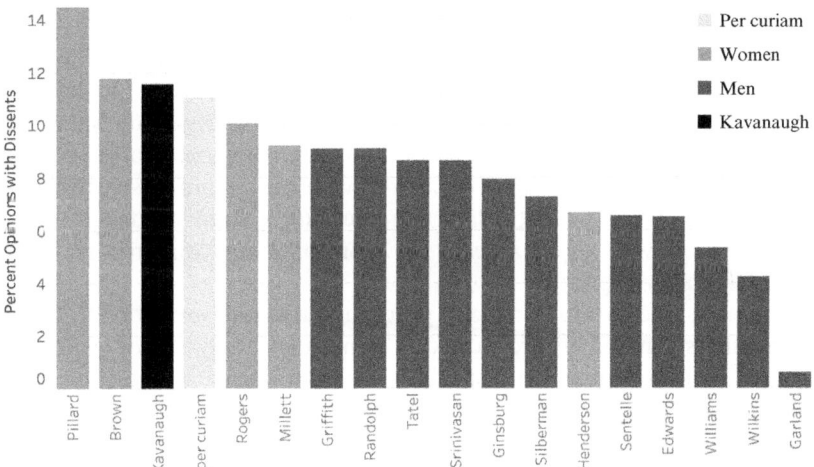

Figure 2.5   Percent of D.C. Circuit Court of Appeals majority opinions with dissents, by judge

---

[31]   The judges tend to cluster by gender on some of the stylistic features I measured as well. Only five women judges are represented in my D.C. Circuit dataset, so we should be wary of generalizing, but I did uncover some similar gender patterns in an analysis of Tenth Circuit opinions. For example, in both circuits, women judges clustered on the low end of expressions of hesitancy as well as certainty.

While Gorsuch's writing style has attracted a lot of pointed and heated commentary, Kavanaugh's style has not attracted nearly as much or as impassioned attention. Guberman (n.d.) calls Kavanaugh's writing "clean"; Lawrence Ebner (2018) observes that Kavanaugh has an "exceptionally clear writing style"; President Trump describes Kavanaugh's writing style as "clear and effective" (Khalid et al., 2018); and Jacqueline Bell (2018) notes that Kavanaugh's writing is "clear" and "concise." The existing commentary about Kavanaugh's writing suggests that his opinions are nothing special, at least stylistically. My quantitative results, for the most part, support that idea. But I did find that Kavanaugh's opinions exhibit some notable patterns in terms of citations to legal authority. My findings also suggest that Kavanaugh's writing is less consistent from opinion to opinion than that of his peers. These characteristics would be difficult to catch using traditional, qualitative methods of analysis alone.

3. SOME LIMITATIONS

First of all, many stylistic features elude machine-recognition and measurement: for example, metaphor, narrative, and irony are all difficult if not impossible to program computers to detect. That said, certain linguistic elements that are amenable to computational methods of analysis—such as sentence structure and tense—may run with these more elusive features of interest.[32] If we want to detect or measure a sophisticated element of style, then, we may be able to use more basic, machine-recognizable textual features as proxies.

Second, some natural language processing methods are more accurate than others, and none are perfect.[33] Sentiment analysis, for example, is known to be unreliable, especially when a sentiment detection tool is employed in a context that differs from its training context.[34] This is

---

[32] See Allison et al., 2013, pp. 5–6 and 20: suggesting that both tense and sentence structure distinguish narrative from other forms of writing; Biber and Conrad, 2009, pp. 109–42: showing that different registers of communication "have systematic linguistic differences" of the type that we can use computers to detect—such as different part-of-speech and tense distributions.

[33] As Malcolm Langford and coauthors note in their chapter in this volume, "[a]s a tool of absolute verifiable truths, stylometrics offer little but indications" (p. 73).

[34] See Rice and Zorn, 2019, p. 3: "'canned' sentiment dictionaries are at best incomplete and at worst inaccurate representations of emotional valence of the words used in a particular context."

because certain words may carry negative valences in one domain but not in another. As others have noted, ideally our sentiment dictionary would be carefully tailored to our textual context of interest (Rice and Zorn, 2019, pp. 2–3). Of the textual features represented in my Kavanaugh study and some of my other computational work,[35] suspense is particularly tricky to estimate. My suspense algorithm, which searches the opening of opinions for outcome keywords such as "reverse" and "affirm," provides only a crude measure of suspense. After all, a judge might reveal the conclusion of a case in a different way.

For example, consider the Supreme Court of Canada's judgment in *Carter v. Canada* (2015) (where the Court held that a criminal prohibition on assisted suicide was unconstitutional), which opens as follows:

> It is a crime in Canada to assist another person in ending her own life. As a result, people who are grievously and irremediably ill cannot seek a physician's assistance in dying and may be condemned to a life of severe and intolerable suffering. A person facing this prospect has two options: she can take her own life prematurely, often by violent or dangerous means, or she can suffer until she dies from natural causes. The choice is cruel.[36]

For a human reading the case, the outcome is readily apparent from the opening. In particular, the final sentence strongly suggests that the court is going to come out against the assisted suicide prohibition. However, given the form in which the outcome is revealed here, the opinion's lack of suspense is not amenable to machine detection, and my suspense algorithm would inaccurately mark this opinion as suspenseful, since no outcome keyword is present in the opening.

Finally, computational studies are typically based on observational data, such as lawyer briefs and judicial opinions. Observational data are good for exploring relationships and patterns among variables of interest, and can also be useful for building predictive models. Causal relationships are another question, however, and observational data do not readily lend themselves to analyses of causality. Nevertheless, we can generate plausible causal hypotheses based on results from observational, computational studies and can then subject those hypotheses to experimental testing. For example, my preliminary tests of the relationship between an opinion's

---

[35]   See Varsava, 2018a, pp. 103–6: testing a set of Tenth Circuit opinions for unresolved openings, and finding that Gorsuch employed suspense at a far greater rate than his peers and that towards the end of his Tenth Circuit career he wrote the majority of his opinions in the suspenseful style.

[36]   Thank you to Jocelyn Downie for pointing me to this example.

style and the number of cases that cite the opinion suggest that writing style may affect citation counts. We can test hypotheses like this one using supplementary empirical research methods, such as survey studies. As Penney counsels, computational legal studies researchers should "combine computational 'big data' case studies . . . with more traditional social [science] research methods and approaches" (p. 20). Such approaches include survey studies as well as qualitative methods, such as focus groups and interviews.

CONCLUSION

Both digital humanists and legal scholars are absorbed by textual data, and have overlapping concerns and commitments. Digital humanists continue to develop creative approaches for analyzing digital textual data; these approaches can reveal aspects of texts that elude the human eye, and can shed light on extra-textual factors, such as authorship, writing process, and context.

In the realm of legal studies, computational and quantitative methods of textual analysis enable us to answer descriptive questions about the opinions of particular jurists, courts, and jurisdictions, as well as about relationships between elements of those opinions and other variables of interest, such as demographics. Moreover, computational methods, applied to observational data, can help us generate causal hypotheses, which we can then test using other, complementary empirical methods.

The fields of digital humanities and computational legal studies have many of the same sorts of concerns and in large part work with the same type of data—that is, digital texts, in large quantities. This chapter represents an effort to connect these two fields, and in particular to highlight the digital humanities methods and sensibilities that legal scholars might wish to borrow and adapt.

REFERENCES

Aldisert, R.J. (2009). *Opinion Writing* (2nd ed.). Bloomington, IN: Authorhouse.
Algee-Hewitt, M., Allison, S., Gemma, M., Heuser, R., Moretti, F., and Walser, H. (2016). Canon/archive: Large-scale dynamics in the literary field. *Stanford Literary Lab Pamphlet 11*. Retrieved 3 January 2019 from https://litlab.stanford.edu/LiteraryLabPamphlet11.pdf.
Allison, S., Heuser, R., Jockers, M., Moretti, F., and Witmore, M. (2011). Quantitative formalism: An experiment. *Stanford Literary Lab Pamphlet 1*.

Retrieved 3 January 2019 from https://litlab.stanford.edu/LiteraryLabPamphlet1.pdf.

Allison, S., Gemma, M., Heuser, R., Moretti, F., Tevel, A., and Yamboliev, I. (2013). Style at the scale of the sentence. *Stanford Literary Lab Pamphlet 5.* Retrieved 3 January 2019 from https://litlab.stanford.edu/LiteraryLabPamphlet5.pdf.

Archer, J., and Jockers, M.L. (2016). *The Bestseller Code: Anatomy of the Blockbuster Novel.* New York, NY: St. Martin's Press.

Ash, E., and Chen, D.L. (2018). What kind of judge is Brett Kavanaugh? A quantitative analysis. *Cardozo Law Review de novo,* 70–100.

Bell, J. (2018). Not a complicated case: Kavanaugh's straightforward style. Law360, 10 July. Retrieved 3 January 2019 from https://www.law360.com/articles/1061755.

Biber, D., and Conrad, S. (2009). *Register, Genre, and Style.* New York, NY: Cambridge University Press.

Black, R.C., and Spriggs, J.F. (2008). An empirical analysis of the length of U.S. Supreme Court opinions. *Houston Law Review, 45*(3), 621–82.

Bodwin, K., Rosenthal, J.S., and Yoon, A.H. (2013). Opinion writing and authorship on the Supreme Court of Canada. *University of Toronto Law Journal, 63*(2), 159–92.

Brigham Young University Law School. (2019). Corpus of Founding Era American English (COFEA). Retrieved 3 January 2019 from https://lcl.byu.edu/projects/cofea/.

Carlson, K., Livermore, M.A., and Rockmore, D. (2016). A quantitative analysis of writing style on the US Supreme Court. *Washington University Law Review, 93*(6), 1461–510.

Carter v. Canada (Attorney General), S.C.C. 5, [2015] 1 S.C.R. 331. (2015).

CBS News. (2017). Supreme Court nominee Neil Gorsuch's writing described as "breezy." CBS News, 8 March. Retrieved 3 January 2019 from https://www.cbsnews.com/news/supreme-court-nominee-neil-gorsuch-writing-style-breezy-clever/.

Choi, S.J., and Gulati, G.M. (2005). Which judges write their opinions (and should we care?). *Florida State University Law Review, 32*(4), 1077–122.

Citron, E. (2017). Potential nominee profile: Neil Gorsuch. SCOTUSblog, 13 January. Retrieved 3 January 2019 from http://www.scotusblog.com/2017/01/potential-nominee-profile-neil-gorsuch/.

Cross, F.B., and Pennebaker, J.W. (2014). The language of the Roberts Court. *Michigan State Law Review, 2014*(4), 853–94.

Domnarski, W. (1996). *In the Opinion of the Court.* Champaign, IL: University of Illinois Press.

Ebner, L.S. (2018, July 10). Recent opinion exemplifies SCOTUS nominee Kavanaugh's lucid legal writing. Capital appellate advocacy blogpost, 10 July. Retrieved 3 January 2019 from https://capitalappellate.com/briefs/recent-opinion-exemplifies-scotus-nominee-kavanaughs-lucid-legal-writing/.

Federal Judicial Center. (2013). *Judicial Writing Manual: A Pocket Guide for Judges* (2nd ed.).

Garner, B. (2013). *The Redbook: A Manual on Legal Style* (3rd ed.). Eagan, MN: West Academic Publishing.

George, J.J. (2000). *Judicial Opinion Writing Handbook* (4th ed.). Getzville, NY: W.S. Hein.

Greenhouse, L. (2017). Trump's life-tenured judicial avatar. *The New York Times,*

6 July. Retrieved 3 January 2019 from https://www.nytimes.com/2017/07/06/opinion/gorsuch-trump-supreme-court.html.

Gries, S.T. (2009). What is corpus linguistics? *Language and Linguistics Compass*, *3*(5), 1225–41.

Guberman, R. (2015). *Point Taken: How to Write like the World's Best Judges*. New York, NY: Oxford University Press.

Guberman, R. (2017a). Judge Gorsuch is a gifted writer: He's a great writer – but is he a "Great Writer"? Part one: Four gifts. Legal Writing Pro blogpost, 7 February. Retrieved 3 January 2019 from https://www.legalwritingpro.com/blog/judge-gorsuch-gifts/.

Guberman, R. (2017b, June 26). Judges speak out behind closed doors: How your briefs might bug them, and how you can make them smile instead. Legal Writing Pro blogpost, 26 June. Retrieved 3 January 2019 from https://www.legalwritingpro.com/blog/judges-speak-out/.

Guberman, R. (n.d.). Five ways to write like Brett Kavanaugh. Legal Writing Pro blogpost. Retrieved 3 January 2019 from https://www.legalwritingpro.com/five-ways-to-write-like-brett-kavanaugh/.

Hinkle, R.K., Martin, A.D., Shaub, J.D., and Tiller, E.H. (2012). The execution of judicial discourse: A positive theory and empirical analysis of strategic word choice in district court opinions. *Journal of Legal Analysis*, *4*(2), 407–44.

Hume, R.J. (2009). The impact of judicial opinion language on the transmission of federal circuit court precedents. *Law & Society Review*, *43*(1), 127–50.

Jockers, M. (2013). *Macroanalysis: Digital Methods and Literary History*. Champaign, IL: University of Illinois Press.

Johnson, G. (2017). Is Neil Gorsuch a good role model for legal writers? Yes and no. *Vermont Bar Journal*, *43*(3), 27–30.

Khalid, A., Liasson, M., and Snell, K. (2018). Analysis: Trump picks Kavanaugh for Supreme Court. NPR, 9 July. Retrieved 3 January 2019 from https://www.npr.org/2018/07/09/627529497/trump-names-brett-kavanaugh-for-supreme-court.

Koppel, M., Argamon, S., and Shimoni, A.R. (2002). Automatically categorizing written texts by author gender. *Literary and Linguistic Computing*, *17*(4), 401–12.

Lebovits, G., Curtin, A.V., and Solomon, L. (2008). Ethical judicial opinion writing. *Georgetown Journal of Legal Ethics*, *21*, 237–309.

Liptak, A. (2017). In Judge Neil Gorsuch, an echo of Scalia in philosophy and style. *The New York Times*, 31 January. Retrieved 3 January 2019 from https://www.nytimes.com/2017/01/31/us/politics/neil-gorsuch-supreme-court-nominee.html.

Long, L.N., and Christensen, W.F. (2008). Clearly, using intensifiers is very bad: Or is it? *Idaho Law Review*, *45*, 171–89.

McCormick, P. (2016). Nom de plume: Who writes the Supreme Court's "By the Court" judgments? *The Dalhousie Law Journal*, *39*(1), 77–128.

Meyler, B.A. (2016). The rhetoric of precedent. In A. Sarat (ed.), *Rhetorical Processes and Legal Judgments: How Language and Arguments Shape Struggles for Rights and Power* (pp. 83–99). Cambridge, UK: Cambridge University Press.

Nussbaum, M.C. (1995). Poets as judges: Judicial rhetoric and the literary imagination. *The University of Chicago Law Review*, *62*(4), 1477–519.

Oldfather, C.M. (2007). Writing, cognition, and the nature of the judicial functions. *The Georgetown Law Journal*, *96*, 1283–345.

Palazzolo, J. (2017). Supreme Court nominee takes legal writing to next level. *The*

Wall Street Journal, 31 January. Retrieved 3 January 2019 from https://www. wsj.com/articles/supreme-court-nominee-takeslegal-writing-to-next-level-1485 912410?mod=e2tw.

Peppers, T.C., and Zorn, C. (2008). Law clerk influence on Supreme Court decision making: An empirical assessment. *DePaul Law Review, 58,* 51–77.

Posner, R.A. (1990). *Cardozo: A Study in Reputation*. Chicago, IL: The University of Chicago Press.

Posner, R.A. (1995). Judges' writing styles (and do they matter?). *The University of Chicago Law Review, 62*(4), 1421–49.

Posner, R.A. (2009). *Law and Literature* (3rd ed.). Cambridge, MA: Harvard University Press.

Pusey, A. (2008). Making your case. Retrieved 3 January 2019 from http://www. abajournal.com/magazine/article/making_your_case.

Reagan, A.J., Mitchell, L., Kiley, D., Danforth, C.M., and Dodds, P.S. (2016). The emotional arcs of stories are dominated by six basic shapes. *EPJ Data Science, 5*, no. 31.

Rice, D., and Zorn, C. (2019). Corpus-based dictionaries for sentiment analysis of specialized vocabularies. *Political Science Research and Methods*, 1–16. doi:10.1017/psrm.2019.10.

Rice, J. (2018). What makes Hemingway Hemingway? The LitCharts Blog, 3 January. Retrieved 3 January 2019 from https://www.litcharts.com/blog/analit ics/what-makes-hemingway/.

Rosenthal, J.S., and Yoon, A.H. (2011). Detecting multiple authorship of United States Supreme Court legal decisions using function words. *The Annals of Applied Statistics, 5*(1), 283–308.

Savage, D.G. (2017). In his first Supreme Court opinion, Gorsuch shows writing flair, strict interpretation of law. *Los Angeles Times*, 12 June. Retrieved 3 January 2019 from http://www.latimes.com/politics/la-na-pol-gorsuch-firstopini on-20170612-story.html.

Schiess, W. (2017). Justice Gorsuch's first opinion shows his style. Blogpost, 20 June. Retrieved 3 January 2019 from http://sites.utexas.edu/legalwriting/2017/06/20/ justice-gorsuchs-first-opinion-shows-his-style/.

Spencer, S.B., and Feldman, A. (2018). The empirical relationship between brief quality and summary judgment success in state and federal courts. *Legal Writing: Journal of the Legal Writing Institute, 22,* 61–108.

State v. Rasabout, U.T. 72, 356 P.3d 1258, 1271–90 (Lee, J., concurring). (2015).

Stern, M.J. (2018). Neil Gorsuch is a terrible writer. *Slate*, 23 January. Retrieved 3 January 2019 from https://slate.com/news-and-politics/2018/01/neil-gorsuch-is-a-terrible-writer.html.

Stern, S. (2011). Detecting doctrines: The case method and the detective story. *Yale Journal of Law & the Humanities, 23*(2), 339–89.

Tyler, T., and Mitchell, G. (1994). Legitimacy and the empowerment of discretionary legal authority: The United States Supreme Court and abortion rights. *Duke Law Journal, 43*(4), 703–815.

Underwood, T., Bamman, D., and Lee, S. (2018). The transformation of gender in English-language fiction. *Journal of Cultural Analytics*, 13 February. doi:10.31235/osf.io/fr9bk.

Varsava, N. (2018a). Elements of judicial style: A quantitative guide to Neil Gorsuch's opinion writing. *New York University Law Review Online, 93*, 75–126.

Wahlbeck, P.J., Spriggs II, J.F., and Sigelman, L. (2002). Ghostwriters on the court? A stylistic analysis of U.S. Supreme Court opinion drafts. *American Politics Research*, *30*(2), 166–92.

Weidman, S.G., and O'Sullivan, J. (2017). The limits of distinctive words: Re-evaluating literature's gender marker debate. *Digital Scholarship in the Humanities*, *33*(2), 374–90.

Wilson, C.R. (2002). How opinions are developed in the United States Court of Appeals for the Eleventh Circuit. *Stetson Law Review*, *32*, 247–68.

APPENDIX

Table 2A.1 Summary statistics for selected style variables by judge

Judge		Word count	Lexical diversity	Case cites/ 1000 words	Statute cites/ 1000 words	Latin/ 1000 words	Intensifiers/ 1000 words	Hedges/ 1000 words	Passive to active voice	Reading level
Brown	μ	3855	0.27	8.7	6.8	3.5	1.9	3.3	0.09	12.2
n = 187	σ	2107	0.05	3.5	5.3	3.5	1.3	1.5	0.04	1.23
Edwards	μ	5690	0.21	7.2	7.4	2.9	1.7	2.9	0.13	12.8
n = 138	σ	2338	0.03	2.8	5.1	1.8	0.84	1.2	0.04	1.08
Garland	μ	4133	0.24	8.2	6.0	3.6	1.5	2.7	0.09	11.6
n = 167	σ	2134	0.04	3.3	4.9	4.1	0.82	1.7	0.03	1.14
Ginsburg	μ	3545	0.26	8.0	7.1	3.0	1.6	3.5	0.09	13.7
n = 151	σ	2933	0.05	3.9	5.1	2.1	0.98	1.6	0.04	1.50
Griffith	μ	3685	0.26	8.6	6.5	2.8	1.6	2.9	0.09	12.0
n = 198	σ	1795	0.04	3.8	4.7	3.0	1.1	1.3	0.04	1.19
Henderson	μ	3722	0.26	9.0	7.0	3.9	1.3	2.7	0.10	12.2
n = 240	σ	1677	0.04	3.9	4.9	2.6	0.84	1.3	0.04	1.46
Kavanaugh	μ	2923	0.27	6.6	9.7	3.1	1.6	3.7	0.09	12.1
n = 190	σ	2688	0.06	4.0	8.3	3.9	1.4	2.3	0.05	1.25
Millett	μ	5399	0.23	7.6	10.2	3.5	1.6	2.6	0.11	13.2
n = 65	σ	3112	0.05	3.0	5.9	2.8	0.92	1.0	0.04	1.15
Per curiam	μ	5119	0.29	8.8	8.7	4.1	1.5	2.9	0.14	12.5
n = 172	σ	7284	0.11	4.6	6.7	3.7	1.6	1.7	0.15	1.53

Table 2A.1 (continued)

Judge		Word count	Lexical diversity	Case cites/ 1000 words	Statute cites/ 1000 words	Latin/ 1000 words	Intensifiers/ 1000 words	Hedges/ 1000 words	Passive to active voice	Reading level
Pillard	μ	5875	0.22	8.1	6.6	3.8	1.2	3.1	0.09	13.3
n = 69	σ	3306	0.04	3.3	4.7	3.9	0.68	1.3	0.03	1.34
Randolph	μ	2566	0.30	9.9	9.3	2.8	1.3	3.6	0.09	11.3
n = 121	σ	1398	0.05	4.5	5.9	2.8	0.96	1.8	0.03	1.32
Rogers	μ	4446	0.24	10.1	8.4	3.2	0.98	2.8	0.12	13.4
n = 121	σ	2325	0.04	4.3	5.8	2.3	0.66	1.2	0.04	1.29
Sentelle	μ	4073	0.23	7.3	7.2	3.2	1.4	2.7	0.10	13.2
n = 183	σ	2371	0.04	3.6	4.9	3.0	0.98	1.4	0.04	1.39
Silberman	μ	3030	0.29	4.9	6.0	3.0	3.1	3.3	0.13	13.4
n = 55	σ	2083	0.06	3.0	5.3	2.0	1.3	1.6	0.05	1.20
Srinivasan	μ	5234	0.22	7.8	7.4	3.1	1.1	2.8	0.08	12.4
n = 81	σ	2636	0.04	3.7	5.8	3.3	0.55	1.4	0.03	1.13
Tatel	μ	4402	0.25	7.4	6.0	3.3	2.1	3.4	0.07	12.9
n = 208	σ	2486	0.04	2.9	4.4	2.7	0.97	1.5	0.03	1.30
Wilkins	μ	4569	0.24	8.1	5.4	3.8	1.5	2.5	0.11	12.6
n = 71	σ	2052	0.04	3.1	3.8	2.9	1.3	1.3	0.03	1.10
Williams	μ	2888	0.30	7.1	7.3	3.4	2.2	3.9	0.09	13.1
n = 150	σ	1345	0.05	3.4	5.1	3.1	1.0	1.7	0.04	1.26

Note: For the sake of space, not all style variables are included here. Full summary statistics are on file with author.

3. Computational stylometry: predicting the authorship of investment arbitration awards

Malcolm Langford, Daniel Behn and Runar Lie

1. INTRODUCTION

The authorship of judicial opinions was an early target of computational legal studies (Oldfather et al., 2012). Principally focused on the US Supreme Court, different methods were deployed to identify the role of "unseen actors" in writing opinions. Motivated *normatively* by concerns about the disproportionate influence of clerks in "judicial ghostwriting" (Rosenthal and Yoon, 2011) and *theoretically* by an interest in the allocation and optimization of time in judicial labour (Choi and Gulati, 2005), research has sought to detect *who* are the authors of judgments, examine *how* they are influenced by unseen actors, and chart *what* variation exists across judges, actors and time.

The methodology is grounded in stylometry, a linguistic theory premised on human authors leaving fingerprints in their writing and a method based on the statistical analysis of measurable patterns particular to literary style. Early stylometry focused on the prominence of "function words" (such as "a", "by", "if", "of" "their" and "who"), which were viewed as the most discernible textual fingerprint. The method permitted ground-breaking qualitative research in identifying authorship, among other things, of the Federalist Papers (Mosteller and Wallace, 1964), by focusing on the use of and placing of 63 function words. Others have sought to identify the authors of books of the Christian Bible (Morton and McLeman, 1966; Burns, 2006) and Shakespearean plays (Seletsky et al., 2007).

This "supervised" approach to stylometry is backed by neurological studies, which show that preferences for function words develop late in children and that function and content words are stored and processed in different brain regions (Menn and Obler, 1990; King and Kutas, 1995). However, in stylometry theory, emphasis is also placed on features like word and sentence length, lexical frequencies, punctuation patterns, rare words and the first word in a sentence. Indeed, the origins of stylometry date at least back to 1851 when Augustus de Morgan suggested in a letter that questions of authorship might be settled by determining if a text "does not deal in longer words" (Morgan, 1882).

Computational methods arrived early in the pursuit of stylometric detection (Holmes, 1998). Automated text analysis methods provided a powerful tool due to the speed in which diverse patterns in large quantities of text can be quickly analysed (Oldfather et al., 2012, p. 1206). This computational research was extended to legal documents in a number of analyses of the US Supreme Court, with the function word approach proving popular. Rosenthal and Yoon's (2011) model tested the *distribution* of the observed count of 63 function words of all opinions of 40 justices over time against a theoretical or expected distribution. The latter was created through the generation of 200 pseudo-documents with 2,000 randomly generated words, in which the probability of a non-function word was 70 per cent and a function word 30 per cent. The null hypothesis was a "V-score" of 1, calculated through a chi-squared analysis. The authors found significant variation in the consistency *across* judgment periods for some judges. V-scores ranged from 2.11 to 3.85, and individual justice scores corresponded with a number of anecdotal observations and clerks' stories over which judges delegated authorship to clerks.

Using 307 function or "non-content" words, Carlson, Livermore and Rockmore (2016) analysed 25,407 opinions of the Supreme Court from 1791 to 2008 to analyse trends in style. They find that there is a "style of the time": judges are more stylistically similar to their peers than to temporally remote justices (ibid., p. 1461). Their results also confirm and extend the findings of Rosenthal and Yoon. Comparing two different measures of stylistic consistency, intra-year on the bench and inter-year for individual judges across time, they find that the "writing styles of individual Justices have become less consistent as clerks have taken on a greater role on the Court" (ibid., p. 1461).

In the earliest known study, Wahlbeck, Spriggs and Sigelman (2002) used instead a broader repertoire of style (eight stylistic features) although with a smaller dataset. Analysing 71 opinions during the 1985 term that were authored by Justices Powell and Marshall, they found, as expected, that Powell's clerks enjoyed less autonomy. Bodwin, Rosenthal and Yoon (2013) also drill down on particular justices, focusing on the hard case of Justice Easterbrook, known for jealously guarding authorship of his own sole authored opinions, but permitting clerks – as they mature – to be more involved in the drafting of his majority opinions. Here, by applying measures of function words, rare words, punctuation and principal component analysis, the researchers were able to detect a distinction between Easterbrook's sole authored and majority opinion texts.

In the last two years, three new studies (including this chapter on investment arbitration) have sought independently to advance computational stylometry.[1] While dramatically different in their research agendas, they share some commonalities. The first is to move systemically beyond function words to embrace a broader range of stylometric fingerprints. The second is to experiment with different stylometric software packages.[2] The third is to seek to build stylometric models for individual adjudicators on independent writing and oral material and subsequently test the model against actual decisions.

This latter iteration is certainly the most challenging. However, building independent individual stylometric models is promising for two reasons. It permits machine learning in different forms and is necessary for analysing *joint* opinions or decisions where authorship is even less certain. Joint decisions are a typical feature in many national and international courts and in various types of arbitration. A single judicial author cannot be identified – at least formally – and depending on the type of adjudicative body, a great degree of variation is thus to be expected theoretically. Given the focus in this chapter on the application of stylometric analysis to the decisions of international courts and tribunals – specifically investor-state arbitration, predictive models based on training sets of texts attributed to individual judges or arbitrators (i.e., texts from sole authored academic journal articles) will provide arguably a surer means at getting at the origins of authorship.

In light of this literature on judicial authorship, this chapter seeks to examine new advances in computational stylometry which focus on a broad range of fingerprints, use of new software, and greater incorporation of machine learning approaches. The remainder of this chapter proceeds as follows. Section 2 examines the arrival of new machine learning logics within stylometry and why it is particularly relevant to studying our field of interest: investor-state arbitration. Section 3 sets out the context for the domain-specific study on investor-state arbitration, section 4 explains our method, including our chosen software, and section 5 our results.

---

[1]   The other two are Pauwelyn and Pelc (2019) and Dickinson (2019).
[2]   With the exception of Dickinson (2019).

2.   MACHINE LEARNING, STYLOMETRY AND INTERNATIONAL INVESTMENT LAW

2.1   Building Individual Stylometric Models

The first fully fledged machine learning analysis within stylometry was arguably the use of neural networks in 1996 to analyse the Federalist Papers. Tweedie, Singh and Holmes (1996) point out that neural networks are well suited to stylometry given their comparative advantage in recognizing the "underlying organisation" of data. Neural networks can learn from data, generalize, capture non-linear interactions between input variables and are capable of fault tolerance (ibid., p. 2). With a focus on function words, the authors use the 54 undisputed separate papers by Madison and Hamilton as a training and testing set to determine the authorship of the 15 joint and disputed papers. They confirmed existing scholarship that Madison was the author of the disputed papers and analyse shares of the joint papers.

Within law, Rosenthal and Yoon (2011) use machine learning logic to test the robustness of their chi-squared results. For example, in their study of 40 justices of the US Supreme Court, they partitioned the data into a training set and a testing set. Working with pairs of justices, the training set is used to develop a model for classifying judgments as being authored by either Justice "A" or Justice "B". Using a linear classifier based on function words,[3] they test whether the algorithm predicts the remaining judgments correctly of both judges; and repeat the training and testing process for every single judgment of the two pairwise judges. They found that the classifier could distinguish fairly strongly between judges even when their V-scores for function word distribution were similar. However, the analysis is not used to draw stylometric conclusions about who wrote a decision or test variability – rather it is a supporting argument for the claim that judicial style varies and that variation is a fact in itself.

In a 2019 study on questions around oral argument at the US Supreme Court, Dickinson provides the most recent application of computational text analysis to judicial decision-making at the US Supreme Court (Dickinson 2019). To build his predictive models from the transcript texts, Dickinson combined a number of techniques for assessing oral argument question "features" such as: analysis of the number and length of questions, when questions were asked, what sentiment can be attributed to the question, and an N-gram analysis that captures the frequency in the

---

[3]   They claim that other stylometric features did not influence the results.

use of certain words. The analysis was combined to create models for each justice; and each model was then trained against a training set of ten samples of the different feature analyses. The trained models were finally used to predict the voting patterns of justices, which could be done with an overall accuracy of 73 per cent.

In the other recent study, Pauwelyn and Pelc (2019) sought to identify the WTO secretariat's role in the drafting of WTO panel reports. Similar to this chapter, the authors use academic papers of a selective group of panellists (formal authors) and secretariats (unseen actors) to establish a baseline fingerprint for each potential drafter. Although, unlike Dickinson, the training set is not tested against a test set. By using Stylo, an R-package, they conduct an exclusionary analysis, showing that the stylometric influence of the secretariat is statistically significant. They conclude that the secretariat appears to have a large role in drafting.

2.2 Stylometry and International Investment Law

In the case under consideration, investor-state arbitration, computational methods and particular machine learning-like approaches are unavoidable. Like other fields, unseen actors play potentially a large role in the authorship of arbitral awards, in which a usually three-arbitrator tribunal determines whether a state has breached certain provisions of an international investment treaty to the detriment of a foreign investor. The remarkable increase in the number of cases brought by foreign investors and which are being decided by a small circle of arbitrators (Langford et al., 2017) increases the likelihood that arbitrators rely on assistants, arbitral institution secretaries and/or members of an arbitrator's law firm to assist in drafting of decisions, orders and awards (see Baetens, 2019).

Stylometric analysis of investor-state arbitration is also relevant for legal, political and policy reasons. *Legally*, some parties have sought to annul or set aside arbitral awards on the grounds that they were substantially drafted by an assistant to the tribunal (Galagan, 2015). Take the famed Yukos arbitrations, wherein Russia's efforts to set aside the awards in the Dutch courts included claims that the assistant was in fact a fourth arbitrator due to the disproportionately high number of hours that were billed.[4] Leaving aside the problematic conflation in calling an assistant an arbitrator – billable hours do not necessarily correlate at all to the amount of an award drafted, let alone to a correlation between drafting an award (what an assistant might do) and deciding the outcome (what an arbitrator does) – there may

---

[4]   Which doubled those of the Chairman (3,006 to 1,592 hours).

nonetheless be a tipping point where drafting turns into improper decision-making. While the Yukos set-aside relied on billable hours, a stylometric analysis of authorship of the award texts could have been conducted and would have potentially led to a similar, and likely better, finding.[5]

Politically, stylometric analysis may help us determine what members of an arbitral tribunal contributed to a collectively written (the norm across most types of international courts and tribunals) opinion or award, by providing insights into the panel dynamics and political manoeuvring of such authorial collaboration.[6] In investor-state arbitration, almost all awards are collectively issued by a tribunal of three members. Dissents and separate opinions still remain relatively rare, although decreasingly so in recent years. This consensus-based approach may be viewed as paradoxical in that the parties typically each select their own party-appointed "wing" arbitrator. Yet, while the initial assumption frequently holds that a system of party-appointed arbitrators would be more prone to fragmentation and dissent,[7] it is often the norm of consensus-building and collegiality that prevails in drafting and deliberations among tribunal members. Common explanations for the prevalence of the consensus norm in investor-state arbitration, and why formal dissents may have less utility (unless wing arbitrators are signalling their positions for future reappointment),[8] is that party-appointed wing arbitrators are more likely to influence the collective deliberation and writing of arbitral awards if they are more involved in the drafting process. However, for the parties and readers of such awards, it is difficult, if not impossible to know who may have written what parts of the award.

From a *policy* perspective, understanding the respective arbitral influences on award writing is important for analysing the likely effects of current policy reform processes that seek to push investor-state arbitration closer to a permanent court system without party appointment. Stylometric analysis may help states and reformers predict what a shift to a judge-centric system might mean by better understanding the role of wing arbitrators.[9] Moreover, we may also want to simply know how arbitral resources are allocated in the award drafting process, including how the distribution of tribunal fees between wings and chairs (chairs are

---

[5] See, e.g., Yuen (2017).
[6] And earlier in the USA: see Urofsky (2017).
[7] On affiliation bias due to party appointment, see Puig and Strezhnev (2017).
[8] See discussion in Langford and Behn (2018) on reappointment strategies.
[9] This is because we do not know whether a decision favourable to a claimant, for example, was the result of (1) the respondent wing having little influence; (2) the respondent wing preventing an even more pro-claimant result; or (3) other factors beyond the party appointment.

almost exclusively allocated a higher percentage of fees than the wings)[10] may or may not affect expected workload.

Moving beyond the domain-specific uses, the recent digitization of the jurisprudence contained in international arbitral awards, our comprehensive database with structured data and the rise of new stylometry programmes provides the possibility for new forms of stylometric analysis and machine learning applications. In the past few years, qualitative insights in stylography have been incorporated into software packages in Python and R. This means that we can analyse instantly hundreds and thousands of legal decisions in order to determine the potential author or share of contributions from different authors. Indeed, international investment *treaties* have already shown themselves susceptible to both automatic text analysis and machine learning (Alschner and Skougarevskiy, 2016).

However, automated text analysis of *jointly authored arbitral awards* provides a polycentric challenge. An arbitral award – equivalent to a court judgment – in any given investor-state arbitration case is issued by three "seen" actors and we do not know whether variations in the award might represent the influence of "unseen" actors (assistants to the tribunal, clerks to the arbitrators and arbitral institution secretaries), "seen" actors (claimant and respondent wing arbitrators) or both. In the first iteration of our research, we tried a *comparative* approach to stylometric analysis. We measured the similarity of tribunal awards written by the same chair. However, like Pauwelyn and Pelc in the first part of their paper, we found that this method was noisy. We could not distinguish the work of different members of the tribunal – cosine similarity scores were difficult to compare across arbitrators. Thus, we moved to a prediction-based model and using different baseline documents, this chapter represents a first step in determining authorship using the Java Graphical Authorship Attribution Program (JGAAP) (Joula, 2009).

The main aim of this chapter is methodological. We seek to develop and showcase a stylometric analysis of opinions that moves beyond function words, tests new software, and most importantly applies machine learning logics that seek to predict the degree of authorship. In this chapter, we describe a computational model that seeks to calculate the stylometric distance scores between an arbitrator's single author writings (principally both academic articles and individual procedural orders) and the awards

---

[10] Does authorship follow the money? This might be expected given that chairs are paid disproportionately more than wings on account of the expected workload. Or does it follow influence and are some wings particularly influential? Parties spend considerable time trying to appoint wings that might both reflect their preferences *and* exert significant influence.

emanating from tribunals they chair. There is an underlying assumption here that in any given arbitral tribunal, the chair of the tribunal is the lead in the drafting process of the award.

To create our model, we first develop a stylometric algorithm on single author writings ("training set") and then seek to predict the actual author of the award. This analysis results in a distance score that allows us to determine whether some arbitrators' awards bear less resemblance to their other writings. The lesser the resemblance to other writings, the more likely that the award is being written with input from the wing arbitrators and/or assistants and arbitral institution secretaries. The empirical focus in this chapter is on the nine most prolific presiding arbitrators, whom we introduce in the next section. Future research will concentrate on a broader range of chairs plus a calculation of distance scores for wing arbitrators in order to assess their influence.

3.   THE INVESTOR-STATE ARBITRATION REGIME

3.1   The Regime

The development of the modern international investment regime represents a remarkable extension of international law in the post-war period. Built on a network of more than 3,500 signed bilateral investment treaties (BITs), regional free trade agreements (FTAs)[11] and a handful of plurilateral investment treaties,[12] it gives foreign investors various substantive protections and commonly the right[13] to investor-state dispute settlement (ISDS).

Arbitration commonly arises when a foreign investor alleges that the beneficiary rights granted under an international investment agreement (IIA) have been breached by the state hosting its investments. For example, Phillip Morris challenged (unsuccessfully) tobacco regulation in

---

[11]   UNCTAD provides an extensive database on IIAs, available at: http://investmentpolicy hub.unctad.org/IIA (accessed 15 March 2017).

[12]   Prominent examples include: North American Free Trade Agreement (NAFTA) (1994); Dominican Republic-Central American Free Trade Agreement (DR-CAFTA) (2005); Comprehensive and Progressive Agreement for Trans-Pacific Partnership (CPTPP) (2018), replacing the Trans-Pacific Partnership (TPP); US-Mexico-Canada Agreement (USMCA) (2020) replacing NAFTA.

[13]   IIAs typically include the following types of protections to foreign investments: prohibitions against expropriation without adequate compensation, full protection and security, fair and equitable treatment (FET), most-favoured nation (MFN) treatment, and national treatment.

Australia[14] and Uruguay,[15] on the basis that it infringed their intellectual property rights while shareholders in Yukos challenged (successfully) the Russian government's taxation litigation against the company, which precipitated its eventual bankruptcy.[16] However, for comprehensiveness, investor-state arbitration is not exclusively treaty-based, but also occurs in cases between foreign investors and host states according to contract-based arbitration agreements allowing for investor-state arbitration[17] or investor-state arbitration provisions embedded within national foreign direct investment (FDI) laws.

The number of investor-state arbitrations has increased exponentially over the past two decades: see Figure 3.1. The data comes from our Pluricourts Investment Treaty and Arbitration Database (PITAD) in which we have tracked and coded all known cases.[18] It is this meteoric rise

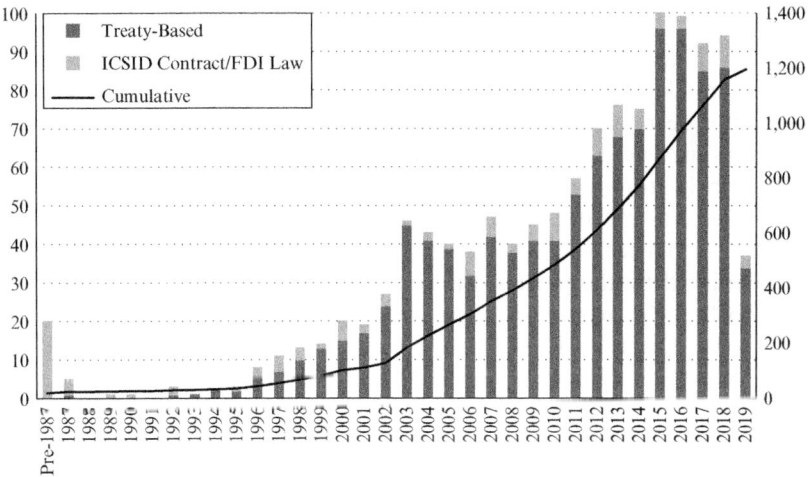

Figure 3.1   Investor-state arbitration cases registered by year
            (1987–2019)[19]

---

[14]   *Philip Morris Asia v Australia*, PCA Case No. 2012-12, Jurisdiction Award (27 December 2015).

[15]   *Philip Morris Brands v Uruguay*, ICSID Case No. ARB/10/7, Award (8 July 2016).

[16]   The three landmark cases collectively granting 50 billion USD to Yukos shareholders: *Yukos Universal v Russia*, PCA Case No. AA 227, Award (18 July 2014); *Hulley Enterprises v Russia*, PCA Case No. AA 226, Award (18 July 2014); *Veteran Petroleum v Russia*, PCA Case No. AA 228, Award (18 July 2014).

[17]   As embedded in various forms of investment contracts or concessions.

[18]   Behn et al. (2019); Behn et al. (2018).

[19]   PITAD, ibid.; 831 cases in total through 1 January 2017.

in the instances of investor-state arbitration over the past two decades that has led some to claim there is "no other category of private individuals" that are "given such expansive rights in international law as are private actors investing across borders" (Simmons, 2014, p. 42).

By the end of the first decade of the 2000s, the use of investor-state arbitration had emerged as a global, prominent and lucrative area of international adjudication, while at the same time coming under increasing scrutiny from a growing number of states, scholars and civil society actors (Waibel et al., 2010). Not all of the cases have been concluded and claimant-investor success rates vary. Of the 1,232 investor-state arbitration cases that have been registered as of 1 June 2019, claimant-investors have won on the merits in 47.2 per cent of cases.

3.2   The Actors

Investor-state arbitration involves a range of actors – arbitrators (wings and chairs), legal counsel, expert witness (legal and quantum) and arbitral institution secretaries/assistants to the tribunal. Each party to the dispute will appoint one of three arbitrators; and in most cases the parties (or the co-arbitrators) will jointly appoint the chair. There is, nonetheless, a large degree of variation in the manner of appointment. While the default is that the parties will appoint the two wing arbitrators, the chair can be appointed by the parties, the two wing arbitrators or by the institution hosting the arbitration. For International Centre for Settlement of Investment Disputes (ICSID) annulment cases, all three annulment committee members are appointed by the Secretary-General of ICSID. Of all the possible configurations for the appointment of arbitrators in investor-state arbitration cases, however, there is an underlying constant. This structure means that for every arbitration, there are individuals (either the parties, legal counsel representing the parties, arbitral institutions or co-arbitrators) that are making selection decisions.

Drawing on a study we produced in 2017, the top 25 arbitrators by numbers of appointments at that time are listed in Table 3.1 (Langford et al., 2017). There is a familiar pattern of well-known grand old men and two "formidable women" (Stern and Kaufmann-Kohler), as Puig (2014) christened them. Most of these top 25 arbitrators also have a sizeable number of influential and prestigious presiding chair appointments. The prominent chairs selected for this study are highlighted in italics in Table 3.1 (except for Andres Rigo Sureda and Gilbert Guillaume, who are in the list of top 10 chairs but are not on the list of top 25 arbitrators by any type of appointment)).

In addition to the number of prominent chairs singled out for the purpose

Table 3.1 Investor-state arbitrators: top 25 by appointments (up through 1 January 2017)

Rank	Arbitrator	Nationality	Presiding	Claimant-appointed	Respondent-appointed	Annulment committee	Total cases
1	Brigitte Stern	France	4	1	82	1	88
2	*Gabrielle Kaufmann-Kohler*	Switzerland	38	15	2	1	56
3	*L. Yves Fortier*	Canada	24	25	2	2	53
4	Charles Brower	US	1	50	0	1	52
5	*Francisco Orrego Vicuña*	Chile	18	27	3	1	49
6	Albert Jan van den Berg	Netherlands	15	16	12	1	44
7	J. Christopher Thomas	Canada	0	1	42	0	43
8	*Bernard Hanotiau*	Belgium	12	18	5	5	40
8	*Karl-Heinz Böckstiegel*	Germany	26	8	2	4	40
9	*V.V. Veeder*	UK	25	6	6	0	37
9	Bernardo Cremades	Spain	14	10	10	3	37
10	Piero Bernardini	Italy	11	13	3	9	36
11	Marc Lalonde	Canada	8	20	7	0	35
12	*Rodrigo Oreamuno*	Costa Rica	15	0	14	5	34
13	Stanimir Alexandrov	Bulgaria	3	25	1	3	32
14	Phillipe Sands	UK	1	4	25	0	30
15	Juan Fernández-Armesto	Spain	21	1	3	4	29
16	Jan Paulsson	France	13	12	2	1	28
16	Horacio Grigera Naón	Argentina	2	24	2	0	28
16	David Williams	New Zealand	10	17	0	1	28
17	James Crawford	Australia	12	2	10	3	27
18	Pierre Tercier	Switzerland	22	0	3	0	25
19	Toby Landau	UK	3	1	20	0	24
19	Vaughan Lowe	UK	13	2	9	0	24
19	Franklin Berman	UK	10	5	4	5	24

of this "proof of concept" study, later iterations may seek to identify the degree of authorship among the wing arbitrators in any given case as well as chairs of lesser caseload than the top 10 chairs selected here. While the number of arbitrators attributable to particular individuals is very high among known investor-state arbitrations, the names and roles of the various unseen actors is decidedly less so. PITAD includes data on the role and name of individuals acting as arbitral institution secretaries as well as data on assistants to the tribunal where disclosed. While often invisible to the outside world, it is often argued that these assistants and secretaries shape and influence different types of international litigation. While earlier studies indicated that the role of an arbitral institution secretary ranged from no drafting to certain non-substantive parts of award drafting (NYC Bar Association, 2006, p. 585), recent accounts suggest that some arbitral institutional secretaries may be more influential (St. John, 2016), but that tribunal assistants are almost assuredly doing significant drafting in certain instances.[20] In PITAD, there is data on these assistants and secretaries in 568 cases.

4. METHOD

4.1 Corpus Selection: Awards

In the first iteration of our stylometric analysis, we adopted the following research design. The aim was to first determine the extent of variation and distance between a chair's award in investor-state arbitrations and a "baseline" of their "personal" writing. This approach cannot disclose whether it is assistants/secretaries or certain wing arbitrators that have also contributed to a chair's award. Rather, it is the first step in identifying whether there is significant variation in some select chair's awards that merit closer quantitative and qualitative examination (to be undertaken in a second iteration).

For this initial pilot study, we have a sample corpus of arbitral awards that maximizes the number of documents that can be analysed. We began by determining the ten most prolific arbitral chairs to date in investor-state arbitration (all treaty-based cases but also ICSID contract-based and FDI law-based cases, and annulment committee decisions). We identified those chairs that have rendered the most final awards (whether a dismissal for lack of jurisdiction or a determination on the merits of the claims). In

---

[20] See also in relation to the WTO: Pauwelyn and Pelc (2019); Langford et al. (2020).

addition to limiting this list to only finally resolved cases, we restrict the sample to identify chairs with the most final awards that are publicly available, and that were written in English. We also include annulment committee chairs where decisions are concluded, public and in English. From these criteria, we are able to select our list of the top 10 chairs. The full set of decisions is set out in the online Appendix[21] and the available corpus is summarized in Table 3.2. From this list, Rodrigo Oreamuno is not analysed because no academic writings in English could be determined.

With these nine arbitrators identified, we created a corpus of investor-state arbitration awards that correspond to each of the cases where each of these arbitrators acted in the role of chair. The number of awards can be higher though when there are multiple awards per case: for example, Gabrielle Kaufmann-Kohler has 17 cases where she was chair that meet the criteria but 38 documents that can be considered awards. There are some jurisdictional awards in addition to final awards in bifurcated cases that we included (as well as interim awards, and cost awards, and so on); and we also included a few jurisdictional awards in cases that ultimately settled or a final award remained pending.[22]

In terms of text for the stylometric analysis, we decided to leave the entire award intact in this iteration. This is because we are partly interested in the overall contribution of different actors (as measured as the likelihood of chair authorship); and different actors are hypothesized as contributing to particular types of texts within each award (e.g., arbitral institution secretaries may produce procedural histories, an assistant to the tribunal drafting the summaries of the position of the parties, and the arbitrators (both the chair and wings) drafting the sections labelled as analysis of the tribunal). Using the award completely intact may be able to show which chairs write more of an entire award; it may not allow for understanding what parts are written by authors other than the chair.

An alternative way is to section the award into parts; and then to analyse each part stylometrically around the most likely type of author for each part. This can be done by looking at the whole award, but with identifiers for each part. Or one could discard all parts of the award except

---

[21] Available at: https://pitad.org/assets/Langford_et_al_Stylometrics.pdf.
[22] These cases were not included in the count to identify the top 10 chairs, but they can be included in the corpus of "awards" rendered by that person in the analysis. Moreover, we only counted one award on jurisdiction and one award on merits for Fortier in the Yukos cases – these are three cases in the selection criteria but six "awards" for the analysis. But in this case, we only used one of the jurisdictional awards and one of the merits awards (because they are identical but for the amount of damages and the names of the parties).

Table 3.2 Corpus sample(s)

Arbitrator		Criteria for selection of top 10		Corpus used for training set		
		Appointed as chair	Total no. of concluded cases as chair	Awards as chair (include jur., liability, quantum, costs)	Sole authored articles	Procedural orders
1. Gabrielle Kaufmann-Kohler	(GKK)	38	17	34	3	62
2. L. Yves Fortier	(LYF)	24	20	22	3	17
3. Karl-Heinz Böckstiegel	(KHB)	26	10	17	3	31
4. V.V. Veeder	(VVV)	25	11	26	3	53
5. Francisco Orrego Vicuña	(FOV)	18	8	18	3	7
6. Albert Jan van den Berg	(AJVDB)	15	8	8	3	38
7. Rodrigo Oreamuno*	(RO)	15	9	NA	0	NA
8. Bernard Hanotiau	(BH)	12	8	12	3	8
9. Andres Rigo Sureda	(ARS)	12	12	16	3	14
10. Gilbert Guillaume	(GG)	9	9	12	3	5
Total				165	27	235

the part identified as most likely to be written by a particular type of actor. A typical investment arbitration award will contain a number of different parts, which might include sections such as: statement of facts, procedural history, summaries of the positions of the parties, and analysis of the tribunal. Additional portioning of the award could remove parts irrelevant to the identification of authorship such as titles, table of contents, information about the parties, addresses, technical annexes, and so on; and finally, it may be useful to portion out citations and quotations in order to reduce text that is known to be the least likely to carry stylometric fingerprints (however, there is an argument that citations may expose patterns of use that could be an identifier of style even if the actual text is not).

We will test these various alternatives in the future. In addition, a final way to dissect investor-state arbitration awards is by paragraph – which we have recently delineated in the text corpus. This will enable us to move from a document-based approach to a paragraph-based approach, which will permit a more fine-tuned stylometric analysis.

4.2 Corpus Selection: Baselines

In order to predict the likelihood that an arbitrator wrote a particular award, we used three baselines of comparable style: academic articles, procedural orders, and their other awards as chair. For each arbitrator, we collected three *academic* articles which arguably provide the best indication of an arbitrator's "personal" writing style. Of course, an academic article cannot be fully representative. It may have been edited or even partly drafted by an assistant and the academic genre of writing is clearly different, at least teleologically, from the arbitral genre.

Procedural orders are quite likely to reflect a presiding arbitrator's "arbitral" style. Many of these are quite long and contain significant tailored and bespoke analysis of particular issues in the case. These orders are usually signed only by the presiding arbitrator, and the preparation of them is a core part of their chair's role in proceedings. To be sure, some of the procedural orders may be written by an assistant, which makes this baseline somewhat endogenous.

Finally, we used as a baseline *other awards* in which an arbitrator was chair. Of course, this method suffers from even greater endogeneity if wing arbitrators played a substantive role in the drafting of those awards. Therefore, we have run separate and joint models for the three baselines. However, given the hypothesis that chairs take the lead in drafting arbitral awards, then we should expect that there is a fairly close relation between these awards. Greater stylometric distance and variation could indicate other players are involved.

Ideally, we will have split this corpus in two in order to test the initial stylometric model against a training set. That was not permitted by the software we used (see next sub-section) but we seek to apply such a method in a future iteration (see discussion conclusion).

4.3   Stylometric Method

As foreshadowed, we have chosen software that examines a broad palette of stylistic features. JGAAP (Joula, 2009) allows extensive analytical customization, such as canonicizers (normalization of texts), analyses function words, ability to sort on word and sentence length, lexical frequencies, punctuation patterns, rare words, first word in a sentence and part-of-speech. Its primary claim to fame is the identification of the ghost novel by J.K. Rowling (Coyne, 2013) although it is not particularly suited to high-volume computational analysis.

While the broad palette of analysis gives further depth to the analytics, it also adds more complexity. To navigate this increased complexity, JGAAP analyses the text in three stages. First, a set of event drivers is applied to each of the training sets and target awards. Each event driver represents a specific method for determining the author. This could be word choice, sentence length, punctuation and so on. Second, the output of each event driver is cumulated in the event culling mechanism, whereby each factor is weighed according to an information gain algorithm, where the event drivers that contribute the most significant contributions to identifying the author are selected. In this second stage, there is a recursive reapplication using several algorithms, including K-means, Markov chain analysis and voted perceptrons on the material as a whole, until the closest match between the texts with unknown authors and known authors is found. Third, the output from stage two is represented as the distance between the known and unknown texts for each possible author. For each iteration the system learns which factors are the most significant identifiers for each document, author and event driver. When this distance iteratively across all texts and authors is minimized to the smallest distance the algorithm stops and outputs the distance of each document to each author. The recent study by Pauwelyn and Pelc used Stylo, which works on a principle of grouping n-grams and comparing these combinations (Eder et al., 2016). However, such a methodology may be vulnerable to common language and drafting standards as well as secondary copy-editing. In this chapter we utilize a broader set of features to enhance the quality of the initial accuracy of the identification.

4.4 Stylometrics as a Tool for Legal Scholarship

As discussed above, so-called "invisible actors" are a simple fact of life in virtually all institutional settings; these actors operate in high numbers in public and private legal institutions around the world, including judiciaries at both the national and international levels. From the clerks and secretaries mentioned above to junior lawyers preparing briefs for senior partners, these actors contribute to the legal reality, and often to the outcome of any given case. While the presence of these actors is not a subject of dispute, their influence and impact is often hard to pin down.

The invisibility of certain actors in the legal output of the arbitral tribunals creates therefore a particular challenge when applying stylometric methods to investor-state arbitration awards. A single paragraph alone may be drafted by a clerk working for one of the wing arbitrators, then reworked and revised by the assistant to the tribunal, before either being edited, or perhaps completely rewritten by the chair of the tribunal with additional review by both wing arbitrators, followed on with proofreading by an arbitral institution secretary. The text may then subsequently be continually edited and modified by all three arbitrators after deliberation, or linguistically corrected and normalized by arbitral institution staff prior to circulation to the parties. When observing an award as a whole – the mixture of text borrowed from the parties, citations of other practice, dry facts of the case, summaries of the parties' positions, and procedural histories – one may perceive an attempt at any coherent analysis as a futile endeavour. Viewed together with the *kakophonia* of potential authors on any one judicial judgment or arbitral award, stylometrics as a tool of empirical truth in legal decision-making may be justifiably questioned. There is, however, a significant difference between the works of J.K. Rowling and an arbitral award – a claimed author.[23] As we may know who *should* be the author or even the authors, we argue that a fruitful use of stylometrics applied to legal decision-making is not the absolute function of author attribution, it is also the study of variance within a single author's written works and decisions. By analysing the degree of variance, we argue that two useful facets of information may be extracted.

The first facet identified is the general variance between the author's (arbitrator's) works compared to the general variance of other authors (arbitrators). We argue that when an author has a greater stylometric variance in their authorship, it is less likely that the work is solely a product

---

[23] At least an assumed one, as it is common and expected that the president of the tribunal also drafts the award.

of their own pen. By applying a comparison of general variance, we also address some of the challenges discussed above. While there are inherent differences in how an arbitral award, a procedural order, an interim decision and an academic article is written, we presuppose that arbitral awards written by the same author (default presumption being the chair of the arbitral tribunal) have roughly the same writing styles. The elements in the awards themselves are also expected to have vaguely similar distribution of quotations and other elements not attributed directly to the author.

The second facet is the identification of outlier cases that warrant further qualitative study. We are of the opinion that in the field of law, empirics alone are not sufficient to explain the vast complexities of the legal world. It should rather be used as a tool of nuance, correction and factor identification. By highlighting that a case is stylometrically different from other works, qualitative studies may be applied to understand why this is the case, even if the case did not warrant further study when investigated in isolation.

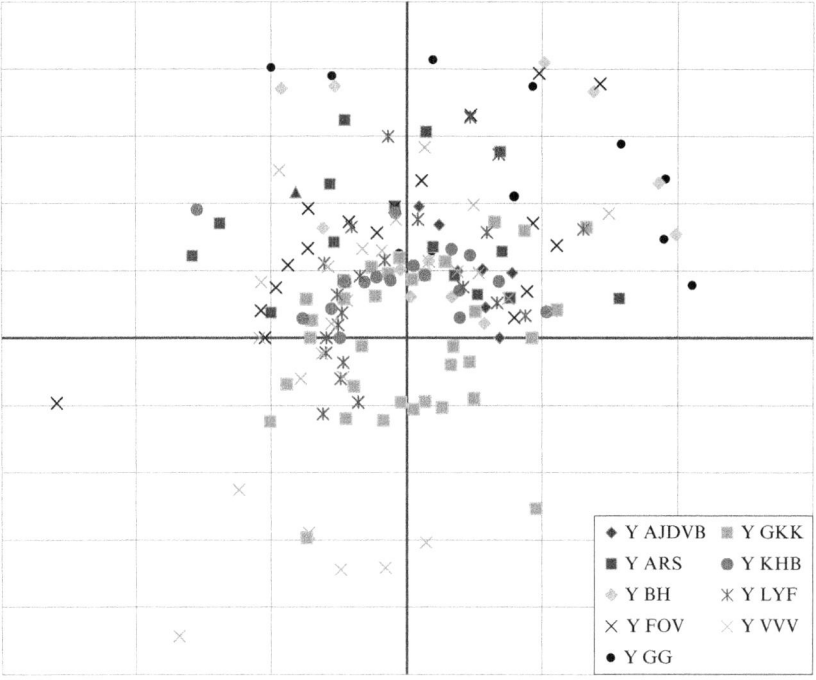

*Figure 3.2   Distance and variation: baseline – academic articles and
                procedural orders*

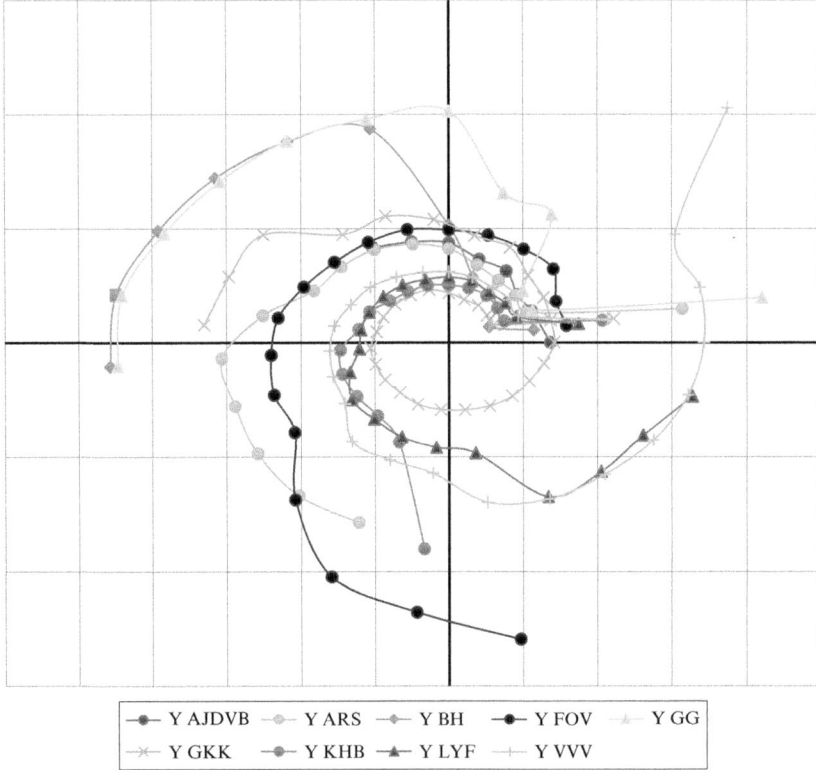

| -●- Y AJDVB | -○- Y ARS | -◆- Y BH | -●- Y FOV | ⊸- Y GG |
| ⊸×- Y GKK | -●- Y KHB | -▲- Y LYF | -+- Y VVV | |

Note: Guidelines are provided for readability.

Figure 3.3   Distance and variation: baseline – academic articles and procedural orders (individually sorted by distance from centre)

5. RESULTS

The results provide support for the hypothesis that there is variation between a particular chair's writings and their awards; and there is also variation between the awards of different chairs in terms of the stylometric fingerprints of the analysed texts. Figures 3.2 and 3.3 display the results for the baseline of an individual chair's academic articles plus procedural orders – the two most theoretically solid baselines. For each of the awards, the computed distance from the baseline is shown. The placement in a particular quadrant is only in aid of readability – the critical feature is distance from the centre. As can be seen, some of the chairs have presided over the writing of awards that exhibit consistent and clear rings and

Table 3.3   Distances and rankings per chair

Arbitrator	Avg. distance	Max. distance	Min. distance	Std deviation	Predicted author rank	Avg. distance from predicted
GKK	0.191455180	0.37502866	0.03068823	0.042319027	5.62	0.03
KHB	0.155873945	0.26308688	0.05338601	0.018107373	4.58	0.03
AJVDB	0.074461303	0.09876399	0.03766525	0.001256029	1.5	< 0.01
LYF	0.147576233	0.27823769	0.03170518	0.030128427	3.13	0.02
ARS	0.185781689	0.27579003	0.06232185	0.026444165	7.44	0.05
FOV	0.157429059	0.28508759	0.08423162	0.051104809	5.61	0.03
BH	0.178953521	0.26270251	0.04124230	0.078244405	5.16	0.04
GG	0.201174781	0.26846347	0.06683364	0.039293022	7.33	0.06
VVV	0.193494691	0.30096136	0.04332618	0.075681522	5	0.04

semi-circles while others appear to have greater variation. It is not unexpected that the distance from the centre varies from chair to chair. While not analysed in detail, we interpret this variance as an expression of the differences in the chair's writing styles between awards, procedural orders and academic articles.

The differences in variation become particularly clear when we compute and compare the standard deviation of distances for each chair. Table 3.3 provides the minimum, maximum and average distances. For some the deviation is very low – for example Albert Jan van den Berg (AJVDB) – although this may be a function of the low number of awards analysed. However, the arbitrator with the greatest number of awards (Kaufmann-Kohler (GKK) with 38) had a fairly average standard deviation. On the other hand, Bernard Hanotiau (BH) and V.V. Veeder (VVV) as well as Francisco Orrego Vicuña (FOV) have significantly higher levels of variation between awards, raising questions as to the reason for variation.

An alternative or complementary approach is to examine for every award by an arbitrator which of the nine arbitrators' individual stylometric models is closest to it stylometrically. We would expect that the actual chair for that award would be ranked first every time. The fifth column, however, indicates otherwise. In the case of AJVDB, he is almost always the predicated author for cases in which he is chair – he has the lowest average distance from his own model to his awards (see also the sixth column). For ARS, it is the reverse – he is ranked lowest as likely author for his own awards based on his stylometric model. The other arbitrators fall within this range.

This form of prediction provides interesting results but possibly the clearest indication of the limitations of the approach. This is because it suggests that for some arbitrators we may lack sufficient training material – whether quantitatively or qualitatively – for developing the individual stylometric models. Gilbert Guillaume is arguably the clearest example given there are only five procedural orders. Yet, for some arbitrators such as GKK we have an extensive text corpus for developing the individual model.

6. CONCLUDING ANALYSIS

This chapter has reviewed existing stylometric analyses of judicial authorship and sought to highlight three new approaches in computational stylometry – the consistent use of a range of stylometric features, new software packages, and the building of individual stylometric models for judges and others to predict the likelihood of their authorship of a judgment.

Our domain study of investor-state arbitration suggests that stylometric variation may be a feature of arbitral awards, suggesting the presence of multiple authorship, particularly in the case of certain chairs (but there is no indication so far that the variation indicating authorship beyond the chair would be contributions from the wing arbitrators or an assistant to the tribunal). Additionally, and given the pilot nature of this study and partly the limitations of computational stylometrics, we cannot yet reach any conclusive results from this study. Regardless, two results and one methodological observation stand out.

First, the variation between the chair's academic articles and procedural orders, in comparison with their awards is significant. This variation raises the question of why the writing styles of the chairs are so different in the different mediums. It may be methodological that the form and content of the documents (training set and awards) are so different that the variation arises as a natural consequence. Or it may be that large parts of such awards are indeed written by others across the board – and that most text is not primarily written by the chair of the tribunal.

Second, within a given chair's work there is substantial stylometric variation. This large internal variation appears odd, particularly considering that the internal variations for a given chair in many cases expand beyond the average difference between awards and baseline materials. We offer three possible explanations for this. First, the particular case may contain large amounts of noise – be it quotes, citations from statements or similar. Second, the wing arbitrators may have made significant contributions to the text, or it may have been subject to significant copy-editing. Third, the chair may have changed the assistants that help in the drafting process.

These multiple possible explanations bring us to the methodological observation. As a tool of absolute verifiable truths, stylometrics offer little but indications. The revelations of the rather odd patterns we discuss in this chapter, however, may serve researchers on two levels. On the general level, it highlights an unexplained anomaly or chair's written product. Unlike courts, arbitrators are hired as individuals and not institutions, and as such the parties to a particular dispute have legitimate expectations that the arbitrators themselves conduct the legal analysis and writings (although it is likely very unclear the extent to which parties – and even their counsel – understand the distribution of writing and decision-making between the chair and wings in any given arbitration). We argue that further scrutiny and transparency in these practices are warranted. As the investor-state arbitration regime is a very heterogeneous and slow-moving system, such changes may take significant time, and subsequently researchers may have to conduct further studies to ensure sufficient transparency.

On the specific level, this chapter has identified several outlier awards that have large stylometric deviations from the other written works of a particular chair. By using automated methods, such identification is possible even given the thousands of pages analysed. The identification of these "odd" cases allows for in-depth qualitative and statistical analysis of why these cases turn out so different. Some interviews with particular chairs have already commenced and will undoubtedly add some clarity in explaining outlier awards. These in-depth studies may also reveal other hitherto unknown information about the inner workings and panel dynamics of arbitral tribunals.

As a final comment, some of these issues may also be resolved by rerunning the analysis using more sophisticated machine learning techniques such as deep learning – together with a testing phase, a larger training sample, and a more finely grained sample. The latter will provide especially two distinct improvements. First, the number of facets used as identifying marks in each sentence is infinitely increased beyond the ones described in this chapter. Second, increasing the resolution down to paragraphs and including more arbitrators will both increase accuracy as well as clearly identifying various authors throughout the text. While traditional author analysis is a powerful tool of identifying outliers and oddities in the texts, sparring further avenues of research, new approaches to computational stylometry may offer accurate evidence to form solid conclusions.

REFERENCES

Alschner, W. and Skougarevskiy, D. (2016). Can Robots Write Treaties? Using Recurrent Neural Networks to Draft International Investment Agreements. In Bex, F. and Villata, S. (eds), *JURIX: Legal Knowledge and Information Systems* (Amsterdam, IOS Press), pp. 119–24.

Baetens, F. (2019). *Legitimacy of Unseen Actors in International Adjudication* (Cambridge, Cambridge University Press).

Behn, D., Berge, T. and Langford, M. (2018). Poor States or Poor Governance? Explaining Outcomes in Investment Treaty Arbitration. *Northwestern Journal of International Law & Business* 38(3), 333–89.

Behn, D., Langford, M., Fauchald, O.L., Usynin, M., Lie, H., Berge, T., St. John, T. and Kirkebø, T. (2019). PITAD: The Investment Law and Arbitration Database. PluriCourts Working Paper, January.

Bodwin, K., Rosenthal, J. and Yoon, A. (2013). A Statistical Approach to Judicial Authorship: A Case Study of Judge Easterbrook. *Advances and Applications in Statistics* 37(2), 123–48.

Burns, K. (2006). Bayesian Inference in Disputed Authorship: A Case Study of Cognitive Errors and a New System for Decision Support. *Information Science* 176(11), 1570–89.

Carlson, K., Livermore, M. and Rockmore, D. (2016). A Quantitative Analysis of Writing Style on the U.S. Supreme Court. *Washington University Law Review* 93(6), 1461–510.

Choi, S. and Gulati, G. (2005). Which Judges Write Their Opinions (And Should We Care)? *Florida State University Law Review* 32(4), 1077–122.

Coyne, J. (2013). Duquesne Professor IDs J.K. Rowling as The Cuckoo's Calling Author. *Pittsburgh Business Times*, 15 July.

Dickinson, G. (2019). A Computational Analysis of Oral Argument in the Supreme Court. *Cornell Journal of Law and Public Policy*, 28(1), 449–82.

Eder, M., Rybicki, J. and Kestemont, M. (2016). Stylometry with R: A Package for Computational Text Analysis. *R Journal* 8(1), 107–21.

Galagan, D. (2015). The Challenge of the Yukos Award: An Award Written by Someone Else – a Violation of the Tribunal's Mandate? *Kluwer Arbitration Blog*, 27 February, accessed at http://arbitrationblog.kluwerarbitration.com/2015/02/27/the-challenge-of-the-yukos-award-an-award-written-by-someone-else-a-violation-of-the-tribunals-mandate/?doing_wp_cron=1591670349.7362859249114990234375.

Holmes, D. (1998). The Evolution of Stylometry in Humanities Scholarship. *Literary and Linguistic Computing* 13(3), 111–17.

Joula, P. (2009). JGAAP: A System for Comparative Evaluation of Authorship Attribution. JDHCS 1(1), 233–334.

King, J. and Kutas, M. (1995). A Brain Potential Whose Latency Indexes the Length and Frequency of Words. *CRL Newsletter* (Ctr. for Res. in Language, UCSD), 1 November.

Langford, M. and Behn, D. (2018). Managing Backlash: The Evolving Investment Arbitrator? *European Journal of International Law*, 29(2), 551–80.

Langford, M., Behn, D. and Lie, R. (2017). The Revolving Door in International Investment Arbitration, *Journal of International Economic Law*, 20(2), 301–31.

Langford, M., Creamer, C. and Behn, D. (2020). Regime Responsiveness in International Economic Dispute. In Gáspár-Szilágyi, S., Behn, D. and Langford, M. (eds), *Adjudicating Trade and Investment Disputes: Convergence or Divergence?* (Cambridge, CUP), pp. 244–84.

Menn, L. and Obler, L.K. (1990). Cross-Language Data and Theories of Agrammatism. In Menn, L. and Obler, L.K. (eds), *Agrammatic Aphasia: A Cross-Language Narrative* (Amsterdam, John Benjamins), pp. 1369–89.

Morgan, S.E. de. (1882). *Memoir of Augustus de Morgan by his Wife Sophia Elizabeth with Selections from his Letters* (London, Green & Co).

Morton, A.Q. and McLeman, J.P. (1966). *The Man and the Myth: A Study in the Authorship of Greek Prose* (New York, Harper & Row).

Mosteller, F. and Wallace, D. (1964). *Inference and Disputed Authorship: The Federalist* (Stanford, CA, CLSI).

NYC Bar Association. (2006). Secretaries to International Arbitral Tribunals: Joint Report of the International Commercial Disputes Committee and the Committee on Arbitration of the New York City Bar Association. *American Review of International Arbitration* 17(4), 575–96.

Oldfather, C., Bockhurst J. and Dimmer, B. (2012). Triangulating Judicial Responsiveness: Automated Content Analysis, Judicial Opinions, and the Methodology of Legal Scholarship. *Florida Law Review* 64(5), 1189–242.

Pauwelyn, J. and Pelc, K. (2019). Who Writes the Rulings of the World Trade Organization? A Critical Assessment of the Role of the Secretariat in WTO Dispute Settlement. Working Paper, 26 September.

Puig, S. (2014). Social Capital in the Arbitration Market. *European Journal of International Law* 25(2), 387–424.

Puig, S. and Strezhnev, A. (2017). Affiliation Bias in Arbitration: An Experimental Approach. *Journal of Legal Studies* 46(2), 371–98.

Rosenthal, J. and Yoon, A. (2011). Judicial Ghostwriting: Authorship on the Supreme Court. *Cornell Law Review* 96(6), 1307–44.

Seletsky, O., Huang, T. and Henderson-Frost, W. (2007). The Shakespeare Authorship Question. Dartmouth College, 12 December, accessed at https://home.cs.dartmouth.edu/~datamining/Final.pdf.

Simmons, B. (2014). Bargaining over BITS, Arbitrating Awards: The Regime for Protection and Promotion of International Investment. *World Politics* 66(1), 12–46.

St. John, T. (2016). Tribunal Secretaries. PluriCourts Investment Arbitrator Behavior Workshop, Oslo, 25 May.

Tweedie, F.J., Singh, S. and Holmes, D.I. (1996). Neural Network Applications in Stylometry: The "Federalist Papers". *Computers and the Humanities* 30(1), 1–10.

Urofsky, M. (2017). *Dissent and the Supreme Court: Its Role in the Court's History and the Nations Constitutional Dialogue* (New York, Pantheon Books).

Wahlbeck, P., Spriggs II, J. and Sigelman, L. (2002). Ghostwriters on the Court? A Stylistic Analysis of U.S. Supreme Court Opinion Drafts. *American Political Research* 30(2), 166–92.

Waibel, M., Kaushal, A., Chung, K. and Balchin, C. (eds). (2010). *The Backlash against Investment Arbitration: Perceptions and Reality* (Alphen aan den Rijn, Kluwer).

Yuen, J. (2017). Arbitral Award Written by the Tribunal Assistant, *Lexology*, 11 December.

4. Automated classification of modes of moral reasoning in judicial decisions

Nischal Mainali, Liam Meier, Elliott Ash and Daniel L. Chen*

1. INTRODUCTION

The legal profession is undergoing a great transformation. The tools of machine learning and causal inference can be used to increase efficiency and fairness of the law. In this chapter, we discuss how these tools can also be used to detect how judges motivate their decisions. What is the role of moral reasoning in judicial decision-making?

Law is divided between two modes of moral reasoning. On the consequentialist view, optimal policy should be based on calculations of costs and benefits. The deontological view holds that policy should be determined from moral duties – what is right and just. One way of quantifying this divide empirically is to identify and measure the use of different modes of moral reasoning in judicial decisions. The goal of this project is to use computational techniques to automatically classify judicial decisions by the type of moral reasoning employed.

Computational linguistics, typically referred to by computer scientists as natural language processing (NLP), utilizes computational techniques to translate, make sense of, and produce material in human languages. Human language is complex, full of ambiguities, encoded knowledge, and variety. Though state-of-the-art NLP systems still struggle with tasks that are simple for humans (disambiguation, for example) statistical techniques that make use of large data sets have been highly successful in sentiment analysis, classification, and more (e.g. Hirschberg and Manning, 2015).

Two broad moral frameworks most often used by philosophers are

---

*   These authors contributed equally.

consequentialism and deontology. For a consequentialist, what one ought
to do is whatever brings about the best consequences. The canonical form
of consequentialism is utilitarianism, according to which ethical agents
are obligated to do whatever brings about the most utility. For hedonic
utilitarians like J.S. Mill and Jeremy Bentham, pain is bad and pleasure
good. While philosophers have debated about how to measure utility,
the idea is broadly in line with preferring happiness over unhappiness
(Sinnott-Armstrong, 2015).

In a deontological framework, an act is right if it conforms to a moral
norm. For Kant, this is the categorical imperative, the first formulation of
which holds that one should act only according to a maxim which they can
will to be a universal law (Alexander and Moore, 2016). The idea is that
morality is a matter of conforming to ethical law instead of acting in order
to bring about certain consequences.

Applied ethicists argue about the morality of various issues from these
positions. Take the permissibility of lying, for example. A consequentialist
might argue that it would be permissible to lie if the consequences of telling
the lie would be better than not telling the lie. In contrast, a deontologist
instead might argue that it is immoral to lie because one could not will the
acting of lying to be a universal law.

Law commonly operates in correspondence with morality. Some actions
are made illegal not because of practical considerations, but because
a society believes that the action is morally wrong. For example, laws
against sex work are often justified on moral grounds.

In the legal system, we can observe when judges reason according to
either of these moral frameworks. In the case of a contract, a deontological judge may hold that breach is always illegal, since it is a break of
a promise. A consequentialist judge may reason that certain breaches of
contract are acceptable, if, for example, a breach of contract would lead to
a better outcome for the relevant parties. Such reasoning is recognized as
"efficient breach" in law and economics.

In this chapter we build a classifier using tools from NLP and machine
learning, trying to identify modes of moral reasoning. Moral reasoning is
often studied in relation to political ideology (Fishkin et al., 1973; Graham
et al., 2009; Emler et al., 1983). Recently researchers (Sagi and Dehghani,
2013) employed computational techniques to measure texts amongst the
five moral dimensions posited by Jonathan Haidt (Haidt and Joseph,
2004). To the best of our knowledge, our work is the first attempt to
computationally classify moral reasoning into the conventional theoretical categories of ethics.

Here we operate on the assumption that patterns in written language
reflect, however imperfectly, different types of reasoning. For example,

a consequentialist would use language associated with ends. We might also expect language that attempts to infer the results of different types of actions and a higher frequency of words that designate consequence. In contrast, a judge reasoning deontologically might tend to use more absolute language and employ words like duty and obligation more often.

To train our classifier, we use a corpus of articles from the applied ethics literature. In these articles, philosophers argue about issues like abortion, vegetarianism, and war. The articles are drawn from an archive of philosophical literature, where they were categorized as either consequentialist or deontological. Our trained classifier assigns holdout samples to the proper class with over 90 percent accuracy.

We then apply the classifier to circuit court opinions, where judges outline their reasoning for the decision on a case. We use these opinions (dating back to 1883) to analyze trends in moral reasoning in the US legal system. We look at rates of consequentialist versus deontological reasoning over time, according to where the individual was born, where the individual attended school, their gender, and the party of the president under which they were nominated.

2. AUTOMATED CLASSIFICATION OF MORAL REASONING

2.1 Training Data

The training corpus comprises all articles from the philosophy paper database PhilPapers.org tagged with "Applied Consequentialism" or "Applied Deontology". We filtered out papers written in languages other than English, papers that had both consequentialism and deontology tags, and papers that obviously did not conform to either category. The resulting training corpus consists of 14 Consequentialist papers and 11 Deontology papers. These were converted to plain text, and artifacts from the PDF conversion were expunged when possible.

Our data set is composed of a few large texts. But most text classification techniques perform better with larger corpora. Accordingly, we separated each of our Consequentialist and Deontology corpa into 100 equally sized chunks. This introduces risk of overfitting, which we address by verifying performance over multiple random seeds that were used for separation of the data into the training and validation set.

Next we featurize the text. We tried many approaches, including bag-of-words, various lengths of n-grams, tf-idf, and so on, for featurizing the text. After some hyperparameter tuning, we chose tf-idf with n-gram featurization, which we found performed best in the holdout test set. The tf-idf statistic is an indicator of the relative importance of a word or phrase to a specific document. We take phrases of up to 3-words-length and adjust them by their document frequency to create a list of tf-idf n-grams. Each document is represented as a sparse vector representing the frequency distribution over these n-grams. Because these vectors are high-dimensional, the algorithm proceeds by using singular value decomposition to reduce the dimensionality to a lower-dimensional manifold.

2.2   Model Training

The preprocessing step leaves us with a vector assigned to each of the texts to use for training the machine learning model. A natural choice for classification problems such as ours is Linear Support Vector Machine (SVM) or Naive Bayes. Initial performance of Naive Bayes was very poor, so we focused our efforts on implementation of the SVM, which is known to be highly effective at text classification (Joachims, 1998).

In broad terms, Linear-SVM tries to find a hyperplane that neatly separates the vectors with "Deontology" labeling and "Consequentialist" labeling. On one side of the hyperplane we find consequentialist text and on the other side we find deontological texts. The prediction is made by locating the vector of the test text in relation to the hyperplane. We use a multi class SVM, with an additional label "other", trained on philosophy papers that did not have the consequentialism or deontological label. This measure reduces spuriously categorizing moral reasoning into the categories when in fact there is no moral reasoning being used at all.

During the initial steps in the training, we separate our data set into training and validation sets. After each training, the model predicts on the validation set and we tweak the training parameters to increase accuracy and get sensible features. Major tuning components in training the model were frequency threshold and stop words. A sensible frequency threshold prevents especially uncommon n-grams from influencing the classification. Stop words are common words filtered out of a data set before introducing the data to a model.

Our model very quickly approached a 100 percent prediction accuracy in the validation set, so the main hyperparameter tuning step was finding junk features in the prediction function and removing them. For example, the papers were downloaded on a university license, so we removed the terms that came from the license watermark. There were other overfitting type terms (e.g. "fetus", from the high-frequency of medical ethics papers), and junk phrases from the PDF conversion such as "x-86". These were also removed.

This was done through examination of the prediction function. Linear-SVM predicts by assigning weights (coefficients) to the n-grams. We looked at the top 50 predictors for both Consequentialist reasoning and Deontological reasoning and weeded out obviously irrelevant n-grams.

We also experimented with n-grams by adjusting the number of words per phrase. N=3 gave good results. Further increasing N helped very little and would have introduced risk of further overfitting.

Finally, we used Latent Dirichlet Allocation (a method frequently used to model topics) to check if any unobserved groups or topic bias are influencing the prediction. We found that the topics were varied and uniformly distributed, an indication that there was no such bias.

2.3   Feature Importance

The end product of the training is a weight assignment to each n-gram in the feature set. We rank the n-grams by their weights. In our model an n-gram with a positive weight means that it tends to occur in deontology articles, while a negative weight signals that the text is consequentialist.

The set of most predictive n-grams for each category are visualized in Figure 4.1's word clouds. Some of the features are somewhat intuitive. For example, "pleasure" is a consequentialist value, while "duty" is a deontological value.

3.   APPLICATION TO US CIRCUIT COURTS

The application corpus is the universe of US Circuit Court opinions from the years 1883 through 2013. Besides the text of the opinions, we have some relevant metadata, such as biographical details of the judges writing the opinions.

3.1   Prominent Paragraphs

To understand better how our classifier works in the judicial corpus, we ranked the paragraphs in the corpus by the mode of moral reasoning used. We list some of those paragraphs here. We can read these paragraphs and see how our classifier works in the new context.

Figure 4.1   Most predictive n-grams for identifying consequentialist (top) and deontological (bottom) reasoning

Strongly deontological prediction

The following paragraphs are considered deontological by the prediction model with high confidence:

> Second, after determining that Congress intended "special dumping duties" to be treated differently than normal customs duties, Commerce compared 201 safeguard duties to both normal customs duties and antidumping duties in order to determine how Congress would have intended 201 duties to be treated in achieving the purposes of the antidumping objectives. Commerce found several significant similarities between 201 safeguard duties and antidumping

duties and determined that 201 duties are "special dumping duties" because they are "more like AD [antidumping duties] in purpose and function than they are like ordinary customs duties." Id.

[I]f an insurer who refuses to defend were estopped from asserting the lack of coverage as a defense in a subsequent action, then the insurer's duty to indemnify would be coextensive with its duty to defend. [The Maine Law Court], however, ha[s] repeatedly stated that an insurer's duty to indemnify is independent from its duty to defend and that its duty to defend is broader than its duty to indemnify.

By reason of its nature as a public institution St. Elizabeth's Hospital owes a duty to the public in carrying out its difficult responsibilities. We have no occasion now to decide, however, whether its public duty included an entirely separate duty to Mrs. Morgan. There was a particular duty to the Court of General Sessions, and in the circumstances of this case it was intertwined with a duty to her. See infra, note 12.

3.2 Strongly Consequentialist Prediction

The following paragraphs are considered consequentialist by the prediction function with high confidence:

No rule of bankruptcy practice and procedure is designed to be considered in isolation. Each rule is to be considered in conjunction with every other rule. What the entire body of rules makes available to the practitioner and the bankruptcy judge is a gestalt designed to constitute a functional whole. The rules are not a melange of independent parts. The Advisory Committee alluded to this in its preface to the rules. "The proposed rules are not divided into chapters related to the different types of debtor relief chapters in the Code. These rules apply in all chapter cases except as a particular rule otherwise provides." Preface to Rules and Forms, 11 U.S.C. XXI. One of the trustee's most vigorous arguments, therefore, is explicitly contradicted by the Preface to the Rules. He argues that Rule 1019(4) does not apply to Chapter 7 cases. This is the rule that specifies that claims filed in the superseded case shall be deemed filed in the Chapter 7 case. The Advisory Committee's preface clearly reveals that the rules apply in all chapter cases "except as a particular rule provides otherwise." Rule 3002(a), requiring the filing of a claim in a Chapter 7 case, does not "provide[] otherwise." So construed, there is but one proper resolution of this case.

Besides the nonrestrictive nature of the ordinary meaning of the claim term "code," the doctrine of claim differentiation provides a powerful argument against construing the term "code" restrictively, to mean "spreading [**1615] code." Independent claim 1 of the '966 patent uses the term "code," and dependent claim 5 recites, in full, "The subscriber unit of claim 1 wherein the same code is a spreading code." The clear implication of narrowing the term "code" in dependent claim 5 by limiting the claim scope to cases in which the claimed code "is a spreading code" is that the term "code" in the independent claim is not limited to a spreading code.

However, the evidence submitted by Clark does not stand alone. Critically, Jerlene Bush and Mildred Bobo, both within job code 1433, testified that at the time of the RIF, they trained two employees, Carolyn Muse and James Russell Hunter, who then replaced them in their positions. See Appellants' App. at 496-98. Yet Hunter was placed in job code 1432, see id. at 171, and Muse in 1402, see id. at 170.10 Muse's placement in another job code generally raises questions about the claimed functional differences between job codes. But Hunter was placed into the very job code that plaintiffs argue was pretextually separated from their own code for purposes of discrimination. On the basis of personal observation, two witnesses from job code 1433 testified that they trained someone to perform their jobs and that the person they trained was placed in job code 1432. That is sufficient for a reasonable jury to find Seagate's differentiation of the two codes pretextual.

First, we see that the statements considered deontological all contain the word "duty," which is intuitive. The statements categorized consequentialist include phrases like "Each rule is to be considered in conjunction with every other rule", emblematic of context-sensitive consequential reasoning.

Time series for consequentialist reasoning
Next we examine trends in consequentialist versus deontological reasoning over time (Figure 4.2). We see there is a discrete jump in consequentialism in the 1930s, indicating a major switch in thought at the time.

There could be many factors driving this change. One possibility is that the hardships of the depression brought disenchantment with prevailing norms; so moral attitudes shifted toward a focus on better outcomes, rather than strict adherence to laws regardless of outcomes. Another potential factor is the legal realism movement of the 1920s and 1930s, which viewed law as a means toward an end, rather than an end in itself (Posner, 1986).

Another explanation for the trend is that over time the language of circuit court opinions has shifted to that of the consequentialist articles. For example, words that are weighted as consequentialist like "code" and "rule" might be appearing more often now compared to the past because there are more cases being decided on statutory grounds instead of common-law grounds.

In the Appendix, we report rankings of legal topics by moral reasoning. Opinions written in estate law and family law have a deontological bent, while administrative law tends to be more consequentialist. As the

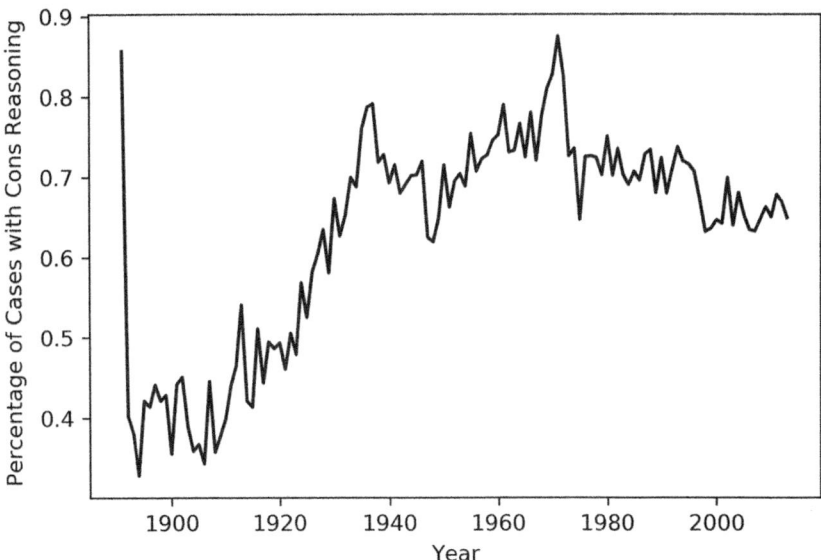

Figure 4.2   Consequentialist reasoning in the Circuit Courts, 1891–2013

popularity in topics has changed over time, some of the rankings may reflect when opinions in that topic were being written, because reasoning has become more consequentialist (e.g. the fact that there has been more administrative law in more recent times explains why more opinions in this topic are consequentialist). This effect could be disentangled in future work.

3.3   Judge Rankings

It might also be illuminating to learn which judges are most consequentialist or most deontological. For example, we might expect pragmatist judges such as Richard Posner to be consequentialist. To ensure a large enough sample size, we filter out all judges who published fewer than 50 opinions in our data set.

Table 4.1 has the most deontological judges. Table 4.2 has the most consequentialist judges. We can see that this appears to be driven by judge cohorts and time effects. Interestingly, the most consequentialist judge, Neil Gorsuch, was recently promoted to the US Supreme Court.

Table 4.1   Top ten deontological judges

Judge	Percent Consequentialist
Trieber, Jacob	21.2
Van Devanter, Willis	21.9
Cotterall, John H.	24.4
Reed, Henry Thomas	24.6
Kenyon, William	25.3
McDowell, Henry Clay	25.8
Hawley, Thomas Porter	26.6
Booth, Wilbur F.	27.5
Philips, John Finis	27.6
Pritchard, Jeter C.	28.1

Table 4.2   Top ten consequentialist judges

Judge	Percent Consequentialist
Gorsuch, Neil M.	92.4
Moore, Kimberly Ann	91.3
Martin, Beverly B.	90.2
Tatel, David Stephen	88.8
Madden, Joseph	88.1
Clevenger, Raymond Charles, III	87.9
Wilkey, Malcom R.	87.8
Rich, Giles Sutherland	87.6
Starr, Kenneth W.	87.5
Patterson, Robert P.	87.3
Chambers, Richard H.	87.0

3.4   Moral Reasoning and Judge Characteristics

Here we look at what biographical characteristics of judges are associated with the use of more consequentialist versus deontological language.

First, we show in Figure 4.3 that there seems to be very little difference across gender in moral reasoning. While it appears that females are more likely to reason consequentially, the difference is not statistically significant. What difference we do see is likely due to more female judges being in office in later years, after the upward shift.

Next, we ask in Figure 4.4 whether political party affiliations matter for modes of reasoning. There appears to be no significant difference in

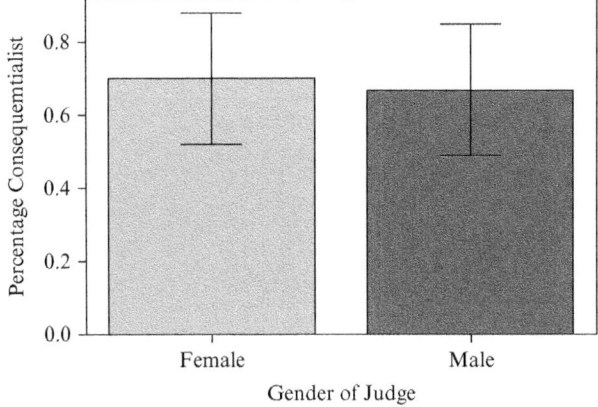

Figure 4.3   Consequentialist reasoning by gender

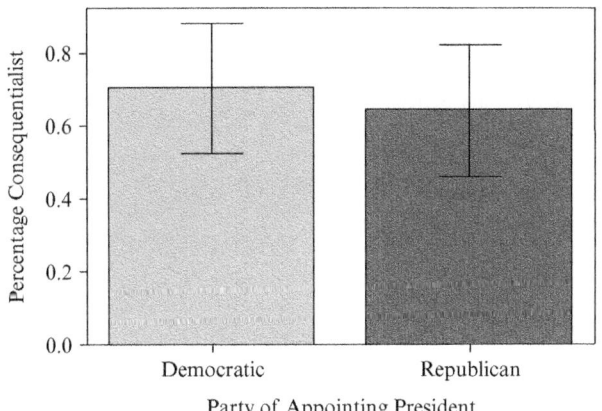

Figure 4.4   Consequentialist reasoning by political affiliation

consequentialist reasoning across party affiliations of the President who appointed the judge.

Another factor determining differences across judges in the mode of reasoning is their legal training. Are there differences between judges that come from different law schools? To answer this question we took the average use of consequentialism for the judges trained at each law school and then ranked them. We include all law schools where at least 1000 opinions by attendees are in the data set. This ranking is reported in Table 4.3, along with the percentage difference of that school from

Table 4.3   Ranking of judge consequentialism by law school attended

School	Percentage
Washington and Lee University School of Law	−19.6
University of North Carolina School of Law	−9.9
University of Wisconsin Law School	−9.5
University of Oxford	−3.5
University of Nebraska College of Law	0.5
St. Louis University School of Law	1.2
University of California, Berkeley	1.7
New York University School of Law	2.3
Columbia Law School	2.8
Cornell Law School	3.1
Syracuse University College of Law	3.6
Fordham University School of Law	4.0
University of Arkansas School of Law	4.3
University of Alabama School of Law	4.5
Harvard Law School	5.9
George Washington University Law School	5.9
Notre Dame Law School	6.0
Northwestern University School of Law	6.1
University of Utah College of Law	7.2
University of Washington School of Law	7.4
University of Southern California Law School	7.6
University of Virginia School of Law	7.8
Louisiana State University Law School	8.4
Yale Law School	8.4
University of Minnesota Law School	8.5
University of Chicago Law School	9.6
Tulane University Law School	9.6
University of Texas School of Law	11.1
University of Mississippi School of Law	11.7
University of Montana School of Law	11.7
Stanford Law School	12.1
Georgetown University Law Center	17.2

Note: Rankings of judge law schools by consequentialism

the global average. So, for example, judges who attended law school at Washington and Lee are on average reasoning consequentially about 20 percent less often than the average judge. There are large differences by law school attended.

Perhaps moral reasoning style is determined by where one grew up as well as where one attended law school. In Figure 4.5, we look at

Filling State Polygons by Consequentialist percentage

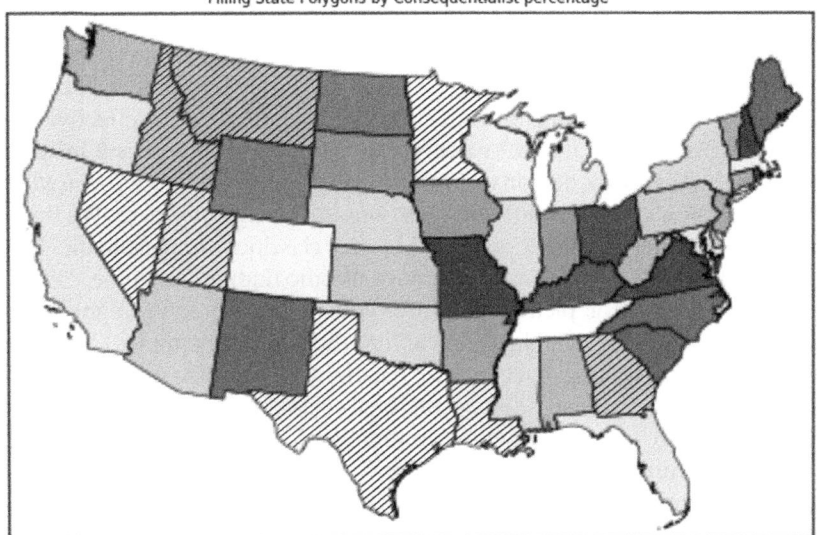

Figure 4.5   Consequentialist reasoning by judge birth state

differences by birth state. We find that judges from coastal states seem to have a relatively deontological leaning.

In the figure diagonal hatching corresponds to highly consequentialist states, while plain shading corresponds to highly deontological states.

4.   CONCLUSION

Utilitarian versus deontological modes of reasoning is a classic divide in moral philosophy and in economics and law. To understand human values, artificial intelligence (AI) systems will likely need to be able to detect and annotate when an argument is utilitarian or deontological. This chapter has demonstrated the use of computational linguistics and machine learning techniques for the problem of classifying moral reasoning in written texts. We show that even a small corpus of training articles can be utilized to reasonably infer patterns of moral reasoning. Such tools can then be used to help understand judging and the practice of law.

That said, we must caution against interpreting these results too strongly. How people reason, morally and otherwise, is a complex psychological and behavioral phenomenon. Oftentimes the reasoner herself cannot correctly identify how they came to some conclusion. To do so from an outside perspective presents even more of a challenge.

Machine learning techniques are far from able to engage in the sophisticated and robust patterns of inference and reasoning that humans exhibit. Current machine learning techniques should be understood as effective but limited, essentially statistical methods that can be used to draw insights from data. This work demonstrates how these techniques might be used to try and answer especially difficult questions in law and elsewhere. We think that the major conclusions suggested by our classifier are reasonable. It is difficult to assess how accurate the more specific findings might be.

There is room for plenty of future work. One approach might be to classify assignments of obligations and authority: for example, "the right is vested in party 1", "party 1 has the right", "the duty is assigned to party 1", "party 1 must", and so on, or to classify conditional language: "if A, then B" constructions. Another could be to observe whether economics-trained judges use different features of defendants consistent with cost-benefit analysis when obtaining sentences. A larger corpus of training data could be obtained, for example, by hand labeling instances of judges' reasoning in a specific way in court opinions. Topic modeling and dimensionality reduction should be further pursued in order to better understand how different populations reason morally.

REFERENCES

Alexander, Larry and Michael Moore (2016), "Deontological Ethics", in Edward N. Zalta (ed.), *The Stanford Encyclopedia of Philosophy*, accessed 1 March 2018 at https://plato.stanford.edu/archives/win2016/entries/ethics-deontological/.

Emler, Nicholas, Stanley Renwick, and Bernadette Malone (1983), "The Relationship Between Moral Reasoning and Political Orientation", *Journal of Personality and Social Psychology*, **45** (5), 1073–80.

Fishkin, James, Kenneth Keniston, and Catherine McKinnon (1973), "Moral Reasoning and Political Ideology", *Journal of Personality and Social Psychology*, **27** (1), 109–19.

Graham, Jesse, Jonathan Haidt, and Brian A. Nosek (2009), "Liberals and Conservatives Rely on Different Sets of Moral Foundations", *Journal of Personality and Social Psychology*, **96** (5), 1029–46.

Haidt, Jonathan and Craig Joseph (2004), "Intuitive Ethics: How Innately Prepared Intuitions Generate Culturally Variable Virtues", *Daedalus*, **133** (4), 55–66.

Hirschberg, J. and C.D. Manning (2015), "Advances in Natural Language Processing", *Science*, **349** (6245), 261–6.

Joachims, Thorsten (1998), "Text Categorization with Support Vector Machines: Learning with Many Relevant Features", in C. Nédellec and C. Rouveirol (eds), *Machine Learning: ECML-98*, Proceedings of the 10th European Conference on Machine Learning, Chemnitz, Germany, 21–23 April 1998, Lecture Notes in Computer Science (Lecture Notes in Artificial Intelligence), vol. 1398. Berlin and Heidelberg: Springer, pp. 137–42.

Posner, Richard A. (1986), "Legal Formalism, Legal Realism, and the Interpretation of Statutes and the Constitution", *Case Western Reserve Law Review*, **37** (2), 179–217.

Sagi, Eyal and Morteza Dehghani (2013), "Measuring Moral Rhetoric in Text", *Social Science Computer Review*, **32** (2), 132–44.

Sinnott-Armstrong, Walter (2015), "Consequentialism", in Edward N. Zalta (ed.), *The Stanford Encyclopedia of Philosophy* (Winter 2015 ed.), accessed 1 March 2018 at https://plato.stanford.edu/archives/win2015/entries/consequentialism/.

APPENDIX

We can rank different legal topics by the percentage of opinions written within the topic that are labeled consequentialist:

Table 4A.1   Topics with consequentialism score

Topic	Percentage
Wills, Trusts and Estates	44.7
Negotiable Instruments	50.2
Torts	52.6
Real Property	54.0
Admiralty and Maritime	54.9
Native Peoples	56.7
Judicial Ethics and Conduct	57.1
Natural Resources	57.7
Mortgages and Liens	58.0
Real Estate Investment Trust	58.6
Damages and Remedies	58.8
Landlord and Tenant	59.1
Debtor Creditor	60.1
Bankruptcy Law	60.4
Alcohol and Beverage	61.2
Motor Vehicles and Traffic Law	61.5
Legal Malpractice	61.9
Personal Property	62.3
Eminent Domain	62.6
Corporate Law	62.7
Entertainment Law	63.3
Contracts	63.8
Professional Responsibility	64.9
Civil Procedure	66.1
Civil Rights	66.3
Medical Malpractice	66.6
Agency	66.7
Criminal Law	66.8
Mergers and Acquisitions	67.1
Class Actions	67.6
Transportation Law	68.5
International Trade Law	68.5
International Law	68.8
Art Law	68.9
Appellate Procedure	69.0
Government	69.5
Constitutional Law	69.7

Table 4A.1   (continued)

Topic	Percentage
Prisoners' Rights	69.9
Partnerships and Non-Corporate Business Entities	70.1
Insurance Law	70.5
Employee Benefits	70.6
Postal Service Law	71.6
Alternative Dispute Resolution	72.0
Habeas Corpus	72.8
Gambling and Lotteries Law	72.9
Workers' Compensation	73.2
Elections and Politics	73.7
Securities Law	74.1
Employment Law	74.5
Franchise Law	74.5
Banking and Finance	74.6
Land Use Planning and Zoning	74.8
Uniform Commercial Code	75.2
Evidence	75.2
Environmental Law	75.7
Products Liability	75.7
Agricultural Law	75.9
Government Employees	76.0
Copyright Law	76.1
Military Law	76.2
Consumer Law	76.5
Patent Law	76.7
Education Law	76.8
Construction Law	77.0
Tax and Accounting	77.5
Professional Corporations	77.8
Antitrust and Trade	77.8
Immigration and Naturalization	77.9
Trade Secrets	78.6
Trademark Law	78.8
Intellectual Property Treaties and Conventions	79.2
Conflict of Laws	79.2
Executive Compensation	80.0
Communications and Media	80.3
Religious and Non-Profit Organizations	80.9
Hazardous Material Law	81.3
Health Law	81.7
Government Contracts	81.9
Privacy and Information Law	82.1

Table 4A.1 (continued)

Topic	Percentage
Sports Law	82.6
Homeland Security	83.3
Social Security	83.4
Administrative Law	84.6
Labor Law	84.6
Energy Law	92.3
Technology Law	93.9

Note: Scores are a percentage of the opinions in that category that were classified consequentialist.

5. On dragons, caves, teeth, and claws: legal analytics and the problem of court data access*

**Charlotte S. Alexander and
Mohammad Javad Feizollahi**

INTRODUCTION

In his 1897 essay, "The Path of the Law," Oliver Wendell Holmes famously defined "the law" as "[t]he prophecies of what the courts will do in fact, and nothing more pretentious. . . ." Holmes' particular brand of what came to be called legal realism was focused intently on judicial behavior: understanding "the law" meant understanding, in a granular, pragmatic way, how and why judges arrived at their conclusions. One can therefore imagine Holmes' delight at the development of legal analytics and computational law, or the application of data science tools and methodologies to legal questions and problems. Indeed, returning to Holmes (1897):

> When you get the dragon out of his cave on to the plain and in the daylight, you can count his teeth and claws, and see just what is his strength. But to get him out is only the first step. The next is either to kill him, or to tame him and make him a useful animal. For the rational study of the law the blackletter man may be the man of the present, but the man of the future is the man of statistics and the master of economics.

* Thanks to Anne Tucker for her practical partnership in the development of the Legal Analytics Lab at Georgia State University and her thought partnership in tackling these and other data access questions; to Mike Lissner, Free Law Project Executive Director, who contributed his extensive knowledge of PACER and its flaws, as well as thousands of PACER documents to the project described here in Section 2; to Ryan Whalen for organizing the 2018 Emergence of Computational Legal Studies Workshop at Hong Kong University; and to all workshop participants for their fascinating research and engaging discussion. The project that is described in Section 2 was funded by the U.S. Department of Labor, Chief Evaluation Office, Labor Research and Evaluation Grant EO-30275-17-60-5-13.

Today's legal analytics practitioners are Holmes' women and men of statistics, who use text mining, natural language processing, machine learning, network analysis, and other techniques to pry insights and extract patterns from masses of legal text. At what rate do judges grant motions for summary judgment to plaintiffs versus defendants, for example? What lawsuit features are the best predictors of grants and denials, holding all else constant? Computational tools allow exploration of these sorts of questions, serving descriptive, explanatory, predictive, and ultimately prescriptive goals, and rooting scholars' analyses in the granular, pragmatic minutiae of how judges actually operate in the civil lawsuits and criminal prosecutions before them.

But to answer these questions – to count the dragon's teeth and claws – we must first get access to court data in bulk, to pull the dragon from the cave. And when the particular dragon to be studied is litigation and its outcomes – "what the courts will do in fact," as Holmes put it – the data access challenges are substantial.

This chapter proceeds as follows. Section 1 briefly reviews other scholarship on court data access and identifies two major themes: limitations on bulk access and problems with usability. Section 2 describes a project that attempted to study all US district court judges' decisions in employee misclassification disputes over a ten-year period, as a case study of court data access problems in real-world computational legal research. Section 3 concludes by proposing solutions.

1.   DATA ACCESS UNPACKED

The observation that court data is inaccessible is not a new one. Peter Martin has produced a career's worth of scholarship detailing the shortcomings of the federal courts' Public Access to Court Electronic Records (PACER) system, its state court analogs, and commercial legal research services.[1] Lynn LoPucki (2002, p. 2162), too, has developed an incisive set

---

[1]   PACER is the system that allows users to access electronic versions of federal court docket sheets and documents, including party-filed documents and judge-issued opinions and orders. It is maintained by the Administrative Office of the U.S. Courts (PACER (Public Access to Court Electronic Records), n.d., webpage: describing the PACER system). State court systems maintain their own, separate systems, with varying coverage and allowing varying levels of public access to court dockets and the underlying court documents (See, e.g., Kourlis and Gagel, 2008: describing both state and federal court systems). See also Martin, 2008; Martin, 2018.

of critiques centered on court transparency, observing that government officials "control access to the data" and withhold the sort of granular, judge-level data that would allow scholars to "study . . . the judges' work." Elizabeth McCuskey (2016, pp. 516–17), in turn, has identified what she calls "submerged precedent," or judges' reasoned decisions that are absent from commercial legal research databases and only available within PACER via "grueling docket-based search techniques." This absence from readily accessible databases "not only limits public *use* of court opinions, but largely prevents public *knowledge* of those opinions' existence" (McCuskey, 2016, pp. 516–17). Pauline Kim, Margo Schlanger, Christina Boyd, and Andrew Martin (2009, pp. 98–9) have sounded a similar alarm, noting that many district court judges' decisions, which "can have a significant impact on the potential outcome and may reflect a judge's attitude toward the case or the litigants . . . are largely inaccessible from traditional data sources" (see also Schultze, 2018). Kim and her collaborators (2009) also note the difficulties in accessing and studying court data of other types: party-filed documents and courts' docket sheets.

Outside of academic legal scholarship, parties as diverse as the American Association of Law Libraries (2006), technologist and public domain advocate Carl Malamud (2013), the late hacktivist Aaron Swartz (Schwartz, 2013), the nonprofit Free Law Project (n.d.: "We seek to collect and freely distribute online all United States court opinions, both state and federal, both historical and current"), and plaintiffs in four separate lawsuits challenging PACER fees (*Greenspan v. Administrative Office*, 2014; *Fisher v. Duff*, 2015; *Fisher v. United States*, 2015; *National Veterans Legal Services Program v. United States*, 2016) have called for serious reform of the delivery, accessibility, and availability of court documents, to bring "the nation's legal system [out from] behind a wall of cash and kludge" (Schwartz, 2009). In short, our country's court systems do an exceedingly poor job of making comprehensive data available on judges' management and disposition of the cases before them. The federal appellate courts are perhaps the most accessible, federal district courts are worse, and most state and local court systems lag substantially farther behind (Kim et al., 2009, p. 99: noting availability of appellate court decisions and lesser availability of federal district court opinions; Martin, 2008, p. 856: "State court systems, lagging far behind the federal judiciary in creating comprehensive systems of remote public access, have in important respects taken quite different approaches").

Taken as a whole, these commentators identify two main, interlocking problems with court data access, defining "court data" here inclusively as lawsuit-level metadata, decisions and opinions issued by judges, documents filed by the parties, and the docket sheets that serve as chronological indices of every action in a matter before the court. These are the twin challenges of bulk access and usability.

A. Bulk Access

The first problem is that of bulk access, meaning the ability of a user to obtain an electronic version of large amounts of court data, with reasonable effort and at a reasonable cost. Of course, court data is nominally always accessible, in that members of the public can request most court files from a clerk's office and, absent a protective order that seals the documents, read them and make photocopies. This is not the "access" that is demanded here, however, or that would enable analysis of large amounts of court data and extraction of patterns and insights, as Holmes envisioned.

As an alternative, users can access court data through commercial providers such as Westlaw, LexisNexis, Bloomberg Law, and their competitors.[2] However, as McCuskey and Kim et al. have demonstrated, while these providers offer user-friendly, detailed search interfaces atop huge troves of data, they also omit large numbers of party-filed documents and judges' decisions, and do not reveal their data collection methods or reasons for inclusion or exclusion. McCuskey's work (2016, p.517), for example, found that 30 percent of reasoned decisions issued by judges from two US district courts on a particular topic were missing from Westlaw and Lexis. Kim and her co-authors (2009, p.99: citing Hoffman et al., 2007, p.682) also summarize multiple studies that document gaps in court data availability, including one in which the authors "were able to access written opinions for less than 20% of judicial orders in the cases they examined."

Further, as the case study in the next section illustrates, commercial legal data providers can return dramatically different numbers of results

---

[2]   Some competitors include Fastcase, Casemaker, and even Google Scholar, all of which differ in their coverage and search architecture. Further, Ravel Law, a legal research and analytics startup that was acquired by LexisNexis, has recently announced the Caselaw Access Project, a partnership with the Harvard Library Innovation Lab, that will scan, digitize, and make available online all materials in Harvard Law Library's collection of published court decisions (Caselaw Access Project, n.d., webpage). However, this service is also limited, in that the collection only contains the "official print versions of . . . court decisions," omitting the unknown number of judges' decisions that are not designated for publication. See also Kim et al., 2009, p.97, fn. 44: noting that "[n]umerous studies have found that published and unpublished opinions differ in systematic ways" and collecting studies.

when provided identical search parameters. This discrepancy renders these sources functionally useless if the goal is to assemble all court data within some given universe: should a researcher rely on Westlaw, on Lexis, on some other provider, on the results that are common to all searches, on the unique set of results, or on some other set? Section 2 returns to these questions in detail.

Moreover, commercial providers commonly prohibit the use of auto-mated search and retrieval techniques such as crawling and scraping, meaning that any user who seeks to assemble court data in bulk, including judges' decisions, parties' filings, and docket sheets, must spend painstak-ing hours manually pointing, clicking, and downloading to gather the relevant set of documents for analysis (see, e.g., Thomson Reuters, n.d., terms of use webpage: Governing all Thomson Reuters legal materials including Westlaw, "[Y]ou will not use any robot, spider, other automatic software or device, or manual process to monitor or copy our website or the content, information, or services on this website without Thomson Reuters' prior written consent"). Even if a researcher were to invest the time and money to undertake a manual search-and-download process, the commercial products' terms of service prohibit sharing the resulting corpus of assembled documents with the public or even fellow researchers (Thomson Reuters, n.d., terms of use webpage: "[Y]ou will not reproduce, duplicate, copy, download, store, further transmit, disseminate, transfer, or otherwise exploit this website, or any portion hereof without Thomson Reuters' prior written consent, except that you may reproduce limited content from this site describing Thomson Reuters' products and services solely to educate users or potential users about Thomson Reuters prod-ucts or services"). Finally, subscriptions to most of these services may be prohibitively costly for anyone outside a university, large law firm, or corporate setting.

As an alternative, a user might go straight to the courts, and attempt to assemble court data in bulk via the federal courts' PACER system or an equivalent state or local court document access platform. The problem here is not selective inclusion and exclusion, as with commercial service providers, because the courts are the original source of the data from which those providers draw. Instead, there are substantial cost and searchability problems. With respect to cost, PACER charges $.10 per page downloaded, which, in a project that requires access to data in bulk, can generate PACER bills that run into the thousands. Under the E-Government Act of 2002, courts are supposed to designate as free any document in which a judge describes the reasoning for his or her decision, exempting those documents from PACER charges, and to make those opinions available online in "text searchable format" (Martin, 2008,

p. 862: describing E-Government Act of 2002, Pub. L. No. 107-347, § 205(a)(5), 116 Stat. 2899, 2915 (2002)). However, as Martin (2018, pp. 4–7: illustrating problems with judge non-compliance with opinion availability mandate) has observed, and as the case study in Section 2 illustrates, judges, or their staff, are shockingly bad at following this rule. Moreover, this fee exemption only applies to judges' decisions, meaning that all party-filed documents, and the docket sheets themselves, generate download costs.

The federal courts do permit researchers to apply for PACER fee waivers, as some legal academics have done.[3] However, data obtained via a waiver may not be transferred or shared with any other party (PACER, 2013, pdf). In addition, the courts have appeared to use grants and denials of PACER fee waivers for self-protective ends. Professor Lynn LoPucki, a bankruptcy scholar who – like Peter Martin – has produced some of the closest and most thoughtful analyses of court data access problems, reports being denied a PACER fee waiver by a court after publishing work that criticized the court's operations (LoPucki, 2009). In the end, as Kim and her co-authors (2009, p. 101: arguing for an expansion of scholars' focus to the totality of judges' role in district court litigation, as gleaned from docket sheets and parties' filings rather than just judges' reasoned opinions) have observed, this system works to sequester an exceedingly rich source of information on litigation's pathways and judicial decision-making behind a paywall.

Turning from the problem of cost to that of searchability, PACER's search architecture is designed primarily for users who are seeking out specific, known cases, rather than assembling large amounts of court data at once.[4] PACER allows users of its front-end search functionality to search only limited, lawsuit-level metadata: court type (district or appellate), case number and title, case type (civil, criminal, multi-district litigation), region, party name and type (plaintiff or defendant), and dates filed and closed.[5] This structure could suffice if a researcher were seeking all cases

---

[3]   PACER Electronic Public Access Fee Schedule, 2013, Sec. 9, pdf. The most famous researcher to which PACER fee waivers were granted is probably now-Senator Elizabeth Warren, who received fee waivers to study bankruptcies when she was a law professor at Harvard. These waivers have now become the source of some (minor) controversy (Jacobson, 2012).

[4]   State and local court data search platforms operate similarly (Martin, 2008; *supra* note 1).

[5]   PACER Case Locator, n.d. a, advanced case search webpage; PACER Case Locator, n.d. b, advanced party search webpage. For all of their flaws, by contrast, commercial legal research providers do allow users to run full-text searches of docket sheets as well as many of the underlying court documents and decisions,

filed in a certain court during a certain time period, but falls short when researchers are interested in studying only a subset of cases brought under a certain statute, or raising a certain issue.

PACER does provide an Application Programming Interface (API), which allows users to write their own customized search-and-download queries, at the same per-page download price, and provides a limited set of additional metadata as search fields (PACER Case Locator, n.d. c, pdf). Yet API access, too, is problematic, as the classification or labeling of cases is often inaccurate or unhelpful. Some of the labels are generated by the parties themselves with little guidance, meaning that their contents vary widely. One such label, the Nature of Suit (NOS) code, is assigned in civil cases by the plaintiff or his/her lawyer at the time a case is filed, chosen from a list on a required document called a civil cover sheet (U.S. Courts, n.d., pdf). This code ostensibly classifies lawsuits by the main set of statutory or common law violations alleged: plaintiffs may choose only one NOS code; they are instructed to select the "most applicable" if more than one could apply (U.S. Courts, n.d., 2, Sec. IV ("Nature of Suit"), pdf).

Though seemingly quite helpful at first glance, NOS codes in fact erase substantial detail. For example, imagine that a plaintiff files an employment discrimination case in US district court against her employer, alleging that she experienced sex and disability discrimination, in violation of Title VII of the Civil Rights Act of 1964 (Title VII) and the Americans with Disabilities Act of 1990 (ADA). She assigns her case NOS code 442, which denotes "Civil Rights – Employment" cases (U.S. Courts, n.d., 2, Sec. IV ("Nature of Suit"), pdf). She chooses 442 over 445, the specific code for ADA cases, because she is allowed only one choice and her sex discrimination claims are forefront in her mind. The assignment of 442 has written the plaintiff's additional ADA claims out of PACER's metadata. It is no surprise, then, that studies that compare lawsuits' NOS codes with the allegations recited in the text of their complaints have revealed substantial mismatches (Boyd and Hoffman, 2017; see also Alexander, 2019).

Researchers who are attempting to assemble court data in bulk via PACER are therefore left to choose between over- and under-inclusive data sets. Returning to the example above, if a researcher is interested in studying the universe of cases in which ADA violations were alleged, she must download *all* cases filed in her court and time periods of interest, and then mine (manually or via automation) the court documents' text to

---

specifying keywords, date ranges, judges, courts, and other features to identify the set of court data to be retrieved.

find ADA allegations. This process, explored further in the section below, would require a substantial investment of money, as well as reading time, coding time, or both.

Alternatively, the researcher may decide to download only cases with NOS code 445, for ADA cases, and just to write off the cases that contain ADA allegations but not the ADA NOS code. Or she might download NOS codes 445 and 442, the next-closest employment discrimination NOS code, on the theory that the ADA cases missing from 445 are most likely to turn up in 442. Regardless of strategy, these approaches cannot produce a reliably comprehensive bulk data set. In addition, the researcher has no way of estimating the number or characteristics of the missing cases, and is unable to hypothesize about the effect of this exclusion on her results.

As Martin (2018, p. 3) summarizes, therefore, after decades of attention to these problems, "effective and comprehensive access" to court data in bulk through any of the sources described here "remains an elusive goal." Whether the source is a commercial legal research provider or the courts' own document access systems, large swathes of data "remain hidden from lawyers, academics, and the general public," or are functionally inaccessible, in bulk, as a practical matter (Martin, 2018, p. 3).

B.   Usability

Closely related to the problem of bulk access is the problem of usability. "Usability" requires, at absolute minimum, that data be machine-readable. At maximum, "usability" demands that court data be substantially more structured than in its current state, requiring much less manipulation in order for users to learn something about the issues at stake and how the judge (or the parties themselves) resolved the dispute.

The section above explored the bulk access problems caused by the absence or unreliability of structured, lawsuit-level metadata within PACER and analogous systems. Moving beyond metadata, similar problems persist on the level of court documents, both party- and judge-filed, and the docket sheets that index them.

Court documents are the richest source of information about "what the courts . . . do in fact," as Holmes put it. Those documents might be party-filed, including pleadings, motions, and briefs, or judge-filed, including both purely ministerial and substantive orders and opinions. Yet court documents are the least structured of any kind of court data, and that messiness can be substantial. First, many court documents, despite being available in electronic form, were originally scanned from hard copies, and remain unreadable in part or in full even after conversion attempts using the best-performing Optical Character Recognition (OCR) pre-processing packages.[6] Second, even with crystal-clear text, party- and judge-filed documents lack a standardized terminology that enables easy identification of the issues and sub-issues at hand, and the judges' disposition of those matters.

Assume, for example, that a researcher is interested in studying US district courts' resolution of ADA claims over a certain time period, focusing in particular on claims that an employer failed to reasonably accommodate an employee's disability. She decides against using commercial legal research providers due to the concerns about the selectivity of their search results described in the previous section. She opts instead for the over-inclusive PACER bulk access option presented above, downloading *all* civil cases from PACER, regardless of NOS code, resolved in the time period of interest, in all 94 US district courts. As a rough measure of the scope of such a download, the Administrative Office of the U.S. Courts reports 821,753 civil cases terminated during three recent federal fiscal years (2015–17).[7] In order to identify the claims at issue and their resolution in each case, the researcher would need to download the docket sheet, complaint, and any dispositive judge's opinion such as a summary judgment decision in each case.

Corpus now assembled, because the NOS codes supplied by PACER's lawsuit-level metadata are unreliable, the researcher's next task is to parse the text of the court documents to identify reasonable accommodation ADA claims, and then to discern the claims' outcome from the court documents, the docket sheets, or some combination of the two.

Starting with the identification of ADA reasonable accommodation claims, the researcher might read all documents associated with the 821,753 lawsuits. Alternatively, she could write a set of regular expressions, or computer code that searches for a pre-defined term or terms, to mine the court documents for keywords associated with reasonable accommodations claims, and then manually classify the lawsuits according

---

[6] This violates the E-Government Act of 2002, which requires that judges' reasoned opinions be made available online in "text searchable format." See Martin, 2008, p. 862: describing E-Government Act of 2002, Pub. L. No. 107-347, § 205(a)(5), 116 Stat. 2899, 2915 (2002).

[7] Federal Judicial Caseload Statistics, 2015–17, webpage (reporting 287,114 civil cases terminated in US district courts in federal fiscal year 2017, 270,515 in 2016, and 264,124 in 2015). Note that this scenario could likely only occur in the realm of the hypothetical. Assuming, charitably, that all judges' decisions would properly be designated as free on PACER, and that docket sheets and complaints would average three pages apiece (for calculation purposes), PACER fees for the documents related to those 821,753 lawsuits would total almost half a million dollars.

to their keyword frequencies. These tasks are complicated by the fact that judges and the parties use varying language to describe the statutes and claims at issue. The name of the Americans with Disabilities Act of 1990, for example, could appear in its complete form, or without the year, or as "ADA." A court document might also include one of the various forms of the statute's citation: Pub. L. No. 101-336, 104 Stat. 328 (1990), 42 U.S.C. § 12101, and/or any of the approximately 100 subsequent sub-sections. And the term "reasonable accommodation" may appear in a decision only in passing, or may indicate that the court actually engaged in a reasonable accommodation analysis.

Machine learning techniques – specifically multi-label classification and various approaches to topic modeling – might offer another path forward. However, more supervised machine learning tools would require a substantial front-end investment of manual review time in creating training, validation, and test sets with all allegations of statutory violations and claims properly classified (see Géron, 2017: for a general discussion of machine learning classification techniques and topic modeling). Less supervised techniques would require less manual classification on the front end, leaving the algorithm to discover patterns autonomously within the text, but may not be able to produce classifications that are sufficiently granular to identify all statutory violations and claims within a given piece of legal text.

Once our hypothetical researcher has identified the relevant set of lawsuits that contain reasonable accommodation claims, by whatever method, she must next determine those claims' outcomes. Here, she is not interested in the overall outcome of the litigation, but rather the outcome of the particular claim of interest. It is possible, for example, that a plaintiff might lose his or her reasonable accommodation claim at summary judgment, but prevail on other claims. Therefore, the researcher's task is to identify the outcome on a granular, claim-specific level.

She might draw on two types of court data in order to do so: judges' opinions and docket sheets. First, docket sheets: federal district court docket sheets available via PACER are relatively structured, in that each entry contains a date, an item number, and a text description of the action taken or document filed. These descriptions may indicate the filing party and the document type, for example, "Complaint," or "Defendant's Motion for Summary Judgment," or "Memorandum Opinion and Order Granting Defendant's Motion for Summary Judgment."[8] However, docket

---

[8]   Note that certain document names need not specify the filing party, as only one party (or the judge) may enter them on the docket. Examples include

entry text is often incomplete, appearing only as "Motion for Summary Judgment," for example, and omitting the identity of the filing party.

Text descriptions also vary with respect to judge-filed entries. The most complete examples identify the filing party, the motion type, and the judge's disposition of the motion. However, opinions might also appear only as "Opinion and Order on Defendant's Motion for Summary Judgment," identifying the filing party but omitting how the judge ruled, or – even less helpful – merely "Memorandum Opinion and Order," failing to detail what type of motion the judge was ruling on, who filed the underlying motion, and how the judge resolved it.

This problem stems from the method by which docket sheet text is generated: it is a combination of user-provided free responses and court-provided categories, and the court-provided categories vary from court to court. In fact, PACER can better be understood not as a single provider of electronic court data, but as a wrapper around 214 separate systems, run by separate district, bankruptcy, and appellate courts, each of which uses its own standardized docket sheet categories to which users provide (or not) additional detail (Herther, 2018).

Thus, at its most complete, the docket sheet text discussed above can signal to a researcher how a case closed. The presence of a docket entry called "Notice of Settlement" indicates that the case settled; a fully identified judge's opinion granting a defendant's motion for summary judgment on all of plaintiffs' claims indicates that the plaintiffs lost and the defendant won. However, beyond these clear indications, learning how a case resolved, and – as in the hypothetical example focused on reasonable accommodation claims in particular – how a judge resolved specific sub-issues within a case, is substantially more difficult. Docket sheet text's sparsity and variation thus drive researchers into the text of the court documents themselves in order to fill out a granular picture of what actually happened – to count the dragon's teeth and claws.

Mining the text of judges' opinions for outcome information presents many of the same problems detailed above in connection with statutory violation and claim type identification. This is because there is no standardized form in which judges deliver their decisions on each sub-issue in a case, let alone any reliable structured data source that catalogs each decision.[9] For example, each of the following sentences represents a

---

"Complaint," which is always plaintiff-filed, and "Memorandum Opinion and Order," which is always judge-filed.

[9] The only existing data sets on judicial decisions come from the Federal Judicial Center (FJC), the research arm of the federal courts. These data contain no information on state courts, and are sparse and unreliable even for the federal

judge's disposition of a reasonable accommodation dispute on summary judgment in three different ADA cases:

- "In light of this conflicting evidence, this Court finds that triable issues of fact exist regarding whether Knowles could be reasonably accommodated in fulfilling the essential function of the production job at Scotts or whether such accommodation would place an undue hardship on defendant" (*E.E.O.C. v. Remedy Intelligent Staffing, Inc.*, 2003).
- "Her claim for failure to accommodate under the ADA therefore fails as a matter of law" (*Watts v. Creative Foundations, Inc.*, 2017).
- "In accordance with these decisions and the unpublished decisions of the Sixth Circuit, this Court concludes that, because, after discovery, the Plaintiff has failed to put forth any evidence that there was a vacancy which would accommodate her disability, the Plaintiff cannot prevail on a claim that the Defendant failed to accommodate her disability by failing to engage in the interactive process" (*Beair v. Summit Polymers*, 2013).

While certainly possible, the task of extracting these and similar sentences – as before – would require a substantial investment of both manual and coding time by our hypothetical researcher.

Whether this state of affairs constitutes "usability" is perhaps open to argument. Considering only the federal court system as an example, it is theoretically possible for a user to invest the money and time to bulk-download all court data across all years, courts, and NOS codes from PACER, producing a set of court documents and docket sheets in the millions. He or she could then invest substantial additional resources to write, train, test, and deploy code that effectively classifies docket sheet entries and the text of the underlying court documents into many categories that are useful for analysis. However, this scenario does not constitute "usability" in the way that Holmes might define the word, as the "dragon" that is the operation of the country's courts would remain firmly in the cave for all but the richest and most computationally savvy consumers of court data.

Stepping back, one might attack the shortcomings identified here from

---

courts that they do cover. Many variables are missing values for half or more of the lawsuits that are reported, and the FJC's own code book cautions against using some of the data, as data collection quality varies substantially across the federal court system (Federal Judicial Center, n.d., integrated database webpage).

an access to justice perspective, arguing, as Malamud (2013) does, that "[p]ublic promulgation of the law," and the documents on which it is written and interpreted, "is a fundamental aspect of a doctrine known as the rule of law, a doctrine reflected in constitutions and treaties throughout the world." Relatedly, Stephen Schultze (2018) argues that court data access problems raise First Amendment implications, as they impede the access of the press to the workings of the courts. Finally, Lynn LoPucki (2002) notes the stifling effect that constricted court data access has on researchers' ability to develop new understandings of our judicial system. Indeed, spinning out this final point, given data access problems, it is very difficult for a researcher to assemble the full universe of judges' decisions, docket sheets, or other legal text. Even assembling anything resembling a "big" dataset is difficult, limiting the application of machine learning and other tools that require large training sets in order to extract insight from masses of text.

Moreover, given the lack of a canonical list of all documents of a given type, it is equally difficult for a researcher to select a random sample from a universe of unknown size and characteristics. This means that whatever biases that exist within the data sets that researchers do assemble are unknown, calling the results of empirical and computational projects into question.

These critiques, combined with Holmes' vision of transparency around "what the courts will do in fact," is where this chapter situates itself. If, as Holmes asserts, the key to the law is judicial behavior, then we now have unprecedented ability to study that behavior, by mining millions of pages of judges' writing. We can also study the behavior of the parties and the courts' resolution of disputes writ large, considering not only cases that end with judicial action, but also those that settle.

Yet the task of assembling a corpus of relevant documents, before even beginning any analysis, is often herculean. Simply put, it is absurd in this era of data that a researcher would have to undertake the hypothetical methodological contortions described above to answer the seemingly simple question of how one type of court resolved one type of claim during a specified time period.[10]

---

[10]   The United States also risks falling behind other countries that face their own legal data access problems, but are taking greater strides to address them. Chinese legal scholars, for example, note a similar set of data access and completeness problems as those identified in this chapter (Tang and Liu, Chapter 6 in this volume). However, China has adopted a "leapfrogging" approach to online transparency and court document availability, investing substantial resources and government backing in "the use of big data and artificial intelligence in the

This chapter now turns to a case study of just such an endeavor – long, costly, and beset with challenges – in a computational law project run by the authors, who are a law professor and a data scientist. It then draws on this case study to consider the implications of court data access for the study and practice of law in the age of analytics, and to offer ideas for solutions.

2.   THE EMPLOYEE MISCLASSIFICATION PROJECT

The employee misclassification project is an attempt to assemble all relevant decisions by all US district court judges over a ten-year period (2008–17), to use computational tools to mine the opinions' text, and ultimately to understand how judges apply the law to distinguish between employees and independent contractors.

"Employee misclassification" refers to employers' practice of improperly classifying employees as independent contractors (Alexander, 2017, p. 907). Despite their label, these workers function like employees: they are controlled by and economically dependent on a single employer, and lack the flexibility, entrepreneurial opportunity, and autonomy of true independent contractors. By virtue of their contractor status, however, misclassified workers are granted few workplace rights and denied access to benefits, as nearly all federal labor and employment statutes apply only to employees (Alexander, 2017, pp. 907–8).

Courts are meant to act as a check on employers' power to classify, as nominally independent contractors may file suit alleging violations of their workplace rights and seek reclassification as employees for purposes of the litigation. However, the law does a poor job of distinguishing cleanly between the two categories of workers. Title VII, for example, the main federal employment discrimination statute, defines an "employee" as "an individual employed by an employer" (42 U.S.C. § 2000e(f)). To fill this gap, courts have developed various legal tests, analyzing between

---

administration of law" id. at 1. For example, unlike the patchwork of federal and state court document access systems in the United States, the Supreme People's Court (SPC) in China "maintains a centralized database of all court decisions in the country, hosted on a [free,] publicly available website" id. Though Tang and Liu have documented holes in the SPC data, the availability of a single, nationwide source of court data – combined with China's larger, state-backed push to become a "number-managed country" – means that China is poised to jump ahead in the application of computational methodologies to litigation-related questions and problems (id. at 11–12).

4 and 13 factors to identify a worker's proper classification (Alexander, 2017). Judges' decisions are thus where misclassification law is created.

The goal of the employee misclassification project is to understand how courts deploy this body of law in distinguishing between employees and independent contractors, and to identify the factors (both the enumerated factors from the caselaw and factors associated with the characteristics of the lawsuits, parties, or judges involved) that most influence their decisions.

In a predecessor project, Alexander supervised a team of law students who hand-coded a set of variables from all 154 employee misclassification summary judgment decisions issued in Title VII cases, 2005–14, that were available via Westlaw keyword searches. This work culminated in a law review article published in 2017 (Alexander, 2017).

While this Westlaw-derived convenience sample yielded interesting results, it was far from representative. A second phase of the project, funded by a grant from the US Department of Labor (DOL), sought to assemble the complete universe of electronically available summary judgment decisions in employee misclassification disputes, from all underlying case types, not just Title VII. The time frame for the study would be 2008, the year when most US district court data became reliably available in electronic format via PACER, to 2017, the most recent complete year of data. The project thus proposed to produce the first comprehensive study of what was expected to be thousands of federal district court employee misclassification decisions, and to use the tools of text analytics and machine learning to understand the on-the-ground operation of this area of law.

As the sections below explain, however, court data access limitations caused substantial problems at nearly every turn.

A. Data Assembly Strategy 1

The research team originally planned a data assembly approach that combined the easy searchability of commercial legal research providers with the comprehensive document availability of PACER. Specifically, the team planned to use Bloomberg Law to search the docket sheet text of all labor and employment lawsuits, identified by NOS code, filed in the study period, to find summary judgment decisions.

Notably, this process would not involve searching Bloomberg's curated set of *opinions*, which would be subject to the same problems of selective inclusion and exclusion described in Section 1.A above. Instead, these searches would crawl the text of the lawsuits' *docket sheets*, which Bloomberg pulls directly from PACER, searching for keywords that identified summary judgment opinions.[11] The intent was to assemble a comprehensive list of all labor and employment law cases during our study period in which a judge issued a summary judgment decision, regardless of issue.[12] Test searches in Bloomberg Law suggested that this process would identify approximately 30,000 employment and labor law summary judgment decisions.

The next step would be to obtain the full text of those opinions. Because one goal of the DOL grant was to produce shareable data, and because Bloomberg Law, like other commercial legal research providers, prohibits sharing, the team would not actually download the 30,000 summary judgment opinions from Bloomberg Law (n.d., About us: Terms of service: Subscription products, Sec. 2(b), webpage). Instead, we would obtain them from two sources: RECAP (n.d., webpage), a free public archive of several million federal court documents, and PACER.[13] After first searching RECAP for any of the 30,000 target documents, the research team would purchase the remaining documents directly from PACER.[14]

By the end of these first two steps, the research team planned to have amassed a superset of all summary judgment decisions, on all topics, issued in employment and labor law cases filed in US district courts in the years 2008 through 2017. The next steps would require text-based classification in order to identify the decisions that addressed the issue of employee misclassification specifically, and then further analysis of those decisions' text to understand the way that judges were deploying the law in the cases before them.

---

[11]   Unlike other commercial legal research providers at the time this project was planned, Bloomberg Law allowed US district court docket sheet searching by keywords, while also allowing filtering by NOS code and year.

[12]   Admittedly, this technique relied on the flawed NOS code system to identify labor and employment lawsuits from the outset. As illustrated above in note 7, however, funding simply was not available to cast a wider net and target all civil cases, as in the hypothetical in the previous section.

[13]   RECAP (n.d., webpage) is a joint project of Princeton University's Center for Information Technology Policy and the Free Law Project (FLP), a federal 501(c)(3) nonprofit. The RECAP archive consists of court documents in electronic form that users have already purchased from PACER, and then voluntarily contributed to the archive.

[14]   PACER fee waivers, if granted, could defray the cost of downloads, but would have prohibited the transfer of any documents downloaded, frustrating the shareability goal of the DOL grant.

B. Data Assembly Strategy 2

It soon became apparent that the above plan was insurmountably time- and resource-consuming. Because, as noted in Section 1.A above, Bloomberg Law prohibits any automation of its search processes, assembling a list of the estimated 30,000 target summary judgment decisions through manual means would occupy too much researcher time.

At the same time, Free Law Project, the nonprofit organization that runs the RECAP archive, began a project to bulk-download all free material on PACER and add it to RECAP. In theory, if all judges' reasoned opinions are designated as free on PACER, as the E-Government Act requires, RECAP would contain the entire summary judgment corpus of interest to this project, at no cost, searchable by court, date, and NOS code. We could replace the resource-intensive Bloomberg Law methodology described above, obtain the full set of summary judgment opinions in one fell swoop from RECAP, and then begin to analyze the text to identify the subset of interest – employee misclassification summary judgment opinions.

Embarking on this revised plan, the research team pulled 110,878 documents that were identified as free on PACER from Free Law Project's RECAP archive, with the relevant set of NOS codes, in the relevant time period, from all US district courts.[15] Notably, this total was almost four times the estimated target of 30,000 labor and employment law summary judgment opinions generated via the Bloomberg Law searches described in the previous section. This, in and of itself, was not troubling, as the free document set on PACER should include not only summary judgment opinions (our target), but also, inter alia, judges' decisions on motions to dismiss, class certification, protective orders, and a host of evidentiary issues. The team would next need to perform substantial filtering to identify the relevant, target subset.

Despite our initial hope, however, once the research team began to engage with the RECAP documents, this plan, too, proved unworkable. We quickly discovered that the 110,878 set was both over- and under-inclusive, in different ways. Some courts appeared to designate anything issuing from a judge as free, including purely ministerial orders that lacked any reasoning. Other courts' free document sets were under-inclusive, omitting reasoned opinions that were readily discoverable via commercial legal research services. The U.S. District Court for the District of

---

[15] Because this method relies on front-end filtering by NOS code, it is subject to the continuing caveat, explained above, about those codes' unreliability.

Wyoming, for example, designated zero documents as free on PACER in any labor or employment case, in the five years between 2008 and 2012, despite at least 50 known opinions issued by that court in those years, located via keyword searches in Westlaw.

Yet without a canonical list of the documents that *should* appear as free on PACER, it was difficult to assess courts' patterns of inclusion or exclusion. As a next-best approach, we created a roughly normalized measure of courts' decision designation practices, dividing each court's number of free documents on PACER each year by the number of lawsuits filed in that court in the previous year, obtained from Federal Judicial Center case-filing data (Federal Judicial Center, integrated data base, civil data, file: Civil cases filed, terminated, and pending from SY 1988 to present, webpage: because these data are recorded by federal fiscal year, we used data from 2009 through 2016 only for this analysis, eliminating any mismatch between fiscal and calendar years in the first and last years of the data set).

Overall, the denominator was designed to account for differences in the number of cases filed in different courts, and in the same courts in different years. The one-year lag assumed that it takes some time after a lawsuit is first filed for the case to generate reasoned judicial decisions, which judges or their staff would then designate as free on PACER.

Thus, though some courts and years might be busier than others as an absolute matter, one would expect the *ratio* of free decisions to cases filed to be roughly the same across courts and years, assuming equal compliance with the E-Government Act of 2002. It is possible that, even after case-filing normalization, some courts would produce fewer reasoned opinions than others, perhaps because of different local norms among litigants, filing more or fewer motions requiring resolution. Yet even if courts differed in this respect, one would at least expect consistent ratios *within* courts, across years.

The data confound both sets of expectations, revealing differences in ratios both *within* and *across* courts during the study period. Figures 5.1 and 5.2 illustrate both within- and across-court variation. Figure 5.1 includes all 94 US district courts, with ratios on the vertical axis and years on the horizontal axis. The lines, representing each district court, are not labeled in this figure due to space constraints; Figure 5.2 provides more per-court detail for a selected subgroup. In Figure 5.1, the key observation is the difference both within and across courts over time. While most lines cluster at the bottom of the graph, indicating a relatively low, consistent ratio of free PACER documents per lawsuit filed, some courts have much higher ratios, and have ratios that vary quite dramatically between years.

Figure 5.2, in turn, isolates the top ten courts by within-court standard

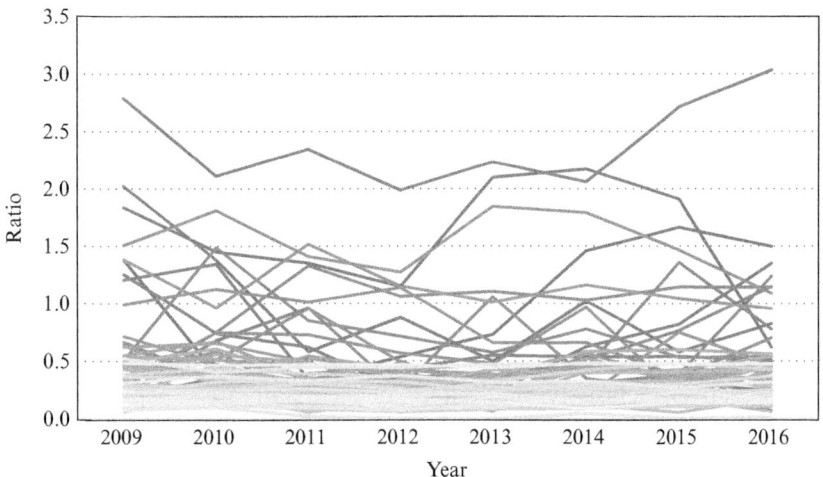

Figure 5.1   Ratio of free PACER documents per year to number of cases filed per year (lagged)

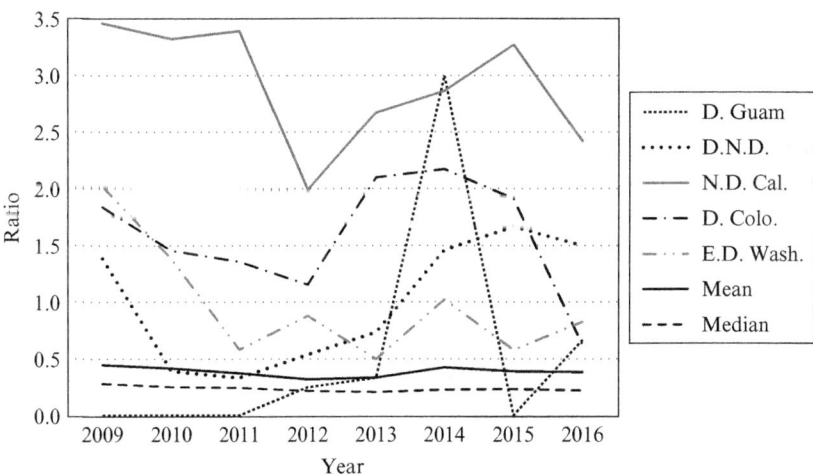

Figure 5.2   Ratio of free PACER documents per year to number of cases filed per year (lagged): top ten courts by standard deviation

deviation. In very rough terms, standard deviation measures the average distance from the mean of a set of data points, capturing the dispersion of the data across the set. Here, each district has eight data points: one ratio per year for eight years. The ratios for the ten courts shown in Figure 5.2

fluctuated the most, year to year, during that time. Figure 5.2 also includes the median and mean ratios for the entire data set for purposes of comparison, revealing that most of the courts that had highly *variable* ratios also had high *value* ratios, relative to other courts. In the Northern District of California, for example, shown as a gray line at the top of both graphs, the ratio of free PACER documents to lawsuits previously filed was substantially higher than in most other districts in all years except one. In addition, that district's ratio was among the most volatile, plunging from 3.39 free PACER documents per lawsuit previously filed in 2011 to 1.99 one year later.[16]

As suggested above, one plausible explanation for the dispersion in ratios both *across* courts and *within* the same courts over the years of the study period is over-inclusivity: that judges, or their staff, are sweeping in more documents than are required by the E-Government Act, and are doing so inconsistently across years. Another explanation is under-inclusivity: that judges are failing to include documents that should be free, again inconsistently. The remainder of this section discusses the research team's solution to over-inclusivity; the next section describes our attempts to identify and fill the gaps that we suspected were caused by under-inclusion.

With respect to over-inclusion, we identified two categories of document that were designated as free on PACER, but were not, in fact, reasoned opinions – the proper target of the E-Government Act. These were party-filed documents such as motions and briefs, and documents that described actions by judges, but contained no reasoning, such as those setting a hearing date or summarily allowing a party to file a brief with extra pages.

To remedy this over-inclusion problem, we constructed a series of filters, applied to the lawsuit-level metadata derived from PACER and to the docket sheet text. We first dropped all documents with two or fewer pages, reasoning that this would exclude purely ministerial judges' orders. We next dropped documents that appeared first, second, or third on the docket sheet. Here, we reasoned that the absolute earliest that a judge's reasoned summary judgment opinion might appear on a docket would be in position four, after the complaint, a motion for summary judgment (assuming no need for discovery), and an opposition. Therefore, items one through three were not likely to be judges' reasoned opinions.

Next, we ran a keyword search on the first three words of the docket entry description text to identify words associated with judges' summary

---

[16] The district of Guam demonstrated comparable volatility around 2014, but that phenomenon can likely be explained by the relatively small absolute number of lawsuits filed there.

judgment opinions, as opposed to party-filed motions or briefs. This produced a set of 49,560 possibly relevant judges' summary judgment decisions from the initial, much larger set of 110,878. Comparing this number to the initial, Bloomberg Law-derived estimate of 30,000 summary judgment opinions in labor and employment law cases over the ten-year period reveals a mismatch, perhaps because our filtering swept in extra documents, or because the initial Bloomberg Law search strategy produced an undercount.

Taking the 49,560 opinions we had identified, we next turned to the document text, to begin to isolate the decisions that engaged with the question of employee misclassification, the issue central to our research question. Here, we performed a very broad, very rough keyword search, identifying all documents in which the word "employee" appeared within the same paragraph (reading three sentences forward and backward) as "independent contractor." This filter produced a working set of 2,360 decisions.

We then shifted to yet another data assembly strategy, to fill the holes that we suspected were present in the data due to courts' failure to comply with the requirements of the E-Government Act of 2002.

C.   Data Assembly Strategy 3

We identified two possible gap-filling strategies by which to locate additional, potentially relevant summary judgment decisions that were not fee-exempt on PACER. First, we went back to the RECAP archive and pulled 38,627 additional court documents that had labor or employment law NOS codes from the target years, but were not tagged as free on PACER. If some judges had failed to designate their reasoned opinions as free, we thought, perhaps another PACER user had paid to download those opinions and then voluntarily contributed them to RECAP. Using the same set of filters employed above to identify likely summary judgment decisions, this strategy yielded an additional 5,394 judges' opinions. We further filtered based on the presence of "employee" and "independent contractor" in the document text, producing a set of 955 opinions.

Second, we returned to the commercial databases. Here, we searched the US district court judicial opinion databases of Westlaw, Lexis, and Bloomberg Law in the relevant time period for the same keywords used above: "employee" within the same paragraph as "independent contractor." Table 5.1 reports the results, and the overlap among the three, and with the RECAP results.[17]

---

[17]   Determining whether a decision was present in more than one set of search

Table 5.1   Search result comparisons

	Westlaw (WL)	Lexis (LX)	Bloomberg Law (BL)	RECAP
Totals	8,318	6,390	5,002	2,360
Also in WL	–	5,617 (88%)	4,461 (89%)	392 (17%)
Also in LX	5,617 (68%)	–	4,431 (89%)	340 (14%)
Also in BL	4,461 (54%)	4,431 (69%)	–	275 (12%)
Also in RECAP	392 (5%)	340 (5%)	275 (5%)	–
Also in any other set	5,864 (70%)	5,786 (91%)	4,638 (93%)	409 (17%)

Within the combined set of results returned from all searches, there were 11,417 unique opinions. Of those, 5,374 were present in only one set of results, whereas 6,043 opinions were present in at least two results sets. There were 4,104 opinions that were present in all three of the commercial legal research providers; only 253 were present in both RECAP and all three commercial providers.

Table 5.1 shows the extent of the overlap among the four sources. Bloomberg Law, as a whole, overlapped the most with other sources, as 93 percent of Bloomberg's results appeared in at least one other result set. Of Lexis' results, 88 percent also appeared in Westlaw's results set, but only 70 percent of Westlaw's own results, in total, appeared in any other results set.

Turning to the RECAP results, only 17 percent appeared in any other set. This could be explained by the vast under-inclusion of reasoned opinions in the set of documents that are free on PACER, as suggested by the analyses above, and the zero results for some districts. This could also be further evidence of the flawed system of NOS code assignment. The RECAP documents were initially filtered to include only the NOS codes for labor or employment law cases, whereas the Westlaw, Lexis, and Bloomberg Law results were keyword-based, across all cases, regardless of

---

results required substantial work. This is because case names are formatted differently across the result sets, and one system's citation does not necessarily apply to the others. RECAP documents, for example, appear with their court-provided civil action number; that number may or may not be listed on the version of the opinion that is retrieved from a commercial provider. Moreover, opinions that are published in the Federal Reporter carry a common citation format that is traceable across the commercial providers, but not RECAP. Unpublished decisions may carry a Westlaw, Lexis, or Bloomberg Law-specific citation, but that citation is not present in the search results of other commercial providers. Matching by case name can be accomplished by using various "fuzzy matching" toolkits, but the results inevitably contain some error.

the NOS code attached. We suspect that many of the results that appear in the commercial providers' result sets but are absent from RECAP carry a non-labor or employment NOS code, and are therefore erased from the lawsuit-level NOS classifications in PACER's metadata.

Thus, we return to the questions from Section 1.A: should a researcher rely on Westlaw, on Lexis, on some other provider, on the results that are common to all searches, on the unique set of results, or on some other set? Given the lack of overlap among the four results sets, there does not seem to be a clear answer to this question.

In the end, the research team adopted a conservative approach, to try to amass the most complete corpus possible of employee misclassification summary judgment decisions. The team assembled all unique documents that were not already included in the RECAP set, regardless of which commercial set contained them. However, the team was pursuing the DOL's grant's goal of generating a shareable dataset, and so could not merely download the opinions from their respective commercial sources. Instead, the team searched Google Scholar's free database of federal court opinions (which requires a case name or case number as a search term), and paid the PACER fees to download the set that remained. In the end, this strategy yielded an additional 7,031 unique opinions, for a total set of 10,923.[18]

The team performed one additional text-based filtering step before finally turning to the project's central research question of how judges differentiate between employees and independent contractors. In order to identify the opinions in which judges actually engaged in an employee misclassification analysis, rather than merely mentioning "employee" and "independent contractor" in passing, the team constructed an additional set of keyword filters based on case names, the names of legal tests, and other language that is particular to the employee misclassification analysis. Deploying these filters further reduced the working set of opinions to 4,326.

As in the hypothetical research project described in Section 1, it is impossible to determine how far short of the mark this 4,326 set of opinions falls, where the goal was originally a comprehensive set of all US district courts' summary judgment opinions that addressed employee misclassification disputes. There is no definitive list of misclassification disputes against which to measure our corpus; due to the flaws in the NOS

---

[18]   This figure cannot be compared directly to the initial 30,000 estimate derived from Bloomberg Law docket sheet searches, because 30,000 is the estimated number of summary judgment opinions in all labor and employment law cases, on all topics, during the ten-year period, whereas the 10,923 was the result of keyword-specific searches to identify probable employee misclassification decisions.

code system, there is not even a definitive list of labor and employment law cases from which a subset might be extracted. Thus, in this real-world computational law project, any insight or findings derived from the set of 4,326 are likely to be biased, but the research team lacks a baseline against which to estimate the size of the bias or theorize about its effects.

The twin problems of bulk access restrictions and limited usability thus severely hamper researchers' ability to achieve the kind of visibility into judicial behavior that Holmes might have imagined, and that today's computational and analytics tools might otherwise enable. The following section offers some solutions, though it is essential to note that Martin, LoPucki, and the other scholars cited throughout this chapter have proposed essentially the same set of fixes for years. Progress remains elusive, though perhaps the new availability of sophisticated legal analytics and computational law toolsets – in search of bulk, usable data on which to operate – will finally prompt change.

3.   PROPOSED SOLUTIONS

This section offers solutions to the bulk access and usability problems detailed above in both hypothetical and real computational law contexts.

As a first, most ambitious proposal, all court data, defined inclusively to include lawsuit-level metadata, docket sheets, and party-filed and judge-filed court documents, should be provided by the court systems in machine-readable electronic format, to the public, for free. As Kim and her co-authors (2009, p. 112) note, only by studying all aspects of civil litigation conducted on the trial court level, and gaining bulk access to the associated data, "can empirical research bring greater understanding of district judge decision-making." Of course, PACER is profitable for the federal courts, generating much more in revenue than is required to maintain the system, according to one of the lawsuits challenging the fee structure (Sullivan, 2016). State and local court analogs are likely also fee-generating for their respective jurisdictions. The elimination of fees for all court data would dry up these income streams, likely generating fierce opposition from the Administrative Office of the U.S. Courts and their state and local equivalents. Yet the fees seem particularly unjust – setting aside whether they are legal – in light of the sorry state of the PACER system, its searchability problems, and the unreliability of the metadata tags attached to the court data that is available.[19]

---

[19]   In September 2018, Rep. Doug Collins (R – Georgia) introduced a bill in the

More modestly, if all court data is not free, all actions by judges should be free, not just reasoned opinions, as is currently required. This change would remove any discretion that currently resides in the judges and/ or their clerks in determining which opinions count as "reasoned" for purposes of the E-Government Act of 2002, and would therefore lessen the administrative burden currently borne by those parties. This change would also bring all courts into compliance with existing government transparency mandates in one fell swoop, as all reasoned opinions would, by definition, be made freely accessible. The problem of "submerged precedent" that McCuskey (2016, pp. 530–31) identifies would be solved, as all judges' work would be transparent and available for study.[20]

These reforms would help remove "the nation's legal system," or at least the federal judiciary, from "behind a wall of cash" (Schwartz, 2009). To remove it from behind "a wall of . . . kludge" (Schwartz, 2009) requires addressing the related searchability and usability problems described in the foregoing sections. Here, the general push is in the direction of structuring court data, or requiring that the records of the lawsuits (e.g. PACER's metadata), court dockets, and court documents be tagged, classified, or labeled when they are made available to the public, such that researchers are not forced to extract basic descriptors of litigation and its outcomes from masses of messy text.[21] In the case of lawsuit-level metadata, one can imagine many better options than the current NOS code system. In their useful study of NOS codes, for example, Christina Boyd and David Hoffman (2017, pp. 1024–7) offer the modest suggestion that filing attorneys classify all causes of action alleged in a complaint, rather than being forced to choose a single NOS.

Even more granularity might be useful, however, as a plaintiff who asserts a claim under Title VII, for example, might also need to assign her case a "sex discrimination" cause of action, as opposed to race, religion, national origin, or color discrimination. Moreover, the underlying fact pattern contains substantial richness as well. Did the plaintiff experience

---

House of Representatives, the Electronic Court Records Reform Act of 2018, that would, among other actions, eliminate PACER fees.

[20] McCuskey notes that: "The widespread failure to tag opinions of the U.S. district courts thoroughly and consistently compromises empirical studies that focus on the work of these courts and emerging systems of data-informed prediction and planning . . . At minimum, empirical work on the federal district courts requires a careful look at the completeness of the data for the court and even the judge in question. As matters now stand, with the majority of districts that cannot be accomplished without a laborious review of docket information."

[21] The current lack of structure also requires researchers to duplicate time, resources, and effort in imposing their own structure(s) on court data.

an allegedly unlawful failure to hire? A termination? Discriminatory discipline, pay, or access to training? Sexual harassment? One can imagine a menu of options from which plaintiffs and their attorneys could choose, with an "other" choice as a fallback. Such a menu could be "smart" and dynamic, analyzing the underlying text of the filing in real time and suggesting the most relevant choices. Moreover, the menu would need to be revisited regularly by experts in the field, to ensure that the descriptors captured any newly available causes of action.

Beyond metadata, docket sheets, while already somewhat structured, would benefit from standardization across filings, actions, judges, and courts. This is an easy fix, as parties and judges (or their clerks) who place entries on the dockets are already required to choose from a drop-down menu. In the federal courts, the items on that menu need only be standardized across the appellate and district courts in order to achieve much greater structure in the data. Moreover, the drop-down menus need also to prompt parties and judges to link their entry to the particular cause of action, motion, and party to which it applies. In such a system, a judge's entry on a docket sheet that appears only as "Memorandum Opinion and Order," with no other identifying or linking information, would become extinct.

Finally, court documents should also be tagged, to provide a more granular picture of the nature of the judge's action, and on the particular claim or issue that he or she is addressing within a case. Here, and throughout, text analytics tools could be useful, to "read" the content of a party's filing or a judge's order, opinion, or decision, and to suggest an array of appropriate tags. The user would have the option to choose one or more, to reject them and supply his or her own tags, or to fill in an "other" blank. In this way, court data would become substantially more shaped, structured, and therefore more usable for researchers interested in studying the granular, pragmatic minutiae of courts' operations and judges' behavior.

One final note is important: while the move toward more structured court data is essential to opening up bulk access and increasing usability, pre-assigned tags, classifications, and labels should not take the place of access to the underlying text itself. This is because substantial insight lies in the specific words, phrases, sentences, topics, and larger structure of the text, insight that may be lost if the text is replaced by a collection of features-cum-data points.

Thus, in the words of Lynn LoPucki (2002, p. 2171), "By offering selective access to data, the courts have controlled legal scholars' research agendas, . . . discouraging research that focused on the actions of judges and the impacts of those actions on both litigants and the public." These reforms would help to open up that access, to grant a view into the actual, on-the-ground operation of our nation's legal system. And when advances in legal analytics and computational law techniques are combined with open access to court data, the dragon will be squarely out of the cave, in broad daylight, ready for the counting of teeth and claws, and a clear-eyed assessment of the ways that our courts succeed or fail at their central tasks of managing their caseloads, resolving disputes, and delivering justice.

REFERENCES

42 U.S.C. § 2000e(f).

Alexander, C.S. (2017). Misclassification and antidiscrimination: An empirical analysis. *Minnesota Law Review*, *101*(3), 907–62.

Alexander, C.S. (2019). Using text analytics to predict litigation outcomes: A preliminary assessment. In M. Livermore and D. Rockmore (eds), *Law as Data: Computation, Text, and the Future of Legal Analysis*, Santa Fe, NM: Santa Fe Institute Press, pp. 275–311.

American Association of Law Libraries (2006). Resolution on no-fee FDLP access to PACER (webpage). 28 June. Retrieved 9 May 2020 from https://www.aallnet. org/about-us/what-we-do/resolutions/resolution-fdlp-acess/.

Beair v. Summit Polymers, Civil Action 5:11-cv-420 (E.D. Ky.) (13 August 2013).

Bloomberg BNA (n.d.). About us: Terms of service – Subscription products, Sec. 2(b) (webpage). Retrieved 9 May 2020 from https://www.bna.com/terms-of-ser vice-subscription-products/.

Boyd, C.L., and Hoffman, D.A. (2017). The use and reliability of federal nature of suit codes. *Michigan State Law Review*, *2017*(5), 997–1032.

Caselaw Access Project (n.d.). Project: Caselaw Access Project (webpage). Retrieved 23 December 2018 from https://lil.law.harvard.edu/projects/caselaw-access-project/.

E.E.O.C. v. Remedy Intelligent Staffing, Inc., Civil Action 3:02-cv-10067 (S.D. Iowa) (22 December 2003).

Electronic Court Records Reform Act of 2018, 115th Congress (2017–18) – H.R.6714. Retrieved 9 May 2020 from https://www.congress.gov/bill/115th-con gress/house-bill/6714/text.

Federal Judicial Caseload Statistics (2015–17). Federal judicial caseload statistics (webpage). Retrieved 9 May 2020 from http://www.uscourts.gov/statistics-reports/analysis-reports/federal-judicial-caseload-statistics.

Federal Judicial Center (n.d.). Integrated database (webpage). Retrieved 9 May 2020 from https://www.fjc.gov/research/idb.

Fisher v. Duff, No. 15-5944 (W.D. Wash.) (2015).

Fisher v. United States, No. 15-1575C, (Ct. Fed. Cl.) (2015).

Free Law Project (n.d.). https://free.law (webpage).

Géron, A. (2017). *Hands-On Machine Learning with Scikit-Learn and TensorFlow: Concepts, Tools, and Techniques to Build Intelligent Systems*. Sebastopol, CA: O'Reilly.

Greenspan v. Administrative Office, No. 14-cv-2396 (N.D. Cal. 2014) (2014).

Herther, N.K. (2018). PACER faces continuing troubles. *Information Today*, 17

April. Retrieved 9 May 2020 from http://newsbreaks.infotoday.com/NewsBre aks/PACER-Faces-Continuing-Troubles-124301.asp.

Hoffman, D.A., Izenman, A.J., and Lidicker, J.R. (2007). Docketology, district courts, and doctrine. *Washington University Law Review*, *85*(4), 681–751.

Holmes, O.W. (1897). The path of the law. *Harvard Law Review*, *10*(8), 457–78.

Jacobson, W.A. (2012). Elizabeth Warren obtained federal fee waivers despite high 6-figure income and 8-figure net worth. *Legal Insurrection*, 14 October. Retrieved 9 May 2020 from https://legalinsurrection.com/2012/10/elizabeth-warren-obtained-federal-fee-waivers-despite-high-6-figure-income-and-8-figu re-net-worth/.

Kim, P.T., Schlanger, M., Boyd, C.L., and Martin, A.D. (2009). How should we study district judge decision-making? *Washington University Journal of Law & Policy*, *29*, 83–112.

Kourlis, R.L., and Gagel, P.A. (2008). Reinstalling the courthouse windows: Using statistical data to promote judicial transparency and accountability in federal and state courts. *Villanova Law Review*, *53*(5), 951–72.

LoPucki, L.M. (2002). The politics of research access to federal court data. *Texas Law Review*, *80*(7), 2161–71.

LoPucki, L.M. (2009). Court system transparency. *Iowa Law Review*, *94*(2), 481–538.

Malamud, C. (2013). On crime and access to knowledge (unpublished essay). 30 March. Retrieved 9 May 2020 from https://public.resource.org/crime/.

Martin, P.W. (2008). Online access to court records: From documents to data, particulars to patterns. *Villanova Law Review*, *53*(5), 855–88.

Martin, P.W. (2018). District court opinions that remain hidden despite a longstanding congressional mandate of transparency: The result of judicial autonomy and systemic indifference. *Law Library Journal*, *110*(3), 305–31. Retrieved 9 May 2020 from https://www.aallnet.org/wp-content/uploads/2018/10/LLJ_110n3_01_ martin.pdf.

McCuskey, E.Y. (2016). Submerged precedent. *Nevada Law Journal*, *16*(2), 515–84.

National Veterans Legal Services Program v. United States, No. 1:16-cv-00745 (D.D.C.) (2016).

PACER (n.d.). About (webpage). Retrieved 9 May 2020 from https://www.pacer. gov/about.html.

PACER Case Locator (n.d. a). Advanced case search (webpage). Retrieved 9 May 2020 from https://pcl.uscourts.gov/pcl/pages/search/findCaseAdvanced.jsf.

PACER Case Locator (n.d. b). Advanced party search (webpage). Retrieved 9 May 2020 from https://pcl.uscourts.gov/pcl/pages/search/findPartyAdvanced.jsf.

PACER Case Locator (n.d. c). Search field overview (pdf). Retrieved 9 May 2020 from https://free.law/pdf/PACER-API-Documentation.pdf.

PACER (2013). Electronic public access fee schedule (pdf). Retrieved 9 May 2020 from https://www.pacer.gov/documents/epa_feesched.pdf.

RECAP Project (n.d.). Turning PACER around since 2009 (webpage). Retrieved 9 May 2020 from https://free.law/recap/.

Schultze, S.J. (2018). The price of ignorance: The constitutional cost of fees for access to electronic public court records. *The Georgetown Law Journal*, *106*(4), 1197–227.

Schwartz, J. (2009). An effort to upgrade a court archive system to free and easy. *The New York Times*, 12 February. Retrieved 9 May 2020 from https://www. nytimes.com/2009/02/13/us/13records.html.

Schwartz, J. (2013). Internet activist, a creator of RSS, is dead at 26, apparently a suicide. *The New York Times*, 12 January. Retrieved 9 May 2020 from https://www.nytimes.com/2013/01/13/technology/aaron-swartz-internet-activist-dies-at-26.html.

Sullivan, C.C. (2016). PACER fees are too damn high, class action alleges (FindLaw's Strategist blogpost). 25 April. Retrieved 9 May 2020 from https://blogs.findlaw.com/strategist/2016/04/pacer-fees-are-too-damn-high-class-action-alleges.html.

Thomson Reuters (n.d.). Terms of use (webpage). Retrieved 9 May 2020 from https://legal.thomsonreuters.com/en/legal-notices/terms-of-use.

U.S. Courts (n.d.). Services and forms, civil cover sheet (pdf). Retrieved 9 May 2020 from http://www.uscourts.gov/sites/default/files/js_044.pdf.

Watts v. Creative Foundations, Inc., Civil Action 2:14-cv-0176 (S.D. Ohio) (27 March 2017).

6. Computational legal studies in China: progress, challenges, and future

Yingmao Tang and John Zhuang Liu

1. INTRODUCTION

Computational legal studies are gaining increasing attention in China. In the contemporary field of legal studies, scholarly discussions are beginning to include such unusual terms as big data, artificial intelligence, and machine learning, to an extent that these may even outstrip traditional legal terminology, like consideration, remedy, and liability. The prosperity of computational legal studies has never appeared so real and close for China. The Chinese government is enthusiastic about the use of big data and artificial intelligence in the administration of law. The Supreme People's Court (SPC) maintains a centralized database of all court decisions in the country, hosted on a publicly available website. In 2017, the SPC also established a so-called internet court in Hangzhou, where the e-commerce giant Alibaba is headquartered. Two more internet courts were established in Beijing and Guangzhou a year later. The SPC is currently in the process of exploring the idea of smart courts that would be able to utilize big data and artificial intelligence. Much research has been published that uses mass data on court decisions to analyze law and judicial behavior (Liebman et al., 2017). An increasing number of empirical research articles have been published by top legal journals over the last decade. These articles cover a wide range of legal topics from criminal law and the judiciary to constitutional law and eminent domain. The acceptance of these empirical articles by top legal journals and the wide assortment of topics that they cover indicate the potential for further expansion of empirical, and hence possibly of computational, legal studies in China.

For the purposes of this chapter, we divide legal studies that use data and statistical methods into four categories. The first includes studies that use descriptive statistics and simple statistical tests. The second encompasses studies that use linear models and conduct multivariate analysis. Then, in the third, we group studies that use various strategies of identification and make causal inferences—typical identification strategies include lab experiments, natural experiments, and field experiments. The last category is composed of studies that use mass amounts of data and employ non-linear models, including machine learning, network analysis, and natural-language analysis.

We admit that this categorization is crude, but we believe that it is sufficient for the purposes of our analysis here in this chapter. Outside China, only the fourth category is generally considered to be authentic computational legal studies. In China, however, legal scholars employ such terms as data legal studies, empirical studies, and computational legal studies quite loosely. Such scholars generally perceive most empirical legal studies, including those in our categories one and two to be computational. In this chapter, we occasionally use the term empirical legal studies to refer to studies in categories one, two, and three and the term computational legal studies to refer to the fourth category. However, we also use the term computational legal studies to loosely refer to studies in all four categories, to reflect the perceptions of the Chinese scholar. This suggests, however, despite the enthusiasm of both the government and legal academia, computational legal studies in China remains in its infancy. Nevertheless, empirical legal studies is certainly accepted in China, and there appears to be potential for a progressive development from studies of category one to those of category four.

The top three journals (三大刊) and the top three law journals (法学三大刊) have traditionally been dominated by articles expressing doctrinal or comparative legal research.[1] These three journals have, however, accepted and published quite a number of articles in recent years that use empirical research methods, including some presenting quantitative and statistical analyses (i.e., category one and two legal studies) (examples of empirical research articles published in the top three journals and the top three law journals over the last decade: Bai, 2010; Cheng, 2015a; Huang, 2012; Lin, 2016). Legal studies in China appear to be even more radical than those in the United States, where empirical legal studies originated, in their move

---

[1] The top three journals here refer to the accepted triad of *Social Sciences in China* (中国社会科学), sponsored by China Academy of Social Science, *China Legal Science* (中国法学), sponsored by China Law Society, and the *Chinese Journal of Law* (in Chinese 法学研究), sponsored by the Institute of Law at China Academy of Social Science. The top three law journals are generally understood to be *China Legal Science*, the *Chinese Journal of Law*, and *Peking University Law Journal* (中外法学), sponsored by Peking University Law School.

from doctrinal to empirical studies. In the United States, articles like these are generally published in specialized or peer-reviewed journals like *The Journal of Legal Studies* or *The Journal of Law & Economics*. However, empirical legal studies have found little resistance in the last decade as they enter top law journals in China.

Other law journals have followed suit and begun to accept and publish empirical research. For example, *Tsinghua University Law Journal* published a special issue in 2018 that contains a series of articles focusing on computational legal studies, including articles based on study of the SPC website (review of the articles in this special issue: He, 2018). Most of these articles nevertheless belong to category one or two computational legal studies, but some appear to have the potential to become category three or four research because of certain strategies of identification that they use, or the relatively large amount of data that their authors retrieved from the SPC website. In addition, the *Jurist*, a journal sponsored by Renmin University Law School, another leading law school, has also published empirical research reporting quantitative statistics (Cheng and Ke, 2018).

The comingling of old-style legal research articles and new-style computational legal studies in these leading law journals has raised concerns regarding the quality of computational legal studies; this question is taken up below. However, it is clear that the acceptance of computational legal studies by leading law journals as a body of methods and approaches has a signaling effect, which pushes other scholars to be more accepting and accommodating of such legal studies than their peers outside China. Furthermore, journals and books edited by legal scholars that focus on empirical legal studies have also emerged. For example, Sichuan University Law School has held an empirical legal studies conference on an annual basis, beginning in 2016. Selected papers submitted to this conference have been published together by Law Press as an annual book.[2]

The publication of empirical research articles in top law journals is only an indication that empirical and computational methodologies have begun to be accepted by mainstream legal scholars. More importantly, the subjects of these articles and their approaches are the key to understanding the breadth and the depth of the acceptance of this type of legal studies by

---

[2]   One volume, *Legal Empirical Studies*, edited by Professor Weiming Zuo of Sichuan University Law School, was published by Law Press in China in 2016. The other volumes that focus on empirical legal studies are *Peking University Law & Finance Review*, edited by Yingmao Tang of Peking University Law School and published by Law Press in China, in 2015. Certain articles published in the *Peking University Law & Finance Review* belong to category three computational legal studies.

the mainstream. The range of topics covered by articles using empirical methods is surprising. Some topics remain traditional and are often seen in similar studies outside China, while certain others are unique, indicating a real expansion of empirical or potentially computational legal studies in the country.

Traditionally, litigation, courts, and criminology are the focus of scholars using empirical research methods. Because of the relative ease of transplanting work on such topics to China, whether this is due to the familiarity of the topics, the availability of data, or the ease of application of the models, empirical legal research in these areas emerged relatively early in China, even before the concept of big data was introduced into the country, just a few years ago. For example, the well-known Priest and Klein litigation model has prompted numerous empirical studies since it was introduced in the 1980s (Priest and Klein, 1984). Scholars borrowed Priest and Klein's model to determine why the enforcement rates on judgments in China were so low (Tang and Sheng, 2006; Tang and Sheng, 2009). Another example relates to studies on crime control. The debates on gun control and crime rates that were happening in the United States in the 1990s stimulated a large number of empirical studies, including the well-known work by Donohue, Grogger, and Levitt (2009). In China, the sharp contrast between the significant increase in criminal penalties and the continuing increase in crime rates has also prompted scholars to study the effectiveness of the criminal law regime on crime control. For example, scholars in China examined these questions using the methods of descriptive statistics, publishing a number of articles in the top three journals (Bai, 2010; Bai, 2017).

In addition to the above topics, which are quite traditional, empirical legal studies in China cover other topics that are unique to China or otherwise largely ignored by scholars outside China. For example, the poor rates of enforcement of judgments is a phenomenon uniquely pertaining to China. About 15 percent of judges in China are responsible for executing all court decisions, and their workload accounts for over 20 percent of the entire caseload of the entire court system. By contrast, the marshals, sheriffs, or police enforcing court decisions in the United States are generally not considered to be part of that country's judiciary. Therefore, judgment enforcement is usually excluded from study of litigation or the courts in the United States.

Many other empirical studies focus on China-specific legal institutions. These studies cover such topics as the Chinese investment law that restricts foreign ownership (Han, 2015), the role of capital-markets lawyers (Cheng, 2015b), local regulation of labor contracts under the China-style federalism model (Cheng and Ke, 2018), and corporate charter amendments to reflect the role of the Communist Party in the corporate governance of Chinese companies (Zhang and Liu, unpublished). In recent years, empirical legal studies have begun to cover almost all areas of law, including contract (Zhao and Liang, 2018), tort (Man, 2018), administrative (Qiao and Mao, 2018), and constitutional law, largely because of the rapidly increasing number of court decisions on the SPC website and the easy access that scholars have to its information (Liang, 2017).

In summary, it is no illusion that empirical legal studies in China have grown. Articles presenting empirical research have been published by top law journals. They also cover a wide range of topics. All of these create potential for computational legal research, especially that falling within category four, to develop. Despite the common pursuit of empirical legal studies and the potential popularity of real computational legal studies in China, this chapter will cast doubt on the sustainability of this popularity.

Empirical legal studies are popular as a result of a leapfrogging movement in contemporary Chinese legal research: it is leaping from a copy and paste style that treats legal research as a means of articulating political propaganda or legal doctrines to a big data-style legal studies environment, with a focus on facts (numbers), trends (big data), and rationales (correlation and causation). The acceptance of empirical legal studies and the potential acceptance of real computational legal studies in China signal enormous opportunities for young scholars to enter into fresh areas of legal study and to shape how they will be understood. However, the nature of the leapfrogging tendency means that certain necessary steps will not be taken, including, for example, a lack of computational training for legal scholars (and journal editors) and the incompleteness of research data for the purposes of computational studies. More fundamentally, those missing steps also include a lack of consensus among scholars on how legal scholarship should be produced and evaluated. These missing steps will continue to pose challenges to how computational legal studies are to be conducted and to what extent they will truly be accepted in China.

2.   RATIONALES FOR THE INCREASE IN COMPUTATIONAL LEGAL STUDIES IN CHINA

Computational legal studies' growth in China is primarily driven by three factors. First, there is a demand for computational legal scholarship that is driven by China's leapfrogging in the internet and data sector. Second, conducting computational legal studies is possible, due to the online transparency initiatives of the Chinese government. The third factor is related to the view of Chinese legal scholars that computational legal studies can be used as an instrument to reshape and to some extent unite different schools of legal scholarship.

A.   China's Leapfrog in E-Commerce and its Implication on Computational Legal Scholarship

It only took China two decades to become a leading country in e-commerce and other internet-driven sectors. Twenty years ago, computers and access to the internet were still luxury commodities. In an interview by 60 Minutes in 2014, Jack Ma, the founder of Alibaba, admitted that he was afraid to type on a computer keyboard during his first visit to the United States in 1995 because computers were "so expensive" and he "did not want to destroy it" (J. Ma, personal communication, 2014). However, access to the internet using laptops and mobile devices is now a daily necessity for many Chinese. China has now become an e-commerce leader, as well as being strongly competitive in fintech and a number of other internet-related economic areas.

China had the largest online mobile population in the world in 2017, at 750 million. A successful e-commerce player in China can reach over 300 million active users, approximately the entire population of the United States. The online shopping platform of Alibaba had 617 million annual active shoppers on mobile as of 31 March 2018 (Alibaba Group Holding Limited, 2018, p. 6). Meituan Dianping, an online delivery company of food and services, had 340 million transacting users on 30 April 2018. Those users completed about 5.8 billion deliveries of food and other services in 2017, with about 20 transactions per each transacting user per year (Meituan Dianping, 2018, p. 5).

The popularity of platforms for e-commerce and other internet-enabled platforms in China has contributed to the rise of internet giants like Alibaba, Ant Financial, Tencent, and Baidu, who are able to compete with their counterparts in the United States such as Amazon, Google, and Facebook. The huge volume of transactions conducted through the online platforms operated by Alibaba and others have led to China becoming a more data-rich, data-driven country. In recent years, almost all China's leading e-commerce and internet companies have created big data analytic platforms, cloud operating systems, and artificial-intelligence technologies (Alibaba Group Holding Limited, 2018, p. 86).

The success of e-commerce and internet-enabled platforms in China has attracted the attention of law schools and legal scholars. For example, Tsinghua University Law School established a research center on big data in late 2017 (Tsinghua University Law School, 2017); around the same time, Peking University Law School established a research center on artificial intelligence (Peking University Law School, 2018). Jilin University Law School has also established a research center that focuses on the use of judicial data, primarily data available at the SPC website (Jilin University Law School, 2017). Jilin University Law School and Southeast University Law School even sponsor commercial organizations to explore the application of big data technology in the analysis of court decisions. Conferences and workshops sponsored by these research centers or by other companies have attracted a huge audience, including legal scholars, practitioners, judges, regulators, and senior officers of internet giants such as Alibaba, Baidu, and Tencent.

Legal scholars continue to interact in traditional ways with judges, regulators, and industry players, by participating in the legislative process of drafting laws such as the E-Commerce Law of 2018 or the Internet Security Law of 2017 or by supporting the judicial decision-making process through consultation on difficult cases. Legal scholars now also interact with industry players, and among themselves, through these new centers and channels and on new topics, such as big data and artificial intelligence. Because these topics are new to almost any legal scholar, they provide a good opportunity for everyone to participate in discussions of them. This has resulted in an interesting mixture: professors of jurisprudence are being invited to give talks on artificial intelligence, administrative law professors are chairing big data discussion panels, and editors-in-chief of journals with international law backgrounds are reviewing articles full of regression models. In a nutshell, legal research is leaping into the data era at the same time that the country is transforming itself into a leading country in the internet and data century.

B.   Open Government Initiative and its Implications for Computational Legal Scholarship

The Open Government Initiative (OGI) was adopted by the Chinese government in 2007 with assistance from international donors. The promulgation of the Regulation on Open Government Information (the OGI Regulation) by the State Council in April 2007 was a key milestone of the OGI. The OGI Regulation mandates that all levels of the Chinese government disclose information by their own initiative or upon citizen request. The effects of the OGI Regulation have not yet been assessed, but its promulgation has placed pressure on all government agencies to increase transparency. It has also created opportunities for computational studies, thanks to the significant amount of data that have now become available to legal scholars.

China's leapfrog into its position as a leading internet country has accelerated the process of implementation of various government transparency initiatives. In the judicial sector, China moved quickly from a traditional open-trial idea to a broad concept of judicial transparency, which contemplates massive publication of court decisions, online acceptance and trial of disputes through internet courts and other innovation-driven initiatives, such as smart courts that would use big data or artificial intelligence technologies. In 2013, the SPC issued a rule that would require every court in China to upload all court decisions, with certain exceptions, to the SPC website and make these court decisions available to the public for free, starting in 2014. Since then, the number of court decisions available on the SPC website is rapidly increasing, with the addition of tens of millions of court decisions each year. The SPC now claims that this website exhibits the largest collection of legal cases worldwide, with 12.5 billion visits from all over the world as of the end of 2017 (Shuzhen, 2018).

The massive online public access of court decisions has a significant impact on legal scholarship in China. There is a huge number of court decisions, and they cover a very broad range of subjects. Decisions of courts from 2008 onward are present at every level and in all geographic locations. Access to the SPC website is free. Free access to a huge number of court decisions now makes computational legal studies a real possibility. The availability of court decisions as text data also allows legal scholars to use more advanced statistical tools, such as topic models, to examine this data. For example, examining 25,921 decisions in administrative lawsuits from Henan province, Liebman and his co-authors (2017) find that litigants in China use administrative litigation to draw the state into private disputes, an underappreciated phenomenon they call the administratization of private disputes.

C.   Continuing Debate on Legal Methodology and its Implications for Computational Legal Scholarship

Legal scholarship in China is still young. Over the last four decades, the advancement of legal scholarship has generally been associated with continuing debates on legal methodology. Early in this century, Professor Zhu of Peking University Law School put forward his trichotomy of legal scholarship to describe the evolution of legal scholarship in China that has occurred since the 1980s. According to Professor Zhu, political legal scholarship was heavily influenced by soviet traditions. Under this influence, it was essentially an instrument for articulating political propaganda. Doctrinal law scholarship has its origin in traditions of German or civil law (Zhu, 2001). It has primarily been used to interpret legal rules or doctrines. On the other hand, scholarship of the social science of law approaches law from a social science or outsider's perspective, asking how the law is formed and what impact it might have on society. Zhu explicitly argues that political legal scholarship has been or will be replaced by the doctrinal law scholarship and the social science law scholarship. He did not say, but his supporters argue, that social science law scholarship is obviously superior to the doctrinal law scholarship. The debate over superiority between the two schools of methodology has continued over the last decade.

The rise of computational legal studies reflects the increasing influence of social science law scholarship in China. The journal *Social Sciences and Law*, edited by Zhu, has published a large number of empirical research papers since 2006. For example, the article on the difficulty of enforcing judgments in China that was noted above was published in the first issue of *Social Sciences and Law*, in 2006. Although empirical legal scholars in China do not share a common objective, they do occasionally challenge doctrinal law scholarship by investigating empirical truths that the latter usually take for granted or simply ignore.

For instance, the SPC rule regarding the cap on interest rates that may be agreed upon by private lenders and borrowers is generally viewed by doctrinal legal scholars as simply being a rule that must be followed. This SPC rule essentially says that the interest rate agreed upon by private parties cannot exceed four times the interest rate for loans extended by state-owned banks. Because of its simplicity, this rule has generated little interest from doctrinal legal scholars. In an article presented at a forum attended by young scholars of the doctrinal legal and social science of law persuasions in 2014, Cheng (2015a) reported that, in his study of 1,421 court decisions made in Zhejiang province, there was a significant deviation from this SPC rule by lower courts, in numerous forms. This finding clearly reveals a blind spot of doctrinal legal scholars, who view legal rules as static, without regarding the surrounding economic and social context contributing to the formation of legal rules, affecting how legal rules operate. Strong empirical support is also thereby provided for a motivation for the subsequent change to the SPC's position in 2015, which essentially removed the interest rate cap on private lending contracts.

As big data, artificial intelligence, and other technologies become increasingly commonly used in China, empirical legal scholars are experiencing reduced satisfaction with being identified as part of the movement of the social science of law scholarship. This discontent is due to the fact that social science of law scholarship in China is heavily influenced by one particular discipline of the social sciences, namely, sociology. Empirical legal scholars often find themselves engaging in dialog with scholars who have backgrounds in economics, political sciences, statistics, and psychology. The focus on case study, comparison, and small-number interviews and the rather narrow scope of topics in sociology of law are further reasons for empirical legal scholars to keep their distance from social science of law. As a result, some empirical legal scholars have begun to propose an agenda that contemplates the unification of the divided field of legal scholarship under the umbrella of empirical or computational legal studies (Zuo, 2017). This new agenda is ambitious, but it is not an impossible mission, for at least two reasons.

First, the wide range of topics that empirical or potentially computational legal studies is able to cover shows that this set of approaches has the potential to fill gaps existing among different schools of legal scholarship in China. For example, several empirical legal articles published by the special issue of *Tsinghua University Law Journal* in 2018 used the same database (the SPC website) and similar methodologies (quantitative statistical analyses), but they cover a number of different topics, ranging from criminal law to eminent domain (He, 2018). Empirical legal scholarship has achieved remarkable things by expanding its research area, as social science of law has not done, which typically focuses on subjects such as jurisprudence or judicial systems that doctrinal law scholars have almost no interest in touching.

Second, the analyses of numbers and the use of models pin empirical legal studies into a category of research that is generally viewed as scientific, objective, and superior. China is transforming itself into a number-managed country (数目字管理), as the well-known Chinese historian Ray Huang once put it. Management of society using numbers, not using instructions or connections, indicates improved governance. For the same reason, articles that examine numbers and trends are generally associated with the appearance of superior legal scholarship. After the Chinese government announced an action plan in 2015 to implement an internet-plus initiative, which included a plan to develop big data, cloud computing, and artificial intelligence, it has become much easier for legal scholars, traditional and new, to accept, and accommodate, number- and calculation-driven research papers generated by empirical or computational legal scholars.

3. CHALLENGES OF COMPUTATIONAL LEGAL STUDIES IN CHINA

Leapfrogging may not necessarily be negative. Every country has undertaken a leapfrogging approach in one area or the other. The move from the former soviet legal tradition to the practice of rule of law in China, as endorsed by the law and development movement and the Washington Consensus in the 20th century, is essentially a leapfrogging approach. Leapfrogging from political and legal scholarship to computational legal studies is certainly a welcome movement. The key is not the leapfrogging approach itself. Rather, the key is that any success story brought about by leapfrogging must be accompanied by limitations, frustrations, or even contradictions, which may be caused by steps that are missed as the result of the leapfrogging. These limits include some that can easily be identified, such as the incompleteness of data or a lack of computational skills, but there are also those that are associated with institutional limits that cannot be bypassed or cured simply by the advancement of technology.

A.   Incompleteness of Data for Computational Legal Studies

Legal scholars have strongly criticized the incompleteness of the court decisions made available at the SPC website, despite the huge number of such decisions that are available (Ma et al., 2016). Our own research reveals that the average disclosure rate—measured by the number of court decisions published on the website, divided by the number of court decisions actually made by the relevant courts—is about only 47 percent at the national level, as of the end of 2016 (Tang and Liu, 2019). The disclosure rates for wealthy cities like Beijing and Shanghai can be as low as 30 percent. Accordingly, many empirical articles that report statistical results derived from the data available on the SPC website and draw conclusions from them could be entirely wrong.

To put it simply, 100 percent of a 50 percent sample or 100 percent of a 30 percent sample may only account for 50 percent or 30 percent of the entire sample when the missing data are provided. Claiming that a certain finding is significant based on a 50 percent or even a 30 percent sample is unfounded because the missing data may support the opposite claim. This is because the decisions available on the SPC website may not be a random sample of all decisions made by the relevant courts. In other words, the SPC website is a black box. Without knowing the process by which the decisions are uploaded and published on the SPC website, it would be very dangerous to draw any conclusions based on statistical results computed from data on the website (Liebman et al., 2017).

The lack of appreciation of the selection bias present on the SPC website by Chinese legal scholars reflects a deeper methodology problem inherent in any research focusing on litigation. As the Priest and Klein litigation model suggests, cases decided by courts are subject to selection problems, meaning that court decisions are not a random sample of all societal disputes. Any effort to generate rules based on litigation research that apply to society at large is doomed to fail. The debate between doctrinal law and social science of law scholarship discussed above largely reflects a lack of appreciation by doctrinal law scholarship of the selection bias inherent in studies of litigation and doctrinal interpretation. The commonality of the use of statistical results computed from the data on the SPC website to support research claims is simply another form of such lack of appreciation in the internet and data era.

On the other hand, the incompleteness of data reflects another fundamental problem with government transparency initiatives associated with leapfrogging that cannot be easily resolved. It would be easy to assume that missing data would be found as time goes by, but it would be naïve, just as naïve as predicting that the 47 percent average-disclosure rates will gradually increase and selection bias will be eliminated as the SPC continues to enforce its mandatory public-access rule. The SPC is not invulnerable. Even under an authoritarian regime, the SPC or any other higher authority may not be able to achieve its goals precisely as it wishes. Our own research suggests that increases in disclosure rates are subject to a number of factors, such as the marketization level of different provinces and the incentive of provincial and lower courts to publish their decisions online. In other words, the mandated goal of massive online public access may not be fully achieved through leapfrogging.

The Public Access to Court Electronic Records (PACER) system that allows access to all decisions of federal courts in the United States from the 1990s onward is a relevant comparison. Its success is qualified by two factors. First, even before PACER was launched, almost all federal courts had their own electronic databases of court decisions, and the launch of PACER was simply a way to connect different databases that already contained all the decisions. Second, the success of PACER cannot simply be transplanted to state courts in the United States because of the funding, institutional, and other challenges that may rise in connection with the massive expansion of the online public-access model (Martin, 2008). The experience of the United States in the online public access of court decisions tells us that the missing steps (i.e., the existence of electronic databases of court decisions in state courts) cannot be simply bypassed, and nor can transparency be achieved without investing money or other resources. China is different from the United States in many ways. It may establish an online transparency model for court decisions, one that the United States may not be able to build. However, the experience of the United States warns us to be cautious of the idea of resolving the incompleteness problem any time soon.

B.   Inadequate Appreciation of Computational Methodology

For computational legal studies to be scientific, objective, and adequate to its subject, general protocols should be followed. This chapter will not be able to discuss such general protocols in detail, but it is sufficient to point out the following three problems that are frequently encountered in empirical or computational legal studies in China.

First, many such articles report numbers, findings, and explanations but are unable to place their findings and arguments within a theoretical framework.

Some scholars may argue that just "reporting facts" is itself enough. Fact-finding certainly makes an important contribution to legal research, especially to legal research in China that is still dominated by doctrinal legal scholarship. However, we believe that valuable legal scholarship should go beyond simply "reporting facts". In our view, numbers and findings are used to support a theoretic claim; computation is a means to achieve an end; hypotheses are made on the basis of existing theories; findings are gathered to support or rebut a theory. Thus, numbers and findings without theoretical claims are facts only. Legal scholarship is ultimately about establishing or rebutting a theory of general applicability. Even technical questions on what variables should be controlled will largely depend on what theories the particular study is testing. The above general protocol for computational legal studies, however, is not appreciated by many legal scholars in China.

For example, a significant amount of empirical studies on civil and criminal procedures have been published in legal journals, including top legal journals, that report interesting findings on matters such as witness testimony rates (Zuo and Ma, 2005), bail decisions (Zuo, 2007), attorney representation (Zuo and Ma, 2012), and other topics. The authors of those articles also provided quite insightful explanations of their findings, together with potential policy considerations. However, these articles do not attempt to link their findings with any theoretical framework, either in criminal or civil procedures, or more generally in judicial or legal processes. The lack of dialog between factual findings and existing theories in these studies has significantly reduced their strength. In other words, simple descriptive work only tells us what the fact is in a specific context. Its strength can be easily challenged by a new finding in another context. However, theoretically informed scholarship that connects factual findings and theories not only reports interesting facts within a specific context, but also place the fact-finding in a more general context with an aim to explore what law is or how law operates in general.

Second, many empirical legal articles fail to describe their methodologies clearly, meaning that their replicability, reliability, and general applicability remain in doubt.

Empirical or computational legal studies require a significant amount of effort to be expended on data collection, coding, testing, and retesting. We believe that good computational legal scholars should always be conscious of the scope of their samples, the way data is collected, and the methods used to test their variables. To the extent that any of the foregoing steps affect the accuracy of any finding or the applicability of the proposed theory, good computational legal scholars endeavor to clearly describe how their studies are conducted. Such articles are generally accompanied by numerous tables, diagrams, appendices, and so on which are intended to describe samples, findings, and methodology clearly.

However, many empirical legal articles in China do not seem to take this seriously. For example, in one empirical article on constitutional law, the author indicated that "taking the 69 court decisions where courts cited the Constitution in 2017 from the SPC website as an example, 42 are meaningful". The author did not explain how something was cited, how the set of 69 decisions were obtained, or why 42 decisions were meaningful (Liang, 2017). Another example is a very brief reference to the "1155 court decisions that are obtained from the SPC website, have research value, and reflect actual adjudication practices" in an article published in the journal *China Legal Science* regarding environmental torts liabilities (Dou, 2017). This chapter was not an empirical study, so it may not be fair to criticize it using a protocol for empirical legal studies. However, as an article published in one of the top three legal journals in China, any claim or theory based on empirical findings demands a higher level of scrutiny.

Third, many empirical legal articles fail to apply statistical tools or interpret empirical results correctly. The most common problem is to conflate correlation with causation. Some empirical legal studies apply multivariate regression analysis and test the correlation between dependent and independent variables. Many authors claim causation too carelessly after observing correlation (usually from a significant coefficient), neglecting possible identification problems (e.g., omitted variable, endogeneity, or reverse causation). This reflects the fact that Chinese legal scholars are generally unfamiliar with the identification strategies brought by the causal inference revolution and that they are less well-trained in empirical research methods than their counterparts in economics, sociology, political science, and other social science disciplines.

The above problems in computational methodology represent a rather disappointing fact about the quality of empirical or potentially computational legal studies in China. This is primarily due to the lack of training in computational methodology among legal scholars and journal editors.

This also reflects the underdevelopment of computational expertise in China. Legal articles that contain complicated formulas and models are typically submitted to professional or peer-reviewed journals for publication, not to law reviews edited by law students in the United States. Law journals are generally edited by law professors in China, but specialized law journals focusing on computational legal studies remain limited. The lack of scrutiny by experts before publication casts doubt on the scientific nature, objectivity, and quality of empirical or computational legal studies in China.

C.   Research Environments Discouraging Computational Legal Studies

Despite the remarkable progress that empirical and potentially computational legal studies have undergone in recent years, the research environment in China is generally not in favor of such studies. The challenges come from two fronts, both of which touch upon fundamental issues within legal scholarship in the country.

The first challenge is posed by the prevailing academic evaluation system in China, which focuses on efficiently evaluating legal scholars by simply counting the number of articles published in legal journals, without regard for their substance. Different law schools have different requirements for evaluating an employee for professorship. In general, the quantity of publications rather than their quality receives disproportional attention when evaluating legal scholarship. Scholars compete for the number of articles published in legal journals. Law schools promote professors in proportion to the number of articles they publish in legal journals. Computational legal studies generally require months or years of effort. More importantly, time spent is not a guarantee of reliable and publishable results. The habit of overlooking the substance of a publication places computational legal research at a disadvantage during evaluation. As a result, serious scholars in China who have better access to data and other resources may not wish to engage in computational legal studies. Quality articles in this vein will likely continue to be generated by scholars outside China who are not subject to the prevailing academic evaluation system. This will continue to cause the problems discussed above to persist even in dominant legal journals in China.

The second challenge comes from institutional arrangements that are intended to protect academic freedom, that may have the unintended consequence of discouraging inter-disciplinary cooperation. One controversial arrangement relates to the explicit or implicit requirements for the authorship of journal articles. Although not every journal or every law school adopts the same requirement, several journals or law schools, including top ones indeed disallow co-authorship of articles published in legal journals. Alternatively, if two or more individuals co-author an article, it will either be rejected, or the order of names of the co-authors will feature in the decision. In other words, the first author will receive more value than a second or third author in a co-authored article. Requirements like this were originally intended to protect young scholars who may have been required to add a senior professor's name for his or her article to be published. Such requirements were also intended to encourage academic and individual freedom and prevent the formation of any interest groups that could monopolize the academic market.

However, such requirements have unintended consequences on the production of computational legal studies in China, which often require close collaboration among scholars in different disciplines or with different skillsets. It is common for legal scholars to collaborate with economists, political scientists, or psychiatrists. Co-authored articles are commonly seen in specialized legal journals. It is difficult nowadays to imagine how any single scholar would be able to complete a meaningful computational study within a reasonable period of time, as such studies must involve a large quantity of data. The rigid and somewhat strange restriction on co-authorship in China makes it difficult for the production and publication of serious computational research that requires multi-disciplinary cooperation. The rationales behind this restriction have brought legal scholars in China to a dilemma between two ambiguous goods. It is not always easy to choose between academic freedom that may discourage collaboration and quality study that may require cooperation. The fact that legal scholars are forced to make such a choice reflects the deeper problem that they are facing in a new and fast-changing academic environment.

4.   FUTURE OF COMPUTATIONAL LEGAL STUDIES IN CHINA

It is the best of times, and it is the worst of times, in computational legal studies in China. Scholars in this field are extremely fortunate because China's leapfrog into an internet leading country makes it much more likely that mainstream legal scholars will be receptive to articles full of numbers, charts, and equations. The evolution of legal scholarship can be very difficult, as seen in China's history. It took a tremendous amount of time and effort for doctrinal law scholarship, which focuses on laws and rules, to triumph over political and law scholarship, which reiterated political propaganda. Empirical legal studies did not encounter any serious opposition before it appeared in top legal journals. However, computational legal scholars may have to double or triple their efforts to win final mainstream acceptance.

The future of computational legal studies in China will largely depend on two factors: whether China's leapfrogging of data use and technology will enable the generation of high-quality research that uses computational methods and how the missing steps that appear as the result of leapfrogging can be addressed so that computational legal studies will be accepted both within and outside China.

A.   Production of Computational Legal Articles to Address the Missing-Data Problems

The incompleteness of data is not merely an issue of data or methodology. It reflects a more fundamental problem, relating to how information is generated in China's rapidly changing society. Unlike the United States and other developed countries, where the evolution of almost everything is gradual and relatively slow, China has essentially undertaken a leapfrogging approach in almost every aspect of its social and economic life. To what extent a new and centralized model of online transparency can be developed and successful under an authoritarian regime in light of the steps that China missed during the pre-internet era is a question that is worth study by itself. It would be even more interesting if China was able to build a transparency model within a short period of time that would offer free access to the public while the United States and its peer countries who are proud of their transparency and democratic traditions would be unable to do so. One piece of supporting evidence for this picture is that the SPC website allows, in principle, free access to all court decisions in China to the entire world, while the PACER system of the United States still charges fees to users and only allows access to federal decisions, not to the larger number of state courts.

The key issue here is not whether China can do better than the United States. That would be a question for further research. Rather, it is how data is generated in different countries, what factors contribute to the generation of data, and what factors impose restrictions on the use of data and by whom. Our research suggests that this is a complex issue. Political authority has been critical for achieving online massive public access to court decisions in China over the last decade, but the resulting transparency is subject to a number of factors, including economic and incentive factors, neither of which is entirely determined by authority. Our research adds to the existing research on the authoritarian transparency done by political scientists. However, during the pre-internet era, authoritarian-transparency literature has been traditionally focused on political institutions like elections (Malesky and Schuler, 2010). The rise of e-government and online court transparency on a worldwide basis demands new theories. Research on the problem of missing data on the SPC website or any other centralized database in China may not only advance our understanding of authoritarian transparency but also help us build new models on data generation and utilization in the era of internet and big data.

B. Production of Good Computational Legal Studies, Acceptable to the International Community

The acceptance of computational legal studies in China will eventually depend on the quality of such studies. The lack of expertise in computational methods among scholars and editors in China implies that quality control will most likely come from scholars and editors outside China. This is unfortunate, but it seems inevitable. It is also largely consistent with China's development experience over the last four decades. For example, leading internet companies, including Alibaba, Tencent, and Baidu all raise funds abroad and list their securities on stock exchanges outside China. This is because foreign investors are able to value these high-tech companies better than Chinese investors can, and foreign markets are deep enough to allow fund raising of billions of US dollars. The domestic Chinese stock market remains closed to these companies, and until the Chinese market is ready, they will remain listed abroad.

If the production of good computational articles largely relies on expertise from outside China, the continuing opening of the academic market in China to the outside world is critical. The continuing opening of overseas academic markets to China is equally important. The two-way opening of academic markets means that young Chinese scholars will be able to study computational methods abroad and, when they return to China, they will receive continuing support from scholars based in the United States and other countries. Academic conferences, workshops, and roundtables that bring computational legal scholarship into China should be encouraged. Collaboration between Chinese scholars and scholars from abroad should be supported.

Academic sympathy for Chinese scholars who collaborate with scholars abroad should also be encouraged because of how difficult it is to produce quality computational works using data from China and other challenges associated with the changing academic environment in general. This is not an excuse to lower standards for computational legal studies. Rather, it is to place the evaluation of computational legal studies within a context where the data are generated and the studies are completed. This is similar to the rationale behind affirmative action, which is intended to afford minorities protection for the time being that may even be disproportionate. The priority or preference placed on China studies may eventually be beneficial to the states of computational legal studies outside China. Above all, computational legal studies lacking an account of China as one of the leading internet and data countries would certainly be incomplete.

C. Production of Good Computational Legal Studies that Would Be Acceptable to Chinese Scholars

The advancement of computational legal studies also depends on the production of good computational works that can be accepted by Chinese scholars. In light of the challenges discussed above, such studies will most likely involve a simplification of the computational element, to the extent that such studies would maintain a certain quality while continuing to be easily understood by Chinese audiences. No clear standard exists for how simple is simple enough to achieve both standards, namely, quality and comprehensibility. This will essentially be assessed by the market. The key, however, is to produce computational legal works that will meet the demands of Chinese readers.

To put it more concretely, simplicity would likely mean greater amounts of descriptive statistics results and fewer regression models, more discussions and fewer equations, more explanations, and fewer numbers. Quantitative studies based on big data will likely be handled by the very few scholars with experience and resources, and they will be targeted to a small audience. Regression models and statistics tables will likely not be found at top legal journals, while a small number of professional or peer-reviewed journals will provide the required platforms for advanced works involving models and tables. A division of labor or expertise will develop to resolve the comingling problem. Traditional top legal journals will publish computational legal articles that are simplified for ordinary audiences.

The simplicity of computational legal studies is necessary for it to gain support. This is consistent with China's development experience in foreign investment and foreign trade. For example, foreign investors were encouraged to establish joint ventures or wholly owned subsidiaries in China in the 1980s that manufacture commodities for export to the United States or other countries. This foreign-oriented investment and trade policy has begun to change in the last two decades. Foreign-invested enterprises and growing Chinese private enterprises manufacture commodities for sale to the growing middle class in China as the Chinese domestic market develops. Although Chinese domestic consumption power has been growing at a gradual and slow rate, ignoring domestic markets would be a poor strategy for private enterprises both abroad and in China. For the same reason, the purpose of pursuing simplicity in computational legal studies now is to train more scholars who would be able to support and use computational methods in the future.

REFERENCES

Alibaba Group Holding Limited. (2018). *The Annual Report on Form 20-F of Alibaba.* Retrieved 30 September 2018 from https://www.sec.gov/Archives/edgar/data/1577552/000104746918005257/a2235254z20-f.htm.

Bai, J. (2010). Researching the relationship among crime causes, crimes and criminal punishments from the perspective of crime rates in China. *Social Sciences in China*, 2010(2), 144–59. (白建军：《从中国犯罪率数据看罪因、罪行与刑罚的关系》，《中国社会科学》2010年第2期).

Bai, J. (2017). A research on criminal law preferences of the Chinese public. *Social Sciences in China*, 2017(1), 143–63. (（白建军：《中国民众刑法偏好研究》，《中国社会科学》2017年第1期).

Cheng, J. (2015a). Adjudication practices of the rules on "four-time interest rates" and an academic attempt to resolve doctrinal questions by using empirical studies. *Peking University Law Journal*, 27(3), 684–716. (程金华：《四倍利率规则的司法实践与重构利用实证研究解决规范问题的学术尝试》，《中外法学》2015年第3期).

Cheng, J. (2015b). Chinese bond issuer and its counsel. *Peking University Law and Finance Review*, 2015(1), 3–28. (程金华：《中国证券发行人及其律师》，《北大法律和金融评论》2015年第1期).

Cheng, J., and Ke, Z. (2018). Federalism practices of legal power in China: A study of labor contract law. *Jurist*, 2018(1), 1–17. (程金华、柯振兴：《中国法律权力的联邦制实践 以劳动合同法领域为例》，《法学家》2018年第1期).

Donohue, J.J., Grogger, J., and Levitt, S.D. (2009). The impact of legalized abortion on teen childbearing. *American Law & Economics Review*, 11(1), 24–46.

Dou, H. (2017). Reconstruction of the types of environmental torts. *China Legal Science*, 2017(4), 264–84. (窦海阳：《环境侵权类型的重构》，《中国法学》2017年第4期).

Han, Y. (2015). A quantitative analysis of the foreign investment law and policy of China between 2007 and 2011. *Peking University Law and Finance Review*, 2015(1), 83–123. (韩一淳：《2007年至2011年中国外商投资法律和政策的定量分析》，《北大法律和金融评论》2015年第1期).

He, H. (2018). Marching to data legal studies. *Tsinghua University Law Journal*, 2018(4), 5–6. (何海波：《迈向数据法学》，《清华法学》2018年第4期).

Huang, H. (2012). Empirical studies on piercing corporate veil theory in China. *China Journal of Law*, 2012(1), 3–16. (黄辉：《中国公司法人格否认制度实证研究》，《法学研究》2012年第1期).

Jilin University Law School. (2017). *Introduction to the Research Center of Judicial Data Application (About Us).* Retrieved 30 September 2018 from http://www.jlulbd.com/2017/07/10/1359.html.＿(吉林大学法学院：《司法数据应用研究中心简介》，2017年).

Liang, H. (2017). Research on implementation issues relating to citation of constitutional law by courts in China. *Politics and Law*, *2017*(7), 60–71. (梁洪霞:《我国法院援引宪法说理的实施问题研究》,《政治与法律》2017年第7期).

Liebman, B.L., Roberts, M.E., Stern, R.E., and Wang, A.Z. (2017). Mass digitization of Chinese court decisions: How to use text as data in the field of Chinese law. 21st Century China Center Research Paper Series, No. 2017-01. 15 June. Retrieved 30 September 2018 from https://ssrn.com/abstract=2985861.

Lin, X. (2016). Empirical studies on the fairness of procedures for penalty reduction in China. *China Legal Science*, *4*(6), 133–52. (林喜芬:《中国减刑程序公平性的实证研究》,《中国法学》2016年第6期).

Ma, C., Yu, X., and He, H. (2016). Big data analysis: A report of online publicity of judicial documents in China. *China Law Review*, *12*(4), 195–246. (马超、于晓红、何海波:《大数据分析:中国司法裁判文书上网公开报告》,《中国法律评论》2016年第4期).

Ma, J. (2014). Personal interview with CBS "60 Minutes". Retrieved 30 September 2018 from https://tv.sohu.com/v/dXMvMTc3MDg2MTAyLzc1ODUzODIwLnNodG1s.html.

Malesky, E., and Schuler, P. (2010). Nodding or needling: Analyzing delegate responsiveness in an authoritarian parliament. *American Political Science Review*, *104*(3), 482–502.

Man, H. (2018). The emptiness trap and the resolution of causality in medical tort liabilities: Comment on article 12 of Supreme People's Court judicial interpretation No. 20 [2017]. *Law Science*, *2018*(7), 83–100. (满红杰:《医疗损害责任因果关系虚无陷阱及其化解-兼评法释【2017】20号第12条》,《法学》2018年第7期).

Martin, P.W. (2008). Online access to court records: From documents to data, particulars to patterns. *Villanova Law Review*, *53*(5), 855–88.

Meituan Dianping. (2018). *The Prospectus of Meituan Dianping for its Initial Public Offering and Listing on the Hong Kong Stock Exchange*. Retrieved 30 September 2018 from http://www.hkexnews.hk/listedco/listconews/SEHK/2018/0907/LTN20180907011.pdf.

Peking University Law School. (2018). *Leading the Production of Jurisprudence, Promoting the Cultivation of Legal Talents, and Powering the Development of the Rule of Law*. Retrieved 30 September 2018 from http://www.law.pku.edu.cn/xwzx/xwdt/58007.htm. (北京大学法学院:《引领法学知识生产、推动法治人才培养、助力法治发展进步》, 2018年).

Priest, G.L., and Klein, B. (1984). The selection of disputes for litigation. *Journal of Legal Studies*, *13*(1), 1–55.

Qiao, S., and Mao, W. (2018). Judicial control of eminent domains: An analysis based on court decisions of provincial high courts. *Tsinghua University Law Journal*, *2018*(4), 68–90. (乔世彤、毛文峥:《行政征收的司法控制之道:基于各高级法院裁判文书的分析》,《清华法学》2018年第4期).

Shuzhen, L. (2018). The visits to the website China Judgment Online amount to 12.5 Billion. *People's Court Daily*, January 3. (罗书臻:《中国裁判文书网访问总量近 125 亿次》,《人民法院报》2018年1月3日).

Tang, Y., and Liu, Z. (2019). Mass publicity of Chinese court decisions: Market-driven or authoritarian transparency? *The China Review*, *19*(2), 15–40.

Tang, Y., and Sheng, L. (2006). Double high rates in enforcement of civil and commercial judgments. *Law and Social Sciences*, *2006*(1), 1–29. (唐应茂、盛柳刚:《民商事执行程序中的"双高现象"》,《法律和社会科学》2006年第1期).

Tang, Y., and Sheng, L. (2009). A quantitative analysis of judicial enforcement difficulties in China. *Law and Social Sciences, 2009*(1), 197–238. (唐应茂、盛柳刚：《中国司法执行难的计量分析》，《法律和社会科学》2009年第1期).

Tsinghua University Law School. (2017). *Tsinghua University Law School Law and Big Data Research Center was Unveiled and the Seminar of "Marching to Data Legal Studies" was Held*. Retrieved 30 September 2018 from http://www.law.tsinghua.edu.cn/publish/law/3567/2017/20171227145350201753074/2017122714 5350201753074_.html. (清华大学法学院：《清华大学法学院法律与大数据研究中心揭牌暨"迈向数据法学"研讨会召开》，2017年).

Zhang, A.H., and Liu, Z. The determinants of political control in state-owned enterprises: Evidence from charter amendments. Unpublished transcript on file with the authors.

Zhao, Y., and Liang, Q. (2018). Prospect of categorical application of "obvious unfairness" clauses under the general principles of civil law: An analysis of "obvious unfairness" cases at the China judgments online. *Law Application, 2018*(1), 70–75. (赵永巍、梁茜：《<民法总则>显失公平条款的类型化适用前瞻——从中国裁判文书网显失公平案例大数据分析出发》，《法律适用》2018年第1期).

Zhu, S. (2001). Maybe it's happening: An overview of the development of legal studies in contemporary China. *Comparative Law Research, 2001*(3), 1–9. (苏力：《也许正在发生——中国当代法学发展的一个概览》，《比较法研究》2001年第3期).

Zuo, W. (2007). Bail and awaiting trial in criminal investigation: A functional analysis based on empirical studies. *Peking University Law Journal, 19*(3), 339–52. (左卫民：《侦察中的取保候审：基于实证的功能分析》，《中外法学》2007年第3期).

Zuo, W. (2017). A new methodology revolution: Uncovering empirical legal studies in China. *Tsinghua University Law Journal, 2017*(3), 45–61. (左卫民：《一场新的范式革命？一解读中国法律实证研究》，《清华法学》2017年第3期).

Zuo, W., and Ma, J. (2005). Testimony rates of criminal witnesses: A theory based on empirical studies. *China Legal Science, 2005*(6), 164–76. (左卫民、马静华:《刑事证人出庭率:一种基于实证研究的理论阐述》，《中国法学》2005年第6期).

Zuo, W., and Ma, J. (2012). Effects and paradox: An empirical studies of attorney representation in criminal defenses. *Tribune of Political Science and Law, 2012*(2), 60–73. (左卫民、马静华：《效果与悖论:中国刑事辩护作用机制实证研究——以S 省D 县为例》，《政法论坛》2012年第2期).

7. Measuring surveillance chill and other regulatory impacts at scale*

Jonathon W. Penney

1. INTRODUCTION

With digital surveillance and censorship on the rise (Fiscutean, 2017; Penney, 2015, pp. 693–4; Volz, 2015), the unprecedented amount of data available online (Boehme-Neßler, 2016, p. 222; Kuner, 2013, p. 4ff), and governments and businesses increasingly employing emerging technologies like artificial intelligence (AI), machine learning, and facial recognition technology (FRT) to automate surveillance, legal enforcement (Hartzog et al., 2015, p. 1763; Pasquale and Cashwell, 2015, pp. 36, 39), and to protect and promote private and corporate legal interests (Carpou, 2016, p. 585; Elkin-Koren, 2017, p. 1084), concerns about the large-scale impact of these state and corporate regulatory activities—particularly their "chilling effects", that is, capacity to "chill" or deter people from speaking freely or exercising other fundamental rights and freedoms (Citron and Penney, 2018–19, pp. 2319–20; Kendrick, 2013, p. 1657; N. Richards, 2015)—have taken on greater urgency and importance (Barocas and Selbst, 2016; Elkin-Koren and Gal, 2019, p. 4; Hartzog et al., 2015, p. 1765).

Yet, skepticism remains among lawyers, privacy theorists, and social scientists about whether such chilling effects exist and, if they do, whether they are anything more than a passing or trivial phenomenon (Jef and Faure, 2014, p. 121; Sklansky, 2014, pp. 1094–100). This skepticism has not been confined to attorneys or the academy—courts have long been skeptical as well, particularly on chilling effects associated with information gathering (Penney, 2016, pp. 120–21). Despite this urgency and

* The author would like to thank Ryan Whalen, Nathan Matias, Frank Pasquale, Nicolas Suzor, Nina Varsava, Dan Katz, Nicola Lettieri, Paul Gowder, Angela Zhang, and Alex Schwartz for helpful feedback and suggestions, as well as other participants at the 2018 Emergence of Computational Legal Studies Conference: The Promises and Challenges of Data-Driven Legal Research, Faculty of Law, Hong Kong University, 28–9 June 2018.

skepticism, and a growing body of related studies (Marthews and Tucker, 2017; Penney, 2017, 2019; Stoycheff et al., 2019; Stoycheff et al., 2017), there nevertheless remains a noteworthy lack of systematic research on chilling effects (Kaminski and Witnov, 2015, p. 517; Kendrick, 2013, p. 1657). This is particularly so for new forms of AI and machine-learning driven automated legal and regulatory enforcement (Denning, 2017, pp. 37–8; Hartzog et al., 2015, p. 1767; Pasquale, 2019; Stevenson and Wagoner, 2015, p. 1352). As a result, questions persist about the nature and permanence of surveillance and other forms of regulatory chilling effects; the factors that influence these impacts; and how different forms of technological surveillance or legal/regulatory enforcement may impact people's behavior differently.

In this chapter, I argue that the emerging field of computational legal studies ("CLS") (Katz et al., 2011, p. 79) can play a unique role in addressing this research gap—helping substantiate, and providing essential insights into, impacts of surveillance and other emerging forms of regulatory activities—like automated legal enforcement. My focus, in particular, will be on chilling effects on people's behavior caused by these state and corporate activities. In Section 2, I illustrate why CLS is uniquely suited to helping fill this research gap. In Section 3, I illustrate this point by describing a case study exploring and measuring the impact of mass surveillance online using computational methods: how public awareness about US government surveillance online, due to intense media coverage of the Snowden revelations in June 2013, had a chilling effect on Wikipedia users. In Section 4, I set out limitations of this case study and make recommendations for computational legal research in this field of study moving forward.

2.   MEASURING IMPACTS AT SCALE: WHY CLS?

Though not exhaustive, I set out in this section three reasons why CLS is well situated, as a new field of legal research, to contribute to our understanding of the impact—particularly the chilling effects—of state and corporate regulatory activities like surveillance and automated legal enforcement.

2.1   Persistent Empirical/Theoretical Skepticism

Chilling effects theory has been with us for at least half a century. Its emergence begins with the US Supreme Court, which began to develop the "chilling effects doctrine"—a First Amendment law doctrine—in the Post War Period, which encourages courts to treat laws or state actions that may chill or deter free speech "with suspicion" (Kendrick, 2013, p. 1636). The doctrine would, through the Cold War years, become established in First Amendment doctrine, as the Court addressed First Amendment challenges to various overreaching anti-communist statutes enacted in this period (Kendrick, 2013, p. 1653; N. Richards, 2015, p. 106). But this legal doctrine, as Frederick Schauer would illustrate in his oft cited 1978 work (Cohen, 1995–96, p. 1011), was based on a theory of human behavior: that certain state and/or corporate actions—information and data gathering, regulations, or statutory enactments—could "chill" or deter citizens from engaging in legal and constitutionally protected activities—like free expression (Schauer, 1978, pp. 687–9). Schauer theorized chilling effects as mainly due to people fearing legal prosecution, sanction, or liability, combined with uncertainties inherent in the law and the legal system, and was most concerned with how overreaching statutes may chill First Amendment protected speech (Schauer, 1978, pp. 687–9).

Privacy theorists like Daniel Solove have extended Schauer's work to explore chilling effects associated with privacy threats. Solove, for example, theorized how surveillance and other information practices can create a kind of "environmental pollution" leading to self-censorship and other chilling effects (N.M. Richards, 2013, pp. 1949–50; Solove, 2006, p. 488). On this account, people are chilled or deterred from exercising their rights and freedoms not due to fear of legal harm or punishment—as Schauer posited—but due to harms that may result from being tracked or having data gathered about you—like reputational harms resulting from public disclosure of private facts or economic harm due to misappropriation of personal information by third parties (Solove, 2006, p. 496). Others like Wendy Seltzer, for example, have theorized chilling effects in relation to specific statutory schemes like the Digital Millennium Copyright Act of 1998 (DMCA) (Seltzer, 2010). Of course, there are other bodies of research and social science—like psychology, privacy research, surveillance studies, and communications, among many others—relevant to chilling effects theory and the behavioral premises underlying it (Kaminski and Witnov, 2015, pp. 483–93).

Yet, as noted earlier, skepticism persists as to the existence and magnitude of chilling effects, beyond mere trivial or passing impacts. This skepticism exists beyond just legal scholars and social scientists. Though courts have recognized and/or cited chilling effects in countless decisions (Kendrick, 2013)—like how vague or overly broad statutes can chill First Amendment speech—they have remained skeptical about other forms of chilling effects, like those associated with government or corporate surveillance or information gathering (Penney, 2016, pp. 120–21). In its 1978 decision *Zurcher v Stanford Daily*, for example, the US Supreme

Court expressed skepticism that police searches of newsrooms would have a chilling effect on news publishing or journalistic activities (*Zurcher v. Stanford Daily*, 1978).[1] And in the often cited 1972 case *Laird v. Tatum* (*Laird v. Tatum*, 1972), the Supreme Court rejected claims about chilling effects due to government surveillance, finding the government information gathering did not constitute an "objective harm or a threat of specific future harm" (*Laird v. Tatum*, 1972, p. 15).[2] This skepticism remains today (*Clapper v. Amnesty Int'l*, 2013).[3]

There are likely many reasons for this persistent skepticism. A key part of the challenge concerns common perceptions and assumptions as to what surveillance impacts or other forms of regulatory chilling effects might look like. On this count, the general public, as well as experts—from courts to legal scholars to social scientists—often expect surveillance and similar forms of government and corporate regulatory activities have clear and obvious impacts on fundamental democratic rights and freedoms leading to obvious and pervasive chilling effects, such as societal-wide suppression of controversial or radical political speech and discussion, or the right to peaceful assembly.

A great example of this assumption or expectation, leading to skepticism about whether surveillance may promote self-censorship or have broader societal chilling effects—is here expressed by University of Chicago Law Professor Eric Posner. Posner, a leading legal scholar who also incorporates empirical methods in his work (Posner and Weyl, 2013), conveys his skepticism about the "threat" posed by National Security Agency (NSA) surveillance in a *New York Times* "Room for Debate" discussion after the Snowden disclosures in June 2013:

> This brings me to another valuable point you made, which is that when people believe that the government exercises surveillance, they become reluctant to exercise democratic freedoms. This is a textbook objection to surveillance, I agree, but it also is another objection that I would place under "theoretical" rather than real. Is there any evidence that over the 12 years, during the flowering of the so-called surveillance state, Americans have become less politically active? More worried about government suppression of dissent? Less willing to listen to opposing voices? All the evidence points in the opposite direction . . . It is hard to think of another period so full of robust political debate since the late 1960s—another era of government surveillance. (Posner, 2013)

---

[1] Zurcher v. Stanford Daily, 436 U.S. 547, 566 (1978).
[2] Laird v. Tatum, 408 U.S. 1, 13–14 (1972) ("Allegations of a subjective 'chill' are not an adequate substitute for a claim of specific present objective harm or a threat of specific future harm").
[3] Clapper v. Amnesty Int'l, 133 S. Ct. 1138, 1152 (2013).

For Posner, the presence of "robust" political debate and activities that are apparent in society is compelling evidence against claims about chilling effects associated with surveillance.

Similarly, Stanford's David Sklansky also finds compelling evidence "all around us" contradicting the idea that surveillance would "chill independent thought, robust debate, personal growth, and intimate friendship" (Sklansky, 2014, pp. 1094, 1097, 1099). Among that evidence is the widespread "sharing of personal information" online (which would not occur if surveillance was having a dampening effect); how employer monitoring has not deterred employee emailing; how freedom of information laws have not deterred "intra-governmental communications"; and how young people that have grown up with the internet and the possibility of surveillance and information gathering concerning their activities online, particularly with social media—are more expressive and experimental than previous generations (Sklansky, 2014, pp. 1099–100). Like Posner, Sklansky finds all of this robust expression, sharing, and experimentation in society as strong evidence that chilling effects do not exist or are not "worth worrying about" (Sklansky, 2014, p. 1101).

These assumptions and expectations—which I have elsewhere argued can be linked to George Orwell's popularized dystopian vision of society under mass surveillance (Penney, 2018)—are further compounded by the aforementioned lack of systematic empirical study of the chilling effect phenomena. This persistent gap in relevant research is particularly salient in relation to new digital contexts and emerging technologies like AI and automation. These areas, and the field more generally, require further research, particularly large-scale systematic studies.

With this lack of study, these common perceptions, and the skepticism they feed about chilling effects, persist. This is the first clear way that CLS, as an emerging field of empirical legal studies that employs tools, methods, and forms of analyses common to computational social science, can play a unique role in this area of research (Katz et al., 2011, p. 79; Lettieri, 2016; Lettieri et al., 2018, pp. 1–2; Lettieri and Faro, 2012). As CLS involves using such tools and methods that are quantitative, computational, statistical, and technology-driven, it is ideally positioned to study people's "interactions with digital technologies", to shed new light on the impact of surveillance and other emerging forms of public/private sector regulatory activities (Lettieri, 2016, p. 3; Lettieri et al., 2018, pp. 1–3). In short, it offers new and innovative tools and methods to address the research gap more generally.

But in particular, I believe CLS can play a unique role helping empirically test these common assumptions held by Posner, Sklansky, and others, about the impact of surveillance and other public and private causes of chilling effects, whether it is surveillance, regulation, or forms of online harassment and abuse. That is, simply because social and political discussion or debate appears today robust in democratic societies there are no such chilling effects. Or if these effects do exist, they are trivial and not worth worrying about. Indeed, the research that *has* been done—a still small but growing body of research— suggests these commonly held assumptions and perceptions are wrong: chilling effects are real, but not always obvious. Rather, people are chilled in more subtle ways—from speaking in certain contexts; from seeking out certain information; from informing themselves about certain controversial topics, among some examples. While not resulting in widespread suppression of speech and debate, these subtle impacts, in the long term, are arguably just as danger-ous to important freedoms and healthy democratic societies (Penney, 2016, pp. 169–71).

These insights are not surprising. It is essentially what experts like Daniel Solove, Julie Cohen, Neil Richards, Danielle Citron, David Lyon, and others have long argued (Citron, 2014, p. 196; Cohen, 2000, p. 1426; Lyon, 2018, pp. 65–9; N. Richards, 2015, pp. 179–80; Solove, 2006, 2007). However, while such impacts may not always be clear or obvious on an individual or group-level basis, such subtle effects may be far easier to detect, measure, and document at larger scales. This is where CLS can offer important insights. It employs tools and methods with capacity for more large-scale studies to better document the subtle impacts of surveillance and other regulatory impacts at large—even mass or population-wide—scale.

In fact, studies employing CLS tools and methods have been among the most important and impactful studies in this emerging body of research. One good example of this would be the 2015 study by lawyer Alex Marthews and MIT Professor Catherine Tucker who found, using sophisticated statistical analysis of Google search trends before and after the June 2013 Snowden revelations, that Snowden's disclosures about gov-ernment surveillance had a chilling effect on what people searched for on Google (Marthews and Tucker, 2017, pp. 5–9). Another would be Sauvik Das and Adam Kramer's research on "self-censorship" on Facebook, which found 71 percent of the 3.9 million users sampled self-censored a post or comment due to concerns about surveillance by multiple audiences (Das and Kramer, 2013). Another example of a CLS study on point would be Urban et al.'s 2016 large-scale study of automated copyright enforce-ment online under the DMCA—which included quantitative analysis of over 100 million DMCA removal requests (Urban et al., 2017, p. 2). These are just some examples of studies—there are others—that employ statistical and computational analysis, along with large data sets, to track and document the subtle but large-scale impacts of surveillance and the automated enforcement of legal rights and norms. And CLS is already having impact.

2.2 Taking Advantage of New Research Possibilities

Another central factor in the aforementioned lack of study is the complex interdisciplinary and methodological challenges involved in designing this kind of research. First, designing this kind of research requires interdisciplinary expertise and training. Studying the impact of legal rules, corporate enforcement legal rights and interests, and other forms of activities undertaken to promote state or corporate interests like surveillance, will require legal expertise to understand the nature and scope of the legal rules, rights, or interests involved. However, legal expertise is not enough—designing empirical research, particularly large-scale studies, can often require training in social science, data science, computer programming, statistics, and familiarity with quantitative methods. Lawyers and legal scholars do not often have that kind of training. Second, it is difficult to document, measure, and explore surveillance and other forms of state and corporate regulatory impacts—particularly chilling effects or self-censorship. This is because demonstrating self-censorship or chilling effects requires showing a counterfactual state of affairs: that a person would have said something or done something but for some surveillance threat or awareness.

These observations are not new. These very challenges have often led many lawyers, theorists, and researchers to conclude that chilling effects, self-censorship, and similar impacts are very difficult, if not impossible, to document or quantify. Privacy theorists like Solove (Solove, 2006, p. 155) and Richards (N.M. Richards, 2013, p. 1964) have both observed the difficulties in producing evidence of chilling effects. Schauer likewise admitted that the behavioral assumptions underlying the "chilling effects doctrine" was "most likely unprovable" (Schauer, 1978, p. 730). Diane Rowland, examining free expression and defamation decades later, would similarly observe that such impacts were "difficult to quantify" (Rowland, 2005, p. 67). Summing up these challenges, Kendrick notes the "intractable empirical difficulties" (Kendrick, 2013, p. 1638) in such research and concludes it is "difficult to establish either the presence or the absence of a chilling effect, let alone to measure the extent of such an effect" (Kendrick, 2013, p. 1638).

One way around these methodological problems is to simply ask people if their behavior changed based on awareness of surveillance or some other state or corporate activity. Would you have said something but for this law or awareness of state or corporate awareness? Indeed, there have been worthwhile qualitative and quantitative survey-based studies—like those by PEN and Pew Internet Research—providing insights into self-censorship and other forms of regulatory chilling effects (Hampton et al., 2014, p. 4; PEN American Center, 2013, pp. 3–4, 2015; Rainie et al., 2013; Rainie and Madden, 2015, p. 4). However, a not insubstantial body of "privacy paradox" research, involving a diverse range of online platforms and contexts, has demonstrated that people's statements or reports about their own behavior are not always reflected in their actual behavior (Bergström, 2015; Kokolakis, 2017). So while these studies provide important insights, relying only on people's statements is not reliable (or not persuasive enough evidence alone). There must be additional research to document *actual behavior* suggesting chilling effects and similar impacts.

These challenges, again, illustrate how CLS can offer an essential contribution. The digital age offers transformative new opportunities for social research. The amount and quality of data and information available is unprecedented and ever increasing, and new advances in digital storage are allowing for new forms of sharing, transmission, and analysis of this "big data" (Salganik, 2017, p. 2). These innovations are coupled with growth in computing power, and its ubiquity—computers are everywhere (Salganik, 2017, p. 3). This, too, facilitates new forms of analysis, transmission, and reproduction. As a result of these important changes, researchers can ask new questions, observe in ways unimaginable before, run innovative new experiments, and collaborate in ways that were just not possible in previous times (Salganik, 2017, p. 2).

These changes, in short, offer important new qualitative and quantitative research possibilities to not just observe, but analyze and understand *actual* behavior. Previously, collecting behavioral information or data was expensive and time-consuming. Now, with more plentiful data, it is much easier to observe behavior—particularly changes in it—across a range of new contexts, for longer periods of time, at a greater scale, and with greater precision (Salganik, 2017, p. 13). In other words, the possibilities to document, track, measure, and explore *chilling effects* are likewise more plentiful than at any time previously. It is thus no coincidence that the new research on chilling effects has emerged in recent years, with the corresponding growth and availability of "big data" sources.

Again, CLS, which investigates law problems using computational social research methods designed to analyze and experiment with these new data sources, is arguably best positioned among other legal research approaches to take advantage of these new research opportunities to study chilling effects and related regulatory impacts. CLS researchers, for example, have statistical and computational training to use new research techniques like mass collaborations or combining traditional research

methods—like surveys—or human information processing with big data
and machine computation (Salganik, 2017, pp. 272–73). Such techniques
will be increasingly important as public and private sector data gathering
and analytics become more sophisticated and their impact more complex
and far-reaching. CLS researchers can likewise take advantage of the
new natural experiments made possible by what Matthew Salganik, a
computational social scientist at Princeton, calls "always-on" big data
systems, that is, always collecting data (Salganik, 2017, pp. 21, 52). This
creates the possibility for large longitudinal data sets to study behavior of
large populations over time. Taking advantage of such "always-on" data
can include studying the effects of legal changes or similar public/private
sector regulatory actions or events, whose impact—like chilling effects—is
captured in the always-on data (Salganik, 2017, p. 52). Here, statistical and
computational analytical methods can help identify and analyze any such
impacts in the data. This offers an entirely new dimension for research on
chilling effects.

2.3   Tools/Methods for New Technological Challenges

Besides opportunity, the digital age—and emerging technologies like AI,
automation, and machine learning—also offers complex new challenges
for the law itself. These technologies, combined with big data, when
deployed in both public and private contexts—like predictive policing,
FRT and AI-driven surveillance and detection, and algorithmic law—
also have the potential to create new large-scale chilling effects, and other
deleterious impacts, on human rights. To meet these complex challenges,
lawyers and legal scholars need new research tools and methods to match
the scale of these new forms of automated, machine, and AI-driven law
and regulation. CLS, I would again argue, is best positioned to employ
the new tools and methods required to meet these challenges. As a
field that already harnesses these very same technologies—including
"Big Data", "machine learning", "Network Analysis", and "Artificial
Intelligence" (Lettieri et al., 2018, pp. 7–8)—to explore legal questions
and issues, it likewise is very well positioned to also interrogate the
technologies themselves—and the new challenges they pose to the law,
and human rights.

   Of course, these arguments in favor of the role CLS can play in measuring surveillance and other regulatory impacts in the digital age come with
important qualifications and limitations. To illustrate these, as well as
the arguments I have here, I set out a case study in the next section that
deploys computational methods to study chilling effect with legal implications. My aim is to demonstrate the new possibilities of CLS methods in

this area of research, but also the need to combine these approaches with more traditional legal and social research methods.

3.   CLS CASE STUDY: SURVEILLANCE IMPACT ON WIKIPEDIA USE

3.1   Design

In the previous section, I talked about CLS researchers being well positioned to take advantage of new natural experiments made possible in the digital age—where the impact of random or unexpected social and political events or forces are captured by "always-on" big data systems. The case study discussed here did precisely that. The Snowden disclosures about NSA surveillance, detailed by *The Guardian* and *The Washington Post* on June 6, 2013 (Bakir, 2015; Gellman and Poitras, 2013; Giles and Hartmann, 2014; Greenwald, 2013; Lyon, 2014, p. 2; Qin, 2015; Wu et al., 2015), created more than just a media fire-storm, with revelations receiving widespread coverage in the US and internationally (Bakir, 2015, p. 132; Giles and Hartmann, 2014, p. 24; Qin, 2015, p. 166). It also offered a new possibility to explore surveillance impacts—like chilling effects—potentially at mass scale.

The Snowden leaks' far-reaching coverage led to widespread public awareness in the US about government surveillance of internet and other telecommunications activities. A Pew study in 2014, for instance, found 87 percent of adults heard something about "the government collecting information about telephone calls, e-mails, and other online communications" as part of "efforts to monitor terrorist activity"(Madden, 2014, pp. 2–3). That kind of deep public awareness about surveillance at a specific point in time would allow one to "test" a chilling effect theory concerning the impact of the surveillance revelations by examining behavior of people before and after the Snowden revelations. But this raised the question—where might the impact, if any, of this unexpected event be captured? Certainly, large online service providers like Google or Facebook might have excellent data about user activity before and after June 2013 that may evidence an impact or lack thereof, but that data was private and very difficult to obtain (Salganik, 2017, p. 27). Similarly, governments might have such data, but why would it release it, in order to help social researchers explore the (possibly negative) impacts of government national security and law enforcement activities like surveillance (Salganik, 2017, pp. 27–28)?

Instead, the "always-on" big data system that I would rely on for this study is better known as a wildly popular website and influential information source—Wikipedia. Why Wikipedia? Over half of internet users use Wikipedia and over a third of Americans visit Wikipedia every year (Penney, 2016, pp. 134–5). This makes it one of the most visited sites in the world. Given its popularity, if there were surveillance impacts from the Snowden revelations, I surmised that Wikipedia may have felt them. In fact, Wikipedia's non-profit governing body—the Wikimedia Foundation—would later make this very claim—that NSA surveillance had a chilling effect on Wikipedia users—in a lawsuit launched against the US government (Newman, 2018). It is still being litigated today.

Most importantly, however, unlike inaccessible data held by private sector platforms and governments, Wikimedia Foundation makes publicly available a wealth of data concerning Wikipedia and its use. Among this available data is aggregated monthly "page view" counts for individual Wikipedia articles—essentially a measurement of how often a Wikipedia article is visited or viewed by internet users in a month (Penney, 2016, p. 119). Wikipedia's logging of this data was "always-on" during the relevant time period, from January 2012 to late 2014. So, I constructed a study that examined Wikipedia article page view traffic or counts before, during, and after June 2013, to test the hypothesis that increased public awareness about NSA surveillance would lead users to be likely to view Wikipedia articles on privacy-sensitive topics (Penney, 2016, p. 134).

To determine what Wikipedia articles to include in the study—ones that may raise privacy concerns for internet users aware of possible government surveillance online—I matched 48 Wikipedia articles with a list of "terrorism" related keywords that the US Department of Homeland Security (DHS) uses to track and monitor social media (Penney, 2016, pp. 139–40). This DHS keyword list categorizes search terms or keywords in relation to a range of different governmental issues including "Health Concern", "Infrastructure Security", and "Terrorism". This 48 Wikipedia articles set included articles on "dirty bomb", "suicide attack", and "Al Qaeda", among others. Using "terrorism" related keywords to construct this set made sense because the US government largely cited the need to track and monitor terrorism threats as a key justification for the surveillance programs themselves (Bakir, 2015, p. 133).

In the previous section I also talked about CLS researchers combining traditional social research tools—like surveys—with computational "big data" methods, which Salganik recommends. I did so here too, conducting an online survey of 415 Mechanical Turkers, wherein each participant in the survey provided a privacy rating for the 48 "terrorism" keywords (Penney, 2016, p. 143). The survey findings provided evidence the 48 Wikipedia articles were privacy sensitive, that is, likely would raise privacy concerns for Wikipedia users aware of government surveillance. I then created a data set that aggregated English language Wikipedia monthly article view counts for these 48 Wikipedia articles over 32 months, from January 2012 to August 2014. To understand the scale of the data, these 48 "terrorism" related Wikipedia articles constituted nearly 81 million total page views over the course of the 32-month period (Penney, 2016, p. 141).

Like other CLS research, this project deployed computational and statistical analysis. I used an interrupted time series (ITS) design with segmented regression analysis. ITS offers a powerful statistical method and design to analyze whether Wikipedia page views for privacy-sensitive topics were impacted by public awareness about NSA surveillance after the June 2013 Snowden revelations (Penney, 2016, pp. 137–8). An ITS design involves a series of observations of the same outcome—in this case Wikipedia article views—collected at identical intervals over time, before and after an intervention event (here the June 2013 Snowden revelations). Analyzing changes in these observations over time allows you to test the immediate and longer term effect of the event. I then used two statistical approaches to analyze the ITS observational trends. First, I conducted a simple means comparison of the total views for all the Wikipedia articles in the dataset before and after June 2013. Second, I used a segmented regression analysis to estimate article view trends before and after June 2013. Segmented regression analysis offers a powerful statistical method to facilitate this, by helping to identify trends, changes in data level, and to isolate the scope of impact from other confounding factors (Penney, 2016, p. 137).

Additionally, I conducted standard statistical diagnostic tests, including examining and correcting data for outliers and autocorrelation, two threats to the validity of results in ITS research designs (Penney, 2016, pp. 144–5). I also added comparator groups—sets of Wikipedia articles on "security", "infrastructure", as well as a set of the most popular (most visited) Wikipedia articles in 2012, 2013, and 2014. These Wikipedia articles comparator sets are similar (the security and infrastructure articles were also created from DHS keywords, while the popular set was created using Wikitrends reports (Penney, 2016, pp. 153–7)) but different: unlike "terrorism" related Wikipedia content, articles on security, infrastructure, or popular articles (the set included articles on "Breaking Bad", "Game of Thrones", and "World War II") would be unlikely to raise privacy concerns for Wikipedia users (Penney, 2016, pp. 156–7). If the "chilling effect" hypothesis was correct, then the "terrorism" Wikipedia articles would be impacted by the Snowden revelations, while the comparator article groups would not.

3.2   Results

The study's results provided compelling evidence of surveillance chilling effects—arguably at mass scale. First, the combined average monthly views for all 48 "terrorism" related Wikipedia articles showed a reduction of 526,614 in the average monthly views for the articles after June 2013, a 19.5 percent drop in article view counts. This difference was statistically significant with a large effect size and consistent with a surveillance chilling effect (Penney, 2016, pp. 145–6).

The findings from the segmented regression analysis were also consistent with a chilling effect hypothesis. The initial set of results showed a large and statistically significant drop in article views in June 2013 of 995,085 article views, also consistent with a chilling effect in that month (Penney, 2016, pp. 147–8). However, once a significant outlier was removed—the "Hamas" Wikipedia article had extremely high view counts for November 2012 and July 2014 likely due to armed conflict between Hamas and the Israeli Defense Force in Gaza during those months (Penney, 2016, pp. 149–51)—an even clearer picture emerges. This can be seen in Figure 7.1 below.

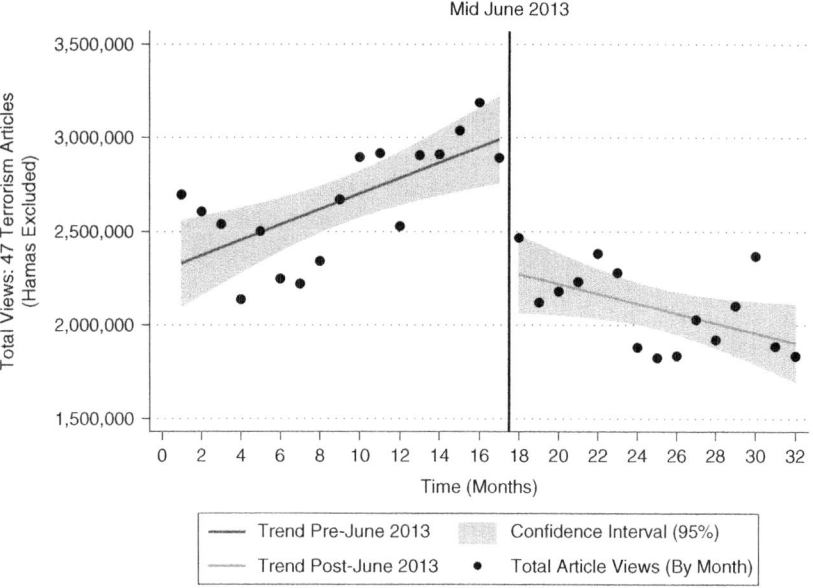

Note: The sudden drop in views and trend shift—from increasing monthly views over to decreasing after June 2013—is consistent with a significant and lasting chilling effect.

Figure 7.1   Pre and post June 2013 article view trends (outliers excluded)

The findings for the 47 "terrorism" Wikipedia articles (Hamas article outlier excluded) likewise showed a large, sudden, and statistically significant drop of 693,617 total article views in June 2013, a 25 percent drop-off. This was consistent with a surveillance chilling effect in June 2013 due to public awareness about government surveillance due to reporting on the Snowden leaks in the US and internationally that month. However, there was *also* a statistically significant change in the overall trend in monthly article views—which went from increasing by 41,421 views on a month to month basis before June 2013, to a decrease of 67,513 in views per month after. This suggests the chilling effect was not just temporary (in June 2013) but also longer term.

These findings are further confirmed by additional analysis of the most privacy-sensitive articles within the set of 47 "terrorism" Wikipedia articles (according to the MTurk survey privacy ratings (Penney, 2016, pp. 149–51)) as well as the comparator Wikipedia articles. The results are set out in Table 7.1.

The most privacy-sensitive "terrorism" Wikipedia articles showed the same large statistically significant drop-off in views in June 2013 with a statistically significant change in the overall monthly article view trend—from increasing monthly before June 2013 shifting to decreasing after. Moreover, none of the comparator groups showed either a statistically significant drop in article views in June 2013 or a statistically significant shift in the overall trend in views after.

Table 7.1   *The highly statistically significant drop in view count in June 2013 and shift to fewer monthly views after June 2013 for the terrorism articles is consistent with a chilling effect. The comparator article groups show no similar statistically significant results*

Wikipedia Article Group	Monthly trend pre-June 2013	Change in view count in June 2013	Change in monthly trend after June 2013	Model fit
47 Terrorism articles	**41,420.51****	**−693,616.9****	**−67,513.1****	**Yes**
	p = 0.000	**p = 0.000**	**p = 0.000**	**F = 0.00**
25 Security articles	11,135.0	−24,638.34	−20,465.87	No
	p = 0.187	p = 0.840	p = 0.120	F = 0.45
34 Infrastructure articles	**−11,079****	−12,721.0	2,431.84	**Yes**
	p = 0.000	p = 0.770	p = 0.610	**F = 0.00**
26 Popular articles	−48,458	−1,716,643	177,324.7	No
	p = 0.798	p = 0.530	p = 0.551	F = 0.79

Note: Statistically significant findings in bold (* $p < 0.05$, ** $p < 0.01$).

All of these findings are consistent with the hypothesis that the public's awareness about possible US government surveillance thanks to intense media coverage of the Snowden revelations in June 2013, and the months after, had a chilling effect on Wikipedia users—leading them to avoid privacy-sensitive "terrorism" content in June 2013 and in the months thereafter. This was the case for the 47 "terrorism" Wikipedia articles as well as the most privacy-sensitive articles within that grouping. Also consistent with the chilling effects hypothesis is that article views for the comparator Wikipedia article sets on security, infrastructure, and popular topics did not show any impact, statistically or otherwise, from the June 2013 Snowden revelations.

4.   MEASURING IMPACTS GOING FORWARD

This case study has offered compelling evidence of surveillance chilling effects, but there are noteworthy limitations too. The data in the case study only extended to August 2014, so the persistence of any chilling effects, over the long term, remains unclear. The data was also not granular. It was not geographically specific, as the article view count data was for English language alone; it would have been insightful, for example, to be able to analyze country-level view count data to understand and compare impacts on different national populations. And it was also not a true experimental design—it was not possible to locate a control group insulated from NSA surveillance; anyone could have been targeted and thus impacted. As such, it was also not possible to control for all confounding variables and factors that contributed to the trends analyzed in the findings, though this is true of any study that does not use a true experimental design.

There are far more questions that could be investigated in exploring, measuring, and documenting surveillance chilling effects and forms of regulatory impacts in the years ahead: *why* are people chilled? Is Solove's privacy-based theory more right? Or Schauer's theory based on legal harms? How are different individuals, groups, or populations impacted or chilled differently from others? Are there disparate or disproportionate impacts due to gender, age, ethnic origins, and other personal characteristics? What are the economic impacts of chilling effects? How are these groups or communities coping with surveillance, targeted or mass scale, if at all? These are just some of the questions that remain for exploration moving forward, and I have argued in this chapter that CLS has an important role to play in helping answer them. This case study, for example, to provide its insights took advantage of typical CLS research tools and methods to explore and document surveillance chilling effects.

It employed a natural experimental design (interrupted time series) that took advantage of an "always-on" big data source (Wikipedia article view count logs); used computational and statistical analyses facilitated by statistical software; and incorporated traditional quantitative social research methods (online survey).

But to *truly* provide a complete picture of surveillance chilling effects and other regulatory impacts, a few things must change. First, private sector service providers—particularly popular social media companies like Google, Facebook, and Twitter, among others—need to be more open to partnerships with social researchers. They possess some of the best "always-on" big data sources that, through analysis, could enrich our understanding of chilling effects. However, they are understandably averse to doing so, due to legal and business risks and ethical obligations to their users (Salganik, 2017, pp. 28–9). On this count, governments could do much more to facilitate such partnerships, by enacting policies, guidelines, and/or concrete procedures through which researchers can obtain access to private sector data, and that also address corporate concerns about legal and ethical risks (Salganik, 2017, p. 29).

Second, CLS researchers need to combine computational "big data" case studies like this one, with more traditional social research methods and approaches as well as granular in-depth qualitative work at the individual, group, and community level. Salganik makes this recommendation for computational *social science* (Salganik, 2017, pp. 358–9), and I think it is just as applicable to CLS, as the law and law-related phenomena are complex with multi-faceted social, political, and economic dimensions and impacts.

Large-scale chilling effect measurements need to be matched with on-the-ground qualitative work that can tell the stories of the individuals or groups impacted, and better understand why they reacted the way they did in the face of the public or private sector activities that chilled or impacted them or their community. For example, while this case study documents surveillance chilling effects at a large scale, it is not clear *why* people felt the need to avoid privacy-sensitive content after learning about NSA surveillance from the Snowden revelations in June 2013. Were internet users concerned about being caught up in mass and indiscriminate surveillance programs, leading to legal harms later? Or were they more concerned about government invasions of privacy, thus avoiding content that may attract government scrutiny? It is possible to hypothesize based on theories like those offered by Solove or Schauer, but without more ground-level qualitative insights as to *why* people acted as they did, our understanding of chilling effects and other impacts is incomplete.

In the end, this case study offered compelling evidence of surveillance chilling effects. And given that there were over 81 million Wikipedia article views represented in the data, it is chilling effects at a large—arguably mass—scale, with the behavioral patterns of many millions of internet users likely captured in the Wikipedia article view count data over the course of the 32 months. As I have discussed elsewhere (Penney, 2016, pp. 161–71), these results have important implications for fundamental rights and freedoms—including free expression; the right to privacy; freedom of information and the right to seek, receive, and impart it, among others—and the broader health of democratic societies. Indeed, while state and corporate surveillance, data gathering, and technologically enhanced law enforcement common today have not led to the widespread suppression of dissent and debate as envisioned by Orwell in his famous text *1984*, this case study suggests that even these subtle chilling effects can have a just as corrosive effect on people's exercise of important freedoms and democratic societies in the long term.

REFERENCES

Bakir, V. (2015). News, Agenda Building, and Intelligence Agencies: A Systematic Review of the Field from the Discipline of Journalism, Media, and Communications. *The International Journal of Press/Politics*, *20*(2), 131–44. https://doi.org/10/gf9pqd.

Barocas, S., and Selbst, A.D. (2016). Big Data's Disparate Impact. *California Law Review*, *104*(3), 671–732.

Bergström, A. (2015). Online Privacy Concerns: A Broad Approach to Understanding the Concerns of Different Groups for Different Uses. *Computers in Human Behavior*, *53*, 419–26. https://doi.org/10/bbg9.

Boehme-Neßler, V. (2016). Privacy: A Matter of Democracy – Why Democracy Needs Privacy and Data Protection. *International Data Privacy Law*, *6*(3), 222–9. https://doi.org/10/gf9ng6.

Carpou, Z. (2016). Robots, Pirates, and the Rise of the Automated Takedown Regime: Using the DMCA to Fight Piracy and Protect End-Users. *Columbia Journal of Law & the Arts*, *39*(4), 551–89.

Citron, D.K. (2014). *Hate Crimes in Cyberspace*. Cambridge, MA: Harvard Univ. Press.

Citron, D.K., and Penney, J.W. (2018–19). When Law Frees Us to Speak. *Fordham Law Review*, *87*(6), 2317–35.

Cohen, J.E. (1995–96). A Right to Read Anonymously: A Closer Look at Copyright Management in Cyberspace. *Connecticut Law Review*, *28*(4), 981–1040.

Cohen, J.E. (2000). Examined Lives: Informational Privacy and the Subject as Object. *Stanford Law Review*, *52*(5), 1373–437.

Das, S., and Kramer, A. (2013). Self-Censorship on Facebook. Presented at the Seventh International AAAI Conference on Weblogs and Social Media (ICWSM-13), MIT Media Lab and Microsoft, Cambridge, Massachusetts, USA, 8–11 July 2013.

Denning, P.J. (2017). Remaining Trouble Spots with Computational Thinking. *Communications of the ACM*, *60*(6), 33–9. https://doi.org/10/gfz5hd.

Elkin-Koren, N. (2017). Fair Use by Design. *UCLA Law Review*, *64*(5), 1082–100.

Elkin-Koren, N., and Gal, M.S. (2019). The Chilling of Governance-by-Data on Data Markets. *University of Chicago Law Review*, *86*(2), 403–31.

Fiscutean, A. (2017). Internet Censorship: It's on the Rise and Silicon Valley is Helping it Happen. ZDNet, 28 November. Retrieved 9 October 2019 from https://www.zdnet.com/article/internet-censorship-its-on-the-rise-and-silicon-valley-is-helping-it-happen/.

Gellman, B., and Poitras, L. (2013). U.S., British Intelligence Mining Data from Nine U.S. Internet Companies in Broad Secret Program. *Washington Post*, 7 June. Retrieved 16 June 2020 from https://www.washingtonpost.com/investigations/us-intelligence-mining-data-from-nine-us-internet-companies-in-broad-secret-program/2013/06/06/3a0c0da8-cebf-11e2-8845-d970ccb04497_story.html.

Giles, K., and Hartmann, K. (2014). Socio-Political Effects of Active Cyber Defence Measures. *2014 6th International Conference on Cyber Conflict (CyCon 2014)*, 23–36. https://doi.org/10/gf9pqf.

Greenwald, G. (2013). NSA Collecting Phone Records of Millions of Verizon Customers Daily. *The Guardian*, 6 June. Retrieved 16 June 2020 from https://www.theguardian.com/world/2013/jun/06/nsa-phone-records-verizon-court-order.

Hampton, K., Rainie, L., Lu, W., Dwyer, M., Shin, I., and Purcell, K. (2014). Social Media and the "Spiral of Silence". Pew Research Center, 26 August. Retrieved 10 October 2019 from https://www.pewinternet.org/wp-content/uploads/sites/9/2014/08/PI_Social-networks-and-debate_082614.pdf.

Hartzog, W., Conti, G., Nelson, J., and Shay, L.A. (2015). Inefficiently Automated Law Enforcement. *Michigan State Law Review*, *2015*(5), 1763–96.

Jef, D.M., and Faure, M.G. (2014). Public Authority Liability and the Chilling Effect. *Tort Law Review*, *22*, 120–33.

Kaminski, M.E., and Witnov, S. (2015). The Conforming Effect: First Amendment Implications of Surveillance, beyond Chilling Speech. *University of Richmond Law Review*, *49*(2), 465–518.

Katz, D.M., Gubler, J.R., Zelner, J., and Bommarito, M.J.I. (2011). Reproduction of Hierarchy: A Social Network Analysis of the American Law Professoriate. *Journal of Legal Education*, *61*(1), 76–103.

Kendrick, L. (2013). Speech, Intent, and the Chilling Effect. *William & Mary Law Review*, *54*(5), 1633–92.

Kokolakis, S. (2017). Privacy Attitudes and Privacy Behaviour: A Review of Current Research on the Privacy Paradox Phenomenon. *Computers & Security*, *64*, 122–34. https://doi.org/10/gffmvx.

Kuner, C. (2013). *Transborder Data Flows and Data Privacy Law*. Oxford: Oxford University Press.

Lettieri, N. (2016). Computational Social Science, the Evolution of Policy Design and Rule Making in Smart Societies. *Future Internet*, *8*(2), 19–26. https://doi.org/10/gf9ppk.

Lettieri, N., and Faro, S. (2012). Computational Social Science and its Potential Impact upon Law. *European Journal of Law and Technology*, *3*(3). Retrieved 16 June 2020 from http://ejlt.org/article/view/175.

Lettieri, N. (principal author). (2018). Ex Machina: Analytical Platforms, Law and the Challenges of Computational Legal Science. *Future Internet*, *10*(5), 37–65. https://doi.org/10/gfxvmj.

Lyon, D. (2014). Surveillance, Snowden, and Big Data: Capacities, Consequences, Critique. *Big Data & Society*, *1*(2), 1–13. https://doi.org/10/gcdw6f.

Lyon, D. (2018). *The Culture of Surveillance: Watching as a Way of Life* (1st ed.). Cambridge, UK and Medford, MA: Polity.

Madden, M. (2014). Public Perceptions of Privacy and Security in the Post-Snowden Era. Pew Research Center, 12 November. Retrieved 10 October 2019 from https://www.pewinternet.org/wp-content/uploads/sites/9/2014/11/PI_PublicPerceptionsofPrivacy_111214.pdf.

Marthews, A., and Tucker, C. (2017). The Impact of Online Surveillance on Behavior. In D. Gray and S.E. Henderson (eds), *The Cambridge Handbook of Surveillance Law* (1st ed., pp. 437–54). Cambridge: Cambridge University Press. https://doi.org/10.1017/9781316481127.019.

Newman, L. (2018). The ACLU's Biggest Roadblock to Fighting Mass Surveillance. *WIRED*, 29 June. Retrieved 16 June 2020 from https://www.wired.com/story/wikimedia-nsa-surveillance-privacy-lawsuit/.

Pasquale, F. (2019). Professional Judgment in an Era of Artificial Intelligence and Machine Learning. *Boundary 2*, *46*(1), 73–101. https://doi.org/10/gf9ngr.

Pasquale, F., and Cashwell, G. (2015). Four Futures of Legal Automation. *UCLA Law Review Discourse*, *63*, 26–48.

PEN American Center. (2013). *Chilling Effects: NSA Surveillance Drives US Writers to Self-Censor*. Retrieved 16 June 2020 from https://pen.org/sites/default/files/Chilling%20Effects_PEN%20American.pdf.

PEN American Center. (2015). *Global Chilling: The Impact of Mass Surveillance on International Writers*. Retrieved 10 October 2019 from https://pen.org/research-resources/global-chilling/.

Penney, J.W. (2015). The Cycles of Global Telecommunication Censorship and Surveillance. *University of Pennsylvania Journal of International Law*, *36*(3), 693–753.

Penney, J.W. (2016). Chilling Effects: Online Surveillance and Wikipedia Use. *Berkeley Technology Law Journal*, *31*(1), 117–82.

Penney, J.W. (2017). Internet Surveillance, Regulation, and Chilling Effects Online: A Comparative Case Study. *Internet Policy Review*, *6*(2), 1–39. Retrieved 16 June 2020 from https://policyreview.info/articles/analysis/internet-surveillance-regulation-and-chilling-effects-online-comparative-case.

Penney, J.W. (2018). (Mis)conceptions about the Impact of Surveillance. Freedom to Tinker blog, 14 February. Retrieved 16 June 2020 from website: https://freedom-to-tinker.com/2018/02/14/misconceptions-about-the-impact-of-surveillance/.

Penney, J.W. (2019). Privacy and Automated Legal Enforcement: The DMCA as a Case Study. *Stanford Technology Law Review*, *22*(1), 412–86.

Perel, M., and Elkin-Koren, N. (2016). Accountability in Algorithmic Copyright Enforcement. *Stanford Technology Law Review*, *19*(3), 473–533.

Posner, E. (2013). The Secrecy Paradox. *New York Times* Room for Debate, 9 June. Retrieved 10 October 2019 from https://www.nytimes.com/roomfordebate/2013/06/09/is-the-nsa-surveillance-threat-real-or-imagined.

Posner, E., and Weyl, E.G. (2013). Benefit–Cost Analysis for Financial Regulation. *American Economic Review*, *103*(3), 393–7. https://doi.org/10/gf9pmh.

Qin, J. (2015). Hero on Twitter, Traitor on News: How Social Media and Legacy News Frame Snowden. *The International Journal of Press/Politics*, *20*(2), 166–84. https://doi.org/10/gf9pqg.

Rainie, L., and Madden, M. (2015). Americans' Privacy Strategies Post-Snowden.

Pew Research Center, 16 March. Retrieved 10 October 2019 from https://www. pewinternet.org/wp-content/uploads/sites/9/2015/03/PI_AmericansPrivacyStra tegies_0316151.pdf.

Rainie, L., Kiesler, S., Kang, R., and Madden, M. (2013). Anonymity, Privacy, and Security Online. Pew Research Center, 5 September. Retrieved 10 October 2019 from https://www.pewinternet.org/2013/09/05/anonymity-privacy-and-sec urity-online/.

Richards, N. (2015). *Intellectual Privacy: Rethinking Civil Liberties in the Digital Age* (1st ed.). Oxford and New York: Oxford University Press.

Richards, N.M. (2013). The Dangers of Surveillance. *Harvard Law Review*, *126*(7), 1934–65.

Rowland, D. (2005). Free Expression and Defamation. In M. Klang and A. Murray (eds), *Human Rights in the Digital Age* (pp. 54–69). London: Routledge.

Salganik, M.J. (2017). *Bit by Bit: Social Research in the Digital Age*. Princeton, NJ: Princeton University Press.

Schauer, F. (1978). Fear, Risk and the First Amendment: Unraveling the Chilling Effect. *Boston University Law Review*, *58*(5), 685–732.

Seltzer, W. (2010). Free Speech Unmoored in Copyright's Safe Harbor: Chilling Effects of the DMCA on the First Amendment. *Harvard Journal of Law & Technology*, *24*(1), 171–233.

Shay, L.A., Hartzog, W., Nelson, J., Larkin, D., and Conti, G. (2016). Confronting Automated Law Enforcement. In R. Calo, M. Froomkin, and I. Kerr (eds), *Robot Law* (pp. 235–74). Cheltenham, UK and Northampton, MA, USA: Edward Elgar Publishing.

Sklansky, D.A. (2014). Too Much Information: How Not to Think about Privacy and the Fourth Amendment. *California Law Review*, *102*(5), 1069–121.

Solove, D.J. (2006). A Taxonomy of Privacy. *University of Pennsylvania Law Review*, *154*(3), 477–564.

Solove, D.J. (2007). The First Amendment as Criminal Procedure. *New York University Law Review*, *82*(1), 112–76.

Stevenson, D., and Wagoner, N.J. (2015). Bargaining in the Shadow of Big Data. *Florida Law Review*, *67*(4), 1337–400.

Stoycheff, E., Liu, J., Xu, K., and Wibowo, K. (2019). Privacy and the Panopticon: Online Mass Surveillance's Deterrence and Chilling Effects. *New Media & Society*, *21*(3), 602–19. https://doi.org/10/gfb7kh.

Stoycheff, E., Wibowo, K.A., Liu, J., and Xu, K. (2017). Online Surveillance's Effect on Support for Other Extraordinary Measures to Prevent Terrorism. *Mass Communication and Society*, *20*(6), 784–99. https://doi.org/10/gf9n69.

Urban, J.M., Karaganis, J., and Schofield, B. (2017). Notice and Takedown in Everyday Practice. Retrieved 16 June 2020 from https://papers.ssrn.com/ abstract=2755628.

Volz, D. (2015). Global Internet Surveillance, Censorship on Rise: Report. *Reuters*, 28 October. Retrieved 16 June 2020 from https://www.reuters.com/ article/us-cybersecurity-report-idUSKCN0SM1M220151028.

Wu, A., Ma, W.W.K., and Chan, W.W.L. (2015). "Whistleblower or Leaker?" Examining the Portrayal and Characterization of Edward Snowden in USA, UK, and HK Posts. In W.W.K. Ma, A. H.K. Yuen, J. Park, W.W.F. Lau, and L. Deng (eds), *New Media, Knowledge Practices and Multiliteracies* (pp. 53–66). Singapore: Springer.

8. Understanding content moderation systems: new methods to understand internet governance at scale, over time, and across platforms*

Nicolas Suzor

INTRODUCTION

Technology companies play a major role in governing the internet. The rules of platforms, content hosts, search engines, and telecommunications providers govern how we interact with each other, and they shape the possibilities and nature of public discourse (Suzor 2019). The rules that these intermediaries set, the policies they enact, and the design choices they make all influence how people communicate and what information is visible. These providers are in turn influenced by market forces, by governments around the world, by industry norms, by their users, and by social pressure from the media, civil society groups, and the public.

There is increasing global concern about how the decisions of internet and telecommunications companies impact on human rights. Governments around the world are learning how to influence intermediaries to control the flow of information, often in ways that skirt or avoid constitutional protections for fundamental rights (Elkin-Koren and Haber 2016). Meanwhile, many worry that platforms are not taking sufficient care to protect their users from harm (Suzor et al. 2018b), prevent the spread of hate and disinformation, or to protect the interests of marginalised groups (Citron 2014; Marwick and Lewis 2017; Caplan et al. 2018; Duguay et al. 2018). At the same time, platforms are frequently criticised for unduly silencing legitimate speech through their copyright takedown processes and terms of service enforcement.

There is now more pressure than ever before for internet intermediaries

* Nicolas Suzor is the recipient of an Australian Research Council DECRA Fellowship (project number DE160101542).

to take a more active role in shaping our social lives. Because intermediaries are the focal points of control of the internet, this pressure is only going to increase. Governments are rapidly becoming more sophisticated and learning how to more effectively regulate the internet – for good or for ill – by better targeting to require intermediaries to regulate users on their behalf. Governments will continue to make new demands that platforms take responsibility for censoring speech they deem to be offensive and for rooting out terrorist propaganda and illicit copyright content. Civil society groups, other businesses, and loose coalitions of individual users are also learning how to exert sustained pressure on intermediaries to change their policies or to resist influence from others. There inevitably will be more social pressure and new laws that push platforms to do more to combat abuse and hate speech, deal with fake news and fake reviews, safeguard elections from foreign interference, protect the privacy of individuals, and so on.

In this context, the task of identifying and developing social, technical, and legal approaches that can improve the legitimacy of online governance is becoming an increasingly pressing issue (MacKinnon 2012; Brown and Marsden 2013; DeNardis 2014; Mansell 2012). Unfortunately, there is little good information about how the policies of internet intermediaries are influencing our online environments in practice. It is often difficult to monitor and understand how internet and telecommunications intermediaries influence and regulate social interaction. The influence of technical architecture in constraining behaviour is often subtle or hidden from view (Lessig 2006). The internal decisionmaking processes of internet companies are frequently kept secret (Gillespie 2018), and the formal rules they apply are often vaguely defined (Suzor 2018). Most problematically, the operations of platforms are complex and interrelated systems that operate at a massive scale (Ananny and Crawford 2018), which means that focusing on individual controversies or shocks that are presented in the media may impair public understanding and ultimately reduce the accountability of platforms (Ananny and Gillespie 2016). Understanding these complex systems is made even more difficult because their architecture, policies, and cultural norms of use change rapidly over time (Burgess 2015).

There have been some important recent advances in transparency reporting – major platforms now report high level figures for copyright takedowns and terms of service enforcement, but these are not often presented in a way that enables detailed analysis. The data they provide are always selective and partial (Parsons 2017), and can sometimes do more to obscure understanding than aid it (Hansen and Flyverbom 2015). Where firms provide transparency reports, they predominantly provide summary statistics that cannot be used to evaluate the accuracy or consistency of decisions (Suzor et al. 2019).

As a key priority, if we care about how intermediaries govern their networks, we need to be able to measure their impact on human rights and work out how we can use this information to help protect them from external pressures that would limit our freedom and how we can hold them accountable for decisions they make on their own initiatives. Understanding the effects that technology companies have on our lives and identifying potential biases and other problems requires careful attention to the inputs and outputs of these systems and how they actually work in different social contexts (Noble 2018; Pasquale 2015; Sandvig et al. 2014). Analysis of this type will require large-scale access to data on individual decisions as well as deep qualitative analyses of the automated and human processes that platforms deploy internally. New methods and new collaborations are required to understand content moderation systems at scale, over time, and to be able to compare across platforms (Suzor et al. 2018a). Improving the public understanding of platform governance and beginning to hold platforms to account will also require better collaborations with journalists (Diakopoulos 2015) and civil society organisations that are able to drive real change (Parsons 2017; Maréchal 2015).

LARGE-SCALE INFRASTRUCTURE THAT ENABLES COMPARISON OVER TIME

This chapter presents the "Platform Governance Observatory": new research infrastructure that was designed to enable the systematic study of content moderation practices on major social media platforms. The core research question that made this infrastructure necessary was to understand, at a large scale, what social media content is moderated and by whom, how this compares between platforms, and how this changes over time. So far, this infrastructure enables the analysis of content removals of public posts on YouTube, Twitter, and Instagram. The infrastructure I created to support this exploration proceeds on a general design principle of building a random sample of public social media content, and then tests the availability of that sample at a later date. I try to assemble the initial sample as close as possible to the time a post is uploaded or made public, and test availability again between 8–20 days later. Some content has been tested outside of this range, because the iterative development process was initially not so strict as it is now. More recently, the data collection has also included retesting content that has been removed in previous tests, two months after it was initially collected, to identify posts that have been reinstated – potentially as the result of a successful appeal or copyright counter-notice. For the purposes of this chapter, however, I will report only on the content that (a) was captured within an hour of being posted; and (b) was tested again between 8 and 20 days later.

I selected the 8–20 day range as an appropriate approximate period to wait before testing availability based on qualitative interviews with social media users who had experienced removal of their content. Generally speaking, content on most social media platforms is at its most visible shortly after it is posted – from seconds, in a primarily date ordered feed like Twitter, to hours and days on a more heavily curated platform like Facebook. For content to be moderated through the flagging system, it is presumably more likely to be flagged when it is more visible, and it may take up to several days to be reviewed. Some of my interview participants who produce commercial content noted that they were most concerned about takedowns within the first days and weeks that they post their content, because this is when their content is most visible and when they earn the most advertising revenue. Two weeks is an approximate figure that reflects an estimate of a long enough time for content moderation processes to have made an initial decision.

Wherever possible, the infrastructure I developed uses Application Programming Interfaces (APIs) provided by social media platforms to build and test the samples. Unfortunately, the APIs of some platforms are not fully featured enough (they do not return as much information as is visible to a human using a web browser), or are not routinely made accessible for researchers. In these cases, the Observatory makes use of web scraping techniques to obtain publicly available data. The collection scripts are written in Python 3, and run on a Virtual Private Server provided by the Australian National eResearch Collaboration Tools and Resources (NECTAR) project. All tests are made from an IP address that is identifiable as originating from Australia.

YouTube

The YouTube scraper has been operational since December 2016, although it has been under continuous development and suffered significant periods of outages over 2017. It has been operating at greater consistency and throughput from February 2018. Since its launch, the YouTube scraper has collected 90 million videos that match the criteria (tested within 8–20 days of publication date). The initial sample of YouTube videos is derived from YouTube's search API ("list" endpoint).[1] The sample is

---

[1]   https://developers.google.com/youtube/v3/docs/search/list (last accessed 16 June 2020).

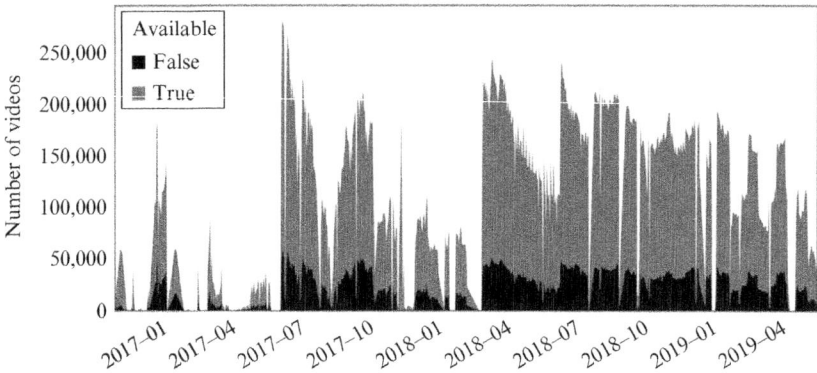

Note: Performance of the YouTube tester stabilised in March 2018.

Figure 8.1   Number of videos tested per day

built by requesting, every ten seconds, 50 videos that were published in a ten second window one minute prior. The metadata available through this API endpoint for each video is limited to time of publication, a unique identifier, and the title and description the uploader has given the video.

The YouTube search API returns only videos that have been made public, and the documentation for the list endpoint notes that it returns results in reverse chronological order. This means the sample is close to a random sample of videos posted to YouTube, although it may capture a slightly higher proportion of total videos posted during low-volume periods. We have no information about the daily or seasonal rhythm of videos uploaded to YouTube, so it is hard to estimate whether this is likely to make a strong difference.

Under live operating conditions and resource restraints, a median of approximately 123,000 videos per day are able to be collected and tested 10–20 days later (Figure 8.1). YouTube do not report accurate numbers about the number of videos they host, but they do report an average figure of 400 hours of video uploaded every minute – or 576,000 hours per day (YouTube 2015). Excluding videos that were no longer available, since March 2018, the Observatory tests a median of 43,742 hours of videos per day. Assuming that removed videos are close to average duration, the sample of videos tested by the Observatory could include as much as 10 per cent of total videos uploaded to YouTube.

Because each video is tested individually the second time, the metadata collected on the second test is more extensive than the information

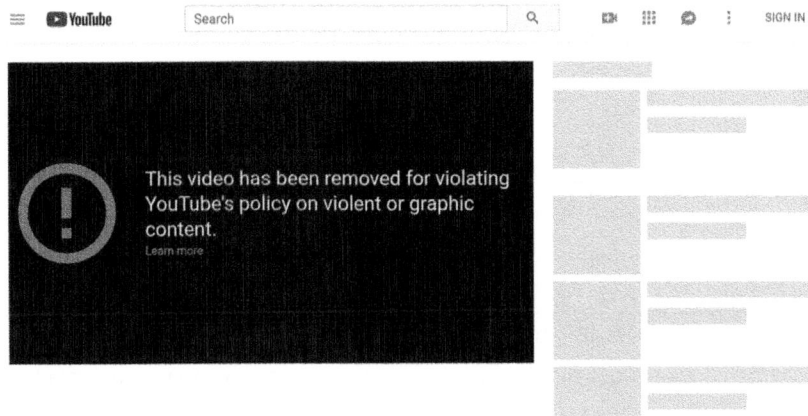

Figure 8.2   Example of the message provided by YouTube when a video has been removed

obtained through the initial bulk search API endpoint. For the purposes of interrogating content moderation, the most important of these extra fields are the content warnings on some videos and the explanations that accompany all videos that are no longer publicly available (see Figure 8.2). I summarise each of the standard explanations into 39 categories. These categories reflect the type of restriction on the video – whether it has been removed completely, whether the user's account has been closed, whether the video is presumably still stored but not available to view, whether it has been geoblocked and is not available in Australia, or whether it has been removed. The categorisations also account for, where possible, the reason that YouTube gave in each instance – including copyright violations, terms of service (ToS) violations, legal complaints, technical problems, or the user's choice to remove the video or make it private (see Figure 8.3).

Overall, the dataset reveals surprising and previously unknown information about the scale of YouTube's content moderation undertaking. The headline figures are interesting: of 90 million YouTube videos tested 8–20 days after they were published, approximately 6.7 per cent are not available because of some form of content moderation. A further 14.9 per cent are not available as a result of the user's choice. Approximately 1 per cent of videos are not available because of alleged copyright infringement – either as a result of detection and blocking by YouTube's ContentID matching algorithm (0.8 per cent), as a result of a copyright takedown or similar complaint (0.1 per cent), or because the user's account has been closed after receiving multiple copyright strikes (0.2 per

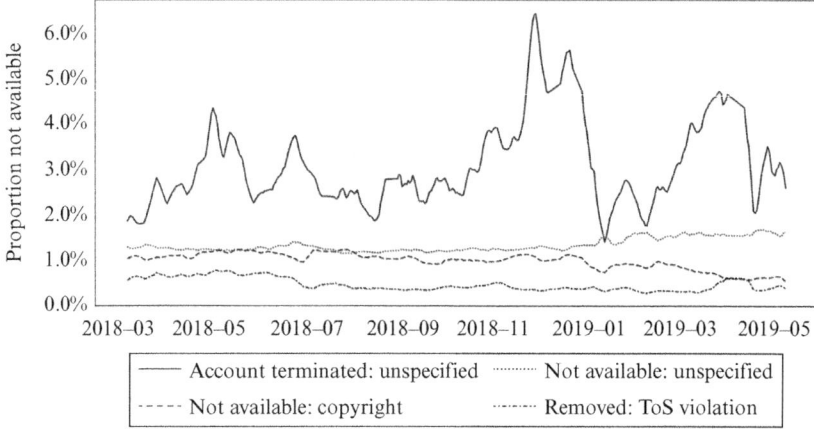

Note: This chart shows removed videos, excluding videos removed by the uploader.

Figure 8.3   *Proportion of videos not available per day since 1 March 2018 (seven-day moving average).*

cent) (note that these figures also include videos that were geoblocked in Australia). Approximately 0.5 per cent of videos are removed for violating some aspect of YouTube's terms of service or community guidelines, and another 1.1 per cent were removed with no reason specified. Another 3.6 per cent of videos tested were not available because their account has been terminated with no public reason provided, excluding accounts terminated as a result of multiple strikes of copyright infringement, and accounts that were closed by the users themselves. Table 8.1 provides a summary of the availability of videos collected and tested.

Content moderation

Of the three social media platforms tested, YouTube provides the most detailed explanations about individual videos that have been removed. It presents users with a digital "tombstone," as Alex Feerst (2018) calls it, that provides an informative message at the specific URL for each video that is not available to the viewer. Google has been an industry leader on transparency in content moderation (Bankston et al. n.d.) and should be commended for the detailed information that it sometimes makes available when videos are removed from YouTube. Unfortunately, while the technical architecture is in place to report detailed reasons when a video has been removed as a result of a breach of the terms of service or community guidelines, a specific message does not appear to be consistently recorded in YouTube's moderation workflows. The most prevalent error

Table 8.1   *Short categorisation of availability of videos (90,492,976 total videos)*

Availability	Number of videos	Proportion
Available	70,849,377	0.783
Not available: user	13,516,453	0.149
Account terminated	3,278,032	0.036
Not available (no further information)	1,003,196	0.011
Not available: copyright	849,617	0.009
Removed: ToS violation	474,333	0.005
Content warning	306,127	0.003
Geoblocked	164,924	0.002
Not available: technical	50,835	0.001
Not available: legal complaint	45	0.000
Geoblocked: legal complaint	30	0.000
Requires payment	7	0.000

Note: A full summary of all categories is available in Appendix Table 8A.1.

messages are still vague, although more specific error messages are sometimes identifiable. So, for example, three of the four most prevalent error messages, not including videos removed by users themselves, are generic messages: "this video is no longer available because the YouTube account associated with this video has been terminated," "this video is not available," "this video has been removed for violating YouTube's terms of service" (including minor variations on these messages as they change slightly over time). More detailed error messages – messages that include the type of ToS violation or legal request, as detailed in Table 8A.1 – are comparatively rare (see Figure 8.4). It appears that YouTube has only partially included more detailed messages as part of its moderation work-flows. YouTube provides no detail when it closes a user's account under its terms of service or community guidelines, even though account closures are the most common reason that videos are not available when tested (3.6 per cent of all videos).

Of the small proportion of videos that have been removed that do present an explanation to the public viewer, YouTube breaks down six categories of rule violations: harassment and bullying, harmful or danger-ous content, hate speech, nudity or sexual content, violent or graphic content, and spam, deceptive practices, and scams. Given the relatively much higher proportion of content that is removed without a public reason, however, it remains difficult to make use of these more granular categorisations.

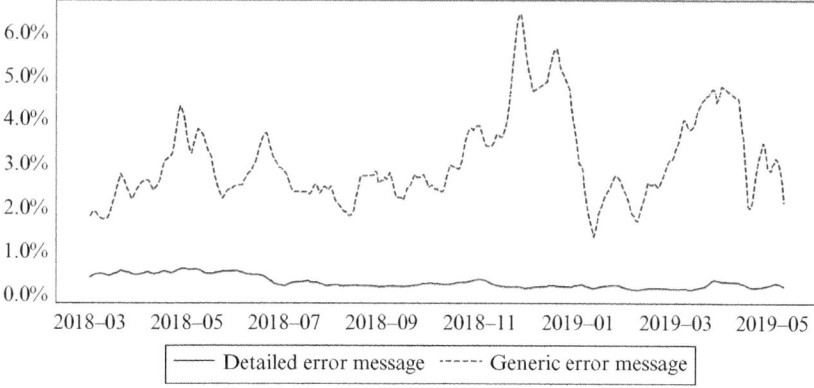

Figure 8.4   *Proportion of videos removed for rule violations by day (seven-
day moving average)*

Copyright removals

The YouTube testing infrastructure allows us to identify with some precision how different tools are used to enforce copyright on the platform.
YouTube's copyright error messages are almost always quite detailed, in
that they provide the name of the copyright owner that requested a video
be blocked or geoblocked. Figure 8.5 shows how the use of different types
of copyright enforcement on YouTube has changed in recent years. Of
the approximately 1 per cent of videos that are no longer available for
copyright reasons, the most common reason are videos that are "blocked"
on copyright grounds – which we assume means that they are videos automatically detected through YouTube's ContentID system that one or more
of the copyright owners have chosen to block, rather than "monetize" (run
advertisements against) or "track" (do nothing, but gain access to the
video's analytics) (Google 2016). A sizeable proportion – approximately
0.2 per cent – are geoblocked in Australia. On a quick qualitative analysis,
many of these videos appear to include copyright music originating
from Korea and Japan, as well as popular US television shows whose
distribution rights in Australia are licensed to the local cable network.

This infrastructure promises to be particularly useful for follow-up
qualitative analysis to improve our understanding of the types of content
that are blocked as a result of copyright. The operation of YouTube's
ContentID system has been opaque, and subject to major criticism from
both YouTube content creators and copyright owners. Unfortunately,
there is no ability to identify when a video has been monetised by a

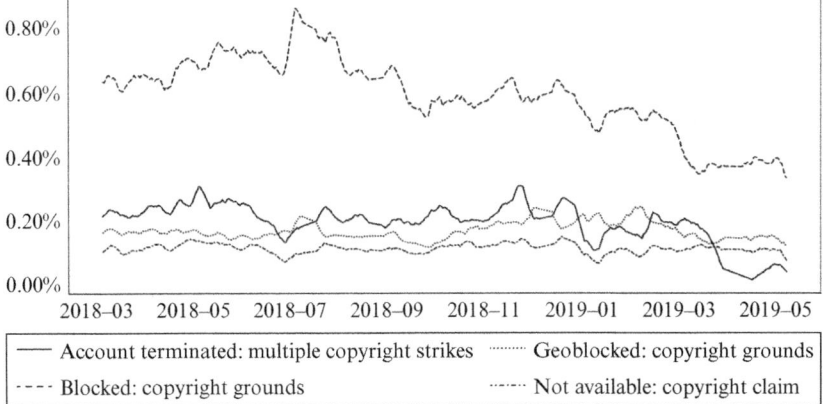

Figure 8.5   Proportion of videos removed on the basis of alleged copyright infringement by day since 1 March 2018 (seven-day moving average)

copyright owner, but this infrastructure does allow new research to be undertaken to identify the factors that influence copyright owners to make a choice to block content. Similarly, it provides insight into how the DMCA Notice and Takedown system, and its regional counterparts, are operating on YouTube. Google reports DMCA notices that it receives to the Lumen database, but does not report DMCA notices sent to YouTube. The error messages reported by YouTube and collected by this infrastructure reveal both the type of complaint and the name of the copyright owner(s) responsible for making the complaint. This information is available at the level of individual videos, not just aggregate statistics, which also opens up the possibility of using metadata of blocked videos to explore patterns in choices to block content on YouTube (actual video content is not collected). The selective enforcement of copyright is an important concern, particularly for fears that copyright owners may disproportionately block critical or political speech (Tehranian 2007; Wu 2007).

Twitter

The Twitter component of the Observatory has been running stably since January 2018. It has tested the availability of 833 million tweets to date since then. The Twitter tester follows the same logic as the YouTube tester: it collects a random sample of tweets as close as possible to the time they are posted, and tests those tweets approximately 14 days later. The initial sample of tweets is collected from Twitter's "statuses/sample"

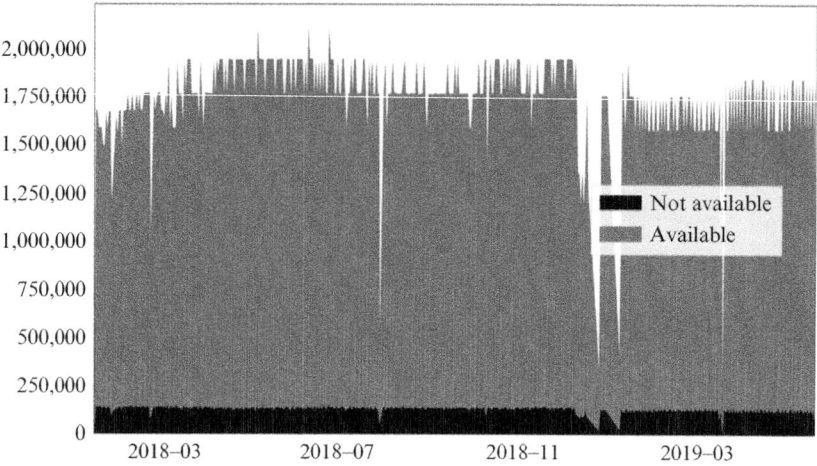

Figure 8.6   Number of tweets tested per day

API endpoint, which Twitter describes as "a small random sample of all public statuses." While there are concerns about the sampling mechanism that Twitter uses to reduce the volume on some of its other public API endpoints, the sample API appears to approximate a random sample of real-time Twitter data (Morstatter et al. 2014). The second test then uses Twitter's "statuses/lookup" API endpoint to rehydrate tweets, recording which tweets are no longer available and which tweets have been geoblocked in certain regions. Each missing tweet is individually queried to find the reason it has been removed. We discard any tweets that are missing because the user has made their account private to respect their preferences. The throughput of the two passes, given Twitter's rate limits, is a total of 1.8 million tweets tested per day. Figure 8.6 shows relatively stable performance over time, with some periods of severe outage.

The error results that Twitter returns when it moderates content are, compared to YouTube, very basic. When Twitter moderates content, it takes action either at the tweet or account level (Twitter n.d.). When Twitter makes a decision to remove an individual tweet, it typically applies a sanction to the user's account which will only be lifted after the user deletes the offending tweet or wins an appeal. For this reason, we are unable to distinguish cases where tweets are deleted because they violate Twitter's rules from tweets that are deleted by the user for other reasons. Accordingly, we only have three main error messages from Twitter: either a given tweet has been deleted, a user's account suspended, or a user's account deleted or otherwise made unavailable (see Appendix Table 8A.2).

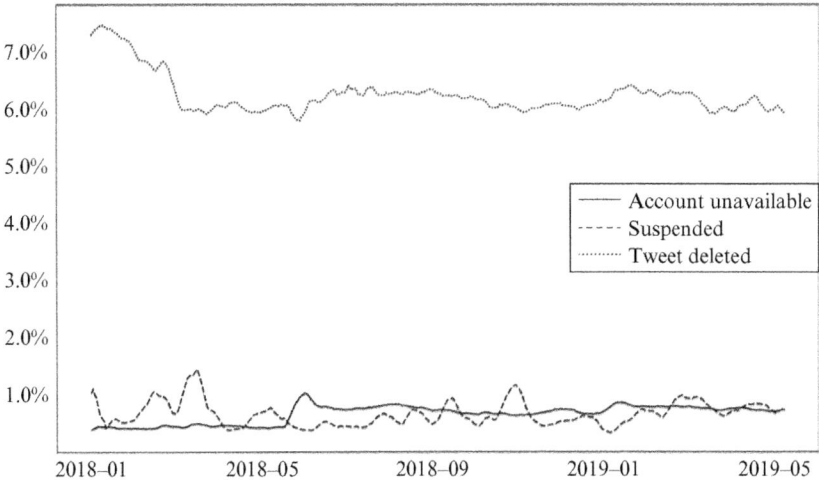

Figure 8.7   Proportion of tweets removed per day by error type

The most common error is that a tweet has been deleted, accounting for 6.30 per cent of all tweets sampled. Twitter provides a message when a user has been suspended (0.70 per cent), but does not explain which rule was broken. Twitter also reports an error when the user's account has been closed or made unavailable (0.69 per cent of our sample). There are two other error messages that indicate the tweet has been hidden by Twitter, but they are almost never visible in our data. Figure 8.7 shows the prevalence of the most common error types over time.

Internally, Twitter keeps better information about why they take action to moderate tweets or suspend accounts. Its most recent transparency report has started to provide aggregate numbers of accounts against which they have taken some enforcement action, broken down into six categories: "abuse, child sexual exploitation (CSE), hateful conduct, private information, sensitive media, and violent threats" (Twitter 2018). It could provide greater transparency by making this information visible on individual tweet pages and user accounts, like YouTube does, but chooses not to.

Instagram

The Observatory tracks several samples of public content from Instagram, but this is one of the more difficult platforms to monitor. One of the most visible – and controversial – mechanisms that Instagram uses to moderate content is to block entire hashtags. Users can add hashtags to their individual posts, and hashtags serve a discursive function as well as a semiotic device through which posts are made visible to other users on the platform (Zappavigna 2015). Blocking entire hashtags can have the effect of making certain types of content harder to find, since hashtags are the predominant method of searching for content from Instagram users that a person is not already following.

In order to track which hashtags are blocked on Instagram, we first developed a super-set of hashtags that had been reported as blocked by news outlets. We supplemented this list with search results on a major search engine for the error messages that Instagram displays when it blocks a hashtag or hides it behind an interstitial content warning. This manual selection generated a list of 1449 hashtags that we checked every day for their availability. In order to identify other tags that might be blocked, every week, we also test 5000 hashtags that have been most frequently used with posts that use hashtags that have previously been blocked in our sample. We test these 5000 posts for up to a month, and do not test them again for at least six months if they have not been blocked in that time. We are then left with a growing sample of hashtags that have been blocked at least once in the last six months, and a rolling sample of 5000 tags that frequently co-occur with those tags. This sampling strategy, taking into account rate limitations in place, currently provides a sample of approximately 12,000 tags tested each day from March 2018. Since inception, the system has identified approximately 12,600 hashtags that have been blocked by Instagram at least once – far more than has ever been reported in any manually compiled list. The information available for each tag includes the title, ID (identifier), and post time for each of the "top posts" and "new posts" displayed by Instagram (usually 9 "top posts" and a median of 57 and up to 72 "new posts").

This hashtag-based sample is not a random sample of hashtags, so should not be used to estimate the total number or proportion of blocked hashtags on Instagram. Because hashtags are practically unlimited in number but vary greatly in popularity, a random sample is not particularly useful for our purposes. More importantly, the hashtag-based sample provides a method to identify patterns in the types of hashtags that are blocked and the methods that Instagram uses to enforce those blocks.

Instagram moderates hashtags in four different ways. First, some tags are blocked using a "hard" block approach; when a user visits these tags in a web browser, they encounter an HTTP 404 error message: "Sorry, this page isn't available." Second, for some tags and periods, Instagram only displays a selection of "top posts" of a hashtag, and hides new posts with a message like "Recent posts from [hashtag] are currently hidden because the community has reported some content that may not meet Instagram's community guidelines." Third, Instagram displays an interstitial "content warning" for tags related to eating disorders, self-harm, the sale of firearms, animal abuse, and opiod or substance abuse, warning users and, in some cases, providing links to third-party help-lines for people at risk. Finally, Instagram also at times chooses to silently block a hashtag by presenting a (false) statement that there are "No posts yet" on the tag. One of the unique features of the Observatory infrastructure is that it can detect these silent types of blocks, which appear for brief periods on tags that are otherwise available.

Instagram's approach to hashtag moderation appears to be an irregular "patchwork" (Duguay et al. 2018). Their little easily discernible pattern that explains why it chooses some forms of blocking over others, and the status of hashtags, sometimes changes frequently over time. The Observatory data reveals that hashtag-level blocking is highly inconsistent, and appears to reflect reactions to some of the controversies that Instagram has faced over the years (Gillespie 2018). As a small example, we can examine some of the tags associated with highly controversial "thinspiration" content (see Figure 8.8). Over many years, internet companies have been criticised in the media for allowing content that encourages eating disorders, but also for blocking content in a way that restricts the ability of vulnerable people to find community and support

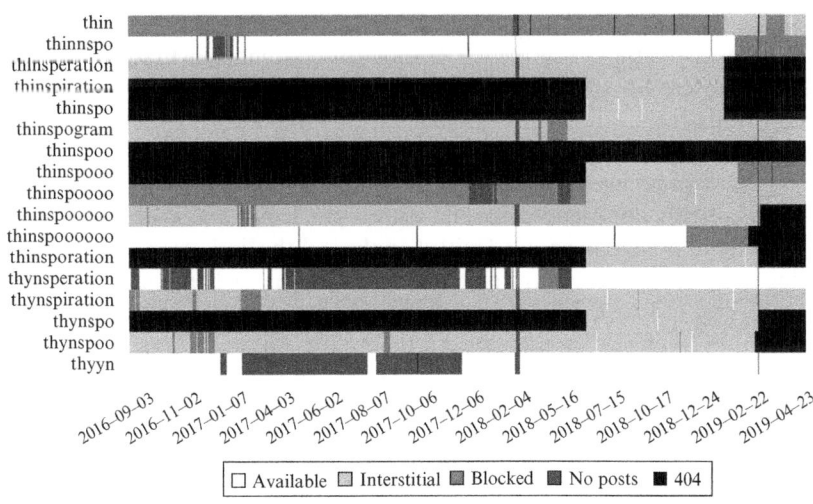

Figure 8.8   A subset of "thinspiration" hashtags, showing moderation status by day

(Gerrard 2018). Figure 8.8 shows how Instagram applies different blocking techniques to different "thinspiration" tags, and highlights the variability in its approach over time.

These tags are all variations on spelling of "thin" and "thinspiration." Some of these tags are consistently blocked with a "404" error, at least until June 2018, when Instagram decided to instead use an interstitial (except one tag, "#thinspoo," which it continues to block with a 404 error). It seems that at least Instagram became more consistent at this time, moving most "thinspiration" tags to an interstitial content warning. Until this date, however, the variability in tag availability is interesting and telling. #thin has been blocked for most of the time we have been tracking it, except for a brief period where it reported "no posts" and several brief periods of 404 errors. Other tags, possibly less utilised – like "thinnspo," "thynsperation," and "thyyn" – report "no posts" with comparatively high frequency and sometimes for extended periods of time. This is a small sample of tags, but it demonstrates the utility of the Observatory infrastructure for tracking policy changes over time, particularly when platforms provide little public detail about their approaches to moderation.

In addition to monitoring hashtags, the Observatory also monitors a sample of posts. Unlike YouTube and Twitter, Instagram provides no public API that can be used to build a random sample of posts. The Observatory builds post-level samples in two ways: by tracking new posts to a small manually selected set of hashtags, and by collecting a larger set of posts that have been posted to Twitter. Neither of these are perfect mechanisms to build samples of Instagram content. Hashtags are not a reliable descriptor of content – Instagram users often use tags selectively and discursively, and will also manage the visibility of their posts by not tagging their content (Gerrard 2018). Nevertheless, hashtag-based sampling can be useful for identifying and studying groups of posts that users explicitly choose to associate with a particular set of hashtags, and this body of posts can enable fruitful analysis if the limitations of the sampling method are carefully considered (Witt et al. 2019). Sampling from Twitter, by contrast, only identifies Instagram posts that are cross-posted to Twitter – either by the posters themselves or by others. Instagram and other third-party tools make it easy for users to cross-post to other networks, and many people do, but we cannot assume that this sample is random.

Like other components of the Observatory, the Instagram post sample checks posts two weeks after they were first collected. In this second check, we focus only on posts that were collected by the Observatory within an hour of being posted – we exclude older posts that are linked to on Twitter.

This component of the Observatory has been running reliably since 1 October 2018, and has collected 3.7 million posts to date (median 25,800 posts per day). Instagram provides no public information about whether it has moderated a post – a post is either available or returns a 404 error. Approximately 3.4 per cent of posts in the Twitter sample are unavailable two weeks after testing.

DISCUSSION

This large-scale data collection infrastructure enables types of investigation that were previously not possible. The view over time is particularly interesting, because platforms are not static objects. Their architecture and affordances, their users and cultural norms, their policies and procedures all change over time (Burgess 2015). As this infrastructure continues to collect information, it should be able to enable scholars to undertake longitudinal analysis of a form not previously possible. For legal scholars interested in the impact of internet regulation, both formal and informal, this is particularly interesting. Twitter, for example, has been under pressure for many years to improve the way that it handles abuse on its network. In 2015, then-CEO Dick Costolo admitted that the company "[sucks] at dealing with abuse and trolls on the platform and we've sucked at it for years," (Tiku and Newton 2015) promising to do better. Researchers and advocates still complain that Twitter has been largely ineffective in this ongoing work (Amnesty International 2018a, 2018b). This infrastructure enables analysis of how practices change over time and provides a useful supplement to annual rankings reports from organisations like Ranking Digital Rights' Corporate Transparency Index (Ranking Digital Rights 2018) and Electronic Frontier Foundation's "Who Has Your Back" (Gebhart 2018) that push internet and telecommunications intermediaries to continuously improve their policies. It also enables detailed analysis of the practical impact of legal change – such as the global and territorial impact of intermediary liability rules, like Germany's Network Enforcement Law 2017 (NetzDG)[2] and the proposed new copyright enforcement obligations in the European Union's Copyright Directive.[3]

---

[2] Gesetz zur Verbesserung der Rechtsdurchsetzung in sozialen Netzwerken (1 September 2017) (Germany), English translation at https://www.bmjv.de/SharedDocs/Gesetzgebungsverfahren/Dokumente/NetzDG_engl.pdf (last accessed 23 June 2020).
[3] Directive (EU) 2019/790 of the European Parliament and of the Council of

The Observatory infrastructure also allows useful and potentially surprising new analysis of the "long tail" of content moderation. Some of the more prominent trends are visible in transparency reports and news reporting, but a systematic random sample also makes relatively infrequent takedowns available for analysis. This allows scholars to investigate the impact of legal rules which differ between jurisdictions – as can be seen, for example, in the relatively very small number of takedowns identified in YouTube for trademark infringement, defamation, bullying content, and hate speech.

The datasets provided by the Observatory enable a range of methodological approaches for follow-up research. Computational tools like topic modelling can be developed to discover clusters of content removals at a large scale, and study patterns of change over time. Machine learning classifiers can be trained to identify particular categories of content in order to examine removal rates – like a machine learning classifier we are building to track removal rates of abuse (Bashar et al. 2018). The Observatory also enables scholars to use statistical methods to study the factors that influence content removals across multiple networks, similar to groundbreaking work undertaken on smaller datasets on, for example, Chinese censorship of Sina Weibo (Zeng et al. 2017) and copyright takedowns on YouTube (Erickson and Kretschmer 2018).

The Observatory datasets and associated computational tools are most useful when combined with deep qualitative work that is able to understand the content and context of social media posts. For example, we have been able to measure takedown rates (false positives and false negatives) on identified categories of Instagram content, investigating allegations of bias relating to gender and body shape (Witt et al. 2019). Our ongoing work investigates how partially automated notice-and-takedown systems are operating to regulate user-generated content, and how hate speech rules around the world impact on both harmful speech and counterspeech.

There are important limitations and opportunities to improve the Observatory's data collection infrastructure. Most obviously, our infrastructure only tracks publicly available content – it is not able to collect information about posts to Facebook, for example. This is unlikely to change in the near future, especially since Facebook continues to move to limit access to researchers (Bruns 2018). With further funding for additional development, however, it might be possible to extend data collection to other public social media platforms, including Reddit, Tumblr,

---

17 April 2019 on copyright and related rights in the Digital Single Market and amending Directives 96/9/EC and 2001/29/EC, Article 17.

Medium, and others. Another core limitation lies in the ongoing refusal of platforms to provide good error messages when they remove content. There are ongoing advocacy efforts to request more granular and accurate information from public platforms – like the "Santa Clara Principles on Transparency and Accountability in Content Moderation" (2018) – but so far these have only been partially successful. Future development work will also aim to better track information about licensed content, advertising, and the operation of search and recommendation systems on platforms, where possible.

One of the core challenges to be addressed in the immediate future is to identify how data sharing between researchers can be improved. It is our hope that this Observatory will be useful to a broader community of scholars studying the governance of digital media. Importantly, however, there are important privacy concerns, both ethical and legal, that need to be carefully considered before this data can be made broadly available. The European Union's General Data Protection Regulation (GDPR),[4] most prominently, imposes obligations on the large-scale collection, processing, and transmission of data. While the GDPR has exceptions for research use, it will be important to develop data sharing protocols that adequately protect the privacy interests of people making public social media posts. Similarly, while the Observatory deals with publicly accessible data, there are ethical concerns about making personal information more visible than the original author intended (Markham and Buchanan 2012). In our work, we strive not to identify ordinary users when we cannot be confident that they intended or should have expected to reach a large audience, even though their selected privacy settings technically allow their posts to be publicly visible. In sharing research data that includes personal information, it will be necessary to carefully consider mechanisms to ensure that downstream access and use follow appropriate legal and ethical safeguards.

CONCLUSION

The Platform Governance Observatory provides an important contribution to research infrastructure that allows scholars to study the curation of

---

[4] Regulation (EU) 2016/679 of the European Parliament and of the Council of 27 April 2016 on the protection of natural persons with regard to the processing of personal data and on the free movement of such data, and repealing Directive 95/46/EC (General Data Protection Regulation), 2016 O.J. (L 119) 1.

internet content on major social media platforms. The infrastructure enables large-scale, longitudinal analysis of the availability of user-generated content on some of the most significant online platforms. There are key limitations about the types and quality of information that are available, but the Observatory presents a major improvement in data collection for scholars interested in how major internet intermediaries regulate online content. Its key strengths are the scale of data collection, the ability to monitor change over time, and the ability to monitor content removal decisions that platforms have generally sought to obscure.

This infrastructure provides a mechanism to monitor not just what platforms themselves are doing to shape our digital media environments, but how they are influenced by governments, private actors, and legal rules around the world. Because internet intermediaries are the focal points of control on the internet (Goldsmith and Wu 2006), they are subject to a great deal of pressure from many different actors to regulate user behaviour – often in conflicting ways. The practices of platforms and those who would influence them are increasingly controversial and are quickly becoming the subject of major potential policy intervention. Our hope is that this infrastructure can provide a mechanism to enable new research that can better inform both scholarly and public understanding of how digital social spaces are mediated. This work can hopefully improve accountability of platforms themselves, as well as informing the ongoing evidence-based development of intermediary liability law and telecommunications policy.

REFERENCES

Amnesty International. 2018a. *Toxic Twitter: A Toxic Place for Women*. Accessed 15 June 2020 at https://www.amnesty.org/en/latest/research/2018/03/online-violence-against-women-chapter-1/.
Amnesty International. 2018b. *Troll Patrol Findings*. Accessed 15 June 2020 at https://decoders.amnesty.org/projects/troll-patrol/findings.
Ananny, Mike, and Kate Crawford. 2018. "Seeing without Knowing: Limitations of the Transparency Ideal and Its Application to Algorithmic Accountability." *New Media & Society* 20 (3): 973–89. https://doi.org/10.1177/1461444816676645.
Ananny, Mike, and Tarleton Gillespie. 2016. "Public Platforms: Beyond the Cycle of Shocks and Exceptions." Paper presented at The Platform Society conference, Oxford, 22–3 September 2016. Accessed 15 June 2020 at http://blogs.oii.ox.ac.uk/ipp-conference/2016/programme-2016/track-b-governance/platform-studies/tarleton-gillespie-mike-ananny.html.
Bankston, Kevin, Ross Schulman, and Liz Woolery. n.d. "Case Study #3: Transparency Reporting." New America. Accessed 16 January 2018 at https://www.newamerica.org/in-depth/getting-internet-companies-do-right-thing/case-study-3-transparency-reporting/.

Bashar, Md Abul, Richi Nayak, Nicolas P. Suzor, and Bridget Weir. 2018. "Misogynistic Tweet Detection: Modelling CNN with Small Datasets." Conference paper. In R. Islam et al., eds, *Data Mining: AusDM 2018 – Communications in Computer and Information Science*, vol 996: 3–16. Bathurst, NSW: Springer.

Brown, Ian, and Christopher T. Marsden, eds. 2013. *Regulating Code Good Governance and Better Regulation in the Information Age.* Cambridge: MIT Press.

Bruns, Axel. 2018. "Facebook Shuts the Gate after the Horse Has Bolted, and Hurts Real Research in the Process." *Internet Policy Review.* 25 April 2018. Accessed 15 June 2020 at https://policyreview.info/articles/news/facebook-shu ts-gate-after-horse-has-bolted-and-hurts-real-research-process/786.

Burgess, Jean. 2015. "From 'Broadcast Yourself' to 'Follow Your Interests': Making over Social Media." *International Journal of Cultural Studies* 18 (3): 281–5.

Caplan, Robyn, Lauren Hanson, and Joan Donovan. 2018. "Dead Reckoning: Navigating Content Moderation after 'Fake News.'" Data & Society Research Institute. Accessed 15 June 2020 at https://datasociety.net/pubs/oh/DataAndSoci ety_Dead_Reckoning_2018.pdf.

Citron, Danielle Keats. 2014. *Hate Crimes in Cyberspace.* Cambridge, Massachusetts; London, England: Harvard University Press.

DeNardis, Laura. 2014. *The Global War for Internet Governance.* New Haven: Yale University Press.

Diakopoulos, Nicholas. 2015. "Algorithmic Accountability: Journalistic Investigation of Computational Power Structures." *Digital Journalism* 3 (3): 398–415.

Duguay, Stefanie, Jean Burgess, and Nicolas P. Suzor. 2018. "Queer Women's Experiences of Patchwork Platform Governance on Tinder, Instagram, and Vine." *Convergence*, June, 1354856518781530. https://doi.org/10.1177/1354856518781530.

Elkin-Koren, Niva, and Eldar Haber. 2016. "Governance by Proxy: Cyber Challenges to Civil Liberties." *Brooklyn Law Review* 82 (1): 105–62.

Erickson, Kristofer, and Martin Kretschmer. 2018. "'This Video Is Unavailable': Analyzing Copyright Takedown of User-Generated Content on YouTube." JIPITEC 9 (1). Accessed 15 June 2020 at http://www.jipitec.eu/issues/jipitec-9-1-2 018/4680.

Feerst, Alex. 2018. "Implementing Transparency about Content Moderation." Techdirt. Accessed 15 June 2020 at https://www.techdirt.com/articles/201801 31/22182339132/implementing-transparency-about-content-moderation.shtml.

Gebhart, Gennie. 2018. "Who Has Your Back? Censorship Edition 2018." Electronic Frontier Foundation. 31 May. Accessed 15 June 2020 at https://www. eff.org/who-has-your-back-2018.

Gerrard, Ysabel. 2018. "Beyond the Hashtag: Circumventing Content Moderation on Social Media." *New Media & Society* 20 (12): 4492–511. Accessed 15 June 2020 at https://doi.org/10.1177/1461444818776611.

Gillespie, Tarleton. 2018. *Custodians of the Internet: Platforms, Content Moderation, and the Hidden Decisions That Shape Social Media.* 1st ed. New Haven, CT: Yale University Press.

Goldsmith, Jack, and Tim Wu. 2006. *Who Controls the Internet? Illusions of a Borderless World.* Cary: Oxford University Press.

Google. 2016. *How Content ID Works.* YouTube Help. Accessed 15 June 2020 at https://support.google.com/youtube/answer/2797370?hl=en.

Hansen, Hans Krause, and Mikkel Flyverbom. 2015. "The Politics of Transparency and the Calibration of Knowledge in the Digital Age." *Organization* 22 (6): 872–89. Accessed 15 June 2020 at https://doi.org/10.1177/1350508414522315.

Lessig, Lawrence. 2006. *Code*. Version 2.0. New York: Basic Books.

MacKinnon. 2012. *Consent of the Networked: The Worldwide Struggle for Internet Freedom*. New York: Basic Books.

Mansell, Robin. 2012. *Imagining the Internet Communication, Innovation, and Governance*. Oxford: OUP Oxford.

Maréchal, Nathalie. 2015. "Ranking Digital Rights: Human Rights, the Internet and the Fifth Estate." *International Journal of Communication* 9 (10): 3440–49.

Markham, Annette, and Elizabeth Buchanan. 2012. "Ethical Decision-Making and Internet Research." AoIR Ethics Working Committee. Accessed 15 June 2020 at http://aoir.org/reports/ethics2.pdf.

Marwick, Alice E., and Rebecca Lewis. 2017. "Media Manipulation and Disinformation Online." Data & Society Research Institute. Accessed 15 June 2020 at https://datasociety.net/output/media-manipulation-and-disinfo-online/.

Morstatter, Fred, Jürgen Pfeffer, and Huan Liu. 2014. "When Is It Biased? Assessing the Representativeness of Twitter's Streaming API." In Chin-Wan Chung et al., eds, *Proceedings of the 23rd International Conference on World Wide Web*, 555–6. New York: Association for Computing Machinery.

Noble, Safiya Umoja. 2018. *Algorithms of Oppression: How Search Engines Reinforce Racism*. New York: New York University Press.

Parsons, Christopher. 2017. "The (In)Effectiveness of Voluntarily Produced Transparency Reports." *Business & Society* 8 (1): 103–31. https://doi.org/10.1177/0007650317717957.

Pasquale, Frank. 2015. *The Black Box Society*. Cambridge, Mass.: Harvard University Press.

Ranking Digital Rights. 2018. *2018 Corporate Accountability Index*. Accessed 15 June 2020 at https://rankingdigitalrights.org/index2018/.

Sandvig, Christian, Kevin Hamilton, Karrie Karahalios, and Cedric Langbort. 2014. "Auditing Algorithms: Research Methods for Detecting Discrimination on Internet Platforms." Conference paper. In *Data and Discrimination: Converting Critical Concerns into Productive Inquiry*, 1–23. Seattle, WA, USA. Accessed 15 June 2020 at http://www-personal.umich.edu/~csandvig/research/Auditing%20Algorithms%20--%20Sandvig%20--%20ICA%202014%20Data%20and%20Discrimination%20Preconference.pdf.

"Santa Clara Principles on Transparency and Accountability in Content Moderation." 2018. 7 May. Accessed 15 June 2020 at https://santaclaraprinciples.org/.

Suzor, Nicolas P. 2018. "Digital Constitutionalism: Using the Rule of Law to Evaluate the Legitimacy of Governance by Platforms." *Social Media + Society* 4 (3): 1–11. https://doi.org/10.1177/2056305118787812.

Suzor, Nicolas P. 2019. *Lawless: The Secret Rules That Govern Our Digital Lives*. Cambridge, United Kingdom; New York, NY: Cambridge University Press.

Suzor, Nicolas P., Sarah Myers West, Andrew Quodling, and Jillian York. 2019. "What Do We Mean When We Talk about Transparency? Toward Meaningful Transparency in Commercial Content Moderation." *International Journal of Communication* 13 (March): 1526–43.

Suzor, Nicolas P., Tess Van Geelen, and Sarah Myers West. 2018a. "Evaluating the Legitimacy of Platform Governance: A Review of Research and a Shared

Research Agenda." *International Communication Gazette* 80 (4): 385–400. https://doi.org/10.1177/1748048518757142.

Suzor, Nicolas P., Molly Dragiewicz, Bridget Harris, Rosalie Gillett, Jean Burgess, and Tess Van Geelen. 2018b. "Human Rights by Design: The Responsibilities of Social Media Platforms to Address Gender-Based Violence Online." *Policy & Internet* 11 (1): 84–103. https://doi.org/10.1002/poi3.185.

Tehranian, John. 2007. "Infringement Nation: Copyright Reform and the Law/ Norm Gap." Utah L. Rev. [2007] 3: 537–50.

Tiku, Nitasha, and Casey Newton. 2015. "Twitter CEO: 'We Suck at Dealing with Abuse.'" The Verge. 5 February. Accessed 15 June 2020 at http://www.thever ge.com/2015/2/4/7982099/twitter-ceo-sent-memo-taking-personal-responsibili ty-for-the.

Twitter. 2018. *Twitter Rules Enforcement, January to June 2018*. Accessed 15 June 2020 at https://transparency.twitter.com/en/twitter-rules-enforcement.html.

Twitter. n.d. *Our Range of Enforcement Options*. Twitter Help Center. Accessed 30 December at https://help.twitter.com/en/rules-and-policies/enforcement-op tions.

Witt, Alice, Nicolas P. Suzor, and Anna Huggins. 2019. "The Rule of Law on Instagram: An Evaluation of the Moderation of Images Depicting Women's Bodies." *University of New South Wales Law Journal* 42 (2): 557–96.

Wu, T. 2007. "Tolerated Use." Colum. JL & Arts 31 (4): 617–35.

YouTube. 2015. *Statistics*. 16 September. Accessed 15 June 2020 at https://web. archive.org/web/20150916171036/http://www.youtube.com:80/yt/press/statis tics.html.

Zappavigna, Michele. 2015. "Searchable Talk: The Linguistic Functions of Hashtags." *Social Semiotics* 25 (3): 274–91. https://doi.org/10.1080/10350330.2 014.996948.

Zeng, Jing, Chung-hong Chan, and King-wa Fu. 2017. "How Social Media Construct 'Truth' around Crisis Events: Weibo's Rumor Management Strategies after the 2015 Tianjin Blasts." *Policy & Internet* 9 (3): 297–320.

APPENDIX

Table 8A.1   YouTube videos removed in sample, from March 2018

Categorisation	Short categorisation	Number of videos	Proportion
Available	Available	70,849,377	0.783
Removed: user	Not available: user	13,295,410	0.147
Account terminated: unspecified	Account terminated	3,278,032	0.036
Not available: unspecified	Not available	963,300	0.011
Blocked: copyright grounds	Not available: copyright	531,783	0.006
Removed: ToS violation	Removed: ToS violation	390,809	0.004
Content warning	Content warning	305,908	0.003
Account terminated: closed by user	Not available: user	219,404	0.002
Account terminated: multiple copyright strikes	Not available: copyright	216,003	0.002
Geoblocked: copyright grounds	Geoblocked	149,849	0.002
Not available: copyright claim	Not available: copyright	101,381	0.001
Not available: duplicate	Not available: technical	49,546	0.001
Not available: unspecified (live stream)	Not available	39,896	0.000
Removed: community guidelines	Removed: ToS violation	34,738	0.000
Removed: spam, deceptive practices, scams	Removed: ToS violation	17,918	0.000
Removed: nudity or sexual	Removed: ToS violation	16,876	0.000
Geoblocked	Geoblocked	15,041	0.000
Removed: violent or graphic	Removed: ToS violation	8509	0.000
Removed: harassment and bullying	Removed: ToS violation	2741	0.000
Removed: harmful or dangerous	Removed: ToS violation	1693	0.000
Not available: user	Not available: user	1444	0.000
Technical: not available on this device	Not available: technical	1196	0.000
Removed: hate speech	Removed: ToS violation	1049	0.000
Not available: copyright content	Not available: copyright	450	0.000
Content warning: inappropriate or offensive	Content warning	218	0.000
Not available: live event ended	Not available: user	194	0.000
Not available: too long	Not available: technical	93	0.000
Geoblocked: legal complaint	Geoblocked: legal complaint	26	0.000
Removed: counterfeit	Not available: legal complaint	24	0.000
Geoblocked: unspecified	Geoblocked	23	0.000
Geoblocked: copyright claim	Geoblocked	11	0.000
Not available: trademark claim	Not available: legal complaint	11	0.000

Table 8A.1 (continued)

Categorisation	Short categorisation	Number of videos	Proportion
Requires payment	Requires payment	7	0.000
Removed: trademark	Not available: legal complaint	6	0.000
Not available: privacy	Not available: legal complaint	4	0.000
Geoblocked: defamation	Geoblocked: legal complaint	2	0.000
Not available: replaced	Not available: user	1	0.000
Geoblocked: trademark complaint	Geoblocked: legal complaint	1	0.000
Geoblocked: government complaint	Geoblocked: legal complaint	1	0.000

Table 8A.2 *Tweets removed in sample from 1 January 2018*

Twitter response	Numerical error code (from Twitter)	Number of tweets	Proportion
Available	n/a	769,627,704	0.92365
Tweet deleted	144	52,067,193	0.06249
Suspended	63	5,813,179	0.00698
Account unavailable	34	5,735,417	0.00688
No longer available: Twitter Rules	422	3855	0.00000
No longer available	421	2327	0.00000

9. Accounting for legal values

Kevin D. Ashley

1. INTRODUCTION

Artificial Intelligence is an area of computer science in which researchers construct computer programs that behave in a manner deemed "intelligent" when performed by humans. In other words, they build computational models of intelligent behavior. In the sub-area of Artificial Intelligence and Law (AI and Law), they try to build computational models of legal practitioners' intelligent behavior, for example, computer programs that can perform aspects of legal reasoning.

Today, subject to certain limitations, computer programs can make legal arguments how to decide a scenario by drawing analogies to past cases and respond to those arguments by distinguishing the cases or citing counterexamples. They can predict outcomes for the scenario based on the strengths of these arguments. In addition, in analogizing, distinguishing, citing counterexamples, and predicting outcomes, they can take into account the values that underlie the legal rules in an area of regulation. This technology offers legal philosophers and practitioners of computational legal studies new tools for studying the role of values in legal reasoning.

Jurisprudential researchers have long theorized about the roles values play in legal reasoning. In his book, *The Nature of the Common Law*, Melvin Eisenberg (1988, p. 43) referred to the values underlying legal rules as "applicable social propositions", "those moral norms, policies, and experiential propositions that it is proper for a court to employ". "[S]ocial propositions always figure in determining the rules the courts establish and the way in which those rules are extended, restricted, and applied" (Eisenberg 1988, p. 2–3).

In this chapter, the term "values" is used to mean social propositions in Eisenberg's sense. Social propositions are distinguished from doctrinal ones, which "purport to state legal rules and are found in or easily derived from textual sources that are generally taken to express legal doctrine" (Eisenberg 1988, p. 1). Social propositions encompass essentially everything else . . ." (Schauer 1989, p. 460). This chapter does not distinguish among types of value-like abstractions; it treats principles, purposes, policies, or social propositions as "values".

According to various philosophical models, values play a role in analogical legal argument. Eisenberg explained the process of distinguishing cases and posing hypothetical cases in terms of applicable social propositions. For example, distinguishing "turns on whether applicable social propositions justify different treatment of the two cases, given the social propositions that support the rule of the precedent" (Eisenberg 1988, p. 75). Similarly, in Scott Brewer's and Cass Sunstein's philosophical models of legal reasoning by example and analogy, the criteria for assessing relevant similarities and differences involve normative values and principles (Sunstein 1993, p. 774; Brewer 1996, p. 932f). Brewer defined relevance criteria in terms of an analogy-warranting rule (AWR) that subsumes the source and target cases and a rationale that supplies the analogy with justificatory weight (Brewer 1996, p. 1020). His account is based on a similar process of analogical reasoning in ethics, in which "relatively precise norms or principles" play the role of AWR (Brewer 1996, p. 979). In Sunstein's model, a principle operating at a low or intermediate level of abstraction informs and is informed by the analogy (Sunstein 1993, pp. 747, 778; Ashley 2018).

These philosophical models of precedent and legal analogy are idealized accounts of real world argument processes. In legal practice, the proponents' argument roles, the factual and legal contexts of the problem scenario, the way an argument has already proceeded, the available precedents and legal rules, and the rules' legal concepts and their underlying values and policies all interact in a manner that is not fully understood (Marshall 1997, pp. 512–13). Philosophers model these processes as they have done for centuries, by conceptualizing and formalizing them and by illustrating their conceptual models with examples drawn from legal decisions or manually constructed.

By contrast, computational models of legal reasoning operationalize these processes in a manner that renders them not only explicit but "runnable" as computer programs. This includes ways that legal reasoners may use the values underlying particular legal rules. As a result, these models can support empirical studies of values' roles in legal reasoning. As explained below, using the models one can investigate how to assign context-sensitive weights to values, perform sensitivity analyses of proposed decisions' effects on values, test legal hypotheses concerning values, and run experiments comparing models' performance with or without values.

For example, with a computer program one can turn on or off, that is, ablate, the various kinds of information the program uses in constructing arguments and making predictions. This includes information concerning values underlying the legal rules. By ablating value-related information, one can demonstrate the effect that taking values into account has on the accuracy of the program's predictions and the nature of its arguments.

In more detail, the models employ argument schemes, a kind of template for generating case-based arguments and predictions, to assign to values context-sensitive quantitative weights reflecting the arguments' strengths. Based on such weights, the programs predict case outcomes and justify them in terms of the arguments. Researchers can then conduct studies, comparing models that do or do not represent values or ablating information concerning values, value-tradeoffs, legal concepts, or chronological ordering of cases in order to assess the effects on the accuracy of the predicted outcomes and on the arguments the program generates. This provides an empirical handle on modeling the significance in legal reasoning of the ablated information, including of values.

In this way, AI and Law computational models of legal argument provide an empirical methodology, a way to conduct certain kinds of experiments, that complements jurisprudential theorizing about the role of values in legal reasoning. This chapter also explains how, in the near future, such models could perform sensitivity analyses, testing a system's arguments and predictions with hypotheticals that modify applicable value effects in a scenario. Finally, newly developed legal text analytics use linguistic, statistical, and machine learning techniques to model some semantic information content in legal text archives (*see* Ashley 2017). A computer program could then support human users in testing hypotheses about cases and values against the corpus of legal cases.

The next section expands upon the description of jurisprudential work explaining the roles of values in legal reasoning and describes efforts in AI and Law to model those roles. Section 3 describes a specific computational model of legal value judgments, how it represents knowledge about the law, values, facts, and cases, and how it uses that knowledge to predict the outcomes of new cases and generate arguments pro and con. In Section 4, we consider how that computational model supports or could support an empirical investigation of the role of values in legal argument through context-sensitive weights, model-comparison or ablation studies, sensitivity analysis, and testing hypotheses. Conclusions follow in Section 5.

2. RELATED WORK

2.1 Jurisprudential Models of Reasoning with Legal Rules, Cases, and Values

When an advocate argues a case before a court, he/she often proposes a rule for deciding the case in favor of the client. The proposed rule may be taken or adapted from a statute, regulation, or precedent, or newly formulated, perhaps by analogy to some other area of law. It typically employs intermediate legal concepts (ILCs), open textured legal terms whose meaning is subject to argument, "in order to characterize abstractly the value-laden factual patterns [an advocate deems] legally significant" (Grabmair and Ashley 2011, p. 164).

In his famous "Tû-Tû" paper, the philosopher Alf Ross (1957) took a skeptical view of legal concepts arguing that while they may make reasoning with legal rules more efficient, they add no semantic content. In response, Lars Lindahl (2003, p. 199) explained that ILCs embody legal values and principles. They are "a mediating link between the requirements and the [normative] consequences" in legal inference (Lindahl 2003). Legislatures and judges choose ILCs with an eye toward anticipating the kinds of scenarios that will arise; the underlying values and principles help to frame the applicability of the legal rules.

When a judge performs legal reasoning, he/she may critique an advocate's proposed rule for deciding a case. One way is to determine if the proposed rule leads to the right result in the current case, in past cases, or in hypothetical cases. In this context, the "right result" is determined by the values underlying the legal rules of the domain. The question is how well the rule accommodates those underlying values.

Here is an example of an argument that a proposed decision does not accommodate the values underlying a legal rule. Under certain circumstances the legal rules of trade secret misappropriation protect competitive information with "independent economic value", an intermediate legal concept. A number of normative value interests underlie the rules including the plaintiff's property interest in competitively valuable information, the plaintiff's interest in protecting confidential relationships, and the general public's interest in the usability of publicly available information. In a particular scenario, a court might argue as follows:

> It must be assumed that plaintiff's product information is not sufficiently economically valuable because deciding otherwise would be inconsistent with the purposes underlying trade secret law. Specifically, regarding the maintenance of secrecy by the plaintiff, the public disclosure amounts to such a clear *waiver of property interest* in a scenario where *usability of public information* is critical,

and such a clear *waiver of confidentiality* interest regarding the lack of maintenance of secrecy by the plaintiff, that the lack of economic value of the information must be deemed sufficiently established despite the lack of strong evidence for the defendant and the fact that the product information was unique.[1]

ILCs also assist in analogical reasoning with cases or examples (Levi 1949, p. 8). As noted, Melvin Eisenberg addressed the roles of legal rules and underlying values with respect to the binding-ness of precedents. In his view, if a court determines in light of applicable social propositions, that is, of underlying values, that there is insufficient reason to treat the case at hand otherwise, it should apply the rule announced in the precedent. On the other hand, if the balance of values favors not applying the rule announced in the precedent, the court may distinguish it and formulate an exception (Eisenberg 1988, p. 87), or if necessary, overrule or radically reconstruct the rule of the precedent (Eisenberg 1988, p. 75).

Interestingly, Eisenberg's account of judges' legal reasoning with social propositions or values does not mention any role for past cases in determining preferences among sets of values. This is not consistent with some of the computational models described below that are based on such preferences. He notes "there will be some cases where the weighting of colliding policies and moral norms must lie within the court's judgment . . . [t]he process of rendering judgment cannot be rendered judgment-free" (1988, p. 35).

His descriptions of analogical reasoning and reasoning with hypothetical cases also involve values; they focus on testing announced or proposed rules against social propositions. In reasoning by analogy, he allows that a court may extend a rule from a case that the rule covers by its terms to one it does not where "neither applicable social propositions nor a deep doctrinal distinction justifies different treatment of the new cases" (Eisenberg 1988, p. 93). Similarly, he says that hypothetical reasoning "turns on the question whether two cases can be distinguished" which "depends on an interplay between applicable social propositions and conceivable doctrinal propositions and cases" (1988, p. 102). A court may reason hypothetically in deciding whether to apply a legal rule to a case, or which legal rule to apply. If a hypothetical case presents different facts from the current case but appears to the court to be easier to decide and cannot be distinguished "under applicable social propositions", the court may apply or extend the rule from the hypothetical (Eisenberg 1988, pp. 99–101; see Ashley 2009, p. 324).

---

[1]   This argument was generated automatically by the VJAP program. See Box 9.2. The underlying values invoked in the argument are italicized.

Scott Brewer's descriptions of analogical reasoning and reasoning with hypothetical cases allow for values to play a greater role in assessing relevant similarities and differences. He treats arguments from hypothetical cases as a kind of analogical argument. (Brewer 1996, pp. 964–5). As noted above, like Eisenberg, Brewer's view also focuses on the role of proposed rules or tests for deciding a case; an AWR provides a legal analogy its rational force; it establishes that the target case is relevantly similar to the source case and warrants the inferred conclusion (Brewer 1996, pp. 971, 975, 1015–16). The analogy is more or less compelling based on the underlying values elaborated in an analogy-warranting rationale (AWRa), which explains why, in the "eyes of the law", "the logical relation among the characteristics articulated by the analogy-warranting rule either does obtain or should obtain" (Brewer 1996, pp. 965, 1025).

Legal philosopher Robert Alexy presents a more elaborated role for values and past cases in analogical legal reasoning. He developed a quantitative model of balancing competing values in specific contexts. His "Weight Formula" combines the abstract weights of principles and the degrees of interference with the principles presented in a given case (Alexy 2003). First, a case is subsumed "under two competing principles"; this establishes that the fact situation is an instance of a legal concept. Then the intensity of interference and the abstract weights of both principles are considered. Finally, the result is discounted by "the degree of reliability of the empirical assumption . . . respecting what the measure in question means for the non-realization" of one principle and the realization of the other (Alexy 2010).

Alexy regards case analogy as complementary to subsumption and balancing, and he provides a basic formal argument scheme for each. Case comparison and balancing are related in that "[T]he analogy scheme cannot achieve coherence exclusively by its own means. The dialectic of reference to features of other cases . . . cannot be rationally resolved without balancing" (Alexy 2010).

Legal philosophers like Brewer and Alexy have tended not to address the question of how to represent such elements of knowledge as case facts, legal rules and their concepts, or values and principles in a form that a computational model can employ for purposes of computing weights, generating predictions, and making arguments. One exception, Jeff Horty, has adopted the AI and Law community's focus on argument models and is developing its techniques for representing factors and their magnitudes with dimensions as in the HYPO program (Ashley 1990) in a way that promises ultimately to connect with underlying values (Horty 2011, 2019).

2.2   AI and Law Models of Reasoning with Legal Rules, Cases, and Values

Since the seminal critique of Berman and Hafner (1993), "Representing Teleological Structure in Case-Based Legal Reasoning: The Missing Link", AI and Law researchers have designed and evaluated computational argument models that include legal values.

For any computational model of case-based legal reasoning to work, one must represent the kinds of legal knowledge that it employs including information about the facts of cases. One influential line of case-based argument models represents cases in terms of legal factors, stereotypical patterns of fact that strengthen or weaken a side's claim (Ashley 1990; Aleven 2003). Factors are essential to the legal reasoning process, and models approximating judicial reasoning need to take them into account. Statutes and restatements in a variety of legal domains identify factors that courts shall or may take into account in deciding legal issues such as who is an employee, whether a trademark has been diluted by blurring, whether an authorized copy is a fair use, or whether information constitutes a trade secret or has been misappropriated.

The work of Bench-Capon and Sartor (2003) and Chorley and Bench-Capon (2005 a, b) models legal argumentation as a kind of theory construction with cases, factors, and values. It relates each of the factors, some of which favor the plaintiff's claim and others favor the defense, to possibly competing values underlying the domain's legal rules. These authors treat precedents as generating preference rules among the competing factors and, by extension, among the competing values. Given a new case, the programs use these preference rules to construct arguments about how to decide the new case and apply theory metrics such as completeness, consistency, and explanatory power in order to pick the most coherent arguments. Completeness is assessed in terms of whether any additional argument construction moves can be performed. Consistency and explanatory power are measured in terms of the number of cases the theory explains. Atkinson and Bench-Capon (2007) extended the model to support multi-level arguments about facts and values that take burdens of proof into account.

As explained in the next section, the Value Judgment-based Argumentative Prediction (VJAP) program provides a more nuanced representation of the effects of factors on values and a refined method for analogically mapping a new case to prior cases that more effectively takes factual contexts into account (Grabmair 2017; Grabmair and Ashley 2011). In this respect, it seems to better accommodate models like Alexy's that incorporate value-balancing and comparison with past cases and to generate more realistic legal arguments.

Prior work on AI and Law has also accounted for values in order to improve legal information retrieval. McLaren (2003) and Ashley (2004) represented abstract normative principles in a professional engineering ethics code that embodied moral values of the profession. A board of ethical review analyzed scenarios submitted by engineers and published their advisory opinions, in which they, in effect, operationalized the principles. That is, the board recorded connections between the principles it deemed relevant and certain events in the narratives of case facts. McLaren developed techniques for representing these connections so that SIROCCO, a computerized information retrieval system, could use them to determine which ethics code provisions and advisory opinions were relevant to newly inputted cases.

2.3 Model-Comparison or Ablation Studies with AI and Law Models of Reasoning

On issues where jurisprudential scholars may differ, an experiment conducted with a computational model of legal argument can provide evidence that sheds some light. For instance, as noted, legal philosophers Alf Ross and Lars Lindahl disagreed as to the extent to which ILCs have semantic content.

Ashley and Brüninghaus (2003) conducted an experiment with the issue-based prediction (IBP) program to assess whether ILCs provide substantive guidance for deciding new cases. Specifically, they evaluated the extent to which ILCs contributed to the program's ability to predict case outcomes based on a database of trade secret law cases. The program employed a model of the rules for trade secret misappropriation and their ILCs, that is, the legal issues. The cases in the database were represented in terms of ILCs and factors. IBP used the ILCs to formulate hypotheses about what the outcome of a new case should be and tested the hypotheses against the cases in the database.

The researchers compared three versions of IBP and measured the effects on the program's predictions: one employed cases and issues, another employed only cases and no issues, and the third employed only issues and no cases. Thus any possible contribution of the ILCs was turned on or off. The results of comparing the three IBP versions confirmed the ILCs' contribution to predictive accuracy; the version that employed cases and issues generated the most accurate predictions. The experiment provided empirical support for concluding that using knowledge about issues to focus hypothesis testing with precedents on the issue-related conflicts leads to better prediction. On the other hand such knowledge does not by itself lead to a strong predictive model; its role in guiding hypothesis testing with precedents is important.

Ethicists have also disagreed about the roles that abstract ethical principles, such as those embodied in engineering ethics code provisions, play in normative reasoning about concrete fact situations. (See Ashley 2004.) In evaluating the SIROCCO program, McLaren ran the program with and without access to the board's operationalizing information, that is, the connections the board recorded between the principles it deemed relevant and certain events in the narratives of case facts. He demonstrated that the ablated information reduced the program's retrieval efficacy and measured the effect. In other words, the ablation experiment provided objective evidence that the board's advisory opinions applying principles to facts fledged out the meaning of the principles.

As described below, model-comparison and ablation experiments can also turn on or off information related to values and empirically assess their effects on the predictive performance of a computational model of argument.

3. VALUE JUDGMENT-BASED ARGUMENTATIVE PREDICTION (VJAP) PROGRAM

The VJAP is one such program that supports model-comparison and ablation experiments with values. The VJAP program assumes that, in deciding a case, a court makes a *value judgment* that the positive effects on applicable values of its decision outweigh the negative effects. It also assumes that the ordering of values underlying a legal regulation is relative to the facts to which the regulation is being applied; there is no single hierarchy of abstract values (Grabmair 2016; 2017).

The program models legal reasoning as mapping and applying value judgments from one set of facts to another. The mappings are based on arguments that the new set of facts presents the same value-tradeoffs as a prior case, thus justifying applying the same conclusion to both. The program also makes arguments against the mappings. These arguments take into account the value interests protected in the particular regulatory domain of interest (Grabmair 2016; 2017).

3.1 Factor Representation

VJAP models legal reasoning in the domain of trade secret misappropriation. In prior work (Ashley 1990; Aleven 2003), 27 factors were identified for the trade secret misappropriation domain, including the four examples illustrated below. In that work, the factors for a case were compiled manually by reading the cases. Experts or trained students identified sentences from which it can be inferred that the court determined that facts cor-

---

BOX 9.1   SENTENCES JUSTIFYING FACTORS IN MASON CASE

F6 p (i.e., pro-plaintiff) Security-measures: He testified that he told only a few of his employees—the bartenders—the recipe. He stated that each one was specifically instructed not to tell anyone the recipe. To prevent customers from learning the recipe, the beverage was mixed in the "back" of the restaurant and lounge.

F15 p Unique-product: It appears that one could not order a Lynchburg Lemonade in any establishment other than that of the plaintiff.

F16 d (i.e., pro-defendant) Info-reverse-engineerable: At least one witness testified that he could duplicate the recipe after tasting a Lynchburg Lemonade.

F21 p Knew-info-confidential: On cross-examination Randle [the defendant's agent] agreed that he had been under the impression that Mason's recipe for Lynchburg Lemonade was a secret formula.

---

responding to particular factors were present or assumed that they were present for purposes of the argument.

The examples in Box 9.1 were drawn from the *Mason* case[2] in which the plaintiff bar owner brought a claim against a distillery for misappropriating the recipe for a cocktail, Lynchburg Lemonade. Accompanying each example are sentences that justify concluding that the factor is present. As explained below, current research in legal text analytics focuses on teaching machine learning programs to identify factors in case texts automatically.

3.2   The VJAP Domain Model

Similar to IBP, the VJAP program employs a domain model representing the legal rules of the trade secret misappropriation domain and the rules' antecedent terms, that is, its ILCs or issues. As illustrated in Figure 9.1, the rules are based on the provisions of the Uniform Trade Secret Act (as amended 1985) and the Restatement (First) of Torts Section 757, which state, in effect:

"Trade secret" means information, . . . that:
(i)   derives independent economic value, . . . from not being generally known to, and not being readily ascertainable by proper means . . . and

---

[2]   Mason v. Jack Daniels Distillery, 518 So. 2d 130 (Ala. Civ. App. 1987).

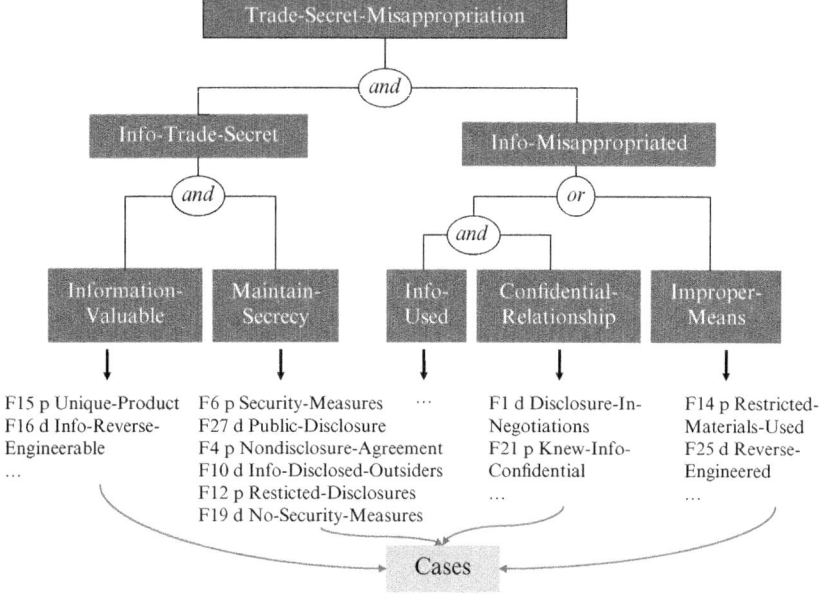

Figure 9.1   VJAP domain model

    (ii)   is the subject of efforts that are reasonable under the circumstances to maintain its secrecy.
    One . . . is liable for trade secret misappropriation if
    (a)   he discovered the secret by improper means, or
    (b)   his disclosure or use constitutes a breach of confidence . . .

According to the domain model, in order to establish a claim for trade secret misappropriation, one must establish that the information is a trade secret (Info-Trade-Secret) and the information was misappropriated (Info-Misappropriated). To show the former, one must show that the information had competitive value (Information-Valuable) and the plaintiff took efforts to maintain the secrecy of the information (Maintain-Secrecy). To show the latter, one must show that the defendant gained access to the information by improper means (Improper-Means) or that it used the information (Info-Used) and breached a confidential relationship (Confidential-Relationship).

The domain model also associates particular factors with each of these issues as indicated in Figure 9.1. The factors, in turn, index cases to which the factor applies. For instance, factor F21: Knew-info-confidential is associated with the issue, Confidential-Relationship. Based on the domain model, the program can infer that a case like *Mason* to which F21 applies also involves this issue.

Like every model, the domain model is an approximation, an interpretation of the legal rules and the facts that matter legally. In an AI and Law context, the question is whether the model is accurate enough to accomplish some useful legal work. Here the task is to improve legal information retrieval enabling a program to find and rank cases relevant to making or evaluating an argument.

3.3   Operationalizing Values Underlying Legal Rules

The VJAP model assumes that the legal rules of trade secret law protect four underlying value interests: (1) the plaintiff's property interest in competitively valuable information, (2) the plaintiff's interest in protecting confidential relationships, (3) the general public's interest in the usability of publicly available information, and (4) the general public's interest in fair competition (Grabmair 2016; 2017).

Factors present in cases can affect those value interests in six complementary ways. A factor can make a value interest more legitimate or less. It can indicate that an interest has been waived or protected. Finally, the presence of the factor can interfere with the value interest or reduce interference (Grabmair 2016; 2017).

As an example of the ways applicable factors can affect a value interest, consider the plaintiff's interest in protecting confidential relationships in Table 9.1. F21 p Knew-info-confidential can protect that value interest. Other factors can make it less legitimate, interfere with it, or waive it.

3.4   VJAP's Rule- and Case-Based Argument Schemes

As noted, argument schemes are blueprints or templates for constructing patterns of argument. (See Ashley 2017, Ch. 5.) They enable a computational model of legal argument to search for, assemble, and respond to arguments. In this way the model deals with legal disagreement, an essential aspect of legal reasoning (Gowder, Chapter 10 in this volume).

In particular, VJAP has schemes for arguing by analogy to a cited case or distinguishing a problem from a cited case (Grabmair 2016; 2017). In these arguments, the analogies are drawn in terms of tradeoffs in the effects of a decision on values. Some of the schemes deal with local tradeoffs, those that pertain to a single issue. Other schemes deal with inter-issue tradeoffs across multiple values. In such arguments, strengths in one issue can overcome weaknesses in another issue. In terms of Figure

Table 9.1 Factor value effects for plaintiff's interest in protecting confidential relationships

Value Effect	Meaning	Factor [plaintiff defendant]
Less-legitimate	Plaintiff's interest in confidentiality is not legitimate because of the public availability of the information, the unspecific nondisclosure agreement and the information being known to competitors	F5 d Agreement-not-specific F20 d Info-known-to-competitors F24 d Info-obtainable-elsewhere
Waiver	Plaintiff has waived his confidentiality interest because of the waiver of confidentiality, the absence of security measures, the public disclosure, the disclosure during negotiations, and the disclosure to outsiders	F1 d Disclosure-in-negotiations F10 d Secrets-disclosed-outsiders F19 d No-security-measures F23 d Waiver-of-confidentiality F27 d Disclosure-in-public-forum
Protection	Plaintiff has protected his confidentiality interest because of the confidentiality of outsider disclosures, the known confidentiality of the information, the security measures, the noncompetition agreement, and the nondisclosure agreement	F4 p Agreed-not-to-disclose F6 p Security-measures F12 p Outsider-disclosures-restricted F13 p Noncompetition-agreement F21 p Knew-info-confidential
Interference	Plaintiff's confidentiality interest has been violated because of the use of restricted materials and the payment to switch employment	F2 p Bribe-employee F14 p Restricted-materials-used

Source: Grabmair (2016; 2017).

9.1's domain model, local tradeoffs involve a single branch; inter-issue tradeoffs involve multiple branches.

3.5 VJAP Argument Graph

Given a new problem represented as a set of factors, VJAP applies its argument schemes and generates *all* the arguments it can about who should win given the cases in its corpus of 121 cases (Grabmair 2016; 2017).

The arguments are recorded in a graph, an abstracted portion of which is shown in Figure 9.2. A graph is a network of connected objects called nodes. The top node is the root, the nodes below a node are its children, and the lowest nodes are leaf nodes. The argument graph comprises arguments, represented as oval-shaped nodes, related to propositions in rectangular nodes, via diamond-shaped confidence propagation nodes (discussed below). The argument graph progresses "from arguments in

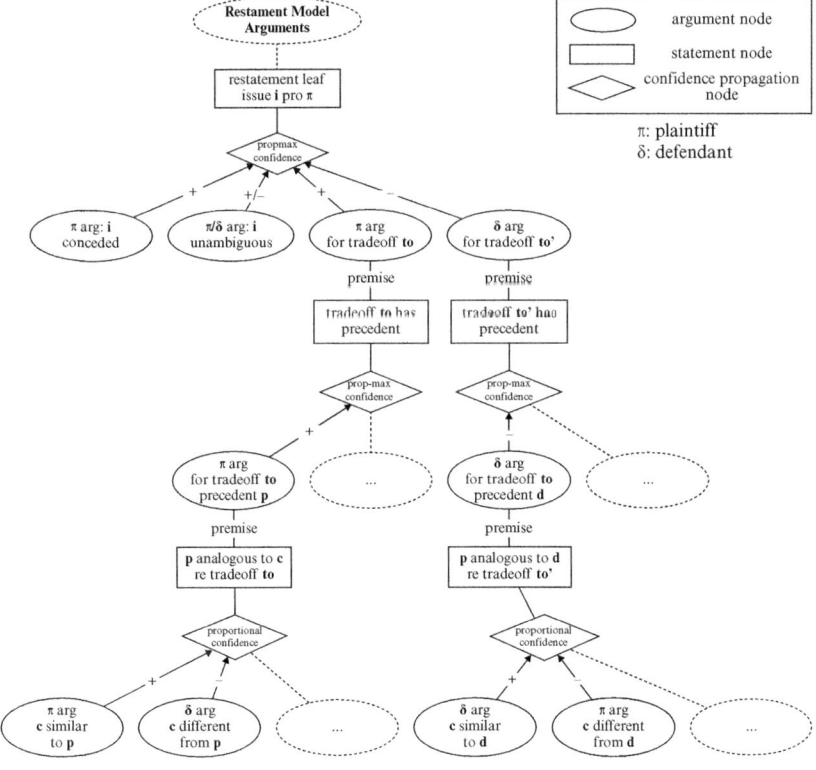

Figure 9.2   VJAP argument graph

the domain model at the top (collapsed to save space) to deep arguments about leaf node issues, tradeoffs, precedents, and analogy/distinction arguments between precedent and the case at bar . . ." (Grabmair 2016, p. 50). In other words, a rectangular node in the upper portion of the graph involves an assertion that an intermediate legal concept such as Confidential-Relationship has been satisfied or not. The children oval nodes represent increasingly detailed case-based analogical arguments in support or contra that proposition (Grabmair 2016; 2017).

The edges connecting the nodes represent consequence and premise relations (Grabmair 2016, pp. 48–51). Each argument scheme is like a procedural rule. When a rule's antecedent fires, the conclusion adds an argument construct to the graph. In order to determine which rule fires next, the system employs backward chaining. That is, given a rule whose conclusion would add a relevant argument if it applied, the system searches for other rules whose conclusions match the target rule's antecedents.

VJAP employs quantitative information about weights in the argument graph to predict the outcome of a problem. The weights represent its confidence in a prediction based on the magnitude of promotion or demotion in past case contexts of the value involved in an argument, and the degree of confidence that argument's premises can be established. That, in turn, depends on the strength of arguments pro and con the premises (Grabmair 2016; 2017).

The weight parameters, which are learned as explained below, represent the persuasive force of the effect a certain fact has on the applicable values. For inter-issue or local issue arguments from precedent, the confidence measure is increased in relation to the strength of the analogy between a precedent and the case at hand and decreased to the extent they can be distinguished (Grabmair 2016; 2017).

The program propagates the quantitative weights across the graph in a learning phase. Using training cases whose outcomes are known, the system tries to learn optimal confidence weight parameters to maximize prediction accuracy. It constructs argument graphs for each case down to the leaf nodes and propagates the weights up through the diamond-shaped confidence propagation nodes to predict an outcome. The construction-propagation-prediction pattern happens in a loop during which the system iteratively searches for the optimal weight map using a technique called simulated annealing. In the course of this construction-propagation-prediction cycle the system learns and optimizes the weights (Grabmair 2016, p. 71). Given the test cases, the program constructs an argument graph but this time applies the learned weights to predict the outcome of the test cases.

Even though VJAP employs quantitative argument weights to predict case outcomes based on value effects, it also translates the arguments

---

BOX 9.2   VJAP'S ARGUMENT FOR DEFENDANT RE
INFO-VALUABLE ISSUED IN DYNAMICS CASE

Plaintiff's product information is not sufficiently valuable because the plaintiff has taken such little efforts to maintain the secrecy of the information that, despite the lack of strong evidence for the defendant, it must be assumed that plaintiff's product information is not sufficiently valuable because deciding otherwise would be inconsistent with the purposes underlying trade secret law.

Specifically, regarding the maintenance of secrecy by the plaintiff, the public disclosure amounts to such a clear *waiver of property interest,* a scenario where *usability of public information* is critical and such a clear *waiver of confidentiality* interest regarding the lack of maintenance of secrecy by the plaintiff that the lack of value of the information must be deemed sufficiently established despite the lack of strong evidence for the defendant and the fact that the product information was unique.

A similar inter-issue tradeoff was made in *NATIONAL-REJECTORS*, which was decided for defendant. There, regarding the maintenance of secrecy by the plaintiff, the disclosure to outsiders amounted to such a clear *waiver of property interest* and such a clear *waiver of confidentiality interest,* the public disclosure amounted to such a clear *waiver of property interest*, a scenario where *usability of public information* is critical and such a clear *waiver of confidentiality* interest and the absence of security measures amounted to such a clear *waiver of property interest* and such a clear *waiver of confidentiality* interest that the reverse-engineerability qualified as the lack of value of the information despite the fact that the product information had been unique (Grabmair 2016; 2017).

---

represented in an argument graph into verbal form. Box 9.2 shows an example verbalization of an argument in favor of the defendant on the issue of Info-Valuable in a case called the *Dynamics* case.[3] VJAP's verbalizations include qualitative arguments about the effects on values. As shown in the figure, the references to value interests and effects have been italicized to illustrate this.

4.   HOW VJAP SUPPORTS EMPIRICAL INVESTIGATION OF VALUES

By operationalizing values underlying legal rules, a computational model like VJAP supports ways and means to empirically study the roles of values in legal reasoning. These include:

---

[3]   Dynamics Research Corp. v. Analytic Sciences Corp., 9 Mass. App. 254, 400 N.E.2d 1274, 209 U.S.P.Q. 321 (1980).

1. Context-sensitive weights: Assigning context-sensitive quantitative weights to values using argument schemes for generating case-based arguments and predictions.
2. Model-comparison and Ablation studies: Comparing models with and without values, for example by turning information concerning values, legal concepts, or chronological order on/off to assess effects on accuracy of prediction.
3. Sensitivity analysis:[4] Testing arguments/predictions with hypotheticals that modify applicable value effects.
4. Hypothesis testing: Supporting testing hypotheses about cases and values.

As discussed below, each of these relates to legal philosophical concerns and could complement jurisprudential theorists' methods and thought experiments about legal values.

4.1 Context-Sensitive Weights

As explained in the previous section, VJAP assigns context-sensitive quantitative weights to value effects using case-based schemes for generating arguments and predictions. It does not rely on some abstract hierarchy of values but bases the weightings on the analogies between the value effect tradeoffs in the concrete fact situation to be analyzed and those in past cases. That is to say, the weights increase the stronger the analogy between a precedent and the case at hand and decrease to the extent they can be distinguished. In a manner that appears roughly to correspond to Alexy's approach, VJAP subsumes fact situations into legal rules, assigns weights in light of specific fact situations, and argues analogically to predict an outcome that coheres with past decisions.

It may well be objected that VJAP's methodology does not correspond to the way in which judges reason with applicable social propositions or values. This may be due to the fact that, presumably, this kind of case-based information has not yet become generally available to jurisprudential theorists or judges, at least not with the same degree of accessibility or in the same form or quantity. While traditional legal information retrieval makes all of the cases potentially available, humans still have to find them. It is unlikely that humans would find or read all of the cases or relate them as systematically to the tasks of prediction and argument-making. Thus, it is interesting to consider whether judges and philosophers might find the

---

[4]   Sensitivity analysis and hypothesis testing are future work based on VJAP.

comprehensiveness and the context-sensitive nature of the value effects weightings to be novel and useful. The weighting scheme, in effect, represents how a new case fits into the corpus of prior decisions, something that judges and philosophers care about and for which the VJAP approach provides new analytical tools.

4.2   Model-Comparison and Ablation Studies

As noted, a computational model like VJAP allows one to compare its performance with other models that do not represent values or to turn on or off, that is, ablate sources of various kinds of information, for example, information about values or the chronological order of legal decisions, in order to assess the effects on the accuracy of prediction. This provides an empirical methodology to probe the roles of values in legal decision-making.

Matthias Grabmair conducted model-comparison and ablation experiments in evaluating the VJAP program (Grabmair 2016; 2017). He compared five models that represent and use values in different ways, VJAP-full, VJAP-local, VJAP-no-precedent, VJAP-timeline, and Global Tradeoff Weight (GTW), with two models that do not represent values, IBP and IBP-noEE, and with three baselines.

The list in Box 9.3 explains the knowledge sources each model employed.

BOX 9.3   LIST OF MODELS' KNOWLEDGE SOURCES

VJAP-full predicts case outcomes with the full argument graph including local and inter-issue tradeoff-based arguments.

VJAP-local functions as VJAP-full, but predicts case outcomes only with local tradeoff argument schemes.

VJAP-no-precedent functions as VJAP-full, but without precedent-based argument schemes. Tradeoffs are solely resolved on the basis of effect weights. That is, global tradeoffs are scoped into smaller issue-based tradeoffs.

GTW predicts a case outcome for the side with highest total factor effect weight on values.

VJAP-timeline functions as VJAP-full, but cases may only be argued on the basis of cases that had been decided at least one year before the year of the case to be predicted.

IBP and IBP-noEE are two variants that employ a domain model and factor associations similar to VJAP's but with no information about values.

Major label is a simple baseline that predicts the label of the majority of the cases in the dataset, namely that the plaintiff wins the case.

Naive Bayes and Decision Tree are two baselines that employ machine learning algorithms.

Table 9.2   Results table of predictive accuracy of baseline and experimental models

Model	LOO	train	5-fold	train	fold-SD
GTW	0.802	0.84	0.805	0.845	0.059
VJAP-full	0.793	0.828	0.779	0.837	0.046
VJAP-local	0.694	0.717	0.691	0.725	0.095
VJAP-no-precedent	0.711	0.727	0.715	0.73	0.097
VJAP-timeline	0.843	0.854	0.821	0.862	0.079
major-label	0.612	n/a	0.612	n/a	n/a
naive-bayes	0.843	n/a	0.851	n/a	n/a
decision tree	0.777	n/a	0.835	n/a	n/a
IBP	0.81	n/a	0.725	n/a	0.112
IBP-noEE	0.587	n/a	0.562	n/a	0.14

Table 9.2 shows the predictive accuracy of the seven models and the three baselines: the number of correctly predicted cases over the total number of predictions made. The middle column marked "LOO", that is, leave-one-out, reports the accuracy in a kind of experiment in which each case is treated as a test case in turn. For each test case, all of the remaining cases are used to train the model anew, the outcome of the test case is predicted, and the prediction is compared with the case's actual outcome. The right column marked "5-fold" involves a similar kind of experiment in which five cases are treated as a test set in each run and the model is retrained from scratch on each run using the remaining cases.

Comparing the results of these models within the LOO column or the 5-fold column enables one to evaluate a number of hypotheses that may be of interest to jurisprudential scholars, as shown in the list in Box 9.4.

Summarizing the evidence from Table 9.2 and focusing on the 5-fold column, it appears to provide evidence that:

1. Accounting for value effects improves the accuracy of prediction.
2. Taking precedents into account improves the accuracy of predictions based on reasoning with values.
3. Taking inter-issue value effect tradeoffs into account improves predictive accuracy as compared to focusing only on local tradeoffs. In other words, strengths and weaknesses in terms of value effects can bleed across doctrinal requirements, with strengths/weaknesses on one requirement compensating for weaknesses/strengths in another.
4. Enforcing a sensible chronological order constraint improves the accuracy of predictions based on reasoning with cases and values.

BOX 9.4   HYPOTHESES TO INVESTIGATE BY ABLATING KNOWLEDGE SOURCES

1. Accounting for value effects improves the accuracy of prediction. Compare Table 9.2 results for VJAP-full versus IBP and IBP-noEE.
2. Taking precedents into account improves the accuracy of predictions based on reasoning with values. Compare Table 9.2 results for VJAP-full, VJAP-timeline versus VJAP-no-precedent.
3. Taking inter-issue value effect tradeoffs into account improves predictive accuracy as compared to focusing only on local tradeoffs. Compare Table 9.2 results for VJAP-full versus VJAP-local.
4. Enforcing a chronological reasonableness constraint improves the accuracy of predictions based on reasoning with cases and values. Compare Table 9.2 results for VJAP-full versus VJAP-timeline.
5. Taking into account intermediate legal concepts (i.e., legal issues) when predicting based on value-tradeoffs improves the accuracy of predictions. Compare Table 9.2 results for VJAP-no-precedent versus GTW.

This seems reasonable since the constraint is realistic; it is especially important if, as Eisenberg and others observe, judicial assessments of applicable social propositions or values change over time reflecting a social dynamic.

5. Taking into account ILCs (i.e., legal issues) when predicting based on value-tradeoffs improves the accuracy of predictions. This may seem commonsensical but, as noted above, jurisprudential scholars like Alf Ross and, more recently, Lewis Kornhauser have questioned the importance of legal concepts. The latter has championed an "eliminativist" approach which replaces the "two-stage theory that requires the agent first to determine what the law requires and then to weigh that requirement against her other reasons for action" with a "one-stage theory that requires the agent to weigh all her reasons at the same time" (Kornhauser 2015). In a sense VJAP enforces a kind of "two-stage theory"; its top-down approach begins with doctrinal requirements and ends with comparing cases in terms of values effects. At the same time, it separates subprocesses and knowledge into elements that can be turned off, that is, ablated or, in a sense, eliminated, or, to some extent, reordered or modified. This makes possible model-comparison and ablation experiments to assess the effects on predictive accuracy or on the types of arguments generated. Such experiments may be a tangible way to operationalize eliminativism that could complement jurisprudential theorizing.

Since the dataset is relatively small, a non-random sample of 121 trade secret cases manually annotated with factors, the results' statistical significance has not been tested. The point here, however, is to illustrate an empirical, if exploratory, methodology for investigating the role of values in legal reasoning.

4.3 Sensitivity Analysis

In making arguments, advocates are often concerned to predict how small changes in facts could affect the argument. They may perform a sensitivity analysis, testing their arguments and predictions by considering hypothetical variations of a fact situation. Sensitivity analysis is especially important in an adversarial context where the facts are not given but depend on which facts the competing advocates are able to prove and which facts a trier accepts. Some of these factual changes have an effect on values and value-tradeoffs.

This suggests that one can test arguments and predictions by posing hypothetical variations to determine how sensitive a predicted result is to changes in underlying value effects. Posing hypotheticals for sensitivity analysis is of jurisprudential interest. Eisenberg and Brewer, for example, focused on examples of hypothetical reasoning akin to a kind of sensitivity analysis and, of course, the Justices of the Supreme Court of the United States are famous for posing hypotheticals to probe advocates' proposed tests for deciding a case (Ashley 2009).

Conceivably, VJAP provides the basis for conducting similar sensitivity analyses. As explained in the previous section, VJAP represents how factors affect various values. To add protection of a value or decrease its legitimacy in a scenario, one could add or remove corresponding factors and determine the effect on the predicted result.

This approach has not yet been tried with VJAP but remains as future work. One of the challenges is determining the kinds of information that are available to guide the program in constructing hypotheticals.[5] VJAP's knowledge about how factors affect values as in Table 9.1 could guide it as to which factor and value effects to add or subtract. In addition, statistical relations among factors could also inform such decisions.

---

[5] HYPO conducted a kind of sensitivity analysis by posing hypothetical variations of the problem scenario that could have a legal effect (Ashley 1990). Near-misses in terms of dimension prerequisites, movement along an applicable dimension's range, and the proximity in a claim lattice of nearby cases with different outcomes guided the program's construction of meaningful hypotheticals.

4.4 Hypothesis Testing: Support Testing Hypotheses about Cases and Values

As human reasoners, attorneys are good at conceiving interesting hypotheses about a domain of law. Legal information retrieval systems should make it easier for them to pose and test the hypotheses. Ideally the systems could enable testing the hypotheses against a whole corpus of cases involving that legal domain.

An example of a hypothesis of interest might be: "In trade secret misappropriation cases, the value of protecting the public usability of information that has become public is paramount." Although not unreasonable on its face, this is a broad claim that begs discovering some counterexamples, for instance with a query like: "What trade secret misappropriation cases involve society's interest in protecting the public usability of information that has become public *and* have been won by plaintiffs?"

It is an enlightening exercise to submit such a query to a commercial legal information retrieval (IR) system. One IR system returned 69 state or federal cases. Perusal of the system's descriptive abstracts suggested that 14 of these involved some kind of public disclosures and yet the plaintiffs still won. These cases involved situations where it would have taken some not insubstantial amount of time to compile or apply the public information, where some aspects or specifics of the information had not been disclosed publicly, where the disclosures were not really public or only for a short time, or where the defendant had acted improperly (an example of an inter-issue effect). Although one of the 14 cases appeared first in the list of 69, the rest were distributed fairly evenly across the top 66 retrieved cases listed. The IR system rarely identified the underlying value effects or made it easy to determine whether the trade secret claimant had won the case.

New developments in legal text analytics may improve this performance, making it easier for humans employing a legal IR system to find positive and negative evidence regarding hypotheses about values. VJAP's computational model includes information for each case about which side won, what factors apply, and how those factors affect values. As argued in Ashley (2017), the new techniques can leverage that information, enabling a computational model of legal reasoning to connect to legal texts, not only of cases in its database but of those in an online commercial corpus of case texts.

A legal app could then assist a human user by translating a query like the above into something like the following: "What trade secret misappropriation cases, won by plaintiffs, have involved some factors from each category?":

value: protection-public-information

- more-legitimate:
- F17 d Info-independently-generated,
- F20 d No-security-measures,
- F24 d Info-obtainable-elsewhere,
- F11 d Vertical knowledge,
- F16 d Info-reverse-engineerable,
- F25 d Reverse-engineered,
- F27 d Public-disclosure

less-legitimate:

- F14 p Restricted-materials-used,
- F21 p Knew-info-confidential,
- F15 p Unique-product

Since such a legal app will have more information about the factors that apply in a case and how they affect the value of interest, it will be able to use that information to improve its ranking of the relevant cases and to summarize why they are relevant to the value-related query.

While identifying factors in case texts is still a technological challenge, some progress has been made. Falakmasir and Ashley (2017) assembled 1600 trade secret cases from CourtListener and employed word-embedding (Doc2Vec) to represent some contextual semantic information. Focusing on the cases in the VJAP corpus, they trained a machine learning (ML) algorithm for each factor and used it to predict factors that apply in a case document. In an evaluation with 70 percent of the documents in the VJAP corpus as a training set and 30 percent of the documents as hold-out test set, the resulting F1 value (the arithmetic mean of precision and recall) was 0.65. While a respectable result, it should be noted that this involves identifying factors by document, not by individual sentences. Nevertheless, it is some evidence that automatically annotating case texts by factors is feasible.

5.   CONCLUSIONS

The history of legal reasoning records many technological developments that have changed the process and substance of legal argumentation, for example, printed case reports, indexing schemes, and computerized legal information retrieval.

The next such technological changes may be computational models of legal argument that take values into account and enable quantitatively and qualitatively fitting new cases into the stream of past decisions and text analytic methods for identifying factor-related value effects.

In the meantime, models like VJAP provide an empirical methodology for investigating the role of values in legal reasoning. These methods include assigning context-sensitive quantitative weights to values using argument schemes for generating case-based arguments and predictions, turning information such as values, legal concepts, or chronological order on and off to assess effects on predictive accuracy, testing arguments and predictions with hypotheticals that modify applicable value effects, and supporting testing hypotheses about cases and values. As such, these AI and Law models complement jurisprudential theorizing and contribute to computational legal studies.

REFERENCES

Aleven, V. (2003) Using background knowledge in case-based legal reasoning: A computational model and an intelligent learning environment. *Artificial Intelligence*, 150(1–2), 183–237.

Alexy, R. (2003) On balancing and subsumption: A structural comparison. *Ratio Juris*, 16(4), 433–49.

Alexy, R. (2010) Two or three? In M. Borowski (ed.), *On the Nature of Legal Principles*, Archiv für Rechts- und Sozialphilosophie, Beiheft 119, pp. 9–18. Stuttgart: Franz Steiner Verlag.

Ashley, K. (1990) *Modeling Legal Arguments: Reasoning with Cases and Hypotheticals*. Cambridge, MA: MIT Press.

Ashley, K. (2004) Capturing the dialectic between principles and cases. *Jurimetrics Journal* 44(2), 229–79.

Ashley, K. (2009) Teaching a process model of legal argument with hypotheticals. *Artificial Intelligence and Law*, 17(4), 321–70.

Ashley, K. (2017) *Artificial Intelligence and Legal Analytics: New Tools for Law Practice in the Digital Age*. Cambridge: Cambridge University Press.

Ashley, K. (2018) Precedent and analogy. In G. Bongiovanni, G. Postema, A. Rotolo, G. Sartor, C. Valentini, and D. Walton (eds), *Handbook of Legal Reasoning and Argumentation*, pp. 673–710. Springer: Heidelberg.

Ashley, K., and Brüninghaus, S. (2003) A predictive role for intermediate legal concepts, legal knowledge and information systems. In D. Bourcier (ed.), *Legal Knowledge and Information Systems: Jurix 2003: The Sixteenth Annual Conference*, pp. 153–62. Amsterdam: IOS Press.

Atkinson, K., and Bench-Capon, T. (2007) Argumentation and standards of proof. In R. Winkels (ed.), *Proceedings of the 11th International Conference on Artificial Intelligence and Law*, pp. 107–16. New York: ACM.

Bench-Capon, T., and Sartor, G. (2003) A model of legal reasoning with cases incorporating theories and values. *Artificial Intelligence*, 150(1), 97–143.

Berman, D., and Hafner, C. (1993) Representing teleological structure in case-based legal reasoning: The missing link. In K. Ashley (ed.), *Proceedings 4th International Conference on Artificial Intelligence and Law*, pp. 50–59. New York: ACM.

Brewer, S. (1996) Exemplary reasoning: Semantics, pragmatics, and the rational force of legal argument by analogy. *Harvard Law Review*, 109(5), 923–1028.

Chorley, A., and Bench-Capon, T. (2005a) AGATHA: Using heuristic search to automate the construction of case law theories. *Artificial Intelligence and Law*, 13(1), 9–51.

Chorley, A., and Bench-Capon, T. (2005b) An empirical investigation of reasoning with legal cases through theory construction and application. *Artificial Intelligence and Law*, 13(3–4), 323–71.

Eisenberg, M. (1988) *The Nature of the Common Law*. Cambridge, MA: Harvard University Press.

Falakmasir, M., and Ashley, K. (2017) Utilizing vector space models for identifying legal factors from text. In A. Wyner and G. Casini (eds), *Legal Knowledge and Information Systems: Jurix 2017 – The 30th International Conference*, pp. 183–92. Amsterdam: IOS Press.

Grabmair, M. (2016) Modeling purposive legal argumentation and case outcome prediction using argument schemes in the value judgment formalism. PhD thesis, University of Pittsburgh, Pittsburgh, PA, USA.

Grabmair, M. (2017). Predicting trade secret case outcomes using argument schemes and learned quantitative value effect tradeoffs. In G. Governatori and J. Keppens (eds), *Proceedings of the 16th International Conference on Artificial Intelligence and Law*, pp. 89–98. New York: ACM.

Grabmair, M., and Ashley, K. (2011) Facilitating case comparison using value judgments and intermediate legal concepts. In K. Ashley and T. van Engers (eds), Proceedings 13th International Conference on Artificial Intelligence and Law, pp. 161–70. New York: ACM.

Horty, J. (2011) Rules and reasons in the theory of precedent. *Legal Theory*, 17(1), 1–33.

Horty, J. (2019) Reasoning with dimensions and magnitudes. *Artificial Intelligence and Law*, 27(3), 309–45.

Kornhauser, L.A. (2015). Doing without the concept of law. https://papers.ssrn.com/sol3/papers.cfm?abstract_id=2640605 (visited, 4 August 2018).

Levi, E. (1949) *An Introduction to Legal Reasoning*. Chicago and London: University of Chicago Press.

Lindahl, L. (2003) Operative and justificatory grounds in legal argumentation. *Associations*, 7(1), 185–200.

Marshall, G. (1997) What is binding in a precedent. In D. MacCormick, R. Summers, and A. Goodhart (eds), *Interpreting Precedents: A Comparative Study*, ch. 16, pp. 503–17. London: Routledge.

McLaren, B. (2003) Extensionally defining principles and cases in ethics: An AI model. *Artificial Intelligence*, 150(1), 145–81.

Ross, A. (1957) Tû-tû. *Harvard Law Review*, 70(5), 812–25.

Schauer, F. (1989) Is the common law law? *California Law Review*, 77(2), 455–72.

Sunstein, C. (1993) On analogical reasoning. *Harvard Law Review*, 106(3), 741–91.

10. Is legal cognition computational? (When will DeepVehicle replace Judge Hercules?)

Paul Gowder

THE SELF-ABNEGATING JUDGE

Let us suppose that we could represent the facts of some legal dispute in some tabular form. As we shall shortly see, that assumption ignores some dicey initial problems, but grant it to me for just a moment.[1]

Since this is sort of a jurisprudence chapter, suppose the law is none other than "no vehicles in the park."[2] Further suppose that we do not have

---

[1] In particular, I am deliberately assuming away the immense practical and conceptual problems that Pasquale and Cashwell (2018) have identified in existing efforts to use machine learning to come to legal judgments: the prior work to identify meaning in those facts, which Pasquale and Cashwell have identified as the core problem, has by assumption already been done. Later on in this chapter I will relax this assumption. I make no claim that this is a project that we are likely to be able to undertake in the immediate future. First of all, any useful machine learning model for adjudication would require lots of training data, which currently does not exist in any useful form for most areas of law. It would be extremely expensive to collect any such data—and it might be that the only way to do it would be to wait for for-profit companies in particularly lucrative areas of law to build predictive models for the use of litigators, and then find some way to capture them for public use. In short, this is a philosopher's thought experiment, not a practical set of recommendations for creating machine learning judges. That being said, the law has often been surprisingly amenable to methodological experimentation in the past; the conclusion to this chapter discusses some practical considerations for managing such experimentation in this context.

[2] This chapter will not spend a lot of energy closely parsing the philosophy of law literature—I assume that the reader is broadly familiar with the ideas extant in conceptual jurisprudence. I do not really intend to contribute directly to either the jurisprudence literature or to the machine learning literature, but rather to put the two in conversation and see if anything interesting comes out. For a preliminary anchor in the former, allow me to here gesture at the notion that contemplating the role of machine learning in adjudication is most productive when we start

Table 10.1   Form of hypothetical table of prior cases

Weight	Number of wheels	Engine	Vehicle?
5	3	T	T
90	2	T	F
10	8	F	F

a prior case "on all fours" with the instant problem—the defendant has brought some novel thing into the park, and the judge is uncertain about whether it ought to be classified as a vehicle. But we do have a tabular representation of every relevant fact about the thing that the defendant brought into the park, and a similar representation of the facts and result of every other of the (by assumption) very large number of cases about the vehicles in the park law. Table 10.1 shows a segment of that table of prior cases, as we might imagine it.

Let us make one more (sadly unrealistic) assumption: our judge (Judge Hercules, of course) is an expert in machine learning. So she reasons as follows: "I could try to use my best judgment to figure out whether the thing Defendant brought into the park is a vehicle. In order to do so, I'm going to have to find a rule from my knowledge of how prior cases came out. But computers can more cheaply and more comprehensively generalize the prior cases, without my biases and idiosyncrasies. So I should fit a machine learning model to all the prior vehicle in the park fact patterns, generate a prediction about the current facts, and rule accordingly."[3]

Ought our judge do that? Ought the legislature mandate that she do so? Would the use of this model (let's call it DeepVehicle) represent a coherent conception of judicial judgment? That is what this chapter considers.

---

from a view that more or less resembles Waldron's (2004) proceduralist reading of Dworkin. (For those who are not jurisprudence people, the no vehicles in the park example is probably the most important thought experiment in 20th century conceptual jurisprudence, and comes from Hart (1958), and Judge Hercules comes from Dworkin (1986).) On the machine learning side, my thanks to Stephen Tu for correcting some of my terminological errors.

[3]   This is not wholly far-fetched: legal scholars have already begun to make efforts to predict judicial results using machine learning, although their approaches have not, thus far, been specifically limited to legally relevant facts (e.g. Aletras et al. 2016; Katz et al. 2017).

ESTIMATING LEGAL TRUTH AS A FUNCTION

So here is one story we could tell, which might lead us to approve of our judge's idea. Within some constraints that are not relevant here, certain popular machine learning techniques (like a neural network) are known, mathematically, to be able to approximate any function (Lin et al. 2017, 1227–8). Judicial decision-making on questions of law (given an absence of dispute of material fact) seems to be something like a function—we can abstractly conceive of the judge as observing (with some error) an underlying legal rule that maps a vector of facts (from within the domain of all possible legally relevant facts) to some vector of legal statements including propositions like "the thing the defendant brought into the park counts as a vehicle."

Moreover, on many interpretations of the normative ideal of the rule of law, it is important that legal rules are determinate—or, rephrased, legal rules ought not to vary with irrelevant facts (facts not properly included in our notional vector) such as the identity of the judge (Gowder 2014a, 1069). That property of law is more or less equivalent to the property of mathematical functions that each input to a function maps to only one output. Furthermore, judges are institutionally constrained from throwing up their hands and saying, "I don't know." In mathematical terms, that is more or less equivalent to the property of functions that they map everything in their domain to some output. So (Judge Hercules reasons) the obligation of a judge to find the exactly one legally correct outcome for a given vector of facts is equivalent to an unknown function called "the legal rule"; we ought to be able to find some machine learning model that approximates that rule.

Furthermore (Judge Hercules continues to reason), ordinary legal practice in common law systems requires judges to discover that legal rule from the prior cases.[4] The process of legal reasoning from those prior decisions is what first-year law students are taught as "following" and "distinguishing" precedent. We can easily interpret this process as analogous to the mathematical operation of finding a line (or plane, or hyperplane, depending on the dimension of the input fact-space) that best separates the points in space that belong to the various legal judgments—coming to the judgment that, for example, the rule that best takes into account the

---

[4] As should be clear, I am assuming something like a common law jurisdiction where (even in the interpretation of a statute) a judge is formally bound to take into consideration the rulings of prior decisions. However, I am imposing the artificial constraint on the system (which I shall briefly relax later on), that we are entitled to ignore any hierarchy of authority or weight between cases.

previous cases is that everything that has an engine, or weighs more than 50 pounds, is a vehicle.

I will restate the previous paragraph a little more precisely. Here is how our data scientist judge might think about the activities of "following" and "distinguishing." To follow a case is just to assert that those facts of that case that mattered for its result are relevantly similar to the facts in the present case. We could represent the set of categories in which those facts fall, or, equivalently, the questions to which each fact is an answer, like "how many wheels does the alleged vehicle have?," as an n-dimensional space where each dimension corresponds to one of those questions. Then we can represent each prior case as some point in that space, and our rule for picking out what is and what is not a vehicle as some n-dimensional hyperplane separating the half-space containing cases in which the thing defendant brought into the park was ruled a vehicle from the half-space where the thing defendant brought into the park was not ruled a vehicle.[5] In that representation, to follow a case is to claim that the facts of the present case are on the same side of the plane as the case you are following; to distinguish a case is to say that it is on the opposite side.

Here is another direction from which to approach the same story. The tech industry routinely makes use of our labor to train machine learning models to reflect human judgment. When we answer a Google image "captcha" that asks us to identify, for example, every segment of an image reflecting a street sign, we are contributing a row of data to be used by artificial intelligence (AI) to identify those signs without our help, by aggregating the wisdom of millions of humans who have somehow figured out how to carry out that task.[6] The goal is to enable the computer to come to the same answer that a human would.

Part of what makes this interesting, I contend, is that street signs are conventionally constructed: the answer to the question "is this a street sign?" is just the one that humans in the appropriate society would ordinarily give. So, too, with legal propositions—for a sufficiently aggressive flavor of legal positivism (or a Holmesian (1997) prediction-ist) we might dare argue that legal correctness is just constituted by what a judge would do, and just like we can use machine learning to answer that question very

---

[5] This representation is drawn from how machine learning practitioners describe the support vector machine algorithm (see, e.g., Burges 1998, 128).

[6] See James O'Malley, "Captcha if you can: how you've been training AI for years without realising it," 12 January 2018, accessed 22 May 2020 at https://www.techradar.com/news/captcha-if-you-can-how-youve-been-training-ai-for-years-without-realising-it.

reliably for arrangements of pixels, we may be able to do the same for arrangements of legal facts.

We might even make a similar claim from a vaguely Fullerian stand-point. Fuller has argued that the meaning of legal propositions is discover-able only with the help of the practical behavior extant in the social world (Fuller 1976, 58–9; see discussion in Postema 1994, 374–6). We might make a weaker variation on this argument, according to which law can be understood only in aid of some kind of practical applications, be those as manifested in community practices or as manifested in exemplars of their application in the form of judicial opinions. We could then understand the work of DeepVehicle as surfacing a kind of latent legal understanding from the aggregation of practical applications of the statute.[7]

Disagreement and Correctness

Let us call the story I just sketched out "legal judgment as function approximation." If it adequately represents how jurisprudence works or ought to work, it might seem reasonable to just sack all the judges. Now let us give it some trouble. What I have just described is the skeleton of a model of legal reasoning (of the judicial sub-type, but it is generalizable). It tends to be useful to test our models of reasoning in any kind of domain by examining the plausibility of their approach to one of the most intractable problems of human social cognition, namely, disagreement.

The approach to disagreement in the story I have been telling most closely resembles an error model: if two judges disagree about the correct evaluation of the vehicleness of something in the park, one of them is wrong—one of the judges is doing a better job at accessing the juridical fact of the matter (in a sense loosely corresponding to Dworkin's right answer thesis).

In particular, this story seems to be in tension with any model of legal disagreement according to which it arises as a result of legitimate differ-ences in context or participants—because there is a true legal judgment out there, which DeepVehicle is just trying to approximate, we do not have the resources to approve of a diversity of legal judgments rooted in things like the different insights that different judges would bring to the problem.[8]

---

[7] Fuller, incidentally, would probably reject this use of his work. See discussion in Postema (1994, 379).

[8] We could approve of different judgments resulting from procedural vari-ations in underlying cases—such as the common situation where a party argues some position on appeal which is, according to the other party, waived by the failure to raise it below—by incorporating information about the procedural

DRAGGING THE HUMANS (KICKING AND SCREAMING) BACK IN?

One thing that the story above seems to miss is the value of procedural justice, as represented in particular by the capacity of parties to engage in legal argumentation, and, moreover, the capacity for that argumentation to actually make a difference to the result of the case. Suppose DeepVehicle completely replaces our judge. There remains an opportunity for the parties to argue about the facts—was the thing that got brought into the park really on wheels, or was the eyewitness just confused?—but not about the law.[9] But meaningful legal argumentation seems like an important part of a legitimate system of adjudication.

How could we reintegrate legal argumentation into the story?

First, we could suppose that legal argumentation serves to shape the form of the model. Here is where we can reintroduce many of the complexities that I assumed away at the beginning of this chapter. The task of figuring out what sorts of things go into our input vector, in machine learning, is known as finding a feature representation. Judge Hercules ought to ask herself a few more questions: why should we extract engine presence, number of wheels, and weight from our prior cases and train our model on that? Why not whether there are wings, whether the user has to pedal, and whether the alleged vehicle goes "neigh" or "woof?" This is a different reading of what lawyers do when we distinguish cases, modifying the support vector machine analogy I made above. Imagine the prosecutor has argued that the defendant's Vespa counts as a vehicle in part because of its weight, and the defendant has pointed (either manually or with a machine learning model) to a collection of cases in which the defendant brought things of similar weights into the park and was

---

history of each case into DeepVehicle's input vector. Although this ignores the distinction between substantive and procedural rules, it does not seem like an obviously incorrect thing to do: the right answer to a legal question as presented in real live cases incorporates not just the facts of what happened in the outside world but also the facts of what happened in the judicial process. (This gets more complicated immediately, as the introduction of machine learning into the adjudicative process would change the space of potential lower-court happenings.)

[9]   Pasquale (2019) has the best extant discussion of how the value of legal process informs how we should shape the relationship between human and automated modes of legal judgment. The remainder of this chapter could be seen as my attempt to supplement Pasquale's argument that we ought to focus on automated augmentation rather than replacement of attorney cognitions with a jurisprudential substructure and some additional examples of how such augmentation might be carried out.

acquitted. Our prosecutor may continue the dialectic by observing that in all those other cases, the heavy object in question was a St. Bernard, and the St. Bernardiness of the prior non-vehicles is relevant as a means to distinguish the Vespa; that is more or less equivalent to arguing to the data scientist that we ought to include being furry and going "woof" in the input vector and (the prosecutor hopes) watch the half-space of couple-hundred-pounds-or-so things separate nicely on that basis.

To be fair to Judge Hercules, some of that stuff can potentially be automated—the lawyer's argument that some heretofore neglected fact was important in deciding the prior case is more or less the same thing as the data scientist's (and even social scientist's) use of various information-theoretic constructs to automate feature selection (Burnham and Anderson 2004). But some of it cannot be automated—we still have to decide on a higher-level feature representation, for example: we have to determine an underlying ontology for legal representation (like how images are made up out of pixels and texts are made up of words, sentences, or documents—what are legal facts made up out of?). We also have to decide what specific instances of that ontology even enter into our feature selection process: we cannot include every piece of knowledge that we have about the whole universe into our input vector; even an automated-feature selection process relies on preexisting legal judgments like the irrelevance of facts about, for example, what the judge had for breakfast that morning.[10]

Moreover, we also would still have to decide on the functional form of the model and its parameters.[11] We could try to automatically select some of this using automated search processes (Mendoza et al. 2016) but we would still require a metric for success, as well as a threshold probability to determine the boundary of a classification.[12] All of those things could

---

[10]   Postema (2014, 92–3) explains that the description of the underlying facts is itself a subject of argument. In data science terms, we could say that unlike, for example, pixels in an image, the value of each of the elements in an input vector in the law is itself subject to contestation.

[11]   Are we doing a deep learning model or a support vector machine? I have shamelessly appealed to features of each in the function approximation story, but they are different algorithms. If a neural network, how many layers? What is the learning rate?

[12]   By a metric for success, I mean that in order to train a machine learning model and judge when one is doing a good job of it, data scientists use a variety of metrics to distinguish better over worse models. For intuition, consider that the true positive rate—the percentage of cases in the training data where a judge labels the object as a vehicle and our model also correctly labels it a vehicle—may be very different from the true negative rate (the percentage of cases where the model, like the judge, says "not a vehicle"). Which of these we care more about may differ

make up the domain of legal argument and human judgment even in DeepVehicle's world. For example, we could imagine a criminal defense lawyer arguing that the rule of lenity implies that we ought not to conclude that the defendant's machine is a vehicle unless DeepVehicle thinks so with very high probability.[13]

And then there are a whole different set of arguments about how we incorporate the formal rules of authority into this predictive process. Could we, for example, represent the hierarchical authority of different prior courts, the impact of recency, the greater significance of landmark cases, the cutting-off of precedent prior to a statutory amendment, and the like in terms of modeling choices such as weights on different (judicial) observations? Perhaps, but this too would require legal argument, and argument closely integrated with the skills of the data scientist to boot.[14]

---

from setting to setting. (For example, minimizing false negatives is much more important in a test for a dangerous, but easily curable with a painless treatment, disease than minimizing false positives, because the harm from one error is much larger than another.) Data scientists have many different metrics, such as accuracy and AUC, to choose from (see Sokolova and Lapalme 2009).

By a threshold probability, I mean that classification models such as DeepVehicle typically do not spit out "yes it's a vehicle"/"no it isn't." Rather they spit out numbers most helpfully interpreted as an estimate of the probability that the observation falls within a given class. It is not obvious that Judge Hercules should rule that an object is a vehicle if DeepVehicle gives a greater than 0.5 probability of vehicleness—perhaps the correct threshold is 0.7, for example, with 0.69 yielding a judicial ruling of non-vehicle. This judgment is going to depend at least in part on what we are trying to achieve with the judgment of vehicleness, as well as on the kinds of considerations that go into other legal probabilistic threshold-setting judgments (like the difference between preponderance of the evidence, clear and convincing evidence, and beyond a reasonable doubt, perhaps?).

[13] Compare Ortner (2016), interestingly using corpus linguistics to apply the rule of lenity.

[14] For example, we might use some kind of model capable of taking into account graph properties of our prior corpus of cases, like citation networks (perhaps using techniques like those described in Hamilton et al. 2017). The choice of which graph properties to use would require legal judgments about how those properties affect the authority of precedent. Some of those judgments will be highly controversial. Consider, for example, what such a model would do with a plurality decision of the US Supreme Court. The Court has articulated a rule in *Marks v. United States*, US 188, 193 (1977): "the holding of the Court may be viewed as that position taken by those Members who concurred in the judgments on the narrowest grounds." While we might be able to imagine ways to represent this in terms of formal properties of cases (such as via concurrence relationships among Justices), it is infamously unclear how to practically apply this rule in ordinary legal analysis (see the discussion in Williams 2017); any particular choice of representation for modeling purposes would be highly debatable.

More troublingly for DeepVehicle, we could suppose that legal argumentation has a generative rather than an epistemic function. That is, suppose the law is open-textured, in that there is necessary linguistic ambiguity in legal propositions, leaving room for judges to make or modify the law in ways that are not fully captured by the record of prior cases (or even an unavoidable need for such lawmaking activity, whether or not the judge recognizes it as part of what she is doing). Or just suppose that legal argumentation raises matters of policy and of justice that may be legitimately used by the judge in making a determination. Imagine, for example, that DeepVehicle has concluded that anything with two or more wheels is always a vehicle, and then, for the first time, someone shows up in the park with a wheelchair. A well-organized legal system ought to give the defendant an opportunity to raise the obvious claim of justice either as an input to the interpretation of the statute or an external side-constraint on it; viewed from a more technocratic perspective we could equally well say that a well-organized legal system ought to have the capacity to take account of true novelty, and it is not obvious how DeepVehicle could do that without a real live judge second-guessing its predictions.[15]

Now we are in a whole new story. Let us call it the "permissible disagreement" story, for the points above suggest that, contra the function approximation story, we may be obliged to put up with persistent legal disagreement: two judges with different conceptions of justice and the

---

[15] This seems important from a machine learning perspective too. Otherwise, over time, such a model would just be training on its own predictions. Consider a model trained on n observations; with the case in which Judge Hercules decides to defer to the model serving as n + 1. From that case until case n + arbitrarily large m, in the absence of additional human judgments, DeepVehicle will be generalizing from the same n actual human judicial determinations, even if the m intermediate (computer-generated) judgments are fed into the training data as they are created. It is not obvious how DeepVehicle could learn how to handle novel situations in which a human judge would not follow the prior cases, such as our wheelchair example. Judge Hercules might need to assure some continuing human intervention in the ongoing docket, perhaps in the form of some kind of reinforcement learning process amounting to stating rules/her judgments in novel cases as "advice" to a learning model, as in Maclin and Shavlik (1996). (Perhaps we could make use of the m intermediate judgments in some kind of semi-supervised learning algorithm, like what Hady and Schwenker (2013, 218) call "self-training," where we bootstrap training data for far-future predictions on the basis of near-future predictions?) Put differently, we must attend to Postema's (2014, 79–81, 86–7) point that the introduction of a new decision, as legal rule, into a dynamic system of preexisting decisions and rules, has to perturb that system, and that way permit change over time; moreover, as he suggests, this process is inherently argumentative.

relative balance of legislative and judicial responsibilities might come to different views on the wheelchair question.[16] This possibility of reaching disagreement arises from the proposition that preexisting law (or the preexisting right decision, all things considered and on top of the law) is indeterminate, or perhaps we could better say incompletely theorized, and so there is not any unique legal conclusion for DeepVehicle to discover on that particular set of facts.[17]

I will just assert that real-world common law legal systems partake of both models.[18] Sometimes, what really matters to us is a correct legal judgment rooted in the context of past judgments—there are cases where there are not real questions of justice or novelty at stake, we are just trying to crunch a technical legal matter, and disagreement seems problematic. Other times, novel questions of law and justice predominate—consider value-laden constitutional litigation, where we would expect reasonable judges to disagree all the time. And in many cases we want a little bit of both.

SCOPING DEEPVEHICLE: SOME NORMATIVE CONSIDERATIONS

Given that we are stuck with judges for the foreseeable future, yet have the inevitable temptation to integrate something like DeepVehicle into their work, it will help us to consider a handful of the many tasks that we,

---

[16] If we were doing proper jurisprudence here, this would be a cue for an excursus into the extent to which these different claims of justice could plausibly be incorporated into the notion of a single legally correct answer—but as I am doing improper jurisprudence, we will ignore this altogether. (At any rate, I do not think the distinction is relevant to judging the capacity of DeepVehicle.)

[17] In mathematical terms, we might think of a function whose domain is not known from the start, and where unknown parts of the domain might not map to a single output. Cf. Morison and Harkens (2019, 13) who identify the indeterminacy of specific legal outcomes with adjudication's character as a social process in which facts and arguments are constructed (and sometimes created as legal novelty) from an open-ended set of potential inputs.

[18] Indeed, I will go further and say (in the spirit of improper jurisprudence) that the usefulness of the two stories I have told so far more or less tracks the Hartian distinction between "easy" and "hard" cases. While I am at it, one more totally undefended allusion to mainline jurisprudence: we could call DeepVehicle a tool to achieve Dworkinian "fit" and say that the continuing employment of Judge Hercules is much more likely to be effective at "justification." Alternatively, we could point to the dynamic tension Waldron (2008, 7–9) identifies between the value of determinacy and the value of participatory opportunities.

normatively speaking, desire that the law carry out, and think about how DeepVehicle might contribute to or undermine those goals.

ORGANIZING LIVES/PREDICTING CONSEQUENCES

One recurrent theme in the rule of law literature (prominent, inter alia, in Hayek and Fuller) is the notion of predictability: individuals are said to be more capable of self-rule, either through or independent of the law, to the extent they are capable of predicting what the law will conclude about their behavior.[19] Predictability likely also encourages economically beneficial settlement.

There is a sense in which DeepVehicle could be said to do a better job of giving guidance to citizens about the legal outcomes of their planned actions than the current method of adjudication. After all, Judge Hercules can always share her code and data, and assuming she uses good reproducibility practices, citizens could generate, in advance, reliable predictions about how a judge would rule on their proposed behavior, at least to the extent they could generate reliable conclusions about the way in which the facts would be labeled.[20] In effect, if the judge only rules on the basis of DeepVehicle's predictions, and the case is one in which it is clear what input vector to pass to that model, there is a potentially unprecedented degree of certainty to the outcome.

Note, however, that I snuck back in the assumption that it is relatively easy to figure out the correct feature representation of a given case. This may be true for some subcategories of cases, such as those where the relevant legal rule rests entirely on some closed part of reality, but will obviously be false for many others.

One domain where such advantages might be available would be in evaluating the facial validity of legal documents. Such document evaluation ("does this lease contain any facially void provisions?") could be the object of a canonical feature representation that would make it relatively

---

[19] For discussion of Hayek's view and more on prediction, see Gowder (2016, 68–70); on Fullerian views, see Postema (1994, 370–73).

[20] This rests on a practical assumption about machine learning, namely, that many aspects of machine learning practice are surprisingly easy, and getting easier every day. For example, while training models requires a certain amount of expertise, as of this writing, a pre-trained model (suitable to generate predictions on new data) can be distributed directly to end-users and can even be executed in an ordinary web browser. (See, e.g., the TensorFlow JavaScript library at https://js.tensorflow.org.)

easy for an individual to pass the correct vector into a preexisting model. This is especially true for those legal rules that are effectively a one-way ratchet—if a lease is invalid on its face, for example, because it has some provision forbidden by a statute, it is typically going to be invalid no matter what extrinsic facts are introduced, while a lease that might look valid on its face could require the introduction of additional facts that still make it invalid—DeepLease could at the very least reduce the range of uncertainty in such cases by allowing some subset of invalid leases to be identified on the spot.[21]

Often, we capture this organizing lives/predicting consequences value of law in terms of a rule of law and due process demand that law provide subjects with notice of how it applies to their behavior. There is some reason to worry, however, that there may be a systematic tradeoff between DeepVehicle's capacity to reach accurate judgments by fully capturing all relevant factors and its capacity to remain consistent with the value of notice.

The "bias-variance tradeoff" (James et al. 2013, 33 *et seq.*) is a core problem in machine learning. Essentially the problem is that you always have to choose between a relatively simple model that can generalize to unseen data but does not take into account all the information we have and a relatively complex model that generalizes less well ("overfits") but is more capable of representing the data we already have. It seems to me that DeepVehicle would be systematically subject to this problem. A model with a complex feature representation would do a better job of capturing all of the considerations that appeared in the prior cases, but would potentially lead to idiosyncratic results in novel cases, results likely to surprise faithful readers of the statutory text. A model with a simple feature representation, or, like parametric machine learning models (logistic regression as opposed to a neural net), one that imposed side-constraints on the relationship between features and result, would discard potentially relevant information from prior cases, to the end of generating outcomes that more resemble human decisions and hence are more likely to be replicable by external human reasoners.

---

21 However, for reasons I discussed in an earlier paper (Gowder 2018) and at more length in a conversation on the "Oral Argument" podcast http://oralargu ment.org/175, 21 July 2018 (last accessed 22 May 2020), this might actually be bad for egalitarian rule of law values. If we create a world in which the landlord has a computer to catch easy facial blunders in his oppressive leases, so that he can rewrite them without the legal errors but with just as much oppression, we have taken away a relatively cheap way for tenants and their legal advocates to have those leases invalidated and eke out a little bit of justice in a system where the decks are already stacked against them.

Michael Livermore's contribution to this volume provides a fascinating example of this tradeoff.[22] He considers a version of DeepVehicle used not to aid judges but to aid the legislature: a statute that specifies a model architecture and a set of features, and simply provides that objects that the model classifies as vehicles are, *ipso facto*, vehicles. This version of DeepVehicle would obviate the need for much of the judicial feature-lawyering on which I have focused in this chapter, and for that reason shows substantial promise.[23]

And yet. For ordinary subjects of law to be able to conform their conduct to Livermore's statute, the model would have to be created with a mind to ensuring that the features over which it was defined were accessible to all. Livermore's example DeepVehicle statute incorporates a computer vision model with an image of specified dimensions. But any such model would have to accommodate variations in the ability to generate such images, in the equipment and positioning of citizen versus police cameras, and so forth—and might be wholly intractable in any event, as such an image could only be generated after the alleged vehicle has already entered the park (or, at least, within-park and outside-park images are likely to look very different)—thus potentially depriving citizens of the opportunity to come to a reasonable conclusion about whether or not their prospective conduct would violate the law until after they carry it out (DeepKafka?).[24]

It seems to me that this example is unlikely to be idiosyncratic, and that this is a kind of bias-variance tradeoff inherent to such enterprises: the more parametric a model embedded in the statute, the more ordinary

---

[22] Michael A. Livermore, "Rule by Rules" (Chapter 11 in this volume).

[23] Although the weights on his neural network would have to come from somewhere—presumably from prior judicial decisions.

[24] It might be that technological change could support the creation of artificial images in advance that could give citizens notice about their plans—for example, by superimposing a picture of the stroller or whatever over a picture of the park and generating predictions from there. However, current computer vision technology is notoriously variable in the face of sometimes minute differences in images; there is an entire subdiscipline of computer vision dedicated to generating "adversarial examples"—images that are imperceptibly different to humans but that yield different predictions from the model (Elsayed et al. 2018). So at least it is an open question under current technology about how much the context shift from observed features of the conduct to pre-conduct simulation of those features could change predictions of the model. Possibly the most fruitful area for application of Livermore's machine learning as legislation concept would be where subjects of law could directly incorporate the model into their behavior. For example, we might imagine a Securities and Exchange Commission regulation of some electronic trading practice where the rules are specified by a machine learning model, and that model can also be deployed by traders to pre-screen trades.

citizens could figure out in advance how it governs their conduct, but the less capable it would be of capturing the diversity of situations that a legislature might want to handle.[25] And this is true whether the citizens are trying to read the text and figure out how an AI-aided judge would interpret it, or trying to prospectively replicate on their own computers the data that a police drone hovering over the park fitting models to their behavior would have.

Of course, this tradeoff exists in ordinary legislation as well—the bias-variance tradeoff is analogous to the rule-standard tradeoff, and a legislature choosing between making law like the First Amendment or making law like the Internal Revenue Code is, arguably, choosing between language that fully represents the legislative intent or law that normal human beings can work with.[26] So DeepVehicle as statute might just represent a shift in our existing domains of human-intractable law. Many individuals with complex financial circumstances are obliged to hire accountants to avoid being punished for inadvertent violations of the tax code; perhaps the lesson of Livermore's example is that some citizens with other complex circumstances in their lives might also be obliged to hire data scientists. But at a minimum we ought to shape our choices about which legal domains to introduce AI into with consciousness of this cost.

CONSTRAINING POWER

A second category of legal value is the law's capacity to constrain official power. The discursive and procedural elements of litigation are central to law's function as constraint, for (as I have argued at some length in Gowder 2016; Gowder 2015) the constraint of power that the rule of law

---

[25]   As Livermore sensibly suggests, the statute could provide a natural language definition in addition to the model specification—but this introduces more difficulties in determining which would prevail in cases of conflict, and what the non-prevailing definition would add to the analysis in such cases (if the natural language wins, the function of the machine learning model again becomes judicial, and the reader may scroll back to the beginning of this chapter). These questions are not insurmountable—but they highlight the overarching point of this chapter, which is that the tasks of lawyers and judges in sorting such things out cannot be laid down.

[26]   Chief Justice Marshall first expressed this in the American tradition: "A Constitution, to contain an accurate detail of all the subdivisions of which its great powers will admit, and of all the means by which they may be carried into execution, would partake of the prolixity of a legal code, and could scarcely be embraced by the human mind." *McCulloch v. Maryland*, 17 U.S. 316 at 407 (1819).

offers inevitably comes through mass action or its threat. The individual capacity to offer legal arguments in such a system is important as a method of communicating claims and outcomes to the rest of the community in order to facilitate broad-based knowledge about official compliance with law.

While this suggests that the value of constraint of power initially might weigh against the acceptability of DeepVehicle, we could imagine some circumstances in which we might be able to use DeepVehicle to help constrain officials in the service of rule of law values. This could be particularly important in criminal law, in which defendants might make plausible arguments from the rule of lenity and due process/*ex post facto* principles barring retroactive criminal law for the claim that if DeepVehicle labels their behavior as non-criminal, any new rule labeling it as criminal can operate prospectively only.

DeepVehicle might also be useful as an external check on government claims of discretion rooted in legal indeterminacy. For example, in the United States, the qualified immunity defense is available under 42 U.S.C. § 1983 to state officials who violate civil rights if the law prohibiting their conduct is not "clearly established"; this doctrine has been criticized for requiring such a high degree of certainty in the wrongfulness of official conduct that it effectively denies the victims of (for example) egregious police abuse any remedy (Reinhardt 2015, 1244–50; Carbado 2016, 1519–22; Feldman 2017). Potentially, something like DeepVehicle could be used as a floor on clearly established doctrine—perhaps if a preexisting model predicts that an official's behavior is illegal with sufficiently high confidence, that misbehavior should count as clearly established. Of course, this idea could also be abused by officials in the other direction, to claim that the illegality of some blatantly abusive behavior is not clearly established because the model does not happen to pick it out.[27]

---

[27] That being said, if "clearly established" is outrageously narrow, there is probably more room for (the hypothetical model that I, in the interest of gallows humor, am tempted to name) DeepBeat to expand rather than contract the set of behaviors subject to liability, at least in the short term. Essentially the question comes down to how much similarity to preexisting facts is required under current doctrine versus under DeepBeat: if qualified immunity doctrine as it currently stands requires the misconduct to essentially be identical to the facts of some prior case, then a machine learning model that can generalize just a little bit from those facts would be an improvement. In machine learning terms, the criticism of qualified immunity doctrine is that it overfits the narrow facts of particular prior cases, and ought to be swapped out with something (DeepBeat *or* a less terrible legal rule) that generalizes better—this is another analogy to the bias-variance tradeoff.

OUTPUT OF DEMOCRATIC SOVEREIGNTY

One of the tasks that we ask of law is that it transmit commands from a democratic sovereign to its members and officials, although the precise details of when law is properly attributable to a popular sovereign is a matter of longstanding debate. At least sometimes, we probably have some pro tanto reason, for the purposes of implementing the democratic or legislative will, to interpret law consistent with its legislative intent or popular understanding. Again, there is endless controversy here, but we also have a regular judicial practice of interpreting statutes in accordance with some notion of legislative intent, so I shall simply rest on that observation and proceed.

We might perhaps put DeepVehicle to work in this context as a tool to connect statutory interpretation and legislative or popular cognitions. Consider the case of a legislature looking to exercise more fine-grained control over how the courts interpret its statutes. As it presently stands, perhaps legislators can make use of things like canons of statutory interpretation to predict and shape how courts will interpret their enactments, but their present ability to use those tools is uncertain at best (Gluck and Bressman 2013). DeepVehicle might enhance shared knowledge between legislatures and courts about how particular provisions in statutory text would be interpreted. If we had, for example, a dataset sufficient to generate predictions about how courts would interpret different formulations of the definitions section in our "no vehicles in the park" statute, we could use it to coordinate judicial and legislative interpretations of that section—legislators could choose the language most consistent with their intent, confident that courts using the same machine learning model would interpret the statute accordingly.[28]

One must observe that qualified immunity does seem to be sufficiently restrictive in terms of the facts that would give rise to liability that we could reasonably expect a machine learning model to do *much* better than current doctrine. For just one example: as this volume prepares to go to press, the supposedly liberal 9th Circuit has recently held that it was not clearly established that a police officer violated any constitutional rights when he *stole* property covered by a search warrant. *Jessop v. City of Fresno*, No. 17-16756 (9th Cir., 4 September 2019). And then there is *Corbitt v. Vickers*, No. 17-15566 (11th Cir., 10 July 2019), which held that qualified immunity applied when a police officer entered the (innocent third-party) plaintiff's property while in pursuit of a suspect, tried to shoot her non-aggressive pet dog for no reason, missed, and hit her child.

[28]   One objection: if the legislature could think of the cases that they wanted to be sure counted as vehicles, they could just write them directly in the text; the problem with statutory interpretation is what to do with the cases the legislators

Alternatively, we might conceive of DeepVehicle as a tool for creating statutory intent. Hurd (1990) has argued that legislative enactments cannot count as communication in a Griceian sense because that account of communication requires both a speaker's intent—notoriously difficult to determine in the case of a legislature—as well as an audience that can receive that intent—notoriously difficult to achieve in the case of mass audiences who at best learn the meaning of statutes through intermediate communicators (the press, their lawyers). Perhaps DeepVehicle could allow us to attribute an intention to the legislature to pick out the cases covered by the predictions the model generates from their language (a slight variation on Livermore's idea), and at least have some hope that ordinary citizens would have access to the tools to "listen" to that communication by repeating the prediction (this obviously requires much more theoretical development).

That being said, DeepVehicle would also require some limitations in order to protect democratic sovereignty, particularly to the extent that sovereignty is understood to consist, in part, in a discursive relationship with legal decision makers.[29] On such a conception of democratic sovereignty, the people must be understood to have some capacity to criticize and (ultimately) change legal conclusions—and thus, in computational terms, to invalidate the labels in the existing datasets. The points I made above about the necessary capacity for judges to make new law, in connection with the wheelchair hypothetical, will apply with equal force to the capacity of legislatures and mass publics to do so. Without more fully developing an account of how exactly the people do make law and engage in discourse with their legal systems I cannot fill out here precisely what the consequent limitations on DeepVehicle would be.

---

could not dream up. This problem can be made to dissolve with a little bit more effort from the computational side: neural networks can generate novel data similar to their training sets—like Chinese poetry (Zhang and Lapata 2014)!—so DeepVehicle could generate imaginary arrangements of facts that are/are not predicted to count as vehicles so that the legislators may see the hidden implications of their text and correct for any that they dislike. In software engineering terms, we can think of this as a kind of intelligent fuzzing (Oehlert 2005), where we use machine learning to generate hypothetical cases for our proposed statute and see if anything goes wrong.

[29] See, e.g., Dworkin (1997, 343–7); Gowder (2014b).

CONCLUSION: LEGAL COGNITION AIN'T JUST COGNITION

In the context of all these points, it may be best to see our philosophical thought experiment of what would happen if we inserted machine learning into adjudication as pointing to the irreducibly discursive nature of legal judgment. Thus, I assert the following propositions.

- *There might actually be a use for DeepVehicle.*   Machine learning could be juridically useful in informing litigants and courts about generalizations from prior decisions and facilitating higher inter-case consistency, particularly in those types of cases that appear with high frequency and that are characterized by well-established factual representations in their domains. Document-based practices may be most amenable to DeepVehicle, such as administrative law in contexts such as securities and patents, and even Social Security disability claims (to the extent medical records are predictive of outcomes) as well as leases, some kinds of insurance claims, and the like.
- *We would have to lawyer it like usual.*   The shape of any model would continue to be subject to ordinary legal process. We would expect lawyers to debate, and judges to decide, things like the success metrics, classification thresholds, and underlying ontology as well as the features represented in the input vector for any model. Indeed, the decisions about many of these inputs to the machine learning process bear a striking isomorphism to ordinary modes of lawyerly reasoning, with the most salient example being the correspondence between the lawyer's practice of identifying relevant facts to distinguish or follow prior cases and the data scientist's task of feature selection. Judge Hercules keeps her job.
- *The uses of and weight placed on any such models would have to be subject to continuing scrutiny and would also vary by area.*   For an obvious example relating to one of the areas noted above: it would be dangerous and almost certainly unjust to deny Social Security disability claims solely on the basis of a machine learning fit from medical records, in light of, among many other reasons, disparities in access to treatment. Similarly, in the criminal law, we might hope that courts interested in basic legal values would choose to use machine learning adjudicative tools in a way heavily favoring defendants—as noted above, perhaps with results that are binding when defendant-favoring but not when prosecutor-favoring. Ordinary principles of law and justice such as the requirement that

ambiguities be resolved in favor of criminal defendants would need to be translated into machine learning terms.

• *Common law methods are well-suited to manage the incorporation of machine learning into law.* The common law might be described as the art and science of muddling through in the context of novelty: evolving robust legal rules in the face of novel facts, via judges doing the best they can on a case-by-case basis, and drawing liberally from adjacent cognitive domains (neighboring doctrines, neighboring intellectual disciplines, and neighboring frameworks for normative decisions in the form of social norms). This is precisely what would be needed to handle the use of machine learning in legal adjudication: we would need to develop meta-rules governing the use of such tools.[30] Thus, Judge Hercules may be wise to borrow rules from the existing law covering other areas of adjudication. For example, we might imagine building on existing rules of precedent to develop rules as to which cases are included in the training data and the weights to be placed on them, depending on jurisdiction, hierarchical level of the issuing court, date, and the like. We might borrow from evidence and civil procedure to figure out what weight to give to the models themselves—drawing analogies between DeepVehicle and, for example, an expert witness, a special master, or a lower court subject to a standard of review on appeal. All of these meta-level legal judgments would likely have to evolve in pragmatic common law fashion, incrementally incorporating prior experience into ongoing judicial experimentation.[31]

• *The legal academy would need to step up.* The story of this chapter has not just been a thought experiment, but also an implicit exercise in speculative disciplinary sociology: it makes some claims about what would have to happen if (when?) the core of the discipline of law is invaded by the tools and methods of the discipline of AI. We have seen this before, in the growth of law and economics, and at a very high altitude, this chapter borrows from the experience of

---

[30] We would also need to finally carry out a long-overdue task: integrate the professional insights and experiences of lawyers with those of ethicists and computer scientists in the burgeoning literature on algorithmic bias (see generally Garcia 2016).

[31] Contemplating those meta-rules reveals an irony at the heart of DeepVehicle. Judge Hercules considered relying on it in order to promote consistency and certainty, but as the second-order rules for making use of DeepVehicle become more complicated, they in turn may become difficult to apply, and the very reasons for DeepVehicle's introduction may begin to slip away.

law and economics to imagine how the development of law and AI might happen. Notably, law and economics was driven by a narrow but influential cadre of intellectual entrepreneurs in the academy and on the bench. In AI, the scholarly cadre is already moving, but it will not get really interesting until (unless?) the judicial cadre forms (as Calabresi, Posner, and the like served the Herculean role in law and economics).[32] If Hercules the Judicial Data Scientist does show up, this disciplinary invasion will have to be integrated within the intellectual framework of law in order to achieve the benefits of AI without the sacrifice of core legal values. On the practical and instructional side, that integration would require a broader training of future lawyers and judges in the methods with which they will be confronted: as every law student now learns at least the rudiments of ideas like the difference between property rules and liability rules, law schools may have to incorporate the epistemology of machine learning into the curriculum in order to prepare the bench and bar for what it may face.[33] On the scholarly side, legal academics may be called upon both to manage the interdisciplinary interface between machine learning methods developed in the academy (and in industry) and legal methods, and to serve their traditional role of systematizing and rationalizing the case-by-case experimentation of judges.

Ultimately, reflecting on machine learning as an element of adjudication should lead us to more vividly appreciate the fact that legal cognition is not *just* cognition. It serves social functions and is embedded into

---

[32]   The sociological predictions of this chapter also mirror our experience with law and economics: despite the ambitions of its founders, economic methods did not take over the field of law; they never did manage to swap out the traditions of the common law for, e.g., Coasean transaction cost economics, although those insights have been put to fruitful use across the discipline.

[33]   This also means that law students will have to be taught to abandon their traditional terror of math. The undersigned has taught an open-source course, entitled "Introduction to Quantitative and Computational Legal Reasoning," which is aimed at making some progress along these lines (readers may access or contribute to the materials for it at https://sociologicalgobbledygook.com); many of the contributors to this volume have conducted similar experiments. I very much hope that the legal academy develops a distinctive mathematical/statistical pedagogy and community of knowledge around such teaching in the near future, one that draws instructional lessons from the experience of our colleagues in computer science and statistics (such as the method of instruction by problem sets) without picking up their vices (such as the shamelessly lazy method of lecturing by reading proofs off a slide).

networks of relationships that mediate hierarchical social categories (cf. Gowder 2018) as well as procedural systems that encapsulate important judgments of political entitlement. Replicating the cognitive operations of legal professionals on either side of the bench is the easy part—that is just engineering—but mapping computational cognition to their social roles is far more difficult and interesting.

REFERENCES

Aletras, Nikolaos, Dimitrios Tsarapatsanis, Daniel Preoţiuc-Pietro, and Vasileios Lampos. 2016. "Predicting Judicial Decisions of the European Court of Human Rights: A Natural Language Processing Perspective." *PeerJ Computer Science* 2: e93. Accessed 1 June 2020 at https://peerj.com/articles/cs-93/.

Burges, Christopher J.C. 1998. "A Tutorial on Support Vector Machines for Pattern Recognition." *Data Mining and Knowledge Discovery* 2 (2): 121–67.

Burnham, Kenneth P., and David R. Anderson. 2004. "Multimodel Inference: Understanding AIC and BIC in Model Selection." *Sociological Methods & Research* 33 (2): 261–304.

Carbado, Devon W. 2016. "Blue-on-Black Violence: A Provisional Model of some of the Causes." *Georgetown Law Journal* 104 (6): 1479–530.

Dworkin, Ronald. 1986. *Law's Empire*. Cambridge, MA: Harvard University Press.

Dworkin, Ronald. 1997. *Freedom's Law: The Moral Reading of the American Constitution*. Cambridge, MA: Harvard University Press.

Elsayed, Gamaleldin, Shreya Shankar, Brian Cheung, Nicolas Papernot, Alex Kurakin, Ian Goodfellow, and Jascha Sohl-Dickstein. 2018. "Adversarial Examples that Fool both Computer Vision and Time-Limited Humans." *Advances in Neural Information Processing Systems* 31: 3910–20.

Feldman, Leonard C. 2017. "Police Violence and the Legal Temporalities of Immunity." *Theory & Event* 20 (2): 329–50.

Fuller, Lon. 1976. *Anatomy of the Law*. Westport, Conn.: Greenwood Press.

Garcia, Megan. 2016. "Racist in the Machine: The Disturbing Implications of Algorithmic Bias." *World Policy Journal* 33 (4): 111–17.

Gluck, Abbe R., and Lisa Schultz Bressman. 2013. "Statutory Interpretation from the Inside: An Empirical Study of Congressional Drafting, Delegation, and the Canons—Part I." *Stanford Law Review* 65 (5): 901–1025.

Gowder, Paul. 2014a. "Equal Law in an Unequal World." *Iowa Law Review* 99 (3): 1021–81.

Gowder, Paul. 2014b. "The Countermajoritarian Complaint." *Transnational Law and Contemporary Problems* 23 (1): 7–33.

Gowder, Paul. 2015. "What the Laws Demand of Socrates—and of Us." *The Monist* 98 (4): 360–74.

Gowder, Paul. 2016. *The Rule of Law in the Real World*. New York: Cambridge University Press.

Gowder, Paul. 2018. "Transformative Legal Technology and the Rule of Law." *University of Toronto Law Journal* 68 (S1): 82–105.

Hady, Mohamed Farouk Abdel, and Friedhelm Schwenker. 2013. "Semi-Supervised Learning." In Monica Bianchini, Marco Maggini, and Lakhmi C. Jain (eds),

Handbook on Neural Information Processing, 215–39. Berlin, Heidelberg: Springer.

Hamilton, William L., Rex Ying, and Jure Leskovec. 2017. "Representation Learning on Graphs: Methods and Applications." *IEEE Data Engineering* 40 (3): 52–74.

Hart, H.L.A. 1958. "Positivism and the Separation of Law and Morals." *Harvard Law Review* 71 (4): 593–629.

Holmes, Oliver Wendell. 1997 (reprint). "The Path of the Law." *Harvard Law Review* 110 (5): 991–1009.

Hurd, Heidi M. 1990. "Sovereignty in Silence." *The Yale Law Journal* 99 (5): 945–1028.

James, Gareth, Daniela Witten, Trevor Hastie, and Robert Tibshirani. 2013. *An Introduction to Statistical Learning: With Applications in R.* 7th ed. New York: Springer.

Katz, Daniel M., Michael J. Bommarito and Josh Blackman. 2017. "A General Approach for Predicting the Behavior of the Supreme Court of the United States." *PLoS ONE* 12 (4): e0174698. Accessed 1 June 2020 at https://journals. plos.org/plosone/article/file?type=printable&id=10.1371/journal.pone.0174698.

Lin, Henry W., Max Tegmark, and David Rolnick. 2017. "Why Does Deep and Cheap Learning Work so Well?" *Journal of Statistical Physics* 168 (6): 1223–47.

Maclin, Richard, and Jude W. Shavlik. 1996. "Creating Advice-Taking Reinforcement Learners." *Machine Learning* 22 (1-3): 251–81.

Mendoza, Hector, Aaron Klein, Matthias Feurer, Jost Tobias Springenberg, and Frank Hutter. 2016. "Towards Automatically-Tuned Neural Networks." In *Workshop on Automatic Machine Learning*, 64: 58–65. Accessed 1 June 2020 at http://proceedings.mlr.press/v64/mendoza_towards_2016.pdf.

Morison, John and Adam Harkens. 2019. "Re-Engineering Justice? Robot Judges, Computerised Courts and (Semi) Automated Legal Decision-Making." *Legal Studies* 39 (4): 618–35.

Oehlert, P. 2005. "Violating Assumptions with Fuzzing." *IEEE Security Privacy* 3 (2): 58–62.

Ortner, Daniel. 2016. "The Merciful Corpus: The Rule of Lenity, Ambiguity and Corpus Linguistics." *Boston University Public Interest Law Journal* 25 (1): 101–42.

Pasquale, Frank A. 2019. "A Rule of Persons, not Machines: The Limits of Legal Automation." *George Washington Law Review* 87 (1): 1–55.

Pasquale, Frank, and Glyn Cashwell. 2018. "Prediction, Persuasion, and the Jurisprudence of Behaviourism." *University of Toronto Law Journal* 68 (S1): 63–81.

Postema, Gerald J. 1994. "Implicit Law." *Law and Philosophy* 13 (3): 361–87.

Postema, Gerald J. 2014. "Law's System: The Necessity of System in Common Law." *New Zealand Law Review* [2014] (1): 69–105.

Reinhardt, Stephen R. 2015. "The Demise of Habeas Corpus and the Rise of Qualified Immunity: The Court's ever Increasing Limitations on the Development and Enforcement of Constitutional Rights and some particularly Unfortunate Consequences Essay." *Michigan Law Review* 113 (7): 1219–54.

Sokolova, Marina, and Guy Lapalme. 2009. "A Systematic Analysis of Performance Measures for Classification Tasks." *Information Processing & Management* 45 (4): 427–37.

Waldron, Jeremy. 2004. "The Rule of Law as a Theater of Debate." In Justine

Burley (ed.), *Dworkin and His Critics: With Replies by Dworkin*, pp. 319–36. Malden, MA: Wiley Online Library.

Waldron, Jeremy. 2008. "The Concept and the Rule of Law." *Georgia Law Review* 43 (1): 1–61.

Williams, Ryan C. 2017. "Questioning *Marks*: Plurality Decisions and Precedential Constraint." *Stanford Law Review* 69 (3): 795-865.

Zhang, Xingxing, and Mirella Lapata. 2014. "Chinese Poetry Generation with Recurrent Neural Networks." In *Proceedings of the 2014 Conference on Empirical Methods in Natural Language Processing (EMNLP)*, pp. 670–80.

11. Rule by rules*

Michael A. Livermore

INTRODUCTION

From at least Leibniz, the dream of removing human beings from the loop of legal reasoning has captured the imaginations of philosophers, lawyers, and (more recently) computer scientists. This project of law-as-computation (sometimes referred to as "computational law") seeks to reduce the law to a set of algorithms that could be automatically executed on a computer, seamlessly translating raw inputs into legal conclusions. Proponents of this approach generally argue that legal automation would increase legal certainty and facilitate the neutral application of law by transcending human biases and errors.

The Leibnizian vision of law has been given renewed life by recent advances in machine learning and artificial intelligence (AI). As has been frequently noted, machine applications are now able to engage in a variety of tasks that, until recently, were the exclusive domain of human beings: from language processing and driving to the mastery of strategic games such as chess, go, and poker. Across many fields, machines are now able to outperform humans in tasks once thought of as at the core of human intelligence, as when IBM's Watson defeated *Jeopardy!* champion Ken Jennings. If a computer can engage in the complex tasks of natural language processing and knowledge management needed to beat the best humans in a trivia game, the natural question arises as to whether computers could perform similar feats in other domains of social life, including law.

Many law scholars may be inclined to object to Leibniz's vision based on some version of a legal realist critique of legal determinism. For many, these objections might begin with the argument that law is an artifact

 * Thanks for helpful comments from Mauricio Guim, Aziz Huq, Fred Schauer, Ryan Whalen, and participants at the Emergence of Computational Legal Studies Conference 2018 at the University of Hong Kong and the Fourth Annual Workshop on Artificial Intelligence and Law at Vanderbilt University Law School.

of natural language and therefore cannot ever be amenable to machine interpretation based purely on symbolic reasoning.

The recent generation of machine learning tools show that this objection is likely to fail. There are currently available information processing tools that are sufficiently flexible that, in principle, they could be used to render legal decision making fully deterministic, even when applied in the real world of human conflict and dispute. If this is true, and natural language does not place an absolute limit on the ability of purely automated systems to execute the law, something like the Leibnizian vision is possible.

But although law-as-computation might be possible, a second question arises concerning whether it is desirable. In coming years, law scholars can help shed light on the many normative and practical questions that will arise as the theoretical possibility law-as-computation moves closer to reality.

One high level question is whether law-as-computation is a project worth pursuing at all. To some, the answer may seem an obvious "yes." Jeremy Bentham, for example, argued that judicial discretion is a necessary evil in the implementation of law, something to be bemoaned and accepted at best (Alfange 1969). From this perspective, it may have been the case in the past that it was impossible for a legislature to craft statutory language in the kind of detailed but supple manner that would be necessary to determine outcomes in every case, making human judges (and their discretion) necessary. But law-as-computation raises the possibility of self-executing statutes where human discretion is no longer necessary for the basic functioning of a legal order. If human discretion is an evil that is only justified on the basis of its necessity, then (presumably) when it is no longer needed, it should be abandoned.

Perhaps, but not so fast. It is worth considering if there are any other reasons why judicial discretion might be justified beyond the simple functioning of a legal system. In particular, there may be characteristics of human judges and the courtroom that are attractive in their own right, even so much so that we could not abandon them without losing something important about the rule of law. Human judges and other persons charged with interpreting legal texts reason in ways that, at least with current approaches, remain over the horizon of machine capacities. For example, although a machine learning algorithm could be trained to accurately predict how a legislature might engage in a classification task, that is not the same thing as reasoning about the purposes of a statutory scheme. Machines do not currently engage in moral or causal forms of reasoning or develop theories of mind and human motivations. These are human capabilities that allow for the co-creation of rich social universes that, in modern society, include law. Crucially, in the courtroom, the subjects of the ultimately legal decision enjoy procedural rights to be involved in this co-creation process—rights that would be severely constrained or even meaningless in the law-as-computation model. Thus, a decision made by a person in a context of robust participatory procedures may carry some special normative weight that cannot be replicated by machine decision of even very high quality.

How one feels about the prospect of law-as-computation may thus turn on relatively deep questions in political philosophy and jurisprudence, rather than on technical issues associated with natural language processing. Although the future of law-as-computation will include a substantial role for professionals and academics in other fields, such as computer science and information engineering, there are a host of normative questions raised by this potential technology that fall within the traditional domain of legal scholarship.

To explore the interaction of technical developments and our normative understanding of law, this chapter will first describe, in rough terms, Leibniz's vision of law and explore some of his intellectual heirs working in areas such as AI and law and computational law, focusing on some of the difficulties that arise from the natural language characteristics of law and past attempts by some researchers to surmount these challenges. The chapter will then turn to a particularly promising approach to achieving law-as-computation based on the machine learning approaches at the heart of the recent renaissance in AI. Techniques such as artificial neural networks (ANN) and other data-based categorization tools may be able to surmount the barriers created by the kind of vague, ambiguous, or open-textured natural language that characterizes the law. Finally, the chapter will discuss the normative consequences of this type of approach. The famous "no vehicles in the park" debate between legal philosophers Lon Fuller and H.L.A. Hart can be updated for an age of law-as-computation through a hypothetical statute that directly embeds a trained ANN for purposes of establishing legally binding categorizations. Such an approach would essentially eliminate the need for judicial discretion in legal interpretation but may raise other troubling issues. Contemplating such a system—where the law is constructed directly and immediately by the rules themselves—helps highlight the promise of law-as-computation but might also illuminate the true value of judges and the courtroom in any system of laws.

LEIBNIZ'S VIEW OF THE LAW

Gottfried Wilhelm Leibniz is most famous for his contributions to mathematics and philosophy, but he also studied and wrote about law and legal philosophy (Armgardt 2014). One of his earlier works, submitted as a doctoral dissertation at the University of Altdorf, was *Disputatio de casibus perplexis*, a tract about the difficulty of "perplexing cases" wherein the application of the law to particular circumstances appears to generate contradictory results (Armgardt 2014; Cairns 1946). That question continues to animate contemporary debates about the determinacy of the legal system and has been taken up by figures such as Hart, Joseph Raz, and Ronald Dworkin, among many others. Leibniz argued that, when both the question and the law are properly understood, there is a unique correct answer to all legal questions (Ben-Menahem 1993), a view that (forgiving the anachronism) places him in opposition to the legal realists and critical legal theorists of today who believe that the law, as written, is at least often indeterminate. Leibniz attempts to solve the problem of indeterminacy by introducing several rules of interpretation and then arguing, using a set of example cases, that his rules are sufficient to resolve them.

Leibniz's thoughts on legal philosophy are most interesting for how they fit in with his larger projects. As noted by Ben-Menahem (1993: 209), "throughout his life Leibniz believed in certainty through formal procedure: in the possibility of constructing simple self-contained algorithms which would yield truth mechanically." This notion is starkly presented in his *Dissertatio de Arte Combinatoria* (1666) as the Universal Mathematics, a theoretical, formal system of propositions and rules that would enable all disputes to be resolved with mathematical precision. Leibniz believed that such a formal system could even be applied to moral questions, arguing that, with a Universal Mathematics in hand,

> if controversies were to arise, there would be no more need of disputation between two philosophers than between two accountants. For it would suffice for them to take their pencils in their hands and to sit down at the abacus and say to each other (with a friend if they wish): Let us calculate. (Leibniz 1666)

Leibniz's legal philosophy was not terribly influential in his time and has been eclipsed by his other contributions. However subsequent philosophers picked up similar themes. Perhaps most importantly, Jeremy Bentham was a strong proponent of legal codification, which he viewed as an antidote to the inaccessible, indeterminate, and confusing common law (Alfange 1969). Bentham's method to achieve this codification was, in many ways, similar to Leibniz's and involved defining legal concepts that mapped onto the world in an unambiguous fashion and then arranging these concepts into a set of relationships that would yield determinate answers to legal questions (Postema 1986). More practically, drawing from the egalitarian principles of the French Revolution and the general aversion to the discredited prior system of feudal law, Napoleon instituted his highly influential codification with the goal of achieving clarity and accessibility in the law. Although the Napoleonic Code did not achieve the kinds of formal perfection sought by Leibniz and Bentham, it did seek to "minimize[] the independent role of judges" (Levine 2005: 63). The general approach taken by the Napoleonic Code has been broadly copied in many jurisdictions throughout the world (Holtman 1981).

In recent years, with both the conceptual and practical advances in computing during the twentieth century, the notion of a mechanical legal system that could be reduced to a set of formal rules that could be used to "calculate" correct legal answers has returned. Computer scientists and software engineers have long been interested in *knowledge representation*, a subset of the field of AI that deals with the problem of how to transform information known about the world into computable code (Hayes-Roth et al. 1983). A knowledge representation approach to machine translation, for example, would seek to directly encode linguistic knowledge concerning the grammatical and semantic structure of different languages into a set of rules that could be deployed on natural language text. For law, knowledge representation could attempt to create code based on the expertise of human lawyers that translates legislative texts directly into executable programs.

Since the 1980s, as part of the first wave of AI research, there have been attempts to use knowledge representation to translate law into executable code.[1] One early approach was to encode statutory language directly from the law. An example of this approach was an undertaking by a group at Imperial College London to model a portion of the British Nationality Act of 1981, which deals with UK citizenship, in the programing language Prolog. The authors recognized that vague statutory terms (such as "good character") are far from self-evident as inputs, but nevertheless believe that there was value in translating legislation into "logical form" because this exercise can help drafters "identify and eliminate unintended ambiguity and imprecision" (Sergot et al. 1986). Early work to address the problem of vague fact-type inputs to statutes (such as whether a person is a "good character") includes a system for representing contract law developed by Anne von der Lieth Gardner (Gardner 1987). Completed as part of a 1984 dissertation, Gardner's model analyzed "offer and acceptance problems" for first year law students, with the goal of separating straightforward applications of vague concepts from those that are less clear. In Gardner's model, legal states (i.e. "offer") are represented via an "augmented

---

[1]   Helpful summaries of the Law and AI movement are provided in Bench-Capon et al. (2012), Rissland et al. (2003).

transition network"—a theoretical linguistic structure based on a Markov process (Woods 1970)—while facts are represented in a syntax developed in Genesereth et al. (1980) called the "meta-level reasoning system." The Gardner model served as an early stage prototype of how knowledge representation could actually be applied to legal decisions, at least in a relatively stylized and simplified setting.

Researchers in this area also recognized early on that legislatures are not the only source of law (Rissland et al. 2006). In Ashley (1990), Kevin Ashley describes work completed as part of his PhD dissertation to construct a computational model of adversarial reasoning in the legal context. Ashley's HYPO software was intended to explore arguments that would arise when prior precedent, drawn from case law, was applied to new circumstances. The core idea was to develop a series of potential modifications to a prior case (i.e. hypotheticals) that could be used to test the types of future cases that would be covered. The HYPO software drew from the work of Ashley's supervisor Edwina Rissland on more general case-based reasoning systems (Rissland 1980). In subsequent work, Rissland incorporated the case-based approach from HYPO into a hybrid system called CABARET that also allowed for rule-based reasoning (Rissland and Skalak 1991). In the same journal issue that reported the CABARET software, Karl Branting described an alternative legal reasoning system based on "exemplar-based explanations" that also incorporated both case-based and rule-based analysis (Branting 1991). Other important work published at around the same time includes Susskind (1987), also based on a dissertation project, which drew on legal philosophy and jurisprudence to investigate the utility of legal expert systems, and Bench-Capon (1991) which reported results from and reflected on a major effort to integrate legal decision making into a knowledge representation system.

Considerable work has expanded on these types of early efforts. An important outlet for work in this vein has been the journal *Artificial Intelligence and Law*, where many of the first movers in the area (including Ashley, Bench-Capon, Branting, and Rissland) remain active as editorial board members. That publication has allowed for a group of researchers at institutions across the globe to continue work on problems related to knowledge representation and law. Academic institutions such as the Stanford Center for Legal Informatics (CodeX), which was founded by Michael Genesereth, and the Leibniz Center for Law of the University of Amsterdam also support work in this area. Beyond academia, Susskind (2013) argues that knowledge representation systems for law have the potential to cause serious disruptions in the profession, and indeed such approaches now serve as the basis for many useful software applications.

One relevant example are various software applications to assist with US federal income tax filing, which are now used by a considerable percentage of filers (Contos et al. 2010). Some commentators have argued that government agencies could use these commercial packages as a template to issue regulations directly as knowledge representation systems rather than as traditional rules (Coglianese 2004).

HUMAN FRAILTY

Both Leibniz and contemporary law-as-computation share a model of law as a formal system of rules. Especially in US legal discourse, this perspective is often derided as simplistic "formalism" that fails to recognize the complexities of legal decision making. Even defenders of legal determinacy—the view that there are correct answers to legal questions—generally do not argue (tracking Leibniz) that the mechanical manipulation of rules as they are written down is alone sufficient. Instead, they typically make room for more flexible and expansive forms of reasoning (Dworkin 1986).

At some level, however, it is difficult to describe the law without invoking rules or something quite rule-like, such as standards or norms (Schauer 1988). Without rules, it is not clear how to distinguish legal decision making from the raw exercise of political power or general moral reasoning. In a rule of law society, judges are expected to apply legal rules to particular facts, not simply impose his or her preferences or select what seems to be the all-things-considered best outcome.

Although it is not enough to simply dismiss Leibniz-style law-as-computation as formalistic, there are two quite powerful challenges to the notion that the law can be fully represented as an executable program. The first is that law fails as a formal system because it lacks internal coherence. Because legal systems arise from natural political processes over time, it would be expected that the law would include conflicting rules, overlaps, lacunas, and other similar problems. Human agents charged with implementing the law can deal in a flexible manner with these failures of logic, but machines are more rigid, and conflicting directives in executable code can lead to wholesale failure.

Such problems are not unique to law and are faced by any large and unwieldy computational system. Within the field of software programming, researchers developed the idea of computational "ontologies" to help address these challenges (Gruber 1993a; Gruber 1993b). Computational ontologies "are a means to formally model the structure of a system, i.e., the relevant entities and relations that emerge from its observation, and which are useful to [the designer's] purposes" (Guarino et al. 2009: 2). A computational ontology renders explicit and formal the "abstract, simplified view of the world" that undergirds the knowledge that is meant to be represented. It is thus an intermediary step between something akin to human understanding and the final coded set of computable logical commands.

Researchers interested in developing knowledge representation systems for law applied these more general lessons to their field. What they began to recognize is that to understand an entire legal system as a formal set of rules would require a generic *legal ontology* for that system. Specifically, to make progress, they saw the "need of an ontological commitment at different levels of abstraction, with explicit specifications of the conceptualization" (Bench-Capon et al. 2012: 267). These ontological commitments would take the form of a shared set of understandings about the entities that are relevant for the legal system and the set of potential relationships between those entities. The effort to develop a working legal ontology can be seen as the most direct descendant of Leibniz's approach to legal reasoning.

The apotheosis of a legal ontology approach would conceive of the legislature as a group of programmers who are writing the law as an executable code. Before they start such a project, coders would agree on an ontology—the basic universe of "stuff" that their code will apply to and the rules for the manipulation of that stuff. A coder-legislature would have as much use for an ontology as would the programmers who design any sophisticated systems, such as an operating system. With the ontological commitments in place, the legislature could divide into committees to work on specific areas of law, reasonably certain that their respective work products will more or less fit together. Indeed, conceiving of a legislature as a group of programmers is not so far removed from the normative enterprise of civil code systems, which seeks internally consistent law.

That said, even in polities that are highly committed to internally coherent law, the real processes of lawmaking make attaining that goal difficult. For example, law revision takes place over time, and even if lawmakers can agree on a legal ontology at some time t_0, that agreement may easily fade, perhaps in ways that are not immediately apparent. If this occurs, inconsistencies can gradually creep into even an initially fully coherent legal order. More to the point, in the contemporary world, legal systems are often very large (involving many rules) and complicated (involving multiple interlocking parts and dependencies). Large and complicated programs are very difficult to maintain bug free. Finally, legal systems are meant to map onto a complex and dynamic social and economic reality, making it even more difficult to achieve internal consistency in practice.

A second set of problems arise from the fact that law is inscribed in natural language (Schauer 2013). A characteristic feature of natural language is *vagueness*, where the applicability of linguistic concepts to certain cases is unclear. For example, although there might be general agreement about the word *hill* and some of the cases that it applies to, there might be other borderline cases where there is disagreement about when a small hill shades into a mound, or a big hill becomes a mountain. For any system of rules to be computable, they must ultimately be reducible to a set of basic logical operations that can be performed in completely definite fashion. If law is inscribed in natural language, and natural language is riddled with vague terms, then the prospect for law-as-computation is dim.

This concern is nicely illustrated in a famous back-and-forth between the legal philosophers Lon Fuller and H.L.A. Hart in the middle of the twentieth century. As explained in Schauer (2008), Fuller and Hart represented two starkly different positions concerning the nature of law, and specifically regarding the relationship between law and morality. Hart maintained that there was a distinction between law and morality, with the former being characterized by the positive law—constitutions, statutes, and judicial opinions—that could be interpreted without recourse to general moral reasoning. Fuller rejected this understanding of the law and argued, in contrast, that it was impossible to make sense of the law without relying on its underlying moral structure.

One line of attack against Hart's position is based on the vagueness of legal language. If the language of a statute is unclear, as applied to a particular case, then something other than purely legal interpretation is necessary to make a decision. Hart accepted that this may sometimes be so, but he argued that it need not always be the case—at least some of the time, the language of the law is sufficient to settle the matter. To make this point, he introduced the classic example of a "legal rule [that] forbids you to take a vehicle into the public park." Hart acknowledged that this hypothetical statute is vague as applied to certain hard cases, such as bicycles and roller skates, but at the same time, he thought that "plainly this [rule] forbids an automobile" (Hart 1958: 607). Thus, the rule had a language-defined "core," even if, at the edges, there was some vagueness.

Fuller introduced the counterexample of a decommissioned military truck that was mounted on a pedestal to strike at Hart's core. For Fuller, the natural interpretation of the word "vehicle" included the truck monument, but this was a plainly absurd (and therefore legally wrong) conclusion. If this was so, even in the core, then the words of the statute alone were insufficient to decide the case because of the inherent limitations of natural language. Fuller's counterexample highlights the "open-textured" nature of language, which is the "potential vagueness in even nonvague terms" (Schauer 2008: 1126). Natural language is open-textured because "even the most precise term has the potential for becoming vague upon confronting the unexpected . . . and so no amount of precision can wall off every possibility of future but now unforeseen and even unforeseeable vagueness" (ibid.). Vehicles might seem like a trivial example, but on even weighty matters, something seemingly obvious, such as who counts as a person for purposes of the crime of murder, can become obscure under examination (Warren 1973).

Open texture has an important relationship to time. The future is always fundamentally unknowable and therefore subject to new cases that were not, or even could not have been, anticipated by the original rule drafter. Mid-century drafters of municipal statutes governing parks could be forgiven for failing to anticipate autonomous aerial drones. This is exactly the kind of case that could create retroactive vagueness even if the term "vehicle" was well-defined at the time of adoption.

The problem of open texture exists for even a well-structured legal ontology. To function, there must be some link between the entities that are described in the law and things that exist in the real world. A vehicle or person might be perfectly well-defined *within* the set of rules that make up the law, but then be vague when applied to objects with wheels, motors, and steering wheels. In the face of vagueness, a system of logical operation that relies on definite categorization will fail.

As noted in Schauer (2013), there is more than one alternative for addressing unanticipated future circumstances and open-textured language. The possibility considered by Fuller and Hart was judicial rulemaking. Under this view, when the language of the law was unclear as applied to an individual case, it is the job of a judge to resolve the ambiguity in some fashion by deciding on a best interpretation (however defined). But an alternative approach was proposed by Bentham, who strongly opposed this type of judicial discretion. Bentham imagined a legal system with a "closure provision" that excluded any new cases not "plainly encompassed" by the rule. Such a closure provision would seem to create the possibility for a "systemic option[] for law other than judicial discretion or judicial lawmaking" (Schauer 2013: 204–5). However, such a closure provision, because it would be encoded in natural language, would also itself be subject to the problem of open texture, creating at least the potential for circumstances in which the law simply cannot provide definite answers.[2]

---

[2] Schauer recognizes the problem of open texture as applied to a closure rule

MACHINE CATEGORIZATION

At first glance, it may seem that the problem of open texture deals a death blow to Leibniz's dream. Recent advances in both the theory and practice of AI and machine learning, however, provide reason to believe that this is not necessarily so.

Although systems for knowledge representation dominated early work in AI, the most recent generation of research in the field has largely moved away from this approach. With breakthroughs in computer science, computational power, and data collection and storage, the field now focuses on flexible machine learning approaches, such as ANNs, capable of making highly accurate predictions without intensive human intervention. Perhaps the best-known example of a modern machine learning approach replacing a knowledge representation system was when Google abruptly switched from a logic-based system derived from linguists' knowledge to an ANN trained on existing multi-language texts to power its Google Translate tool (Agrawal et al. 2018). Another recent example is the success of the program AlphaZero, which is a naïve learner that develops entirely through self-play, compared to traditional game playing software programs that use data on prior human games (Silver et al. 2017).

These same flexible, data-driven tools also have the potential to address some of the challenges that traditional knowledge representation systems have faced in the context of law-as-computation. Specifically, Wolfram (2016) proposes that categorization systems such as ANNs provide a mechanism to create a vagueness-proof legal system that can operate deterministically. Such a system would eliminate the need for human judgment in legal decision making, reviving Leibniz's vision of law-as-computation.

Figure 11.1 is an illustration of a very simple neural network. On the left is an input layer of four nodes, on the right is an output layer with a single node, and in the middle is a hidden layer with three nodes. Each node in each layer is connected to all the other nodes in the neighboring layers. The links are assigned weights, and the nodes in the hidden and output layers are assigned activation functions. Data in the input layer is translated into outputs via the weights and activation functions: the same data generate different outputs if the weights or activation functions are changed.

Neural networks can be used to make categorizations based on the

---

but proposes that the law need not "run out" *if* "a closure rule's language were determinate" (Schauer 2013: 205).

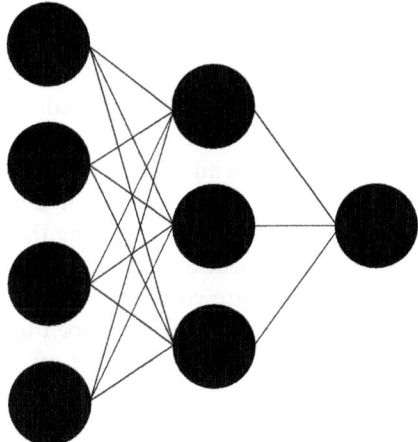

*Figure 11.1   A representation of a simple artificial neural network
(ANN)*

features of the tokens to be categorized. The input layer is populated by
the values taken for each feature for a particular example, and the weights
and activation functions represent a mathematical function for deterministically translating those values into a final value in the output layer.
To take the example of a "vehicle" for the vehicles in the park case, the
output could be a 1 or 0, with "1" signifying "vehicle" and "0" signifying
"not vehicle." The features to be fed into the input layer might be weight,
volume, number of wheels, and maximum speed.[3] Training examples
would be a hand-labeled sample of vehicles and non-vehicles—say cars,
planes, boats, and skateboards, plus drones, toy trucks, shoes, and picnic
baskets. An algorithm can be used to estimate a set of weights to minimize
prediction error in the training set. The model's performance is then tested
on data that was withheld from the training set.

Contemporary neural networks, backed by the "big data" revolution,
have received due praise for their ability to engage in fairly complex
categorization decisions. For example, given a sufficiently large sample
of photographs that are labeled as containing a dog or not, a trained
neural network will be able to categorize out-of-sample photographs
with a degree of accuracy roughly equivalent to that of a human being.
Similar techniques have been used to train neural networks to recognize

---

[3]   These values would typically be normalized for the relevant population.

handwriting and process visual data from telescopes to make astronomical categorizations.

For purposes of law-as-computation, the accuracy of ANNs is important, but what is most consequential is that, once trained, they operate entirely deterministically. Given a set of input values, the ANN can always make an unambiguous characterization, with an output layer taking an output value of either 0 or 1 and nothing else.[4] When engaged in a prediction task, that value might be wrong, in the sense of not matching the pre-assigned label. But there will always be a categorization one way or the other. The ANN thus acts akin to Bentham's closure rule, with the additional advantage of not itself being subject to natural language open texture. Any natural language closure rule is incapable of fully sealing off a legal system from the destabilizing influence of new circumstances. ANN classification would seem to create the genuine possibility of a formally airtight legal system that is not subject to gradual decompression though open texture.

DEFINITION BY ANN

An ANN (or other similar classification algorithm) provides a means to mechanically translate observations concerning the features of objects in the real world into legal categorizations, bridging the gap between a legal ontology of "persons" and "vehicles" and the real world of actual people and things.

This could be done simply through statute of the form:

Statute No. 1123 for City of Annsville
Sec. 1. Vehicles are prohibited in the park.
Sec. 2. Vehicles are to be defined through the application of an ANN with the following characteristics:
    i.   input layer generated by color images of size 400x400 pixels; weight, volume, number of wheels, maximum speed;
    ii. activation functions [A]
    iii. weights [W]

The activation functions [A] and weights [W] would be explicitly defined in the statute, so that any computer with sufficient processing power and

---

[4]   Note that an ANN need not be so constructed—the final output could take any value between 0 or 1, or any real number, for example. The point is that the ANN *could* be constructed to output either a 0 or a 1, for example via a logistic activation function and the rule: output = 1 for all $y > 0.5$; output = 0 for all $y \leq 0.5$.

memory running the relevant software would always produce the same outputs, given a set of inputs. For any suspected vehicle, the relevant information would be collected and inputted into the statutorily specified ANN and an output would be generated, classifying the object as a vehicle or not, triggering the appropriate legal consequences.

The weights, activation functions, and other features of the ANN would be constructed as part of bill drafting. Likely the most efficient way to generate this information would be by collecting training data and feeding that data to a supervised learning system. There would necessarily be considerable human input in this part of the process, through curation and labeling of the training data. In the vehicles in the park example, legislators (or their designees) would identify instances of vehicles and non-vehicles in training data, presumably based on the goals of the underlying statutory regime. In this way, the training data can be understood as deriving from something like legislative intent. This data would then be used to train the model. After the training is complete, activation function and weights could be read off the trained model and stated explicitly in the statute.

Because all of the information necessary to implement the ANN would be contained directly in the statute, the categorizations necessary to implement that statute in any given case would operate as an automatic function of the language in the statute itself. This feature of an ANN statute breaks down the traditional distinction between the creation of legal rules in a legislative process and their implementation in individual cases in an adjudicatory process. An ANN statute would be *self-executing* in the sense that the statute contains the code necessary to apply the law to the facts in all possible cases.

One set of objections naturally presents itself here concerning how the measurements are made. Essentially, these questions raise the issue that, even if the ANN is directly included in the statute, there may be room for discretion in how the measurements are taken: what is the distance from the object when the picture is taken? What about lighting conditions? Is the weight to be taken on a rainy day when the object is soaking wet? The response is that these factors could be specified in the statute, or more to the point, automated via some other ANN—for example, one that controls a drone that continuously surveys the park for potential vehicles and then, when one is suspected, takes the relevant measurements.

Whether these types of objections can be fully satisfied is outside the scope of this project. Perhaps it is possible to eliminate all human discretion; perhaps not (what if the drone breaks down? and the repair drone too?!). For our purposes, let's assume that human discretion can be effectively eliminated, so that human judges are no longer interpreting the meaning of concepts like "vehicle," but instead at most are deciding questions such as whether a scale is functioning properly. In these cases, the statute is operating automatically or near automatically, with the capacity to apply law to facts directly instantiated into itself as code.

If we take it to be roughly plausible that an ANN-based statute, or something similar, is possible, the next set of questions is whether such an approach would be desirable.

ADVANTAGES

The defenders of an ANN-based statute, and law-as-computation more generally, can note several advantages that such a system would have. Generally, an ANN-based statute would be complete, in the sense that there would be no case that could not be classified through the direct application of the statutory definition. As a consequence, the law would be more *legislative* because it would be the legislature that directly decides the shape of the law, without the need for downstream assistance from judges or administrative bureaucrats. To the extent that legislatures are superior venues for lawmaking (in particular due to their democratic legitimacy), this is an important advantage of law-as-computation.

An additional advantage of an ANN-based statute, at least in some contexts, is that the law would be explicit and transparent. If the construction of the ANN appeared in the public laws, then it could be instantiated on any appropriate piece of hardware, allowing the subjects of the law to determine exactly how the law would apply to particular cases. This explicitness would, in general, advance the rule of law value of notice.

It is worth noting that an explicit ANN might also create the potential for gaming, as the subjects of the law test alternatives and then conform their behavior to the letter of the law while undermining legislative purposes. Such an outcome could be avoided if a narrative definition was made public, but the ANN was kept hidden. Hiding the ANN, though, would raise countervailing considerations of notice and secret laws. There is an interesting set of potential tradeoffs to be made in terms of explicitness versus gaming, but they will not be followed here. These tradeoffs are not uniquely presented by law-as-computation; indeed, they are commonplace and faced whenever a legislature must decide between precise rules that can be gamed versus imprecise standards. The possibility of an ANN-based statute or similar law-as-computation approach simply raises the stakes.

Finally, an ANN-based statute might have important *performance* advantages, taken from the perspective of the legislature. One is that randomness related to the assignment of cases to individual judges would be eliminated. There is a long and well-established literature documenting that judges decide similar cases differently—one particularly egregious example is documented in research showing widely divergent grant rates for asylum cases before immigration judges (Ramji-Nogales et al. 2010). The ANN-based statute would not be subject to this kind of random and arbitrary difference in the application of the law to individual cases.

More generally, an ANN might simply outperform judges in terms of achieving legislative purposes. Presumably legislatures adopt statutes for some reason or reasons. Judges, when interpreting those statutes and applying them to individual cases, may simply do a worse job at vindicating the goals of the legislature than the ANN. These failures may arise because of principal-agent costs between the legislature and judges (which would not exist for an ANN) or based on simple human error. Given the choice of human decision makers, with all their foibles, versus a well-trained and accurate ANN, the legislature might choose the latter purely to better achieve the goals of the statute. Just as an autonomous vehicle might outperform a human driver in accomplishing the goal of safely transporting a passenger from point A to point B, an ANN might outperform a human judge in effectuating statutory purposes.

LEGAL OPEN TEXTURE

It is clear that an ANN-based statute would be a terrible idea if it simply functions poorly, leading to worse outcomes than the status quo of human judges. But this is not the interesting case, because then the value of human judges would be obvious. The more interesting case is where the ANN functions well and generates the advantages just discussed, including simply outperforming human judges from the *ex ante* perspective of the legislature. In such cases, the value of human judges is less clear.

One possible reason to favor human judges implementing natural language definitions over an ANN is that the latter might fail in particular problematic ways in individual cases, say by not accounting for some seemingly obvious feature, or treating two cases differently that seem identical on all reasonable grounds. Such outcomes might be particularly offensive, arising from a technical "glitch" rather than on the basis of some interpretive difference over which reasonable people might disagree. Even if, in the aggregate, the ANN generates better results than human judges, failure due to glitch might raise concerns that failure due to disagreement does not.

In his discussion of the Hart-Fuller debate, Schauer (2008) explores a similar question. The important case, for Schauer, is not where the term "vehicles" is linguistically vague (as was suggested by Fuller), but where a term is linguistically clear but is applied to a new case in a way that conflicts with people's judgments about what a sensible rule might be. Schauer contrasts linguistic open texture with such situations, which he refers to as *legal open texture*, where "our language does not fail us but our law does":

> The language is clear, and the application is linguistically clear, but following the clear language will lead to what appears to be a wrong or unjust or unwise or inequitable or silly result. In such cases we do not have linguistic open texture, but we might have legal open texture, and it is in such cases that legal decisionmakers must decide what to do. For Fuller, the law should always in such cases seek to come up with the reasonable result, and from this premise Fuller derives the conclusion that there are no purpose independent, clear, easy, or core cases. . ..[But under an alternative view] sometimes the language of a rule generates a bad result, and sometimes we have to live with that bad result as the price to be paid for refusing to empower judges or bureaucrats or police officers with the authority to modify the language of a rule in the service of what they think, perhaps mistakenly, is the best outcome.

Cases of legal open texture are not merely speculative. Perhaps the most famous example is *Riggs v. Palmer*,[5] where the New York State Court of Appeals heard a case concerning the disposition of the estate of Francis B. Palmer, a man who was murdered by his grandson. The plain language of the will and the relevant statutes implied that the grandson should inherit the estate, but the court found that background normative principles—that a person ought not profit from his misdeed—barred the grandson's claim on the estate. Dworkin (1977) used this case as a core example in his argument against Hart's version of legal positivism. What is most relevant for our purposes is that this is not a case of natural language open texture: all of the relevant terms are well-defined as applied to the case at hand. Rather, the outcome—a murderer taking his grandfather's estate—offends nearly universal notions of justice in ways that imply legal open texture.

The hypothetical ANN-based statute translates all cases of potential linguistic open texture into legal open texture. The law would always be clear, in the linguistic sense, because it would be self-interpreting. But that does not mean that it might not also generate outcomes that are "wrong, silly, absurd, unjust, inequitable, unwise, or suboptimal" (Schauer 2008: 1131). An ANN does not evaluate outcomes against any of the normative criteria that humans use, and so would not be directly sensitive to even

---

[5] 115 N.Y. 506 (1889).

very deep moral concerns arising from injustice or gross negative consequences for individual or collective well-being. Similarly, an ANN might arrive at conclusions that flatly contradicted the purposes of a legislative regime according to any common sense understanding of the human motivations behind the law.

The question is how to feel about the ANN-based statute in light of this possibility. This question essentially recapitulates classic debates between legal formalists and their critics. Formalists believe, roughly, that linguistic meaning ought to control, even when outcomes seem to conflict with a legislative purpose, or equity, or commonly accepted notions of justice. The critics, on the other hand, believe that judges play a critical role in supplementing legislative action with judicial judgment designed to avert negative consequences (Calabresi, 1985). For the sake of convenience, these advocates of legal discretion can be labeled legal purposivist.[6]

Formalists might be relatively more comfortable with an ANN-based statute. The virtues of such an approach, including determinacy and the reduction (or elimination) of judicial discretion, should be particularly attractive to formalists, who are willing to accept some bad outcomes in individual cases to preserve the rule-based nature of legal decisionmaking. Purposivists, on the other hand, might be expected to seek to protect a place for judges to make corrections to avoid patently bad outcomes. If judges are expected to gloss or even negate the express language of the law to promote broader normative goals, then an ANN-based statute that makes such judicial intervention difficult or even impossible, would seem—to a purposivist—to be highly undesirable.

Of course, it is possible that the combination of an ANN with human oversight (based on a natural language definition) would produce the best outcomes. In those cases, there might be good reason to adopt a hybrid approach, although there would still be room for legal open texture to create space between best outcomes and legally required outcomes. But the more interesting case, for our purposes, is where the introduction of human oversight increases the overall error rate and leads to worse outcomes from the *ex ante* perspective of the legislature. Human judgment, in this hypothetical, would have costs in the aggregate, but would also change the nature of the error in some at least plausibly normatively

---

[6]   This label is for convenience only and for purposes of contrast. Critics of formalism include many who would not accept the label of purposivist. As noted by Schauer (2008), these two positions loosely map onto the civil and common law legal traditions, with civil lawyers more comfortable with formalism and common law lawyers more comfortable with a larger discretionary role for judges.

important way: avoiding glitches while introducing more human forms of error.

The law-as-computation proponent might argue that glitches (i.e. errors that are particularly machine-like) are not worse in kind than other types of error. If the goal is to reduce error, then the system that does so should be chosen: machine, human, or hybrid. On the other side is the position that glitches are, for some reason, unacceptable in a way that bad outcomes from the unforeseen consequences of applying a linguistically clear statute (which formalists must accept) or judges departing from the letter of the law (which legal purposivists must accept) are not. This objection to glitches should be conserved even when they are not worse from a consequentialist perspective.

PARTICIPATION

Why might the glitches of an ANN-based statute be more troubling than the linguistic error of a legislature or the mistake of a judge? One possible answer to this question grounds the particular problem of glitches on the participatory rights of legal subjects.

Solum (2004: 279) defends an account of procedural justice where legislation and adjudication cannot be "legitimate" if "the norms of participation are violated." Legitimacy is itself a slippery concept and encompasses multiple meanings (Fallon 2005). From a sociological perspective, legitimacy concerns whether the relevant institution commands the respect and obedience of the relevant population. Morally, legitimacy concerns whether such respect and obedience are justified. Participatory rights could contribute to both sociological legitimacy and moral legitimacy, based either on their importance for felt obligation or their genuine normative value. The following discussion will focus on moral legitimacy, which is also Solum's emphasis. Because it is (or would be) a social fact, the sociological legitimacy of a future ANN-based statute is best understood as the object of empirical inquiry, which is not the focus of this chapter.[7] Moral legitimacy, however, is important in its own right, and may track sociological legitimacy, at least to the extent that people's actual respect and obedience tend to be justified.

Solum defines the "right of participation" as "the right to observe, to make arguments, to present evidence, and to be informed of the reasons for a decision." These rights assure the legal subject that his or her "view

---

[7]   One way to empirically inform speculation about future sociological legiti-

of the law and fact" was "considered" in the proceeding. If these rights are violated, a proceeding would lack legitimacy "(a) even if the outcome of the particular adjudication would be considered right by independent norms of political morality, (b) even if the procedure was generally reliable, and (c) even if the outcome would have been the same had the required participation actually occurred."

If one accepts either Solum's or a related view that participation is necessary for the legitimacy of a legal proceeding, an ANN-based statute raises concerns, which we can refer to as a *participatory objection*. When an individual case is adjudicated via machine, the subject of the proceeding has little opportunity to either "make arguments" to the decision maker or "be informed of the reasons for [the] decision." The relevant features and their weights are determined directly by the statute, and the outcome follows mechanically—there is no room for argument (at least after a law has been adopted) concerning what the features should be, or how they ought to be weighed. Similarly, although the outcome is a consequence of the feature values plus the statutory algorithm, that combination does not add up to "reasons" in the traditional sense and does nothing to make the outcome comprehensible to the legal subject.

Human judges operating according to courtroom procedures, by contrast, are the paradigmatic givers and receivers of legal reasons. Human reasoning is mutually recognizable, based on notions such as causality, morality, and shared mental models of the world. Human beings all learn and use language in ways that are roughly similar, and people in a shared language community have the capacity to make claims about how language ought to be interpreted. Most broadly, human beings share an *umwelt* that allows for mutual recognition, comprehension, and communication (Sebeok 1976). Even a machine with high general intelligence capable of passing a Turing test would not have this shared physical and social reality that makes true communication—and argumentation—possible.

One response to the participatory objection is that the participation rights that exist at the legislation stage are sufficient. We can distinguish between two types of participation: "democratic participation," which exists at the rulemaking stage, and "due process participation," which exists at the adjudicatory stage. This distinction tracks the classic divide in US constitutional law between rulemaking and adjudication that determines when individualized process is required when life, liberty, or

---

macy of an ANN-based statute would be to survey average people about their impression of a hypothetical system. This type of research could provide useful insights into the social acceptability of future legal developments.

property is at stake.[8] If there is robust democratic participation when an ANN-based statute is adopted, and the terms of the statute alone are sufficient to determine the outcomes of all possible cases, then, perhaps democratic participation is sufficient, with no due process rights necessary.

There are several potential replies to this argument from democratic participation. One is that an ANN-based statute would somehow undermine democratic participation at the legislation stage. Perhaps such statutes would be incomprehensible to the public because they are not expressed in natural language. This reply seems weak, however. In complex modern societies, legislatures often generate statutes that are incomprehensible to the general public. If incomprehensibility alone is sufficient to defeat democratic participation, then the law already has a pervasive legitimacy problem. It is not clear that an ANN-based statute would be less comprehensible than any other piece of legislation. Indeed, as discussed above, an ANN-based statute could be tested as applied to individual cases, and thus might be more, not less, comprehensible to the public.

An alternative reply to the argument from democratic participation draws on the notion of legal ontologies introduced above. Perhaps it is the case that any legal system that is sufficiently coherent to be self-interpreting could not possibly arise from democratic contestation with sufficient participatory rights in a diverse and pluralistic polity. If this is true, for an ANN-based statute to function, it would require a degree of coherence that is not achievable through even a minimally satisfactory participatory legislative process.

This reply has more force than the earlier objection based on the comprehensibility of an ANN-based statute. It may well be true that a general legal ontology is unobtainable in a democratic pluralistic society. Nevertheless, computation-as-law could function on the basis of purely local coherence. The "no vehicles in the park" statute appears to be an example where a single ANN-based statute could operate without requiring wholesale coherence across the entire body of law. Even if *all* of law cannot be reduced to computation, there may be important pockets where an ANN-based statute or similar approach is possible, even in a democracy with many competing views.

Another version of the participatory objection is that democratic participation at the legislation stage is insufficient, period. We can refer to this as the *insufficiency objection*. Under this argument, legitimacy requires participation both at the legislative stage and the adjudication stage, and

---

[8] Bi-Metallic Investment Co. v. State Board of Equalization, 239 U.S. 441 (1915).

one cannot be substituted for the other. Very different forms of participation are involved in legislation and adjudication, with different procedures, and legal subjects face very different incentives in the two contexts. If one believes that participation at the adjudication stage is necessary for the legitimacy of a legal decision, then an ANN-based statute may simply be unacceptable, without some hybrid decision making process that also involves a human judge.

There are several possible responses to the insufficiency objection. One is to accept the basic premise that democratic participation and due process participation are independently important, but then argue that alternative modes of participation are possible that at least partially compensate for the loss of due process participation. This is the view argued in Citron (2008), which endorses a new form of "technological due process" based on an "inquisitorial model of quality control" meant to ward against injustice in individual cases. To the extent that Citron's alternative is an adequate substitute for traditional due process participation, it provides one way to respond to this version of the participation objection.

A second response to the insufficiency objection attacks the independent value of due process participation, at least in some contexts. Under this view, due process participation is important when, for whatever reason, judges have discretion to decide the outcome of individual cases. But when judges are constrained by the law—for example, when a formalist judge applies linguistically clear statutory language—then due process participation has little value, because the legal subject cannot shape the ultimate outcome of the decision. All an ANN-based statute would do would extend the field of low-discretion law, which itself is not problematic and where the value of participation is at a nadir, to cover more topics.

Solum addresses this argument, in the context of "points that either cannot, or likely will not, have any effect on the outcome of the proceeding" (Solum 2004: 281). For Solum, the application of linguistically clear statutes after a judge-led courtroom proceeding provides sufficient participation, even if the subject's arguments cannot sway the judge's decision. An adopter of Solum's (or a similar) view on this point would not be swayed by the argument that a human judge is, in any context, equivalent to an ANN-based statute, merely because he or she is bound by clear law. A judge is capable of at least hearing and evaluating arguments in a way that an ANN is not.

A final response to insufficiency objection is that it is inapposite because it conflates the application of an ANN-based statute with an adjudication when the two are, actually, entirely different from one another. When an ANN-based statute is applied in an individual case, perhaps that is more akin to a legal subject voluntarily complying with a general legal rule or a government official lawfully spending revenue from the public fisc, than to a trial or appellate hearing. There are many examples where the law is applied in individual circumstances, but where due process participation rights are not typically thought to arise. Under this line of thinking, an ANN-based statute could be implemented entirely without adjudication, and thus it is inappropriate to import notions of participation from the adjudicatory context to this new setting.

Indeed, given that an ANN-based statute would itself provide an unambiguous response to any relevant query, there would seem to be few settings in which an adjudication, as commonly understood, would be necessary. Disputants simply could not maintain alternative interpretations of the law in the face of an easily accessible and automatic authoritative interpretation. Nevertheless, these non-adjudicatory settings could still give rise to glitches, as defined above. In such cases, where errors arise that simply would not be generated by human beings collectively reasoning over the meaning of a statute, it seems troubling that there is simply no recourse, other than the legislative process. The existence of glitches in the application of an ANN-based statute is not bad per se, at least when their consequences are not worse than human errors. But the prospect of glitches highlights the limited opportunities for participation when the law meets the world.

A related point concerns the educative function of process. The discussion so far has focused on an ameliorative function of participation rights whereby state coercion—which might be understood as presumptively illegitimate—is cured through adequate process. But there may be an additional, more positive understanding of participation as contributing to the civic education of legal subjects. Under this interpretation of participation, which is alluded to in Solum (2004), process serves an educative function of expressing the nature of law and socializing people into legal culture. If this educative function has social value, then one of the costs of an ANN-based statute is that there would be fewer settings for this type of legal education to take place, gradually eroding the cultural foundations for a rule of law society.

CONCLUSION

Leibniz believed that even the most difficult questions of morality or law could be solved with an adequate formal system of computation. His dream is alive and well among researchers and thinkers working in the area of law-as-computation, and new tools in AI and machine learning may, one day in the not-too-distant future, make it technically possible to realize a version of Leibniz's dream. This reality may soon force societies to decide whether pursuing a vision of law-as-computation is consistent with their commitment to the rule of law.

Law-as-computation may present many advantages, some of which bear on core rule of law values. Today, when legal subjects go to court, the selection of the adjudicators who will hear their cases can have major consequences for outcomes, a fact that offends basic notions of natural justice. The unfairness and arbitrariness associated with such random factors affecting case outcomes is acceptable at least in part because it is not clear that there is any suitable alternative. Similarly, the large discretionary role played by non-elected adjudicators is, at least to some, at odds with the system of democratic accountability that lends the law its legitimacy.

However, were law-as-computation to be fully realized, with human decision makers cut out of the loop, it would raise fundamental concerns about participation rights. At the legislative stage, the techniques of law-as-computation may be alienating and undermine democratic participation, and the kind of general coherence required for wholesale adoption of law-as-computation may be impossible to achieve in a diverse society operating according to democratic principles. Furthermore, if participation rights at the adjudicatory stage are required, then a human being must serve as the final decision maker. No matter how lifelike and intelligent, machines will not share an *umwelt* with human beings, a fact that fundamentally disrupts legal subjects' confidence that their arguments have been truly heard and considered by the decision maker. In addition, were law as computation to eliminate the need for human-led adjudication, it could interfere with the educative function of legal process that helps maintain and perpetuate the cultural and political conditions necessary to maintain the rule of law.

One of the most frightening prospects raised by law-as-computation— for law professors at least—may be the potential to deemphasize or even eliminate the forms of reasoning familiar in the practice of law and in legal scholarship: the mix of doctrinal, normative, and interdisciplinary scholarship that comprises discourse in contemporary law practice and the legal academy. If this were the case, notwithstanding all of the exciting research opportunities created by the digitization of legal sources and new techniques of text analysis (Livermore and Rockmore 2019), legal scholarship would become more of a historical discipline, focused on understanding a past practice, rather than one that also makes contributions to an on-going social project.

As this chapter has shown, law scholars have little to fear, at least in the short term. The gradual unfolding of whatever contribution law-as-computation will make to the actual legal system will raise a host of normative and legal questions that will demand thoughtful attention by jurists, law scholars, and the legal profession more generally. Law-as-computation is neither inevitable nor necessarily desirable, and the question of whether, when, and how much to automate the execution of the law is one that is likely to be turned over by legal scholars for many years to come.

REFERENCES

Agrawal, Ajay, Joshua Bans, and Avi Goldfarb (2018) *Prediction Machines: The Simple Economics of Artificial Intelligence* Boston: Harvard Business Review Press.

Alfange, Dean, Jr. (1969) "Jeremy Bentham and the Codification of Law" *Cornell Law Review* 55(1): 58–77.

Armgardt, Matthias (2014) "Leibniz as Legal Scholar" *Fundamina* 20(1): 27–38.

Ashley, Kevin D. (1990) *Modeling Legal Arguments: Reasoning with Cases and Hypotheticals* Cambridge, MA: MIT Press.

Ben-Menahem, Hanina (1993) "Leibniz on Hard Cases" *Archives for Philosophy of Law and Social Philosophy* 79(2): 198-215.

Bench-Capon, Trevor (ed.) (1991) *Knowledge-Based Systems and Legal Applications* London: Academic Press.

Bench-Capon, Trevor, principal author (2012) "A History of AI and Law in 50 Papers: 25 Years of the International Conference on AI and Law" *Artificial Intelligence and Law* 20: 215–319.

Branting, L. Karl (1991) "Building Explanations from Rules and Structured Cases" *International Journal of Man-Machines Studies* 34(6): 797–837.

Cairns, Huntington (1946) "Leibniz's Theory of Law" *Harvard Law Review* 60(2): 200–232.

Calabresi, Guido (1985) *A Common Law for the Age of Statutes* Cambridge, MA: Harvard University Press.

Citron, Danielle Keats (2008) "Technological Due Process" *Washington University Law Review* 85(6): 1249–313.

Coglianese, Cary (2004) "E-Rulemaking: Information Technology and the Regulatory Process" *Administrative Law Review* 56(2): 353–402.

Contos, George, John Guyton, Patrick Langetieg, and Melissa Vigil (2010) "Individual Taxpayer Compliance Burden: The Role of Assisted Methods in Taxpayers Response to Increasing Complexity" *IRS Research Bulletin: Proceedings of the IRS Research Conference* 2010: 191–220.

Dworkin, Ronald (1977) *Taking Rights Seriously* Cambridge, MA: Harvard University Press.

Dworkin, Ronald (1986) *Law's Empire* Cambridge, MA: Harvard University Press.

Fallon, Richard H., Jr. (2005) "Legitimacy and the Constitution" *Harvard Law Review* 118(6): 1787–853.

Gardner, Anne von der Lieth (1987) *An Artificial Intelligence Approach to Legal Reasoning* Cambridge, MA: MIT Press.

Genesereth, M., R. Greiner, and D. Smith (1980) "MRS Manual" Memo HP80-24, Stanford Heuristic Programming Project.

Gruber, Thomas R. (1993a) "A Translation Approach to Portable Ontology Specifications" *Knowledge Acquisition* 5(2): 199–220.

Gruber, Thomas R. (1993b) "Toward Principles for the Design of Ontologies Used for Knowledge Sharing" *International Journal Human-Computer Studies* 43(5–6): 907–28.

Guarino, Nicola, Daniel Oberle, and Steffen Staab (2009) "What is an Ontology?" In *Handbook on Ontologies: International Handbooks on Information Systems* Steffen Staab and Rudi Studer (eds) Berlin: Springer pp. 1–19.

Hart, H.L.A. (1958) "Positivism and the Separation of Law and Morals" *Harvard Law Review* 71(4): 593–629.

Hayes-Roth, Frederick, Donald Arthur Waterman, and Douglas B. Lenat (eds) (1983) *Building Expert Systems* Reading, MA: Addison-Wesley Pub. Co.

Holtman, Robert B. (1981) *The Napoleonic Revolution* Baton Rouge, LA: Louisiana State University Press.

Leibniz, Gottfried Wilhelm (1666) *Dissertatio de Arte Combinatoria* Leipzig: apud Joh. Simon Fickium et Joh. Polycarp. Seuboldum, Literis Spörelianis.

Levine, Ross (2005) "Law, Endowments and Property Rights" *Journal of Economic Perspectives* 19(3): 61–88.

Livermore, Michael A., and Daniel N. Rockmore (2019) *Law as Data: Computation, Text, and the Future of Legal Analysis* Santa Fe, NM: Santa Fe Institute Press.

Postema, Gerald J. (1986) *Bentham and the Common Law Tradition* New York: Oxford University Press.

Ramji-Nogales, Jaya, Andrew I. Schoenholtz, and Philip G. Schrag (2010) "Refugee Roulette: Disparities in Asylum Adjudication" Stanford L. J. 60(2) 295–411.

Rissland, Edwina L. (1980) "Example Generation" In *Proceedings of the Third National Conference of the Canadian Society for Computational Studies of Intelligence*, Victoria, BC, pp. 280–88,

Rissland, Edwina L., and David B. Skalak (1991) "CABARET: Rule Interpretation in a Hybrid Architecture" *International Journal of Man-Machines Studies* 34(6): 839–87.

Rissland, Edwina L., Kevin D. Ashley, and L. Karl Branting (2006) "Case-Based Reasoning and Law" *The Knowledge Engineering Review* 20(3): 293–8.

Rissland, Edwina L., Kevin D. Ashley, and R.P. Loui (2003) "AI and Law: A Fruitful Synergy" *Artificial Intelligence* 150(1–2): 1–15.

Schauer, Frederick (1988) "Formalism" *Yale Law Journal* 97(4): 509–48.

Schauer, Frederick (2008) "A Critical Guide to Vehicles in the Park" *NYU Law Journal* 83(4): 1109–34.

Schauer, Frederick (2013) "On the Open Texture of Law" *Grazer Philosophische Studien* 87(1): 197–215.

Sebeok, Thomas A. (1976) *Contributions to the Doctrine of Signs* Bloomington, IN: Indiana University.

Sergot, M.J., F. Sadri, R.A. Kowalsi, F. Kriwaczek, P. Hammond, and H.T. Cory (1986) "The British Nationality Act as a Logic Program" *Communications of the ACM* 29(5): 370–86.

Silver, David, principal author (2018) "A General Reinforcement Learning

Algorithm that Masters Chess, Shogi, and Go through Self-Play" *Science* 362(6419): 1140–44.

Solum, Lawrence B. (2004) "Procedural Justice" *Southern California Law Review* 78(1): 181–321.

Susskind, Richard E. (1987) *Expert Systems in Law: A Jurisprudential Inquiry* New York: Oxford University Press.

Susskind, Richard E. (2013) *Tomorrow's Lawyers: An Introduction to Your Future* Oxford: Oxford University Press.

Warren, Mary Anne (1973) "On the Moral and Legal Status of Abortion" *Monist* 57(1): 43–61.

Wolfram, Stephen (2016) "Computational Law, Symbolic Discourse, and the AI Constitution" *Wired.com* (12 October) accessed 24 May 2020 at https://writings.stephenwolfram.com/2016/10/computational-law-symbolic-discourse-and-the-ai-constitution/.

Woods, William A. (1970) "Transition Network Grammars for Natural Language Analysis" *Communications of the ACM* 13(10): 591–606.

12. Purposes and challenges of legal citation network analysis on case law

Dafne van Kuppevelt, Gijs van Dijck and Marcel Schaper

1. INTRODUCTION

Legal scholarship can pursue various objectives. It may aim to analyze what the law is and how it should be understood, to evaluate existing rules, to understand the law as a social phenomenon, or to understand the conceptual bases of legal principles (e.g. Hutchinson, 2010, pp. 7–8). Case law functions as a pivotal source of information in a substantial proportion of legal scholarship.

When analyzing court decisions, a variety of questions can emerge. Researchers may observe that textbooks differ in the sub-topics that can be distinguished. It may not be clear which decisions can be studied to obtain a proper overview of the relevant case law. There may be a discussion among scholars about which decisions should be considered the most relevant precedents. Researchers might be interested how the relevance of decisions changes over time (i.e. whether decisions gain or lose relevance over time). Or they might want to explore whether legal scholars have overlooked possibly relevant precedents.

Traditionally, legal scholars rely on human analysis when determining which court decisions are relevant or authoritative. Legal researchers search, read, and interpret legal documents to synthesize court decisions and to determine their relevance. The method of case synthesis is commonly applied by legal researchers and law students to assess the importance of a case (Nievelstein et al., 2013). It essentially entails that case outcomes are compared with the facts of the cases, with the purpose of explaining the differences in outcomes by the differences in facts (Gionfriddo, 2007).

With hundreds, thousands or tens of thousands of court decisions, even in a specific field, computational analysis has the potential to assist researchers in answering research questions regarding the trends, patterns, structure, and organization of the legal system. Network analysis in particular fits this purpose, as it allows mapping, measuring, and possibly visualizing relationships between information (Fowler et al., 2007; Schaper, 2014; van Dijck, 2017), which relates to the information legal scholars are often interested in when analyzing court decisions.

In this contribution, we explore the potential and challenges of Legal Network Analysis (LNA). After discussing for which research questions LNA may be used (Section 2), it will be explained that LNA lacks a proper reference point for evaluating the results (Section 3). Consequently, a methodology needs to be developed in order to produce results that are valid. This contribution is structured around four specific aspects, which are explored more in-depth: (1) how to select sub-networks, (2) which community detection method to select, (3) estimating the probability that the network and its relationships as observed in the data did not occur by chance, and (4) which centrality measure to select to determine the extent to which a decision is a precedent (Section 4). Issues regarding these topics will be discussed, and avenues for solutions will be explored. We conclude that the way in which sub-networks are selected can have a substantial impact on the findings, that community detection algorithms perform differently in different contexts, that statistical significance testing may allow for estimating the probability that the network and its relationships as observed in the data are not likely to be the result of chance, and that centrality measures commonly used in LNA produce different results in different contexts. By exploring the purposes and challenges of LNA, we aim to develop a research agenda for conducting LNA.

This contribution focuses on network analysis applied to case law, citation analysis in particular, as this is the most common type of data to apply LNA to. However, network analysis can also be applied to other domains or areas, including legal social networks (Beaverstock, 2004; Heinz and Laumann, 1982; Lazega, 2001; Lazega and Krackhardt, 2000; Lazega and van Duijn, 1997), networks of statutes and regulatory codes (Bommarito II and Katz, 2010; Boulet et al., 2011; Katz and Bommarito, 2014; Koniaris et al., 2017), and patent citations (Whalen, 2016, pp. 550–51 (providing an overview)).

When discussing the challenges and possible solutions for them, we draw upon literature on network analysis in other disciplines. Because there is an abundance of literature, a selection needed to be made. The references included in this contribution may be used to obtain more knowledge and insight in the challenges and solutions.

2.   WHY CONDUCT LNA?

LNA seems to be predominantly used to identify relevant precedents (Olsen and Küçüksu, 2017; Olsen and Sadl, 2017); that is, decisions or rules set in a prior legal case that are used to decide subsequent cases (Derlén and Lindholm, 2015, pp. 1075–6; Lupu and Voeten, 2012, pp. 416–17). Determining to what extent a court decision is a precedent is an important aim of legal scholarship. Computational analysis offers the advantage of scalability (compared to human analysis): hundreds, thousands or tens of thousands of cases can be investigated. Treating court decisions as nodes and court citations as edges (links), a precedent network can be construed that allows testing how central precedents are (Fowler et al., 2007, p. 325). For example, LNA has been applied in order to identify the most important precedents in the corpus of US Supreme Court majority opinions in the 1754–2002 period (Fowler et al., 2007; Fowler and Jeon, 2008). For this, the authors analyzed the complete network of 30,288 and the cases that cite them. Similarly, others have analyzed the body of case law of the Court of Justice of the European Union (CJEU), formerly known as the European Court of Justice. They found that the importance of judgments such as *van Gend en Loos*, *Costa v. ENEL*, *Brasserie du Pêcheur*, and *United Brand* is overemphasized, and the importance of other judgments like *Bosman*, *PreussenElektra*, and *Schumacker* underestimated (Derlén and Lindholm, 2014, p. 686). In similar fashion, LNA has been used to measure the centrality of CJEU rulings in the field of VAT (Knops and Schaper, 2014) or direct taxes (Schaper, 2014), of the International Criminal Court decisions (Tarissan and Nollez Goldbach, 2016), of Canadian case law (Neale, 2013), and of Italian constitutional court case law (Agnoloni and Pagallo, 2015).

One assumption implicit in much LNA is that citation frequency is an indicator for how authoritative the decisions are: case law that is cited more frequently is presumed to be more important than cases cited less frequently. Thus, *centrality measures* are calculated based on, for example, *in-degree* (number of times the decision is cited) and *out-degree* (number of citations cited in the decision). Centrality, however, does not necessarily coincide with relevance, importance, or authority. This has to do with the quality of the citations, that is, the reasons for citing case law. Court decisions may be cited as a matter of courtesy, to add authority for the interpretation of a rule or for solving a case, to indicate the same rule is applied that was laid out in previous cases, to distinguish the case at hand from other cases, or to stress that the deciding court departs from a rule laid down in a previous case (Derlén and Lindholm, 2014, p. 674; van Dijck, 2017, p. 28; Whalen, 2016, p. 556) Consequently, there might be a gap between the centrality of precedents and their relevance, importance, or authority.

Several studies have explored the relationship between centrality and relevance by comparing network centrality scores with expert rankings. Fowler and Jeon (2008, p. 21), in their study on US Supreme Court cases, report that the "top 10" cases in their analysis are considered in one or more of the legal sources they compared their results to. Similarly, the research that analyzed the centrality of CJEU decisions reported high levels of agreement regarding which decisions belong to the "top 10" judgments, although textbook authors significantly disagree as to which judgments are the most important:

> 65% of the 117 judgments only occur among the frequently cited in a single text-book, 76% of the judgments are among the frequently cited in only one or two textbooks, only 10 judgments are frequently cited in five or more textbooks, and only two cases are among the top 30 cited in all seven textbooks. (Derlén and Lindholm, 2014, pp. 668–9)

The finding led the authors to the conclusion that textbooks "overemphasise the importance of van Gend en Loos, Costa v. ENEL, Brasserie du Pêcheur and United Brands", and that regarding van Gend en Loos, "its status as a source of law is questionable, at best" (Derlén and Lindholm, 2014, p. 686).

LNA can also be used to identify characteristics or events related to the centrality of a court decision. In another study on US Supreme Court decision citations, it was found that "decisions written in years when the mean judicial age is low and judges are more stable in their use of precedent, more conservative in terms of the age of precedent cited, and the yearly citation network is less complex are more likely to be cited in future years" (Whalen, 2013). For CJEU decisions, LNA has shown that CJEU case law is particularly central in preliminary reference rulings, rulings that concern fundamental freedoms, competition law in particular (Derlén and Lindholm, 2015). The same study reports that the number of Member States submitting an observation in a preliminary reference procedure predicts the frequency with which a case will be referred to in subsequent decisions. LNA has also been used to measure how long decisions remain central in a network. A Canadian study reveals that case citation typically has a lifespan of 3 to 15 years, depending on the jurisdiction (Neale, 2013). Only the Supreme Court of Canada persist longer, namely 50 years, while reporting that 19 percent of Canada Supreme Court cases are regularly cited over time, as opposed to less than 3 percent in other jurisdictions.

Furthermore, LNA has been used to determine characteristics of over-ruled decisions. In a study that used a Supreme Court decisions dataset, it was found that overrulings are likely to be reserved for decisions that are more central than for decisions that remain salient longer (Whalen, 2014). Finally, LNA has been used to consider the structure network of decisions on a meso-scale, and thus discern clusters (or communities) of decisions that are closely related in the network. In a study of employer liability cases of Dutch Supreme Court decisions, several communities are identified and interpreted that seemingly provide a meaningful clustering from a substantive perspective (van Dijck and van Kuppevelt, 2018).

3.   VALIDATING LNA RESULTS

Although, intuitively, the added value of LNA is large, a thorough evaluation of the new methodology requires a criterion to measure the success and usefulness of LNA. As the studies discussed in the previous sections illustrate, expert opinions are often used as the baseline against which the results of a LNA are evaluated. At the same time, the way in which the expert opinions are measured varies. Fowler and Jeon (2008, p. 20) mention the *Congressional Quarterly's Guide to the United States Supreme Court*, the *Oxford Guide to Supreme Court Decisions*, and the *Legal Information Institute* as sources that use opinions of judicial specialists to compile rankings of the most important Supreme Court decisions, with the rankings being based on the case's historical and/or social significance, its importance to the development of some area of law, and its impact on the development of American government.

If expert ratings are not available, they may be constructed based on existing sources. In their study of CJEU decisions, Derlén and Lindholm (2014) did so by counting textbook citations and citations by the Advocates General. Scholars that analyzed Canadian case law with LNA used the frequency with which the analyzed cases were viewed on *Canadian Legal Information Institute* (CanLII's) website. They concluded that in-degree centrality and PageRank scores are associated with the viewing frequency on CanLII's website (Neale, 2013). Another measure to compare centrality scores to is to count the number of scholarly opinions, comments, and annotations devoted to the cases analyzed. Applying this strategy to Italian constitutional law cases resulted in the finding that several cases discussed by experts turned out not to be central in the network analysis that was conducted, whereas a number of cases central in the network were scarcely debated or ignored by legal scholars (Agnoloni and Pagallo, 2015). Based on this result, the authors argued that results of LNA and the web of scholarly opinions should be combined in order to determine the relevance of court decisions.

Considering that LNA can bring insights that are not noted by previous scholars, the evaluation of LNA is inherently problematic. LNA that studies case law sometimes confirms scholarly commentary, and sometimes it deviates. As far as the purpose of LNA is to confirm scholarly commentary, the latter can serve as a proper baseline to measure LNA's effectiveness. This way, LNA can be seen as a faster and more powerful alternative to human analysis, at least when it comes to determining the centrality of decisions, which may be seen as an indication of relevance, importance, or authority of precedents. Interesting in this respect is the observation in the Fowler and Jeon study, where it was concluded that it had taken judicial specialists 18 years to recognize the significance of *Speiser versus Randall* (1958) as an influential decision (Fowler and Jeon, 2008, pp. 21–2), whereas the partitioning of the network to cases before 1979 allowed to detect the *Speiser* case as a central case in the network (although the network analysis was conducted 50 years after *Speiser versus Randall*).

In contrast to replicating scholarly expertise, LNA also provides a quantitative approach to answer research questions different from traditional legal research. When network statistics deviate from an expert baseline, this does not necessarily imply a shortcoming of the method, it can expose new insights in the data. An informed choice of methods and metrics is required to determine whether legal scholarship has overlooked information or whether LNA produced results that lack meaning. As will be further explained below, one approach is the formulation of clear hypotheses that can be statistically tested on the network data. In addition, awareness of the sensitivity of methods to noise in the data is required. When the proper method is used and significant findings do not match the expected result, additional analysis can reveal relationships between the network structure and expected structure.

LNA applied to case law is therefore partly confirmatory and partly exploratory, in that it produces new hypotheses that need to be tested by conducting additional analysis. The fact that it cannot be predicted beforehand whether an LNA will confirm or deviate from the findings in scholarly commentary further stresses the importance of a proper methodology for LNA and, consequently, of identifying and addressing challenges.

4.   CHALLENGES OF LNA

When discussing the challenges that an LNA scholar might encounter, and the robustness of the methods available to address those challenges, we turn to other disciplines, as valuable lessons can be learned from other fields that have extensive experience using network analysis as a tool for research, most notably the social sciences (Social Network Analysis, or SNA).

We illustrate the challenges with examples of a citation network of Dutch court decisions. The data, which originates from the LiDO tool,[1] contain cases related to employer liability, which concern situations where the employee suffers a loss for which the employer is liable. Employer liability is covered by the Articles 7:658 and 7:611 of the Dutch Civil Code. All cases with computer-identified references to these articles were selected. An API provided by LiDO allowed for the automated selection of these references, as well as the references between the selected cases.

4.1   Selecting a Sub-Network

The complete network of all available court decisions is very large, which makes the network difficult to visualize and interpret. In addition, often in LNA, only a small portion of the decisions are relevant to the research questions. For example, a researcher may be interested in the topic of employer liability in case of traffic accidents instead of in all decisions on employer liability. The scope of the network can be decreased by selecting a sub-graph of (mostly) relevant cases. The smaller network is easier to visualize and interpret than a larger network, and results do not get confounded by irrelevant cases for the research question at hand.

Tarissan et al. (2016) show that selecting a sub-network of a certain body of case law reveals more landmark cases than the complete network. However, selecting a part of the network has consequences for the network properties of the sub-graph. Overall statistics, such as degree distribution and clustering properties, are likely to be different for the sub graph than for the complete graph. Such deviations may be of interest to the researcher, as they reveal specific properties of the selection. An example of this is the work of Henrik Palmer Olsen and Magnus Esmark, one of the other contributions in this book (Chapter 13), where centrality scores within sub-networks are compared to centrality in the overall network, to highlight judgments that contain general legal principles. However, there are caveats to be aware of when using sub-networks.

Firstly, the method of selection needs to be carefully considered. One way of selecting a sub-graph is based on the network structure, for example the sub-graph of all nodes within a fixed degree from one node of interest. In the employer liability example, this would mean the researcher chooses one or more cases of interest and subsequently selects all decisions

---

[1]   http://linkeddata.overheid.nl.

citing that decision, and possibly also the cases that refer to those decisions (and so on). It is also possible to sample based on network independent criteria, such as keyword search (e.g. searching for "employer" and "liability"). Finally, one may combine the methodologies, for example by selecting all nodes that satisfy a keyword plus nodes linked to those nodes. Any method used is likely to be imperfect, resulting in a selection that both excludes relevant documents and includes irrelevant documents. Consequently, conclusions drawn from the sub-network might be incorrect due to incomplete or incorrect data.

Secondly, the way in which the sub-graph is embedded in the larger network can provide valuable information. Suppose, for example, that one of the selected cases has many citations from cases outside the selection, but few from within the selection. Although the case clearly has some relevance (centrality), it receives a low centrality score in the sub-network. Of course, whether the case is relevant (central) is ultimately determined by the research question.

In the network for employer liability, we first selected a sub-network based on a network independent criterion, namely those cases that refer to statute articles related to employer liability. We will refer to these cases as the "seed cases". We then created a second network by extending the selection to include cases that cite the seed cases. These citing cases are expected to have some relevance related to the topic.

The networks are plotted in Figure 12.1 and network statistics are shown in Figure 12.2. Note that the extended network is much denser, and indeed the average degree is higher in this network, especially in the later years. This can be explained by the fact that we extended the dataset specifically with cases that were citing one of the seed cases, which gave them at least one outgoing citation by default. As a result, the "extended" cases have different properties than the original set of cases.

We also find that centrality measures are different for the extended sub-network. If, for example, we look at the "authorities" score (from the Hyperlink-Induced Topic Search (HITS) algorithm, Kleinberg, 1999), the highest ranking case in the extended network is ECLI:NL:HR:2008:BD1847, with an authority score of 0.51. However, in the original, non-extended network, this node has an authority score very close to zero, even though in both networks it is the node with the largest in-degree. Apparently, the nodes that we added in the extended network often cite cases that cite ECLI:NL:HR:2008:BD1847, giving the node a different, more influential, role in the extended network. The substantive explanation is that the decision is on a topic not related to employer liability (yet still about article 7:611 Dutch Civil Code). The importance of the node is thus very different in the context of

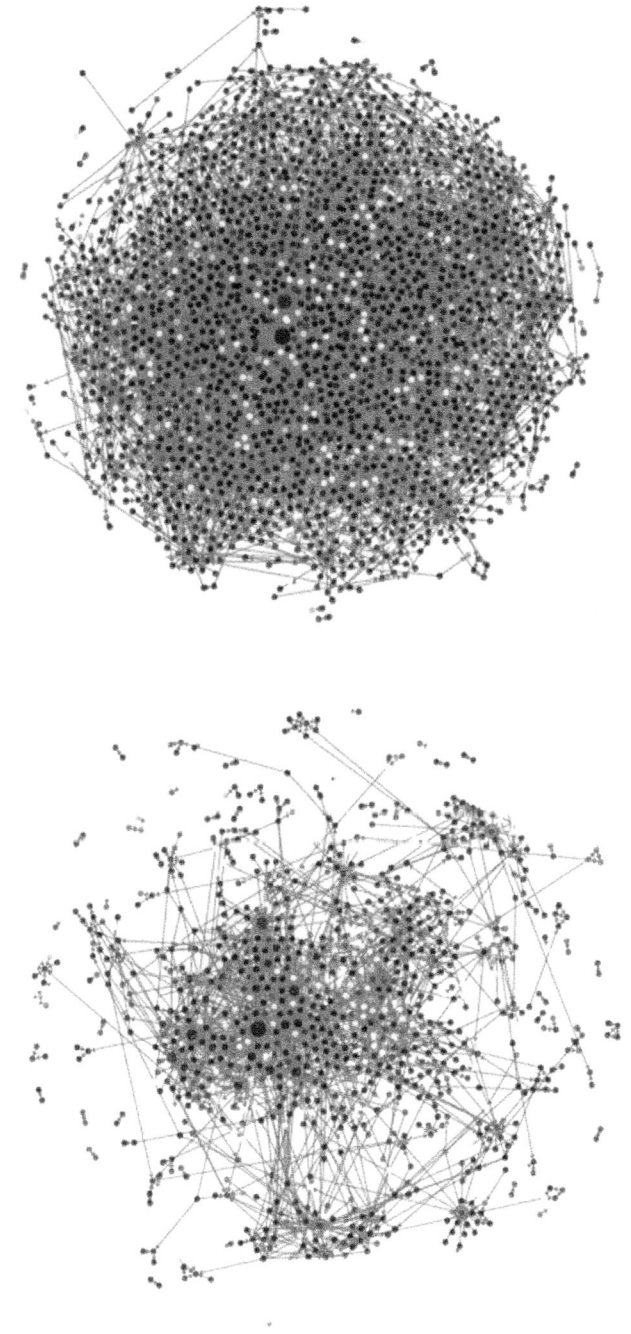

Note: Left: sub-network for employer liability; right: the sub-network, extended with cases citing the original sub-network.

Figure 12.1   Network plots, created with ccse-law-app (DOI: 10.5281/zenodo.823668)

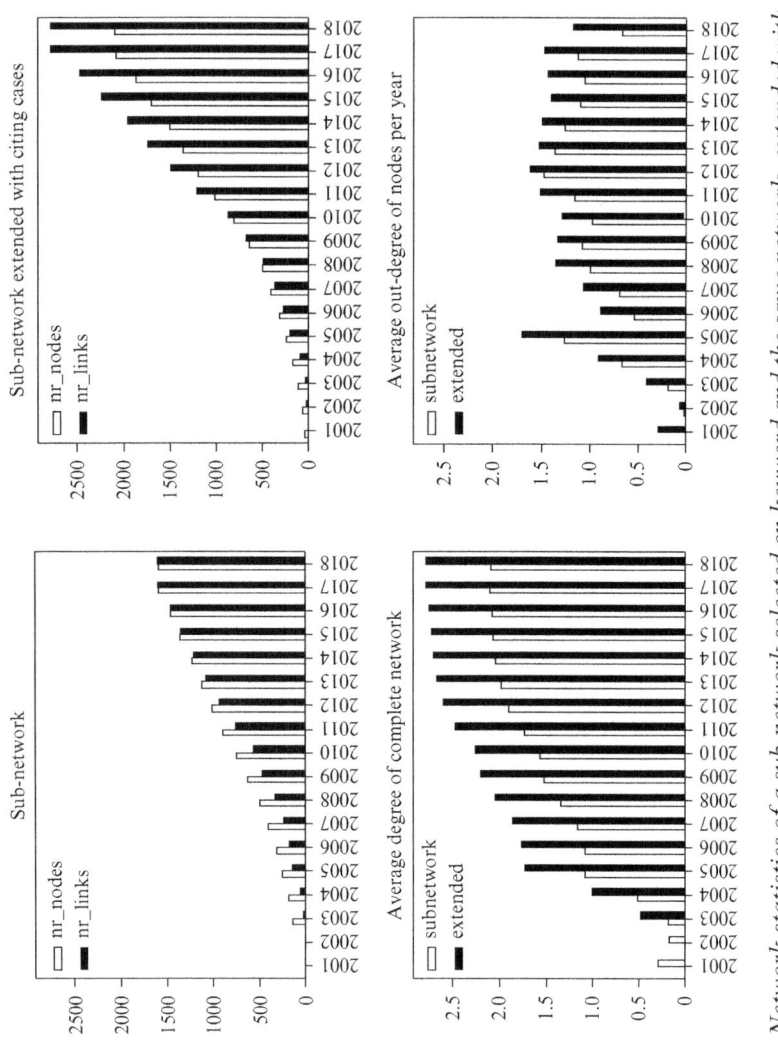

Figure 12.2   Network statistics of a sub-network selected on keyword and the same network, extended with all cases that cite one of the cases in the original sub-network

employer liability, than in a broader context, which coincides with the way the network was constructed. In other instances, a researcher may conclude that such a decision is an influential precedent if the sub-network is analyzed, but deemed irrelevant in the extended network. In summary, the method of selection should be chosen with care and match the research question.

The effects of selection can be measured, by comparing generic network statistics of the smaller network to the larger network. If large differences are found, it is worth investigating whether this is to be expected.

Decisions on network selection thus have substantial implications on the results of LNA, leading to differences in network structure and centrality scores. We therefore propose more extensive studies to the effects of sub-network selection in LNA, which to our knowledge have not been researched. Experiments need to be conducted in order to analyze the implications and to develop best practices as to how to select networks when one is interested in a sub-graph. Similar research has been done for social networks, where the effects of choice "network boundary" on centrality have been investigated (Laumann et al., 1983; Valente et al., 2013). A systematic approach in which network statistics for several sub-networks are calculated can shed further light on sensible choices of selection.

4.2 Challenges of Community Detection Algorithms

Community detection methods provide a clustering of the nodes based on the network structure, giving an overview of the organization and meso-scale structure of the network. Each node in the network gets assigned to a group, so that within-group nodes have relatively many connections between them. In LNA, community detection can be used to find structure in the legal domain, for example by defining legal sub-areas. It allows exploring what cases surround a certain precedent or landmark case, visualizing clusters of case law on similar topics, and testing whether certain decisions were cited more frequently in certain periods of time compared to other decisions.

There are many methods available for community detection, and there is an ongoing debate about the usefulness of the different methods and how they should be evaluated. In LNA, as well as in other domains, it is difficult to define a criterion that can serve as a reference point for how well a particular community detection performs. One strategy is to use metadata as reference point, for example metadata about the field the decision belongs to, but unfortunately it is very well possible that even high-quality metadata does not align well with the community structure.

Moreover, the definition of what constitutes a "community" dictates how well a given algorithm performs, but "community structure" generally has no objective definition. This makes it difficult to distinguish whether the algorithm performed poorly, or whether the algorithm found a structure that is valid but fundamentally different from, for example, the traditional division made in terms of legal disciplines, topics, sub-topics, and so on. Nevertheless, comparing to metadata can be useful, particularly if the objective of community detection is to find a partition that is similar to the division into metadata categories.

Another issue with many community detection algorithms is the number of communities and sizes of the communities. Popular algorithms based on modularity optimization suffer from a resolution limit: the method prefers communities of sizes proportional to the square root of the number of nodes (Fortunato and Barthelemy, 2007). Consequently, the sizes of the communities depend on the number of nodes, with the expected community size being larger for larger networks.

As a result of resolution limits, the sizes of the communities that result from the algorithm do not always match the desired resolution, as small communities get merged into large ones when the network size increases. Several methods have been proposed to overcome this issue, including a resolution parameter in the equation that allows the user to control the sizes of communities (Reichardt and Bornholdt, 2006). A larger value for the resolution parameter results in larger, but fewer communities. Figure 12.3 shows network communities for two different resolution parameter values. It can be useful to take into account multiple resolution communities and to "zoom in" until the desired resolution is obtained. However, with no reference point available, it is difficult to say what the desired resolution of communities is.

In addition to decisions about resolution size, decisions need to be made regarding the method of community detection. Each method has different designs and assumptions (Ghasemian et al., 2018; Schaub et al., 2017). It is therefore necessary to consider what assumptions are valid for legal citation networks. Directed links and ordering of nodes in time are not taken into account by many methods, whereas this is crucial in networks on court decisions, as citations by courts are only backward in time (i.e. to decisions that were already made, not to future decisions). This stresses the importance to consider what assumptions are valid for legal citation networks. Bommarito II et al. have signaled these shortcomings and introduced an alternative clustering method aimed specifically at citation networks (Bommarito II et al., 2010). Based on a qualitative evaluation, they claim it results in an informative clustering of US Supreme Court cases.

Additional methods have been specifically designed for citation

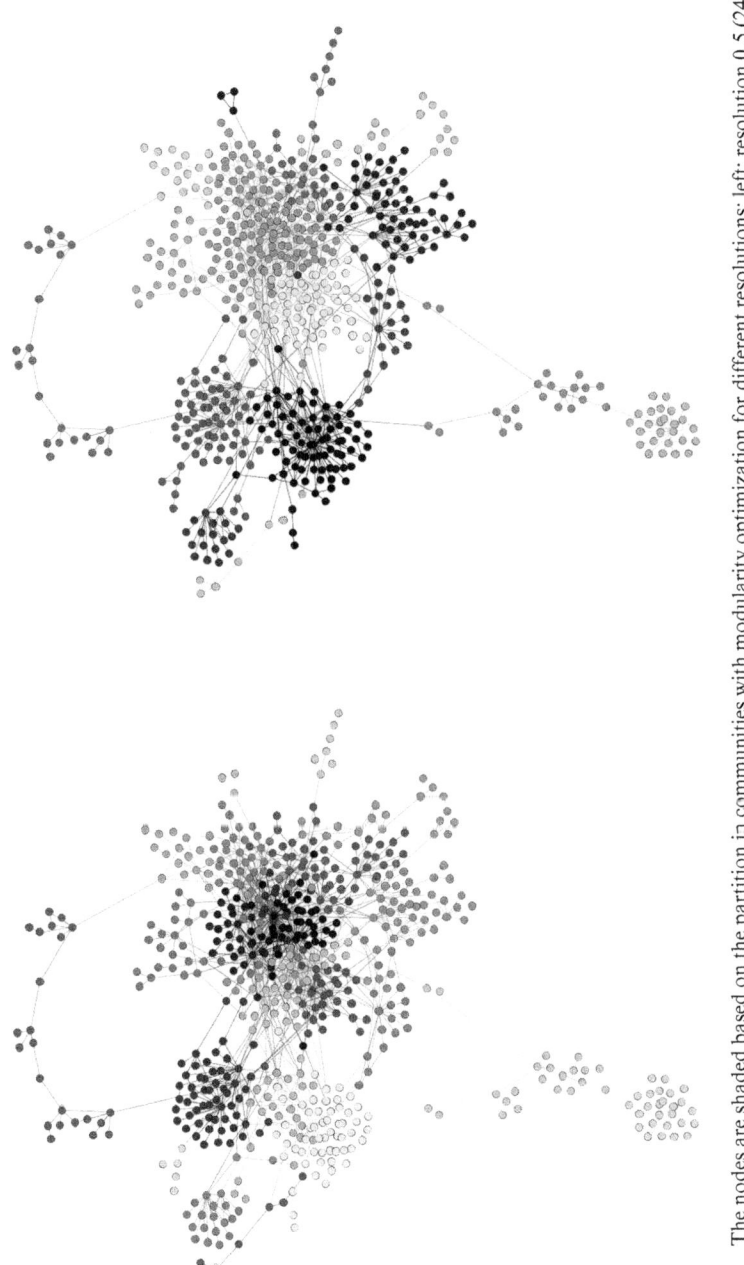

Note: The nodes are shaded based on the partition in communities with modularity optimization for different resolutions: left: resolution 0.5 (24 communities); right: resolution 1.0 (17 communities).

Figure 12.3   The largest component of a network of cases about employer liability

networks, which consider the growth of the network over time. In Leicht et al. (2007), a method is proposed to cluster nodes based on in which years they either cite or are cited, to distinguish "eras" in the data. They apply the method on US Supreme Court cases.

We illustrate the difficulty of algorithm selection by comparing two methods of community detection, namely the widely applied Louvain method (Blondel et al., 2008) and the specialized method of Bommarito et al., which we refer to as the citation distance method. We apply both of these methods to the network of employer liability cases and we perform a qualitative assessment of the resulting clusters. We run the Louvain method with different resolution parameters. The citation distance method results in a hierarchical clustering, and we choose different cut-off values to obtain several resolutions of clusters, where a higher cut-off threshold corresponds to fewer communities.

First, we observe the number of communities that are produced by both methods for the employer liability network, which are plotted in Figure 12.4. The number of communities for the citation distance is shown, for different threshold values. The higher the chosen threshold value, the lower the number of communities, but the minimum number of communities for this network (threshold value=1) is 45. In addition, for threshold values higher than 0.8, more than half of the nodes are put in the largest community. In contrast, the number of communities for the different resolution values in the Louvain method is much lower.

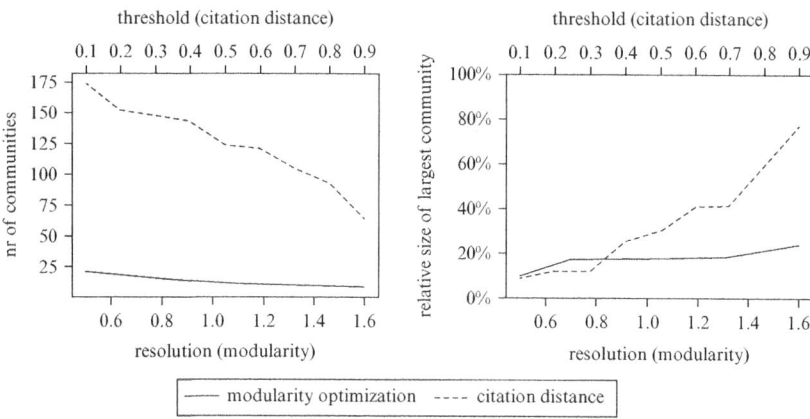

Figure 12.4   The number of communities (left) and the fraction of nodes that is in the largest community (right) for different thresholds in the citation distance clustering method, and different resolutions in the Louvain method for modularity optimization

For the topic of employer liability, the low number of communities is closer to what is to be expected. In legal literature, between approximately 7 to 20 sub-topics can be distinguished on the topic of employer liability, depending on the textbook that is used as a reference point (van Dijck and van Kuppevelt, 2018). The substantially higher number of clusters in the citation distance method does not align with what would be expected from a substantive perspective.

We further inspect the individual communities to add meaning to the clustering. For this, we only select communities that contain Dutch Supreme Court decisions that have been cited at least ten times in order for the selection to include communities with at least one substantially relevant decision. The number of decisions that the selection resulted in was sufficiently small so that a human expert could inspect and categorize the decisions in the networks in order to determine precision levels. Accuracy and recall were beyond the feasible scope of this chapter, as they would require the expert to categorize a large number of decisions.

For each of the clusters in the complete network, we looked at the Supreme Court decisions in that cluster and manually classified the number of decisions that belonged to either the cluster of (a) duty to insure decisions and/or traffic accidents or (b) causality. The topics chosen resemble important topics in the field of employer liability in the Netherlands. The results of the number of clusters and number of decisions per cluster for each topic is shown in Table 12.1.

The comparison reveals that, overall, the Louvain method of community detection results in higher percentages of positive observations (TP) compared to all observations in the selected clusters (TP + TN) (precision) than does the citation distance approach. For most of the resolutions, the citation distance approach produces a lower proportion of "on-topic" decisions in clusters than the Louvain method. Moreover, when the resolution size increases in the citation distance approach, it results in a limited number of large clusters that include a variety of decisions that are substantively different. Compared to the Louvain method, the citation distance approach often either overlooks relevant decisions in the networks that were analyzed, or it clusters together too many decisions that are substantively different.

Only the 0.2 resolution of the citation distance approach produced high precision levels, but this resolution also resulted in numerous small clusters that are not substantially meaningful. As to the Louvain method, the 0.7 and 0.5 resolution resulted in the highest precision levels, grouping together relevant decisions while distinguishing clusters that are substantively different. Nevertheless, higher resolutions (e.g. 1.3 or 1.6) with the Louvain method also result in clusters that include a variety of

Table 12.1   Results of community detection for employer liability network

Approach	Resolution	Topic	No. of clusters	True positives	True positives + false positives	Precision (%)
Citation distance	0.2	Causality	2	4	4	100
		Duty to insure/ Traffic	2	9	14	64
	0.4	Causality	3	5	25	20
		Duty to insure/ Traffic	1	11	21	52
	0.6	Causality	2	7	37	19
		Duty to insure/ Traffic	2	11	38	29
	0.8	Causality	1	7	46	15
		Duty to insure/ Traffic	1	10	46	22
Louvain	0.5	Causality	2	9	13	69
		Duty to insure/ Traffic	2	7	10	70
	0.7	Causality	1	10	13	77
		Duty to insure/ Traffic	2	8	12	67
	1.0	Causality	1	10	13	77
		Duty to insure/ Traffic	2	8	13	62
	1.3	Causality	1	10	13	77
		Duty to insure/ Traffic	2	10	19	53

substantively different decisions, although not to the extent the citation distance approach does. This observation suggests the citation distance approach is more sensitive to resolution changes than is the Louvain method, at least in the network that was analyzed.

We suspected that the relatively small network size might explain why the Louvain method produced more substantively meaningful results than did the citation distance method – the latter produces a minimum of 40 communities, whereas the literature on employer liability indicates no more than approximately 20 communities – we subsequently turned to a larger and denser dataset. We constructed a citation network between 1233 rulings decided by the CJEU on the subject matter "(FISC) Taxation" before 1 January 2018.[2] We again applied the Louvain and citation distance methods to the giant component of the network (1143 nodes, 5284 edges) at different resolution and threshold values. As an indication of the quality of the communities, we compared with the topic of each ruling, extracted from the metadata provided by EUR-Lex. EUR-Lex distinguishes between four topics in the subject matter Taxation (FISC), namely: Excise duties (ACCI), Indirect taxation (INDR), Internal taxation (INTE), Value added tax (TVA). We could not assign 193 rulings to any topic, whereas 922 rulings were assigned to one topic, 28 to two topics, and 1 to three. Most rulings were assigned to topic TVA, the fewest to ACCI. A meaningful community detection method would identify communities around these four topics, considering that they represent different taxes that relate to different EU legal acts, each with their own rules.

The citation distance method did not provide such meaningful results. Figure 12.5 gives the number of communities detected and the relative size of the largest community at different thresholds. At threshold 0.1 the results were very scattered: we found as many as 272 communities, but

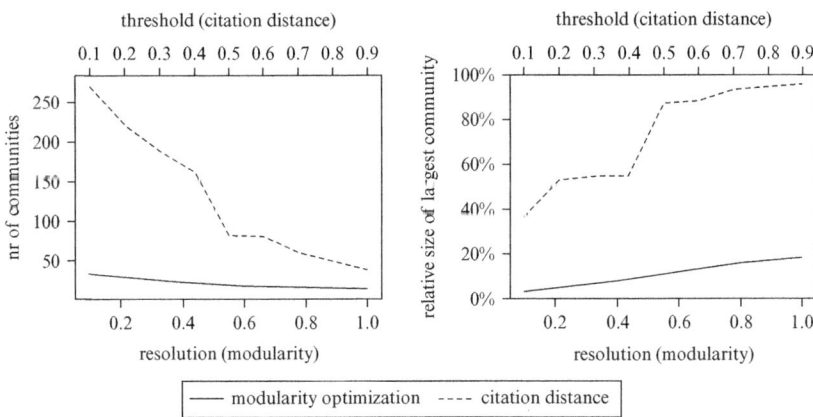

Figure 12.5   *Communities in EU tax network: the number of communities (left) and the fraction of nodes that is in the largest community (right) for different thresholds in the citation distance clustering method, and different resolutions in the Louvain method for modularity optimization*

---

[2]   The data was gathered on 1 January 2018 from EUR-Lex: https://eur-lex.europa.eu.

only 8 comprised ten or more rulings. A threshold value of 0.5 resulted in clearly fewer communities (82), but already placed 87 percent of all nodes in the same community. That largest community also comprised the largest proportion of cases on each of the four topics (TVA: 92 percent, ACCI: 92 percent, INDR: 71 percent, INTE: 71 percent). For higher thresholds (0.6–0.9), the proportions increased. Given the lack of proper results, we do not present the results of the citation distance method as we did for the Louvain method.

For the Louvain method, the results are different. It identified fewer communities than the citation distance method and the relative size of the largest community was smaller (see also Figure 12.5). At the lowest resolution that we tested (0.1), 56 of 86 communities had ten or more rulings (relative size of 1 percent or more). A resolution of 0.5 considerably reduced the number of communities (from 86 to 22) and increased the relative size of the largest community (from 3 percent to 10 percent) and the smallest community (relative size of 2 percent at 20 rulings). At resolution of 1.0, the smallest of the 14 communities comprised 24 rulings (relative size 2 percent) and the largest community had a relative size of 18 percent.

We analyzed how the Louvain method performed at these three resolutions. Table 12.2 illustrates in detail how the four topics were distributed over the 14 communities of Louvain for resolution 1.0. The distribution is very clear with regard to rulings on INTE (N = 137) and INDR (N =

Table 12.2 Distribution of topics over Louvain communities on tax law network

Community	TVA	ACCI	INTE	INDR	Total
0	73	2	0	0	75
1	3	1	1	2	7
2	5	0	4	65	74
3	144	3	0	0	147
4	83	2	2	0	87
5	188	0	0	0	188
6	38	1	0	0	39
7	0	13	0	1	14
8	17	15	0	0	32
9	25	0	0	0	25
10	3	4	1	0	8
11	83	0	0	0	83
12	27	0	0	0	27
13	37	9	129	0	175
Total	726	50	137	68	

68): 94 percent (129/137) of INTE rulings were in community 13 and 96 percent (65/68) INDR rulings were in community 2. The fact that TVA rulings can be found in several communities is consistent with the fact there are many sub-topics (e.g. exemptions, deductions, and so on) within Value added tax. Furthermore, in 11 of 14 communities, the proportion of rulings belonging to a specific topic comprised 70 percent or more (100 percent in 4 communities) of the rulings in that community. Although a lower resolution of 0.5 distributes the topics over more communities, 20 of 22 communities still have a high proportion (70 percent or more) of rulings belonging to a specific topic (100 percent in 10 communities). There are more and smaller communities at resolution 0.1, but we still found that in 74 of 86 communities the proportion of rulings belonging to a specific topic comprised 70 percent or more of the rulings in that community (100 percent in 60 communities). We therefore conclude that the Louvain method provides meaningful community structure to this second citation network, at least from a substantive perspective and in this network.

It is not surprising that the two methods result in observably different clustering. Both methods are based on fundamentally distinctive principles. The citation distance method assumes that the topic of a decision is merely based on the decisions that preceded it, and uses the notion of "sink nodes" (decisions without outgoing citations) to determine what topics exist, and then clusters decisions based on these topics. The Louvain method does not have such assumptions, but optimizes the *modularity* value, which compares the number of links within the communities to the expected number of links, which does not take into account the direction of the links.

Although the inventors of the citation distance method (Bommarito et al., 2010) show the value of the method on US Supreme Court cases, its success there does not appear to extrapolate to our datasets. Future research should investigate the relationship between the performance of the different methods and network properties, such as size, density, and number of triangles, to provide insight into which situations require which method.

Another difficulty with community detection is the apparent instability of the methods. As most community detection methods provide no significance score for the found partition, it is often unclear to what extent the methods are sensitive to noise in the data and randomization effects. For modularity optimization, Good et al. (2010) have shown that due to randomization in the algorithm, multiple iterations result in many different solutions which are all almost equally good. Depending on the application, conclusions drawn based on community detection are prone to be inaccurate, when not considering this uncertainty. Stability over multiple iterations can be achieved with consensus clustering (Lancichinetti and Fortunato, 2012). In this method, the results of multiple iterations of regular community detection methods are combined to find a stable community structure.

Note that there is no "perfect" community detection method, and the choice for one should always depend on the application. Some methods, such as modularity optimization, tend to overfit, meaning that they find patterns in a sample of the data that do not generalize well to the complete dataset, whereas other methods give a too generic description of the network (Ghasemian et al., 2018). We cannot give a complete overview of community detection methods here, and we refer to Fortunato (2010) for a survey on the subject.

4.3   Testing for Significance

Since a "truth" is not always available to validate the methodologies used in LNA, other techniques are required to provide trust in the result of the analyses. Not only do we need to choose an approach that matches our research question, the result of the methods should also be statistically significant if used beyond exploration. Statistical significance testing allows for estimating the probability that the network and its relationships as observed in the data occurred by chance rather than by some systematic process.

Statistical testing in networks is not straightforward, because nodes are by definition not independent from each other. In addition, we generally have only one observed network instead of a large sample. Nevertheless, several methods have been developed for significance testing in networks, with some being more suitable for legal citation networks than others.

In SNA, two popular models for statistical testing are Stochastic Oriented Actor Models (SOAMs) and Exponential Random Graph Models (ERGMs). Both methods can be used to obtain the importance of local structures in the complete network, possibly related to external node-level attributes. These models are used in SNA to statistically test, for example, whether girls prefer to be friends with girls, or if one is more likely to become friends with a friend of a friend. A legal example is whether certain courts favor the citation of certain cases over others.

SOAMs (Snijders, 2001) model the formation of local network structures, with the assumption that nodes are actors that deliberately form or destroy ties. As an implication, SOAMs are specifically designed for dynamic ties in a fixed set of nodes (actors). This is a valid assumption in social networks, but less applicable to citation networks, where the number of nodes grows but links never disappear. Adaptation of the models to growing networks are possible, but applications of SOAMs do not seem to be a proper fit to analyze citation networks.

ERGMs (Robins et al., 2007) are a specific type of random graph model, which consider not only the observed network, but also the complete set of possible networks with the same network statistics. The model holds a free parameter for each of the chosen network statistics, or configurations, such as the degree sequence or number of triads. The values of these parameters are chosen in such a way that the probability of the observed network is maximal. This gives insight into the importance of the different configurations for the network: for example, a high value for the parameter for number of triads suggests that triads form a significant structure in the network.

Networks of court decisions have the special property that they have a particular ordering in time, based on their publishing date. This makes them Directed Acyclic Graphs (DAGs), meaning that the links have a direction, and no cycles are present. Cycles (e.g. A cites B and B cites A) do not generally occur in case law, because decisions can only cite decisions in the past. The DAGs that have been studied most extensively are scientific citation networks, so we can use methodologies from bibliometrics and scientific networks for LNA.

A model to generate random networks for DAGs was proposed by Karrer and Newman (2009), who showed that networks generated by this model appear similar to real-life networks, including the network of US Supreme Court cases. However, applications of random graph models in citation networks remain sparse, possibly due to the fact that software packages do not contain models for DAGs. The applicability of these models for LNA should be investigated further.

Furthermore, many existing community detection algorithms do not provide a significance value for their results, but there are some exceptions. Peel et al. (2017) propose a method to retrieve the relationship between community structure and metadata, by comparing the entropy of the network under the model against networks where the data is randomly permuted.

Significance of communities can also be estimated by rewiring the edges of a network, or by comparing to a sample of similar networks. In Mirshahvalad et al. (2012) this approach is applied to the European Court of Justice citation network. The random network model of Karrer and Newman (2009) was used by Speidel et al. (2015) to formulate a variant of modularity for DAGs.

We note that much of the research of statistical methods on DAGs is rather theoretical, and established research methods similar to the SOAMs and ERGMs for SNA are not present yet for citation networks. We propose further research to connect these domains and provide researchers in LNA with out-of-the-box statistical tools for legal citation networks.

4.4 Centrality Measure Selection

Algorithm selection is not only relevant with respect to the selection of communities, but also regarding the measures used to determine the centrality of decisions. The many available centrality measures are based on different assumptions and will thus capture other properties of the network structure. Authors have evaluated several centrality measures on legal citation networks (Carmichael et al., 2017; Derlén and Lindholm, 2014; Fowler et al., 2007; Van Opijnen, 2012). Some have introduced specific centrality scores for citation networks, such as relative in-degree (Tarissan and Nollez-Goldbach, 2015) and a log-transformed degree measure (Van Opijnen, 2012).

Nevertheless, no guidelines exist in LNA as to which algorithms should be applied in which situations. Algorithm selection is important, as the application of different algorithms yields different results. This is partly caused by differences in underlying assumptions and calculation methods of the algorithms – they simply measure and capture different information. In addition, and importantly, the composition of the network also affects the results. To illustrate, we turn to the example of employer liability in the Netherlands.

When analyzing employer liability networks, we focus on commonly used centrality measures: degree centrality, in-degree centrality, out-degree centrality, relative in-degree, PageRank, HITS (authorities and hubs), closeness centrality, and betweenness centrality. We start with the non-extended sub-network that includes decisions at all levels (i.e. Dutch Supreme Court, courts of appeal, courts of first instance). In this network, which includes 338 nodes and 549 edges, several measures correlate in a statistically significant way, as is shown in Table 12.3. Out-degree centrality (6), in-degree centrality (5), PageRank (5), closeness centrality (5), and degree centrality (4) are related to various other measures (the number of statistically significant relationships reported between parentheses), with substantial variation in effect sizes across all measures.

The correlations change when the network changes. Taking a smaller and less dense sub-sample of the network that counts 40 nodes and 40 edges between decisions from and to the Dutch Supreme Court, correlations between other measures emerge, as we see in Table 12.4. In contrast to the previous network, betweenness centrality (6), authorities (5), and hubs (4) are now also positively associated with various other measures.

The results demonstrate that the outcomes that the centrality measures

Table 12.3 *Correlations between centrality measures (complete network)*

Variables	authorities	betweenness_ centrality	closeness_ centrality	degree_ centrality	hubs	in_degree_ centrality	out_degree_ centrality	pagerank	rel_in_ degree
authorities	**1.00**	-0.01	**-0.16**	-0.03	-0.03	0.02	**-0.15**	0.10	0.01
betweenness_centrality	-0.01	**1.00**	0.06	0.02	0.00	0.01	0.05	0.00	0.01
closeness_centrality	**-0.16**	0.06	**1.00**	0.10	0.05	**-0.20**	**0.96**	**-0.22**	**-0.15**
degree_centrality	-0.03	0.02	0.10	**1.00**	-0.07	**0.95**	**0.13**	**0.78**	**0.90**
hubs	-0.03	0.00	0.05	-0.07	**1.00**	-0.06	-0.01	-0.06	-0.06
in_degree_centrality	0.02	0.01	**-0.20**	**0.95**	-0.06	**1.00**	**-0.19**	**0.84**	**0.94**
out_degree_centrality	**-0.15**	0.05	**0.96**	**0.13**	-0.01	**-0.19**	**1.00**	**-0.21**	**-0.15**
pagerank	0.10	0.00	**-0.22**	**0.78**	-0.06	**0.84**	**-0.21**	**1.00**	**0.76**
rel_in_degree	0.01	0.01	**-0.15**	**0.90**	-0.06	**0.94**	**-0.15**	**0.76**	**1.00**

Note: Significant correlations ($p < 0.05$) in bold.

Table 12.4 Correlations between centrality measures (sampled network)

Variables	authorities	betweenness_centrality	closeness_centrality	degree_centrality	hubs	in_degree_centrality	out_degree_centrality	pagerank	rel_in_degree
authorities	1.00	0.60	0.11	0.67	0.27	0.70	0.11	0.38	0.45
betweenness_centrality	0.60	1.00	0.25	0.69	0.35	0.55	0.29	0.36	0.39
closeness_centrality	0.11	0.25	1.00	0.58	0.74	−0.26	0.98	−0.37	−0.20
degree_centrality	0.67	0.69	0.58	1.00	0.65	0.62	0.60	0.38	0.37
hubs	0.27	0.35	0.74	0.65	1.00	0.07	0.72	−0.12	0.14
in_degree_centrality	0.70	0.55	−0.26	0.62	0.07	1.00	−0.27	0.81	0.66
out_degree_centrality	0.11	0.29	0.98	0.60	0.72	−0.27	1.00	−0.37	−0.23
pagerank	0.38	0.36	−0.37	0.38	−0.12	0.81	−0.37	1.00	0.42
rel_in_degree	0.45	0.39	−0.20	0.37	0.14	0.66	−0.23	0.42	1.00

produce can be different for different networks. Consequently, in the practice of doing research, researchers may want to (1) inspect and even report the results of several network analysis measures and (2) compare these results to the ones found in the literature in order to provide a reference point to compare the results to. Assuming that centrality resembles relevance of precedents, at least to an extent, significant deviations from legal commentaries may either raise additional research questions (e.g. did legal scholarship overlook important decisions?) or indicate that a sub-optimal or even wrong centrality measure is chosen.

5. CONCLUSION

As we described in the previous sections, additional research is required to better understand the applicability of different network methods for the legal domain. It seems that different legal domains vary greatly in the type of networks, and consequently in the network methods and algorithms that are applicable.

An additional challenge in comparing methods and legal domains is the availability of data and software. The accessibility of citation data differs greatly for legal systems, making standardized comparisons difficult. In addition, it is not yet common practice among computational legal researchers to publish code and datasets used, along with written articles. We strongly advocate these "open science" practices, since it not only improves reproducibility, but it also allows for larger comparative studies over datasets and methods.

REFERENCES

Agnoloni, T., and Pagallo, U., 2015. The case law of the Italian constitutional court, its power laws, and the web of scholarly opinions, in: *Proceedings of the 15th International Conference on Artificial Intelligence and Law: ICAIL'15.* ACM Press, New York, pp. 151–5. https://doi.org/10.1145/2746090.2746108.

Beaverstock, J.V., 2004. "Managing across borders": Knowledge management and expatriation in professional service legal firms. *Journal of Economic Geography* 4(2), 157–79.

Blondel, V.D., Guillaume, J.-L., Lambiotte, R., and Lefebvre, E., 2008. Fast unfolding of communities in large networks. *Journal of Statistical Mechanics: Theory and Experiment* 2008, P10008. https://doi.org/10.1088/1742-5468/2008/10/P10008.

Bommarito II, M.J., and Katz, D.M., 2010. A mathematical approach to the study of the United States Code. *Physica A: Statistical Mechanics and its Applications* 389(19), 4195–200.

Bommarito II, M.J., Katz, D.M., and Zelner, J.L., 2010. On the stability of community detection algorithms for longitudinal citation data. *Procedia: Social and Behavioral Sciences* 4, 26–37. https://doi.org/10.1016/j.sbspro.2010.07.480.

Bommarito, M.J., Katz, D.M., Zelner, J.L., and Fowler, J.H., 2010. Distance measures for dynamic citation networks. *Physica A: Statistical Mechanics and its Applications* 389, 4201–8. https://doi.org/10.1016/j.physa.2010.06.003.

Boulet, R., Mazzega, P., and Bourcier, D., 2011. A network approach to the French system of legal codes-part I: Analysis of a dense network. *Artifical Intelligence and Law* 19, 333–55. https://doi.org/10.1007/s10506-011-9116-1.

Carmichael, I., Wudel, J., Kim, M., and Jushchuk, J., 2017. Examining the evolution of legal precedent through citation network analysis. *North Carolina Law Review* 96(1), 227–69.

Derlén, M., and Lindholm, J., 2014. Goodbye van Gend en Loos, hello Bosman? Using network analysis to measure the importance of individual CJEU judgments. *European Law Journal* 20, 667–87. https://doi.org/10.1111/eulj.12077.

Derlén, M., and Lindholm, J., 2015. Characteristics of precedent: The case law of the European Court of Justice in three dimensions. *German Law Journal* 16(5), 1073–98.

Fortunato, S., 2010. Community detection in graphs. *Physics Reports* 486, 75–174. https://doi.org/10.1016/j.physrep.2009.11.002.

Fortunato, S., and Barthelemy, M., 2007. Resolution limit in community detection. *Proceedings of the National Academy of Sciences of the United States of America (PNAS)* 104, 36–41. https://doi.org/10.1073/pnas.0605965104.

Fowler, J.H., and Jeon, S., 2008. The authority of Supreme Court precedent. *Social Networks* 30, 16–30. https://doi.org/10.1016/j.socnet.2007.05.001.

Fowler, J.H., Johnson, T.R., Spriggs, J.F., Jeon, S., and Wahlbeck, P.J., 2007. Network analysis and the law: Measuring the legal importance of precedents at the U.S. Supreme Court. *Political Analysis* 15, 324–46. https://doi.org/10.1093/pan/mpm011.

Ghasemian, A., Hosseinmardi, H., and Clauset, A., 2018. Evaluating Overfit and Underfit in Models of Network Community Structure, arXiv:1802.10582 [stat.ML].

Gionfriddo, J.K., 2007. Thinking like a lawyer: The heuristics of case synthesis. *Texas Tech Law Review* 40, 1–36.

Good, B.H., de Montjoye, Y.-A., and Clauset, A., 2010. Performance of modularity maximization in practical contexts. *Physical Review E* 81, 046106. https://doi.org/10.1103/PhysRevE.81.046106.

Heinz, J.P., and Laumann, E.O., 1982. *Chicago Lawyers: The Social Structure of the Bar*. Russell Sage Foundation.

Hutchinson, T., 2010. *Researching and Writing in Law*, 3rd ed. Thomson Reuters, London.

Karrer, B., and Newman, M.E.J., 2009. Random acyclic networks. *Physical Review Letters* 102, arXiv:0902.4013v1. https://doi.org/10.1103/PhysRevLett.102.128701.

Katz, D.M., and Bommarito, M.J., 2014. Measuring the complexity of the law: The United States Code. *Artificial Intelligence and Law* 22, 337–74. https://doi.org/10.1007/s10506-014-9160-8.

Kleinberg, J.M., 1999. Authoritative sources in a hyperlinked environment. *Journal of the ACM* 46, 604–32. https://doi.org/10.1145/324133.324140.

Knops, M., and Schaper, M., 2014. Holding complexity: Analysing the CJEU's VAT case law as a network. *World Journal of VAT/GST Law* 3(3), 141–65.

Koniaris, M., Anagnostopoulos, I., and Vassiliou, Y., 2017. Network analysis in the legal domain: A complex model for European Union legal sources. *Journal of Complex Networks* 6(2), 1–29. ArXiv, abs/1501.05237. https://doi.org/10.1093/comnet/cnx029.

Lancichinetti, A., and Fortunato, S., 2012. Consensus clustering in complex networks. *Scientific Reports* 2, 336. https://doi.org/10.1038/srep00336.

Laumann, E.O., Marsden, P.V., and Prensky, D., 1983. The boundary specification problem in network analysis, in: Burt, R.S., and Minor, M.J. (eds), *Applied Network Analysis: A Methodological Introduction*. Sage, Beverly Hills, CA, pp. 18–34.

Lazega, E., 2001. *The Collegial Phenomenon: The Social Mechanisms of Cooperation among Peers in a Corporate Law Partnership*. OUP, Oxford.

Lazega, E., and Krackhardt, D., 2000. Spreading and shifting costs of lateral control among peers: A structural analysis at the individual level. *Quality and Quantity* 34, 153–75.

Lazega, E., and van Duijn, M., 1997. Position in formal structure, personal characteristics and choices of advisors in a law firm: A logistic regression model for dyadic network data. *Social Networks* 19(4), 375–97.

Leicht, E.A., Clarkson, G., Shedden, K., and Newman, M.E.J., 2007. Large-scale structure of time evolving citation networks. *European Physical Journal B* 59, 75–83. https://doi.org/10.1140/epjb/e2007-00271-7.

Lupu, Y., and Voeten, E., 2012. Precedent in international courts: A network analysis of case citations by the European Court of Human Rights. *British Journal of Political Science* 42, 413–39. https://doi.org/10.1017/S0007123411000433.

Mirshahvalad, A., Lindholm, J., Derlén, M., and Rosvall, M., 2012. Significant communities in large sparse networks. *PloS One* 7, e33721. https://doi.org/10.1371/journal.pone.0033721.

Neale, T., 2013. Citation analysis of Canadian case law. *Journal of Open Access Law* 1(1).

Nievelstein, F., Van Gog, T., Van Dijck, G., and Boshuizen, H.P.A., 2013. The worked example and expertise reversal effect in less structured tasks: Learning to reason about legal cases. *Contemporary Educational Psychology* 38(2), 118–25.

Olsen, H.P., and Küçüksu, A., 2017. Finding hidden patterns in ECtHR's case law: On how citation network analysis can improve our knowledge of ECtHR's Article 14 practice. *International Journal of Discrimination and the Law* 17(1), 4–22.

Olsen, H.P., and Sadl, U., 2017. Can quantitative methods complement doctrinal legal studies? Using citation network and corpus linguistic analysis to understand international courts. *Leiden Journal of International Law* 30(2), 327–49.

Peel, L., Larremore, D.B., and Clauset, A., 2017. The ground truth about metadata and community detection in networks. *Science Advances* 3, e1602548. https://doi.org/10.1126/sciadv.1602548.

Reichardt, J., and Bornholdt, S., 2006. Statistical mechanics of community detection. *Physical Review E* 74, 016110. https://doi.org/10.1103/PhysRevE.74.016110.

Robins, G., Pattison, P., Kalish, Y., and Lusher, D., 2007. An introduction to exponential random graph (p *) models for social networks. *Social Networks* 29, 173–91. https://doi.org/10.1016/j.socnet.2006.08.002.

Schaper, M.G.H., 2014. A computational legal analysis of acte clair rules of EU law in the field of direct taxes. *World Tax Journal* 6(1), 77–108.

Schaub, M.T., Delvenne, J.-C., Rosvall, M., and Lambiotte, R., 2017. The many facets of community detection in complex networks. *Applied Network Science* 2, 4. https://doi.org/10.1007/s41109-017-0023-6.

Snijders, T.A.B., 2001. The statistical evaluation of social network dynamics. *Sociological Methodology* 31, 361–95. https://doi.org/10.1111/0081-1750.00099.

Speidel, L., Takaguchi, T., and Masuda, N., 2015. Community detection in directed acyclic graphs. *European Physical Journal B* 88, 203. https://doi.org/10.1140/epjb/e2015-60226-y.

Tarissan, F., and Nollez-Goldbach, R., 2015. Temporal properties of legal decision networks: A case study from the International Criminal Court. *Legal Knowledge and Information Systems* 279, 111–20. https://doi.org/10.3233/978-1-61499-609-5-111.

Tarissan, F., and Nollez-Goldbach, R., 2016. Analysing the first case of the International Criminal Court from a network-science perspective. *Journal of Complex Networks* 4(4), 616–34. https://doi.org/10.1093/comnet/cnw002.

Tarissan, F., Panagis, Y., and Sadl, U., 2016. Selecting the cases that defined Europe: Complementary metrics for a network analysis. Proceeding of the 2016 IEEE/ACM International Conference on *Advances in Social Networks Analysis and Mining (ASONAM)*, San Francisco, California, 661–8. https://doi.org/10.1109/ASONAM.2016.7752308.

Valente, T.W., Fujimoto, K., Unger, J.B., Soto, D.W., and Meeker, D., 2013. Variations in network boundary and type: A study of adolescent peer influences. *Social Networks* 35, 309–16. https://doi.org/10.1016/j.socnet.2013.02.008.

van Dijck, G., 2017. *MoneyLaw (and Beyond)*. Eleven International Publishing, The Hague.

van Dijck, G., and van Kuppevelt, D., 2018. Deelonderwerpen en precedenten in het kader van werkgeversaansprakelijkheid ex art. 7:658/7:611 BW: een netwerkanalyse. Ned. Juristenblad.

Van Opijnen, M., 2012. Citation analysis and beyond: In search of indicators measuring case law importance. *Legal Knowledge and Information Systems* 250, 95–104. https://doi.org/10.3233/978-1-61499-167-0-95.

Whalen, R., 2013. Modeling annual Supreme Court influence: The role of citation practices and judicial tenure in determining precedent network growth, in: Menezes, R., Evsukoff, A., and González, M.C. (eds), *Complex Networks: Studies in Computational Intelligence*. Springer, Berlin, Heidelberg, pp. 169–76.

Whalen, R., 2014. Bad law before it goes bad: Citation networks and the life cycle of overruled Supreme Court precedent, in: Winkels, R., Lettieri, N., and Faro, S. (eds), *Network Analysis in Law*. Edizioni scientifiche italiane, Naples, pp. 1–23.

Whalen, R., 2016. Legal networks: The promises and challenges of legal network analysis. *Michigan State Law Review*, 539–65.

13. Needles in a haystack: using network analysis to identify cases that are cited for general principles of law by the European Court of Human Rights

Henrik Palmer Olsen and Magnus Esmark

INTRODUCTION

In recent years a new approach to legal studies, generally subsumed under the category of "computational legal studies" has emerged. This approach to legal studies has a broad range of different applications (Katz et al., 2017; Aletras et al., 2016). For a broader overview, see Whalen (2016, p. 539). Computational Legal Studies has emerged out of two conjoined developments: (1) the emergence of digital and on-line collections of case law from an increasing number of courts and administrative agencies both domestic and international and (2) the realization that data science methods can be used to analyse these new large collections of case law and provide insights that either it were not previously possible to obtain or which may now be produced much faster than previously, thereby allowing for more comprehensive studies of legal practice than before.

This study focuses on a specific branch of computational studies that is characterized by using network analysis to access, process and understand legal information. More specifically, on the background of previous studies, we seek to develop a method to identify the most actively cited cases that are used as precedent for general principles of law in the European Court of Human Rights.

The chapter contributes to the developing knowledge of how repeated case-citation by courts and other law applying agencies can be used to leverage information about what cases are important as precedent in legal practice. Knowledge of this kind is useful for a number of purposes. Litigants, who are seeking to build a legal argument, may wish to know what cases are cited more by the court for the purpose of using these in their arguments. Referring to cases that the court itself uses frequently to justify their own decisions may give legal arguments more appeal. For teachers and students of law, it may be useful both to learn how to use these tools and to apply them in teaching. Recent studies have shown that textbooks sometimes cite cases that the court itself only rarely or never uses (Christensen and Olsen, 2016; Frese and Olsen, 2019). It is useful for a better and more realistic scenario of what is going on in actual court practice to use network analysis as a basis for critically engaging with textbooks to enhance the quality of learning. Finally, network analysis may serve as a legal informatics tool that can present large samples of case law in new ways, thereby providing a basis for asking new questions about a court and its jurisprudence.

This chapter will focus on a specific use of network analysis applied to the case law of the European Court of Human Rights (ECtHR). We build from previous research that has applied various approaches to case law analysis with a focus on finding legally important cases in a given part of the case law relating to *specific substantive rights provisions* (e.g. ECtHR case law on freedom of religion (art. 9) or the protection against discriminatory treatment (art. 14)). From a starting point in the methods applied previously, we move towards a way of identifying cases that are characterized by having a high impact (measured by citation frequency) as precedent for general principles of law. By general principles of law, we mean principles of law that *cut across the specific rights provisions* in the convention. Examples of such principles could be general rules on "admissibility", the "prescribed by law" requirement or other well-known topics such as the "exhaustion of national remedies" or the principle of proportionality. These principles are used across many different kinds of cases, and they are therefore frequently relied on to determine the outcome of new cases. Our study seeks to identify those cases that are most frequently relied on by the court as precedent for these kinds of principles. Developing a computational method that allows for the identification of these principles will allow legal scholars as well as practitioners to see more clearly what cases are used by the court in its reasoning on the specific points of law that are embedded in these principles and thereby to better comprehend the reasoning involved. For lawyers involved in litigation before the court, having more comprehensive knowledge of the court's citation practice will allow for better situating a specific argument in the context of this practice, thereby advancing the chances of winning the case. For a legal scholar, it will allow for more accurate representations of what cases are important when describing the court's adjudicative practice.

We first will provide a brief and non-exhaustive overview of the developments in the field of network analysis applied to case law. This will serve to clarify the most important underlying basis for our work in this chapter. Then, in the following two sections, we will present two different methods to search for important cases that are cited for general legal principles. We use these methods to search through the formal citations between the more than 17,000 judgments that constitutes the entire set of judgments in the period up to and including 2013 from the ECtHR. In the last section, we will evaluate and compare the results of the two methods proposed.

THE DEVELOPMENT OF NETWORK ANALYSIS IN LEGAL STUDIES

The application of network analysis – and other quantitative methods already known to other social sciences – opens up the possibility for more empirical approaches to doctrinal studies and provides a way of asking questions and gaining insights that are not available through more traditional methods. Based on Supreme Court citation data combined with data on the Court and its decisions available in the Spaeth dataset,[1] Fowler, Johnson, Spriggs, Jeon and Wahlbeck (2009) put network analysis to use on the United States Supreme Court (USSC) as an alternative to former subjective measurements of the precedent value of a majority opinion (e.g. if the opinion was referred on the front page of the *New York Times*). Another important lesson from the study, which has laid ground for several later studies, was that the structure of legal citations networks largely mimics the structure of other types of social networks.

Network analysis has since been used to structure and gain overview over a large corpus of precedent and investigating the way courts use citations. Lupu and Voeten (2012) used the HITS-algorithm to show when and how the ECtHR embed its decisions deepest into existing case law by looking at the hub-score of a judgment by the time it was handed down by the court. Derlén, Lindholm, Roswall and Mirshahvalad (2012) used clustering to group the practice of the Court of Justice of the European Union (CJEU) and classify the mathematically identified clusters manually by reading through selected judgments in each cluster. The study showed how the EU case law consisted in part of different legal areas than previously thought by legal scholars, as well as showing through the citations patterns how some legal areas were close to or far from others, in a pattern that had not before been discovered in the theory.

More recently Olsen and Šadl (2017), focusing on the CJEU, showed

---

[1]   The database is available at http://scdb.wustl.edu/.

how network analysis could be combined with collocated word clouds to reveal new information about the emergence of new trends in case law. Whalen, Uzzi and Mukherjee (2017) have measured citation patterns in common law courts in terms of reach (average age of cited works) and range (variance of ages cited) and have found that some citation profiles are much more likely to occur than others. Other recent studies put focus, not on the macrostructure of a network, but on determining the precedent value (or some proxy for that) and compare citation behaviour in the ECtHR to the selection of cases by various textbook authors to measure similarities and differences (Frese and Olsen, 2019). Nollez-Goldbach and Tarissan (2015) introduced *relative in-degree* as a unit of measurement to include the temporal aspect in the ascertainment of the precedent value of judgments from the International Criminal Court. Christensen, Olsen and Tarissan (2016) have built a bi-partite network that, based on the judgments citing a judgment and the articles from the convention mentioned in these citing judgments, can be used to predict the legal content (by article number) for which the judgment is mostly cited. This latter method assumes that if a judgment is cited by a number of other judgments, and these judgments recurrently mention a specific article in the convention more often than other articles, it is most probably because the judgment has some legal content that is used in the interpretation of that specific article. In practical application, a score for each article in the convention is calculated for each judgment in the network, and the highest scoring article is designated as the MainIn (i.e. dominant/main article in the inwards citations to the judgment in question – see Figure 13.1). In a sample, the study shows that the method gets the legal main content of a judgment right roughly nine out of ten times. We will be relying on the use of this method in the present study.

What seems to be a common aim for legal doctrinal approaches to network analysis research applied to sets of case law is the determination of methods that can be used to identify specific legal content and/or patterns of legal content and thereby supplement or even critically assess traditional doctrinal accounts of law. The overall aim then is to translate the network findings into legal meaning. The assumption that individual legal judgments should be seen as fitting into a larger scheme of legal practice that constitutes a coherent system of legal normativity allows one to infer the legal meaning and significance of a judgment not only from its own textual content but also from its relation to the rest of the precedent body (Olsen and Šadl, 2017). This is an important methodological step in the utilization of quantitative methods on legal studies, on which we will elaborate further in this study.

USING CENTRALITY SCORE DIFFERENCE AS AN INSTRUMENT TO FIND GENERAL PRINCIPLES OF LAW

Much of the existing research that applies network analysis of sets of case law with a view to examining doctrinal legal questions focuses either (1) on determining precedent value in a given subfield of law determined by specific legal provisions – say article 14 in ECHR (the right not to be discriminated (Christensen and Olsen, 2016; Christensen et al., 2016)) or (2) on mapping the legal content of a set or subset of a court's case law (Derlén et al., 2012). In this chapter we attempt to take doctrinal oriented network analysis one step further. We will try to use existing techniques – pagerank (Page et al., 1998) and MainIn (Christensen et al., 2016) – to calculate values for each judgment in the entire corpus of case law from the ECtHR in order to determine which judgments contain precedent value for principles of law that are *not* associated with a specific article in the European Convention on Human Rights (ECHR), but are instead general principles of law that are broadly used across the different substantive rights provisions in the convention. We will try out two different methods of calculation and test the results by manually reading those judgments that have the best scores in order to check whether those judgments are indeed cited as precedent for general principles of law.

METHOD

The first method we will examine in this chapter relies on the use of the above-mentioned method for identifying main legal content of a given precedent (MainIn). We use the MainIn score to divide the entire network of cases into sub-networks consisting of judgments with the same MainIn. We then compare the centrality score of judgments within their sub-network to their centrality in the overall network. Our hypothesis is that if a judgment is more central in the overall network than in its own network, then it is precedent for a legal principle that is relevant not only to the interpretation of the substantial rights provision that defines which sub-network it belongs to (its calculated MainIn) but to a range of different types of cases. This legal attribute of the judgment is shown by pagerank flowing from other areas of law to the judgment, thus giving it a relatively higher score in the overall network than in its own. Attracting citations from judgments in other sub-networks is interpreted as a sign that the judgment contains a general legal principle that is relevant across more than one single rights provision. We call these judgments polymorph precedents.

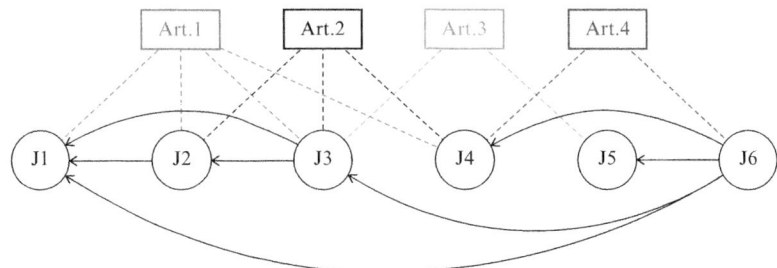

Figure 13.1   Judgment 1 only cites article 1. However, it is cited by judgments 2, 3 and 6, and the predominant articles cited by these are articles 1 and 2. Since article 2 is overall cited more rarely, J1 is designated with MainIn art. 2

DATA AND INITIAL COMPUTATION

Our data consist of the entire set of judgments from the ECtHR up to and including 2013 as published in the Court's own case database, HUDOC. We have used the Court's own metadata to identify, for each judgment, which previous judgments it cites and also which articles it cites.

On the basis of this data we have computed a MainIn score for every judgment. We have attached in Figure 13.1 a model illustration of a double bound network as a crude example of how the MainIn of a judgment is determined. Of the little more than 17,000 judgments in the total dataset, a MainIn is only computable for 7,718.[2] We assume that these other decisions have no value as precedents. We have therefore removed these judgments from the dataset.

Following the identification of a MainIn score for 7,718 judgments we group these judgments together in sub-networks. Each sub-network is composed of judgments that all have the same MainIn value, each value corresponding to an article in the convention. We then calculate two pagerank scores for each judgment: one score for its pagerank in the overall network and another score for its pagerank in the sub-network. When calculating the score for a sub-network, we only use the citations between judgments in that particular sub-network, thus cutting all the ties to other sub-networks. We have illustrated this in Figure 13.2.

---

[2]   This is due to the fact either that the concerned judgments have never been cited at all, or that they have been cited just once by another judgment that in turn does not refer to any of the articles in the convention.

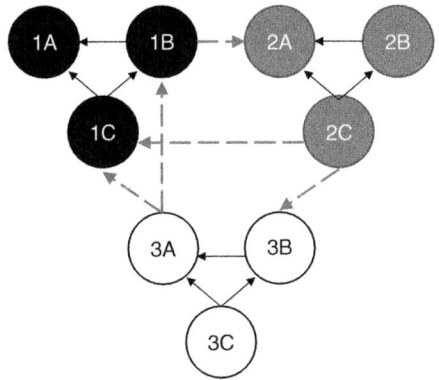

Figure 13.2 *Three sub-networks 1, 2 and 3, each with different judgments.*
When we calculate the pagerank in the overall network,
we take all the citations (arrows) into account. When we
calculate the pagerank in the individual sub-networks, we
remove the citations across different sub-networks (stippled
arrows)

OPERATIONALIZING PAGERANK SCORE FOR A NETWORK OF CASE LAW

We measure the centrality of the judgments in our network and sub-networks with the pagerank algorithm (Page et al., 1998; Derlén and Lindholm, 2017; Derlén et al., 2012), having adjusted its damping factor to 0.66. We use this damping factor because we see this as the best balance between two competing considerations. On the one hand, a high damping factor will likely generate too much pagerank in older judgments, which will distort the distribution over time and make older judgments look disproportionately more important than more recent ones. This is because the network is directed backwards in time; a judgment can only cite earlier judgments. On the other hand, a damping factor set too low will fail to catch the depth in the jurisprudence. By this, we mean that it will fail in accounting for the fact that legal principles often flow through several generations of citations. Taking these two opposing considerations to mind, we find 0.66 to be an acceptable balance.[3]

Pagerank applied to a case-to-case network gives us a mathematical

---

[3]   To our knowledge, there is no study on how to optimally adjust the damping factor for studies of case-to-case networks.

indication of the centrality of a judgment, because it is a measurement of the probability that a reader working randomly through the jurisprudence following the citations to other judgments will read this particular judgment. However, the overall centrality of a judgment is of limited value if we are unable to infer some notions of the legal content of the judgment. Judges do not cite random cases as precedent when they write up judgments. They cite relevant cases. This is why the division of cases into sub-groups of cases with specific content is important. Although the MainIn method described above does not break down the entire set of case law into individual legal principles it does break it down into smaller units that relate to the individual rights provisions in the convention. Using pagerank we can then also show how central each of the judgments are within the scope of their own substantial rights provision. Centrality scores can be combined with different kinds of keyword search, presumably as well as natural language processing technologies to further sort and refine the cases within each rights provision. In this chapter, however, we have set out to search cases that embody general principles of law, and we shall therefore not pursue this line of inquiry.

In order to find the judgments, which contain general principles of law, one cannot settle for the pagerank scores in the overall network. The overall network is not just a uniform collection of judgments; it consists of a collection of different sub-networks each with their own internal citation-structure. Cases on, say, freedom of expression are more likely to cite other cases on freedom of expression, but less likely to cite, say, cases on the right to a fair trial. Simultaneously, some types of cases are much more frequent than others – there are, for example, many more cases on the right to fair trial than there are on the right to freedom of religion – cases that are cited a lot overall do not necessarily receive their citations from many different types of cases.[4] For this reason, one cannot rely solely on the pagerank value in the overall network as a way of finding cases that are cited for generic principles of law. If, however, we compare the pagerank score of a case in its own sub-network to its score in the overall network, we may be able to identify those cases that are cited for general principles of law. Our assumption is that, if a case has a higher pagerank score in the overall network than it does in its own sub-network, then it attracts pagerank value from cases outside its own sub-network. We take that to be an indication that it is cited for a broader legal principle.

It might also be that the value is higher in the overall network because

---

[4]   As an example, of the top ten scoring judgments in pagerank, eight judgments have MainIn art. 6 – a massive overrepresentation of this particular article.

the judgment is cited for two different principles, both relating to a specific rights provision. It is thus not impossible that a judgment contains something significant about, say, article 3 on the prohibition of torture *and* article 9 on freedom of religion, and therefore receives numerous citations from both of these sub-networks. However, one will rarely see judgments that are cited many times for different legal content, and only a few of the sub-networks are large enough to significantly alter the results on their own in the overall network. Therefore, even if these cases might cause small errors, we regard them sufficiently unlikely and rare to disregard them.

Making the comparison between the two values in the right way, however, is not straightforward.

If one compares the pagerank score of a judgment within its own network directly to the same judgment's score in the overall network, with a view to finding those judgments that have highest difference in favour of overall pagerank score, the result will be misleading. Judgments from smaller networks will receive a numerically higher value in their own network than judgments from the large networks, simply because there are fewer judgments to share the total pagerank score of 1. This makes it misleading to compare the difference in pagerank score for cases that belong to a small sub-network (e.g. article 9) to that of a case that belongs to a big sub-network (e.g. article 6). In order to solve this problem, we seek to convert the pagerank scores in the entire dataset into comparable values.

NORMALIZING PAGERANK SCORE AND MEASURING PAGERANK SCORE DIFFERENCE

To be able to carry out an accurate comparison between sub-network pagerank score and overall pagerank score, we normalize the pagerank scores in the following way.

Our starting point are two variables: $PR_o(v)$ which expresses the pagerank score of the judgment v in the overall network, and $PR_s(v)$ which expresses the pagerank score assigned to the judgment v in its local sub-network. As explained above, these two are not directly comparable. In the following, we will explain how we transfer these scores into values that are directly comparable.

Setting off from these variables, we first introduce a variable that neutralizes the effect of a judgment belonging to a particular sub-network. This value k expresses the factor that the sum of the pagerank score of the cases in a given sub-network has been assigned in the overall network must be multiplied by, before this sum becomes 1. To give an example:

1. Identify all cases that have a MainIn of art. 3,
2. Identify the pagerank of each of these cases in the overall network,
3. Add these scores to a new sum,
4. 1 divided by this sum will be the value k for every case that belongs to the MainIn-art. 3 sub-network.

It follows from the varying sum of pagerank values in the overall network for the different sub-networks that a separate value for k must be calculated for each sub-network. We define k to the sub-network of article i as:

$$k_i = \frac{\sum_i PR_{G_{arti}}(v)}{\sum PR_G(v)} = \frac{1}{\sum PR_G(v)}, \; where \; v \in i \qquad (13.1)$$

And where:

$$G_{arti} = \{v \in G, \; s.t. \; MainIn(v) = i\} \qquad (13.2)$$

The calculated k for the sub-network i is used to calculate an average pagerank score in the overall network for all the judgments belonging to the sub-network i. This average value can be understood as a *presumed* value $PR_p(v)$, where we can use k to infer what $PR_o(v)$ "should" be if it followed the average:

$$PR_p(v) = \frac{PR_o(v)}{k_i} \qquad (13.3)$$

If the actual $PR_o(v)$ is higher than the presumed value, this indicates that the judgment is more important in the overall network than what we expect it to be (i.e. on average). In mathematical terms, this means that it draws pagerank from judgments in other sub-networks. In legal terms, it means that it is cited by cases that have another MainIn than itself. We therefore expect these cases to be cited for legal principles that are generally applicable across several substantive rights provisions. Since we are not only looking for judgments with a higher $PR_o(v)$ than presumed, but looking for those cases that stand out most in this regard, we measure the difference $PR_{dif}(v)$ for all cases by a simple subtraction:

$$PR_{dif}(v) = PR_o(v) - PR_p(v) \qquad (13.4)$$

Having performed these calculations we rank all cases according to their $PR_{dif}(v)$ score and we then examine the cases with the highest score for legal content.

RESULTS

We have calculated the PR_{dif} for all judgments in the overall network containing the 7,718 judgments for which a MainIn can be calculated. For the top 100 scoring judgments, we have read all the individual paragraphs that have received 20 or more citations.[5] We have included this filter to ensure that the paragraphs we identify are not only polymorph, but that they also are precedents, that is, that the court uses them in practice. The number 20 has been chosen as a balance point between including paragraphs that are not necessarily the top-scoring paragraphs in the whole network (since these will often occur in cases on a specific subject matter), and selecting only those paragraphs that receive a significant number of citations. To be in the top 10 per cent in-degree in our network, a judgment needs 125 citations, 4 citations to be in the upper 25 per cent, the median value being 1 citation. We consider 20 citations a decent compromise between searching in a broad population of judgments and still eliminating initially the obviously not important judgments.

On the basis of the content of these paragraphs, we have concluded whether the judgment is or is not one of the sought-after types. The results can be summed up as follows.

Out of the 100 judgments, 67 contained at least one paragraph with a minimum of 20 citations. Of these 67 judgments, 42 contain at least one polymorph precedent, some cases contain more than one. Examples of these precedents could be the standard of evaluation of proofs before the court[6] or that the court can award costs and expenses incurred before not only the court, but also before the national courts.[7] Based on a reading of the paragraphs, we have sorted the precedents contained in the 42 judgments into different groups, shown in Table 13.1. We will later use this categorization to compare what kind of judgments this method leads us to, compared to the alternative method for finding these judgments that we will present in the next section.

We deem this amount of polymorph precedents to count as a success for the method. Since this study is one of the first of its kind, there are no proven and recognized baselines from which to evaluate the method,

---

[5] We are aware, as has been pointed out in a series of other studies, that in-degree centrality has some serious flaws when it comes to the temporal dimension of the network. Although methods to treat this issue have been developed, we have chosen in this study – to limit the scope and length of it – not to apply these, and our results should be read in that context.

[6] Case 21986/93 *Salman v. Turkey*, pr. 100.

[7] Case 25181/94 *Hertel v. Switzerland*, pr. 63.

Table 13.1   The seven topics of the precedents

No.	Subject/rule	PR_{dif}	Overlap	Subordinate scores
1	Interpretation of art. 13	7	2	2
2	Exhaustion of national remedies	6	4	5
3	Interpretation of the exceptions to arts 8–11	5	0	1
4	Assignment of compensation	9	2	6
5	The role of the ECHR and the ECtHR	6	1	4
6	Procedural rules before the court/admissibility	7	2	3
7	Interpretation of the treaty in general or specific wordings	8	3	4

Note: The numbers show how many cases fall into each topic, with the overlap column indicating how many cases are identified by both of the two methods.

and the estimation of the results is essentially a question of (qualified) gut feelings until more research on the area is published.

In the following section, we will introduce another method to find the same kind of principles.

PROXIMITY OF SUBORDINATE SCORES IN THE MAININ COMPUTATION

In the above section, we investigated how the MainIn variable can be utilized to divide the cases of the ECtHR into groups that are cited predominantly for the same legal content determined by convention article. We subsequently compared pagerank scores in the overall network to scores in each of the sub-networks to identify cases containing general principles of law. In this section, we will use an enhanced MainIn analysis for the same purpose.

As explained earlier in this chapter, the MainIn computation identifies a score for each article mentioned in the judgments citing the primary judgment. The article that receives the highest score is designated as the MainIn. This is the only part of the calculation that has been utilized in the above and former usages of this variable. However, the computation will often administer scores for many different articles for each judgment, thus providing not only a MainIn (= PrimaryIn), but also a SecondaryIn, a TertiaryIn and so on. We will put those numbers to use in this section under the common designation "subordinate scores". Some judgments will receive only a few different subordinate scores, some not even one, while some will receive more than 20 subordinate scores.

When the MainIn is a measurement of the influence a given judgment has had on the designated area of law, the relative score of the different articles provides a measurement of the distribution of importance between several legal areas. If a judgment receives a very high score for article 6, but very low scores for all other articles, it will indicate that the judgment is not only *primarily* influential in the area of article 6, but *almost exclusively* so. Conversely, a judgment that receives almost equal scores for a range of different articles has had almost equal influence on many different areas of law.

Just having a high score for a couple of articles will not make a judgment "generically applicable", though. Many judgments will contain elaborate sections on the alleged breach of several different articles, and the citations to the judgment may therefore very well be distributed accordingly, thus just indicating that the judgment holds substantial precedents in some legal areas, but not a single precedent applicable in all types of cases. However, if the values of the subordinate scores of a judgment are relatively close over a broad range of articles, say, 8 or 9, this might indicate that the judgment holds something that can be used regardless of the substantial content of a case.

On this basis, we measure the proximity of the different subordinate scores to a given judgment in order to measure the likelihood that this particular judgment will hold a principle that can be – and is in the courts' practice – used across a broad range of cases.

DEVELOPING A MATHEMATICAL MEASURE OF LEGAL BROADNESS: PROXIMITY OF SUBORDINATE SCORES

In order to compute the MainIn of each judgment, one score is calculated for all the articles cited in the judgments citing the judgment in question. The highest scoring article is then designated as the MainIn article. In this section, we assume that if the different scores assigned to the different articles for one judgment are close to each other, this is an indication that the judgment could be equally important for many different types of cases.

However, the numerical value of the scores cannot be compared directly, since the total number of citations influences the number calculated. We therefore construct a measurement that compares the proximity of the different scores to the highest possible proximity, where all scores are equal. For the judgment v, we can compare the proximity of the scores S of the articles a, b, c and so on:

$$P(v) = \frac{S_a S_b \ldots S_n}{S_a^n} \tag{13.5}$$

To translate this into a legal context: if the values of the individual subordinate scores are close to the primary score, this might be an indication that there is a polymorph precedent in the judgment, and that it therefore is cited in many different contexts. Since not one article stands out, but instead the judgment is used (relatively close to) equally in the interpretation of several different articles, the judgments that are receiving a high score in our calculations should be the subject of further investigation.

We have made the aforementioned calculation for each judgment with all the possible number of subordinate scores. This has provided us with the preliminary requisites for further investigation.

HOW MANY SUBORDINATE SCORES?

A challenge for the use of subordinate scores is that judgments receive a different number of subordinate scores depending on the number of different articles cited in the judgments citing the primary judgment. This forces us to confront the question how to measure which number of different subordinate scores that gives the best output.

For a series of different numbers of subordinate scores,[8] we have calculated the number of judgments with at least one paragraph that has been cited 20 or more times. From these calculations, we can see a clear pattern in which a higher number of subordinate scores results in more judgments containing often-cited paragraphs within the top 100, indicating that working with a high number of scores yields better results. We have also observed that all important judgments reoccur in the groups with a higher number of subordinate scores, meaning that we do not lose anything important by

---

[8]   We calculated for 4, 7, 10, 11 and 12 different scores. They gave 1, 5, 16, 23 and 27 judgments respectively. Going higher than 12 different scores would leave too few judgments to sort.

looking at a higher number of scores.[9] However, using the highest possible number of subordinate scores is better if and only if they give us not only more judgments with paragraphs cited 20 times or more, but also only if the additional judgments contain the sought-after principles.

Using only judgments with a considerable number of different scores, a large number of judgments are cut out of the dataset before we start using the method to rank the judgments. This forces us to strike a balance between choosing a high number of scores while not limiting the size of the dataset so much that in reality there is no data to sort. We found that this balance is struck by measuring judgments with at least 12 different scores, which gave us a little more than 500 judgments for which to calculate a proximity score.

The 100 top-scoring judgments measuring all judgments with at least 12 different scores results in 26 judgments containing one or more paragraphs with an in-degree of at least 20. Of these 26 judgments, we deem 19 of them to contain the kind of generically applicable principles we were looking for. In Table 13.1, we have categorized the judgments in the same system as in the former section.

In the following section, we will compare and discuss the results of this and the above section.

DISCUSSION AND EVALUATION OF THE PROPOSED METHODS

First, it is important to note that there is a methodological issue related to the categorization of the legal content in the judgments that have been singled out by our computational approach. While we have conducted most of the analysis based on objective data about the judgments and relations between them, the legal categorization is based on a reading of the material. Furthermore, we made up the categories *after* reading the cases and after and gaining an initial idea about the distribution of cases across topics. In this way the categorizations we have made have taken shape after the results instead of using pre-existing categories to describe the results. However, not only does it seem difficult to avoid such a step if some conclusions are to be made about the qualitative properties of the results. We also believe that the categories we have identified are generally

---

[9] The single exception to this pattern should be mentioned; 9310/81 occurs in the group 11, but not in 12. We consider this single exception not important enough to change our above conclusion.

accepted by legal scholars as representing general legal issues relevant to the ECHR. Hence all of these issues are subject of analysis and discussion in doctrinal legal research.

As we have already mentioned above, evaluation of the methods is complicated by the lack of recognized baselines. Trying to quantify the comparison of the two methods in terms of precision and recall is tempting, but risks simplifying the case by forcing the wrong metrics on the methods in question. To compare the two methods, PR_{dif} receives a precision score of 0.66 while the proximity of subordinate scores receives a precision score of 0.77. However, since the latter finds fewer important cases in the top 100, the fact that we chose to take exactly the top 100 scoring judgments and read these heavily influenced the results. Evaluating a classificatory this way is not easy, and gets even more complicated when computing the recall: what is a false negative in this context? If every judgment with the sought-after content that did not make it into the top 100 is a false negative, there surely would be a lot, but coming around this seemingly arbitrary threshold would require us to actually read every single one of the more than 7,000 judgments. Not only cumbersome, this is also contrary to the philosophy of our quantitative approach.

Overall, these considerations prevent us from doing a simple comparison on the lines of precision/recall. The assessment has to be based on a somewhat subjective evaluation until the point where there is sufficient research with this approach to create a generally recognized baseline.

In general, the PR_{dif}-method finds more judgments with more than 20 citations – 67 as compared to the 26 in the method of subordinate scores. PR_{dif} contains around one-third false positives in the selection from the top 100, while subordinate scores have around one-quarter false positives. Even though the latter slightly outperforms the former in this respect, it should be seen in the context that it overall finds a lot fewer true positives. These two differences between the methods do not have an obvious explanation. One way of looking at it could be that PR_{dif} consists of a combination of two metrics (MainIn and pagerank respectively), where the method of subordinate scores uses only the MainIn computation. By using two different metrics in combination, a double-selection of the material could have happened, where less important (read: rarely cited) judgments are filtered out. At the same time, this could also explain the bigger quota of false positives, since applying two methods will also combine the weaknesses of both. This is, however, an abstract and not very conclusive explanation of the differences in overall results between the two methods.

IS ARTICLE 13 A GENERIC PRINCIPLE?

In our categorization of results, we have listed "interpretation of art. 13" as a true positive. One could argue that article 13[10] is more a substantial rights provision than a generic principle applicable across a broad range of cases. This is true to the extent that the court invokes the provision in the judgments as a section separate to other substantial rights provisions in the judgments, and that it – along with other substantial provisions – deals with the rights of the individual within the member state. This is contrary to many of our other findings that tend to be mentioned in the judgments as parts of other discussions, or at the end of the judgment outside the discussion of any breach of a provision (e.g. the judgments about assignment of compensation). Another possible objection to our categorization of article 13 is that article 14 could as well be applied in a wide array of different cases, so both should be either in or not in our results.

In spite of these objections, we have chosen to include article 13 in our results as a true positive. In the beginning of the chapter, we defined the polymorph precedents as some that find use broadly on the practice of the ECtHR independently of the substantial specificities of the case. Since article 13 regulates the right to have a case about a breach of a substantial provision tested before the national courts, it does not regulate what constitutes a breach in itself. In line with other research on article 13 (Annabel, 2015) we do not consider article 13 to be a freestanding right. Also, article 13 is interpreted in close conjunction with the rule in article 35 on exhaustion of national remedies (Kjølbro, 2010); another procedural rule that falls clearly under our initial definition.

To the objection related to article 14,[11] we hold that this convention is closely linked to the substantial part of the case, because it is used to decide whether the sequence of events to be adjudicated on constitutes a breach of the convention. On the contrary, article 13 does not become relevant as an object of adjudication unless there is some kind of case that is not manifestly ill-founded (violation or not). Only in this situation does article 13 provide procedural guarantees to a plaintiff. Our decision to distinguish between articles 13 and 14 in this way is backed by the fact that the application of article 14 demands tying it directly to another

---

[10]   Article 13 protects the right to have an alleged violation of the substantial rights provisions trialled in the national legal systems.
[11]   Article 14 of the convention protects the right not to be discriminated against relating to any of the other rights in the convention. Article 14 is always used in conjunction with another provision, for example when the right to a fair trial (article 6) is violated due to a person's sexuality.

substantial provision, which means that it does not fulfil our definition of a polymorph precedent, namely that it should be applicable "independently of the substantial content of the case".

CONCLUSION

The two methods presented above both provide some promising results. Since these computational methods can be automated, it provides an efficient way of identifying a group of cases for further qualitative scrutiny.

Both methods can also be seen as a more general contribution to computational legal studies, since they can be applied also to other contexts. While the MainIn computation is developed specifically for the practice of the ECtHR, meaning that the exact method might not be translated 1:1 into a different legal context, the method of dividing a practice into subnetworks of different legal areas and comparing centrality across these is probably useful in many places. For example, American constitutional law practice of the USSC shares many traits with the practice of the ECtHR, that we have studied in this chapter. In addition, more specialized national jurisdictions or legal areas such as the French Conceil d'Etat[12] and the Australian Family Court[13] provide the amount of data and the necessary demarcation of legal content to provide corresponding studies. The PR_{dif}-method seems to be superior to the method of subordinate score in the sense that it finds a larger number of polymorph precedents. The difference in the share of false positives between the two methods does not seem to be of considerable size to change this conclusion.

Based on the above discussion comparing results of the two methods, it seems that combining different metrics yields good results – given that the metrics individually are good. If this is considered a general methodological conclusion to draw, one might expect even better results coming from network analysis studies as this field continually develops and adds new and more refined methods for exploring the law.

---

[12]   Data available at https://www.data.gouv.fr/en/datasets/jade/ (last accessed 25 May 2020).
[13]   Data available at http://www.austlii.edu.au/cgi-bin/viewdb/au/cases/cth/ FamCA/ (last accessed 25 May 2020).

REFERENCES

Aletras, N., Tsarapatsanis, D., Preoţiuc-Pietro, D. and Lampos, V. (2016). Predicting judicial decisions of the European Court of Human Rights: A Natural Language Processing perspective. *PeerJ Computer Science* 2:e93, https://doi.org/10.7717/peerj-cs.93.

Annabel, L. (2015). Focus on Article 13 ECHR, *Judicial Review*, 20:1, 33–41.

Christensen, M.L. and Olsen, H.P. (2016). Netværksanalyse som bidrag til juridisk (forsknings) metode. *Juristen*, issue 3, 110–23.

Christensen, M.L., Olsen, H.P. and Tarissan, F. (2016). Identification of case content with quantitative network analysis: An example from the ECtHR. In: Bex, F. and Villata, S. (eds) *Legal Knowledge and Information Systems* (53). Amsterdam: IOS Press.

Derlén, M. and Lindholm, J. (2017). Is it good law? Network analysis and the CJEU's internal market jurisprudence. *Journal of International Economic Law*, 20:2, 257–77.

Derlén, M., Lindholm, J., Roswall, M. and Mirshahvalad, A. (2012). Coherence out of chaos: Mapping European Union law by running randomly through the maze of CJEU case law. *Europarättlig Tidsskrift*, issue 3, 517–35.

Fowler, J.H., Johnson, T.R., Spriggs II, J.F., Jeon, S. and Wahlbeck, P.J. (2009). Network analysis and the law: Measuring the legal importance of Supreme Court precedents. *Political Analysis*, 15:3, 324–46.

Frese, A. and Olsen, H.P. (2019). Citing case law: A comparative study of legal textbooks on European Human Rights law. *European Journal of Legal Studies*, 11:1, Special Issue, 91–131.

Katz, D.M., Bommarito, M.J. II and Blackman, J. (2017). A general approach for predicting the behavior of the Supreme Court of the United States. *PLoS ONE* 12(4): e0174698. https://doi.org/10.1371/journal.pone.0174698.

Kjølbro, J.F. (2010). *Den Europæiske Menneskerettighedskonvention: for praktikere* (3rd ed.). Copenhagen: Jurist- og Økonomforbundets Forlag.

Lupu, Y. and Voeten, E. (2012). Precedent in international courts: A network analysis of case citations by the European Court of Human Rights. *British Journal of Political Science*, 42:2, 413–39.

Nollez-Goldbach, R. and Tarissan, F. (2015). Temporal properties of legal decision networks: A case study from the International Criminal Court. In: Rotolo, A. (ed.) *Legal Knowledge and Information Systems* (111). Amsterdam: IOS Press.

Olsen, H.P. and Šadl, U. (2017). Can quantitative methods complement doctrinal legal studies? Using citation network and corpus linguistic analysis to understand international courts. *Leiden Journal of International Law*, 30:2, 327–49.

Page, L., Brin, S., Motwani, R. and Winograd, T. (1998). The PageRank citation ranking: Bringing order to the web. Technical report. Stanford InfoLab.

Whalen, R. (2016). Legal networks: The promises and challenges of legal network analysis. *Michigan State Law Review*, 2016:2, 539–65.

Whalen, R., Uzzi, B. and Mukherjee, S. (2017). Common law evolution and judicial impact in the age of information. *Elon Law Review*, 9:1, 115–70.

14. Agent-based modeling for legal studies

Alex Schwartz

1. INTRODUCTION

Agent-based modeling is a computational method for building "bottom up" simulations. Typically, it is used to investigate how the actions and interactions of individual autonomous units (or "agents") generate systemic effects or patterns. Although agent-based modeling has been widely applied in the natural and social sciences, it has seldom been used to study law or legal phenomena. But as computational methods become ever more accessible and popular, a flowering of agent-based models in legal studies may well be on the horizon. With a view to encouraging this nascent trend, this chapter provides a brief introduction to agent-based modeling. In the first part, I explain the basic nature and purposes of agent-based modeling, distinguish agent-based modeling from other methods, and canvass several ways in which agent-based modeling has already been applied to legal studies. In the second part, I present a basic version of an original agent-based model of judicial review to illustrate how the method might be used to shed fresh light on old questions in comparative constitutional law.

2. WHAT IS AN AGENT-BASED MODEL (AND WHAT IS IT GOOD FOR)?

As the name suggests, the fundamental building blocks of an agent-based model ("ABM") are autonomous "agents". Agents behave according to pre-programmed "procedures". Typically, the procedures that agents follow are relatively simple behavioral responses to events that occur within the "world" of a simulation. Agents may have individual characteristics and states that change over the course of the simulation. Agents may be mobile, moving around the world and interacting with other agents according to their respective procedures. Agents may also be sedentary units that affect—or are affected by—neighboring agents. An ABM will play out over a time series (or "steps"), but the world of the simulation need not be an explicit geometric space; it may represent a logical or network space in which relationships between agents are arranged and interactions between them occur.

It is a characteristic feature of an ABM that the interactions of many autonomous agents—each following relatively simple behavioral rules—can lead to complex system-level patterns (see Axelrod 1997). The emergent complexity displayed by an ABM, though not readily predictable from the initial state of the simulation, can be made intelligible by comparing how the model performs with different procedures or under different parameters. For this reason, agent-based modeling lends itself to answering certain types of questions: it provides a distinct way to explore the macro-level implications of micro-level theories and assumptions (see Epstein 1999).

Technically speaking, agent-based modeling does not require a modern computing device. For instance, Thomas Schelling's famous segregation model (Schelling 1971)—arguably the first ABM ever—can be easily built and run with just (1) a checkerboard to represent the residential space of a city; (2) pennies and dimes to represent individual agents belonging to one of two different ethnic groups; and (3) a simple procedure that instructs each agent to prefer a location in a mixed neighborhood over a location in a homogenous neighborhood, *but only if* most of the agent's neighbors would be from the agent's group. This simple model demonstrates that a mild preference for locations in majority in-group neighborhoods quickly generates a dramatically segregated outcome, even if the initial state is an integrated one (i.e., pennies and dimes are evenly distributed throughout the checkerboard). The result is just the sort of emergent macro-level pattern that agent-based modeling is particularly good at illuminating.

Examples like Schelling's segregation model aside, the potential for agent-based modeling has been greatly enhanced by leaps and bounds in computational power over the last few decades. A personal laptop computer can now build and run an ABM that would have required a supercomputer 30 years ago. Moreover, the rise of "big data" means that that agent-based modeling can be informed by rich real-world information. Rather than modeling behavior and parameters based on our intuitions or stereotypes, researchers can now use vast amounts of granular data to calibrate an ABM to very specific real-world circumstances (Kavak et al. 2018). Hence, for example, an ABM exploring different urban planning strategies can be informed by millions of data points on pedestrian flows, traffic congestion, social media use, and the real estate market of an actual city (see Scheutz and Mayer 2016).

Another important development in ABM is the advent of several purpose-built programming languages that substantially lower the barriers to entry for researchers who lack experience in computer programming (Abar et al. 2017). Indeed, the most popular software for agent-based modeling—Uri Wilensky's NetLogo—was designed to be both "low floor" and "high ceiling" (Wilensky and Rand 2015). Wilensky's idea was that NetLogo would provide both an educational tool to be used by school children as well as a research tool to be used by scientists. Accordingly, the language of NetLogo is both intuitive and extremely flexible. NetLogo can also produce easy-to-interpret graphical displays that facilitate real-time understanding of a model's performance as well as large datasets for more sophisticated quantitative analysis of a model's outcomes.

Agent-based modeling has some passing resemblance to formal game theory. Both approaches begin with the micro-foundations of the phenomena they model. Indeed, the "agents" and "procedures" of an ABM can often be redescribed in the language of game theory as "players" and "strategies". There are, however, several fundamental differences between the two approaches that should not be overlooked. Unlike the equation-based models typically employed by game theory, agent-based modeling does not require a mathematically tractable "solution" (De Marchi and Page 2014; Bonabeau 2002). An ABM can easily incorporate "bounded rational" (or even irrational) heuristic behavioral rules inspired by intuitions or empirical evidence about how fallible actors in the real world pursue their goals (see Axelrod and Tesfatsion 2006). Furthermore, agents can be as numerous and dissimilar as the modeler wants to make them (Wilensky and Rand 2015, 37). In short, because mathematical tractability is not a constraint for agent-based modeling, there is virtually no limit—apart from computing power—to the number and heterogeneity of the agents that an ABM can accommodate. For this reason, the method facilitates lines of inquiry that might otherwise be closed off.

Closely related to this difference between agent-based modeling and game theory is another: the ability to explore the path-dependency of systems. Game theory specializes in finding equilibrium and comparative statics, but it is not well-suited to modeling the downstream consequences of early contingent choices. In contrast, agent-based modeling is particularly well-suited for this sort of enterprise. Agents can have individual memories, they can learn (or fail to learn) from their respective histories, and the consequent system-level outcomes can be "non-marcovian", in the sense that future states of the system are not exhaustively determined by present states but also—and perhaps more importantly—by earlier states of the system (see Bonabeau 2002, 7281; and Axelrod and Tesfatsion 2006).

Agent-based modeling also shares some passing similarities with more conventional empirical methods, especially with experimental research design. By systematically varying agent characteristics and simulation parameters one can perform controlled computational experiments. The results of these experiments can be structured as a dataset and imported into a software package for quantitative analysis. For such purposes, NetLogo includes a purpose-built app for performing ABM experiments—"BehaviorSpace"—that allows multiple parallel runs of a model. In this way, the researcher can explore the "space" of possible behaviors and determine which combinations of settings cause the patterns or outcomes of interest.[1] In contrast to conventional empirical research—where research design attempts to overcome the fundamental problem that the counterfactual can never be observed—an ABM can be subjected to a "parameter sweep": the model's parameters can be systematically varied in multiple simulations to show how the results or outcomes covary or are robust to alternative model specifications. In this way, we can see how the *same* agents behave both with *and* without the treatment. The catch, of course, is that the resultant observations are simulated data. These data may tell us something about how the real world might look, given the model's assumptions, but they are not actually observations of the real world itself.

Agent-based modeling has been widely applied to a variety of topics. In the natural sciences, it has been used to simulate phenomena such as contagious diseases (Perez and Dragicevic 2009), wildlife habitat (McLane et al. 2011), and ant colonies (Pratt et al. 2005). And in the social sciences, agent-based modeling has arguably had an even greater impact (see Squazzoni 2010); it has been used to study topics as diverse as cooperation (Axelrod 1997), ethnocentrism (Hammond and Axelrod 2006), civil war (Epstein 2002), prehistoric archaeology (Dean et al. 2000), and financial markets (LeBaron 2001). Often, agent-based modeling has given social scientists a new way to answer an otherwise intractable question. For example, Michael Laver and Ernest Sergenti (2011) use an ABM to model party competition for the support of voters in a multidimensional policy space, showing how different vote-seeking strategies do or do not pay off over time. Agent-based modeling allows Laver and Sergenti to drop the unrealistic assumption of unidimensional policy that would be necessary to make a formal equation-based model of the same phenomenon yield a mathematically tractable solution. More generally, agent-based modeling

---

[1]   See the explanation online at https://ccl.northwestern.edu/netlogo/docs/behaviorspace.html (last accessed 10 June 2020).

is said to facilitate a distinct research paradigm of "generative social science" in which macroscopic social regularities are explained in terms of "decentralized local interactions of heterogeneous autonomous agents" (Epstein 1999).

Though still relatively rare, agent-based modeling has been applied to legal studies in inventive ways. Broadly speaking, the use of agent-based modeling for studying legal phenomena clusters into three broad categories. In the first category are those studies that use agent-based modeling to simulate how different regulatory regimes influence individual agent behavior and how that agent-level behavior in turn generates systemic effects (see e.g., Hokamp and Pickhardt 2010; Balke et al. 2013). For example, Sascha Hokamp and Michael Pickhardt (2010) use an ABM to assess the impact of alternative policies on the prevalence of tax evasion. This category of agent-based modeling would also include studies that show how emergent social patterns are robust to regulatory choice. For example, Daria Roithmayr (2004) uses an ABM to demonstrate how residential segregation along racial lines can "lock in" despite laws that formally prohibit racial discrimination.

A second broad category includes studies that use agent-based modeling to investigate the diffusion of legal norms or legal knowledge within a network. Work in this vein would include the ABM developed by Katz et al. (2009) to complement a computational model (Katz et al. 2011) of intellectual influence within the American legal academy. Agent-based modeling was put to similar purposes by Rouchier and Tubaro (2011) to study the diffusion of legal knowledge within the peer network of the Commercial Court of Paris.

The third category of agent-based modeling in legal research focuses on how individual strategic choices interact and evolve within a system of heterogeneous actors. An example of this application would include the ABM developed by Mayor, Izquierdo, and Sartor (2009) to simulate and compare various litigation strategies in the context of medical liability litigation. Other examples of this sort of ABM research—though more in the domain of criminology than legal studies—would include simulations of strategic criminal behavior (for an overview, see Groff et al. 2018).

These examples aside, it cannot be denied that ABMs are still very few and far between in legal scholarship. Why is this? One simple explanation is that legal scholarship is a late adapter of new methods in general. It is only after a method becomes very well-established in some other field—say economics or political science—that it trickles down, so to speak, into the legal academy. Because agent-based modeling is only just coming into its own in other disciplines, it may yet be some time before ABMs become more familiar in legal scholarship. But agent-based modeling—at least when developed using a low-barrier platform like NetLogo—is arguably a more accessible method than either game theory or quantitative empirical methods. To illustrate how agent-based modeling might be extended to familiar questions, the next section walks the reader through the structure and results of a basic ABM of judicial review.

3. THE ABM OF JUDICIAL REVIEW

The ABM presented here is a simulation of how judicial review evolves over the course of a sequence of interactions between a constitutional court ("the Court") and the political branches.[2] It is designed to show how a newly established constitutional court might build its authority (or fail to do so) depending on its strategic choices and the conditions of its encompassing institutional environment. As constitutional challenges arise, the Court must decide to uphold or invalidate a challenged policy. In doing so, the Court is influenced by the direction and strength of its own policy preferences, its belief about how likely the political branches are to comply with its decisions, and its strategic sensibilities (i.e., a heuristic decision rule it follows in each case). If the Court invalidates a policy, the political branches may decide to comply with or defy the decision. In doing so, the political branches are influenced by the direction and strength of their own policy preferences, as well as existing expectations about compliance with the Court's decisions. If at any time the political branches decide that the Court costs them too much in preferred policy outcomes, they can attempt to coordinate a court-curbing attack. If they succeed in doing so, the simulation ends (because the Court will no longer be an independent organ of constitutional review).

How Does the ABM of Judicial Review Work?

At the very beginning of the simulation, NetLogo "breeds" the Court and *N* Government Agents that represent the political branches. The number of Government Agents is determined by an adjustable parameter

---

[2]   This ABM is programmed and run in NetLogo. A more extensive discussion and exploration of a version of this simulation is published in *The Journal of Law* (Schwartz 2019a). The NetLogo code for a simplified version of the simulation (Schwartz 2019b) can be inspected online at http://modelingcom mons.org/browse/one_model/6039#model_tabs_browse_info (last accessed 10 June 2020).

(NUMBER-OF-GOV-AGENTS). This parameter allows the simulation to model varying degrees of institutional complexity. A very simple context would include the Court and just a single Government Agent; a more complex context—for example, a federal system—might include dozens of Government Agents representing a set of autonomous legislatures and/or executives.

Two adjustable parameters—POLARIZATION and FRAGMENTA-TION—model the policy preferences of the Court and Government Agents. POLARIZATION determines how likely the Court is to disagree with existing policy and how likely, on average, the Government Agents are to disagree with the Court. FRAGMENTATION models the variance in policy preferences among Government Agents, that is, how likely the Government Agents are to disagree with one another.

At the beginning of each "step" in the simulation, a case is generated and assigned a random CASE-SALIENCE value, ranging from 0 to 1 (drawn from a normal distribution). This variable represents how politically important the case is to the agents in the simulation. As in the real world, not all cases will attract the same level of attention. Some cases will be very high profile and divisive; think of the US Supreme Court's decision in *Obergefell v. Hodges*,[3] finding a constitutional right to the legal registration and recognition of same-sex marriage. Other cases will be relatively low profile. Each case in the simulation is also assigned a random CASE-SCOPE interval that determines the range of Government Agents that may be affected by the Court's decision. As in the real world, some cases will have broad policy consequences across the system while others—even if highly salient—will have relatively narrow consequences. For example, despite the attention it received, *Obergefell* only had direct legal consequences for those 14 states that had not already legalized same-sex marriage in one way or another.

Once a case is generated, POLARIZATION will determine if the Court agrees or disagrees with the challenged policy. If the Court disagrees, it must decide either to invalidate the policy or, alternatively, uphold the policy even though it disagrees with it. This decision is a function of a decision rule determined by COURT-STRATEGY. The *Default* decision rule is a probabilistic one: if the Court disagrees with a policy, it will decide to invalidate it with a probability equal to the CASE-SALIENCE value (so the more salient the case is, the more likely the Court will be to invalidate it). An alternative decision rule—called *Avoider*—will invalidate policy it disagrees with but with a probability *inversely* proportionate to the

---

[3]   576 U.S. (2015).

CASE-SALIENCE value. In other words, *Avoider* aims for policy victories in relatively low-salience cases.

In response to the Court's decision, the affected Government Agents (as determined by CASE-SCOPE) will each make an independent decision to comply or defy. The most basic version of the simulation makes compliance/defiance a function of two variables: CASE-SALIENCE and EXPECTATION-OF-DEFIANCE (the mean of these two values in a given case determines the probability of defiance). In the default setting of the simulation, EXPECTATION-OF-DEFIANCE is simply equal to the proportion of previous decisions that have been defied in the past. Hence, other things being equal, the Government Agents start the simulation with a strong inclination to comply with the Court (because, in that initial state, EXPECTATION-OF-DEFIANCE = 0). However, this parameter is adjustable so that varying baseline expectations of compliance/defiance can be set to model a continuum of contexts, from a context in which there is a very strong initial expectation of judicial power to one in which judicial power is tenuous and expected to fail from the outset.

Once the Court and affected Government Agents have made their decisions, each agent collects a payoff in utility according to the following scheme:

1. If the Court invalidates a policy, then the Court collects utility equivalent to the product of CASE-SALIENCE and the number of *affected* Government Agents that comply with the decision. Meanwhile, affected Government Agents that agree with the policy suffer a loss equivalent to CASE-SALIENCE.
2. If the Court upholds a policy that it disagrees with, affected Government Agents that agree with the policy collect utility equivalent to CASE-SALIENCE. Meanwhile, the Court suffers a loss equivalent to the product of CASE-SALIENCE and the number of affected Government Agents.
3. If the Court upholds a policy that it agrees with, then the Court suffers no loss and affected Government Agents that agree with the policy collect utility equivalent to CASE-SALIENCE.

When a Government Agent's utility score drops below zero, it becomes UNHAPPY and it will consider launching a court-curbing attack (e.g., impeachment of judges; jurisdiction stripping; suspending the Court, and so on). The success of this attack depends on two final threshold parameters. The first of these—DEFIANCE-THRESHOLD—represents theoretical expectations about the influence of past defiance on the probability of a present court-curbing attack. Setting this parameter very high models an expectation that Government Agents are cautious about court curbing and so, even if they are UNHAPPY, they will not attempt an attack until a recent history of defiance suggests that the Court's authority is already failing. Conversely, setting this parameter at a relatively low level represents an expectation that Government Agents are more cavalier about the costs of court curbing and do not need to perceive much, if any, weakness in the Court's authority before launching an attack. The second threshold parameter—DISSATISFACTION-THRESHOLD— determines the proportion of Government Agents that must be simultaneously UNHAPPY for a coordinated court-curbing attack to succeed. The idea here is to model the influence of institutional veto points that make a court-curbing attack require the coordinated effort of several Government Agents at once.

Like any model, this ABM makes several simplifying assumptions: (1) the Court and the Government Agents are single-minded policy seekers; (2) the policy preferences of the Court and Government Agents are static and fixed at the outset; (3) the Government Agents' response to a Court decision invalidating policy is a simple binary choice (to comply or defy); and (4) all agents within the simulation know if compliance or defiance has occurred. These simplifying assumptions are not merely for the sake of modeling convenience. By subtracting much of the complexity one would expect to see in the real world, the idea is to try to isolate the influence of the parameters we are most interested in on the outcomes we are most interested in.

Things to Notice about the ABM of Judicial Review

Though very basic, the ABM outlined above can be explored in various ways. For one thing, by systematically varying parameter settings we can investigate the varying probability of a court-curbing attack under different stylized conditions. Figure 14.1 graphs the cumulative hazards of court curbing over time—that is, the probability that the Court will have been attacked at each step in the simulation—depending on which decision rule (COURT-STRATEGY) is followed.

As the figure illustrates, a Court that can survive the first 100 steps of the simulation will tend to survive until the end of the simulation. Moreover, the Court's decision rule really does make a difference on the probability of a successful court-curbing attack. Adopting the *Default* strategy, the Court's cumulative hazard of attack rises rapidly to roughly 35 percent and then gradually stabilizes as the simulation goes on. In contrast, the *Avoider* decision rule only just barely accumulates more than a 10 percent hazard of attack, and this hazard stabilizes much earlier in the simulation.

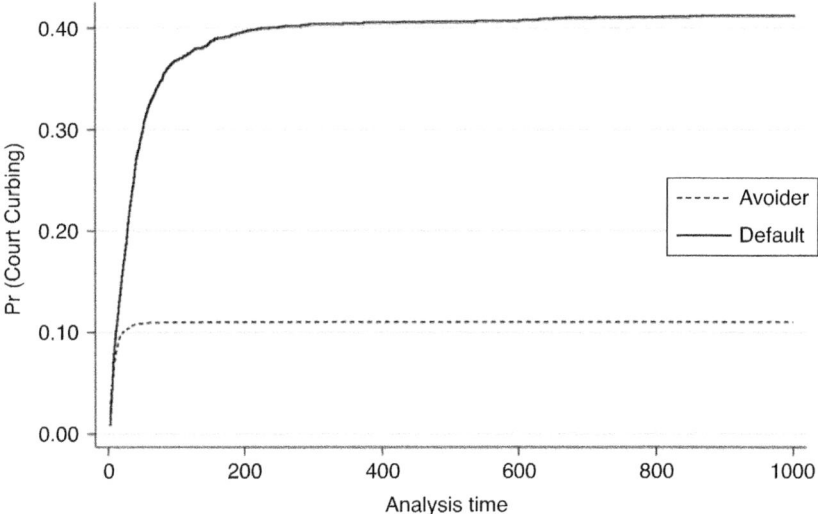

Figure 14.1   Cumulative hazards of court curbing

In other words, a Court adopting the *Avoider* strategy not only has a better chance of surviving the conditions that might otherwise encourage a court-curbing attack but it also benefits from a much shorter window in which such an attack is likely to occur.

The parameter sweep of this ABM experiment also allows us to identify how individual parameters contribute to the cumulative hazard rates depicted above. The most obvious contributor is POLARIZATION. A Court that finds itself in an environment in which there is broad agreement about policy will invalidate less policy and the political branches will also be less likely to disagree with the Court's decisions. If the political branches infrequently disagree with the Court, they will not defy it and, more importantly, have no cause to attack it. Figure 14.2 shows what one would expect: the probability of court curbing increases considerably with increases in policy polarization.

At the lowest levels of POLARIZATION, the two decision rules make little difference because there is so little chance of court curbing anyway. But the difference is already substantively meaningful where the probability of policy disagreement is 0.4. At the highest level of POLARIZATION, in which the Court and Government Agents will disagree 100 percent of the time, there is an almost 100 percent chance that a Court adopting the *Default* rule will be successfully attacked. At this extreme level of POLARIZATION, the *Avoider* rule is also more likely to provoke a

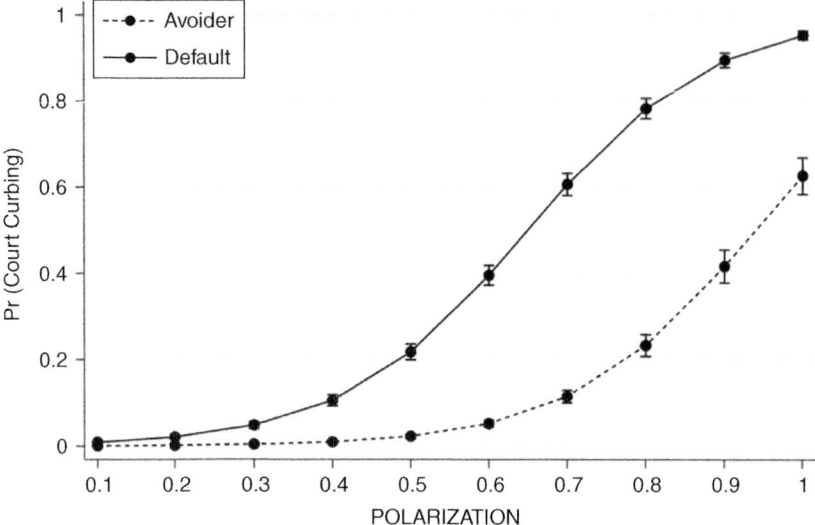

Figure 14.2   Predicted probabilities of court curbing

successful attack than not. However, the *Avoider* rule is still a much safer heuristic (at only a 0.6 probability of court curbing).

Extending the Model

The ABM presented here is a relatively simple one. There are many things here that are either not modeled or are only modeled in a very abstract way. One of the great advantages of developing a basic ABM like this, however, is that it is flexible; it can easily be extended to include other parameters or decision rules, different payoff functions, and other kinds of agents and different kinds of events.

In the case of this ABM, one potential extension is to model the influence of occasional elections. Adding elections would make the simulation more dynamic by introducing shocks that may suddenly change the probability of policy disagreement. Thus, a Court that is relatively safe may abruptly find itself in a much more hostile political environment.

A simple way to model the influence of elections is to periodically reset policy preferences (POLARIZATION and FRAGMENTATION) and the Government Agents' attitudes towards the Court (UNHAPPY or not). Extending the model in this simple way, Figure 14.3 shows the cumulative hazard estimates of court curbing over time by COURT-STRATEGY (*Avoider* or *Default*).

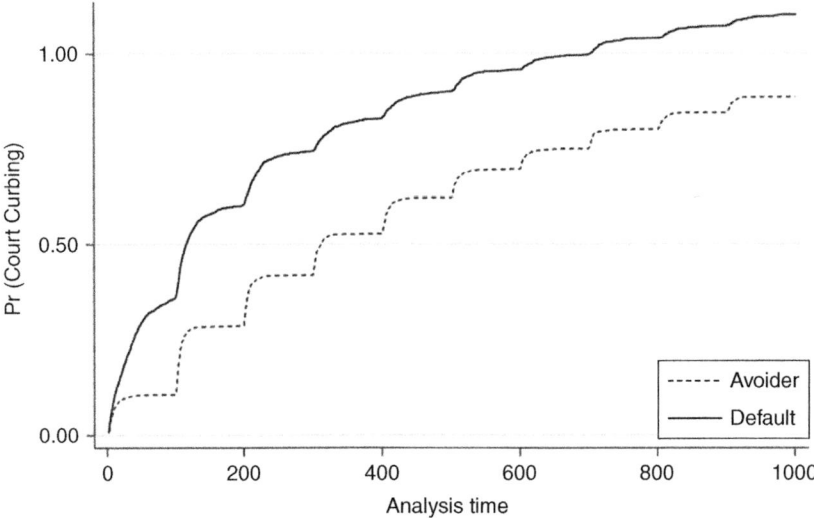

Figure 14.3   Cumulative hazards of court curbing (with elections)

As can be seen above, elections create a much more erratic environment for the Court. Every time the ideological environment is reshuffled, there is the potential for the political branches to become more hostile to the Court's policy preferences. Accordingly, Figure 14.3 shows a sizable jump in the probability of court curbing just after each election. But the difference between the two Court strategies in the version of the ABM that includes elections is much less dramatic than in the version of the model without regular elections. Although the Court adopting the *Avoider* strategy still has a better chance of surviving to the end of the simulation, this advantage is substantially curtailed by the occasional shock of elections.

Naturally, this model could be extended further to make it more realistic. For example, the competitiveness of elections might be included as an adjustable parameter and this parameter could then influence the utility calculus of the Government Agents; the more competitive elections are believed to be, the more Government Agents might tolerate the Court's interventions. The Court could also be assigned a procedure that takes the competitiveness of elections into account in deciding how assertive it will be in invalidating policy. These extensions of the model would be in line with theory and evidence about the influence of competitive electoral democracy on judicial empowerment (see Ginsburg 2003; see also Ramseyer 1994; and Stephenson 2003).

There are of course many other possible extensions of this ABM that might be explored; the literature on judicial power and court curbing is rich with hypotheses to be tested. Increasingly, there is also real-world cross-national data to compare with the results of simulations like the one presented here.[4] The point to take away here is that—once a simple basic skeleton of an ABM is in place—agent-based modeling can be extended in virtually any direction by incrementally adding new elements or parameters.

One should also be wary, however, of a false sense of realism. Although ABMs can accommodate more complex (and therefore seemingly realistic) assumptions, there is always a tradeoff between apparent realism and parsimony. The more realistic the model is the more assumptions it must make about the phenomena it models. Each assumption comes with the potential cost that the model is either relevant to a narrower range of circumstances than it might otherwise be or—if the assumption is really misguided—to nothing at all. For these reasons, ABM methodologists recommend building models that are only as complex as they need to be for the modeler's purposes (Wilensky and Rand 2015).

4.   CONCLUSION

Legal scholars are already interested in the systemic effects of individual behavior; "macroscopic social regularity" is presumably what law is designed to achieve and what many legal scholars want to study. But we cannot manipulate the real world and its legal rules to conduct society-wide experiments. Observational studies can help, particularly if a legal intervention creates the conditions for a kind of quasi-experiment. But waiting patiently for nature to deliver a convenient research design is not a great strategy for mortal beings with urgent research agendas. Nor can we always rely on formal equation-based models to make up the difference; the myriad ways in which individuals and legal rules interact within dynamic path-dependent systems will inevitably outrun our mathematical capacities. This is where agent-based modeling comes in, to supplement conventional empirical methods and formal models with a third approach. By growing artificial societies "from the bottom

---

[4]   For example, the Varieties of Democracy ("V-Dem") project has cross-national data on judicial independence, judicial power, and various kinds of court-curbing retaliation. See the project's website at https://www.v-dem.net/en/.

up", we can gain a new perspective on the mechanisms that generate the real world of law and human behavior. This chapter has tried to show that this computational approach to legal research is both accessible and promising. For those readers who have been persuaded, the still untapped potential of computational legal studies and agent-based modeling awaits.

REFERENCES

Abar, S., Theodoropoulos, G.K., Lemarinier, P., and O'Hare, G.M. (2017). Agent Based Modeling and Simulation Tools: A Review of the State-of-Art Software. *Computer Science Review, 24,* 13–33.

Axelrod, R. (1997). *The Complexity of Cooperation: Agent-Based Models of Competition and Collaboration.* Princeton, NJ: Princeton University Press.

Axelrod, R., and Tesfatsion, L. (2006). Appendix A A Guide for Newcomers to Agent-Based Modeling in the Social Sciences. In L. Tesfatsion and K.L. Judd (eds), *Handbook of Computational Economics, Vol. 2* (pp. 1647–59). Amsterdam: North-Holland.

Balke, T., De Vos, M., and Padget, J. (2013). I-ABM: Combining Institutional Frameworks and Agent-Based Modeling for the Design of Enforcement Policies. *Artificial Intelligence and Law, 21*(4), 371–98.

Bonabeau, E. (2002). Agent-Based Modeling: Methods and Techniques for Simulating Human Systems. *Proceedings of The National Academy of Sciences, 99*(suppl 3), 7280–87.

De Marchi, S., and Page, S.E. (2014). Agent-Based Models. *Annual Review of Political Science, 17,* 1–20.

Dean, J.S., Gumerman, G.J., Epstein, J.M., Axtell, R.L., Swedlund, A.C., Parker, M.T., and McCarroll, S. (2000). Understanding Anasazi Culture Change through Agent Based Modeling. In G.J. Gumerman and T. Kohler (eds), *Dynamics in Human and Primate Societies: Agent-Based Modeling of Social and Spatial Processes* (pp. 179–206). New York: Oxford University Press.

Epstein, J.M. (1999). Agent-Based Computational Models and Generative Social Science. *Complexity, 4*(5), 41–60.

Epstein, J.M. (2002). Modeling Civil Violence: An Agent-Based Computational Approach. *Proceedings of the National Academy of Sciences, 99*(suppl 3), 7243–50.

Ginsburg, T. (2003). *Judicial Review in New Democracies: Constitutional Courts in Asian Cases.* Cambridge: Cambridge University Press.

Groff, E.R., Johnson, S.D., and Thornton, A. (2018). State of the Art in Agent-Based Modeling of Urban Crime: An Overview. *Journal of Quantitative Criminology, 35*(1), 1–39.

Hammond, R.A., and Axelrod, R. (2006). The Evolution of Ethnocentrism. *Journal of Conflict Resolution, 50*(6), 926–36.

Hokamp, S., and Pickhardt, M. (2010). Income Tax Evasion in a Society of Heterogeneous Agents: Evidence from an Agent-Based Model. *International Economic Journal, 24*(4), 541–53.

Katz, D.M., Bommarito, M.J., and Zelner, J. (2009). Model of Intellectual Diffusion upon the American Legal Academy. Accessed 23 June 2020 at https://computationallegalstudies.com/2009/04/22/the-revolution-will-not-be-televised-but-will-it-come-from-harvard-or-yale-a-network-analysis-of-the-american-law-professoriate-part-iii/.

Katz, D.M., Gubler, J.R., Zelner, J., and Bommarito, M.J. (2011). Reproduction of Hierarchy-A Social Network Analysis of the American Law Professoriate. *Journal of Legal Education*, *61*, 76–103.

Kavak, H., Padilla, J.J., Lynch, C.J., and Diallo, S.Y. (2018, April). Big Data, Agents, and Machine Learning: Towards a Data-Driven Agent-Based Modeling Approach. In *Proceedings of the Annual Simulation Symposium* (pp. 1–12). Baltimore, MD: Society for Computer Simulation International.

Laver, M., and Sergenti, E. (2011). *Party Competition: An Agent-Based Model*. Princeton, NJ: Princeton University Press.

LeBaron, B. (2001). A Builder's Guide to Agent-Based Financial Markets. *Quantitative Finance*, *1*(2), 254–61.

Mayor, E., Izquierdo, L.R., and Sartor, G. (2009, July). Nice and Nasty Lawyers, is the Legal System to Blame? Agent-based Simulation Insights. In G. Governatori (ed.), *Proceedings of the 2009 Conference on Legal Knowledge and Information Systems: JURIX 2009 – The Twenty-Second Annual Conference* (pp. 126–35). Amsterdam: IOS Press.

McLane, A.J., Semeniuk, C., McDermid, G.J., and Marceau, D.J. (2011). The Role of Agent-Based Models in Wildlife Ecology and Management. *Ecological Modeling*, *222*(8), 1544–56.

Perez, L., and Dragicevic, S. (2009). An Agent-Based Approach for Modeling Dynamics of Contagious Disease Spread. *International Journal of Health Geographics*, *8*(1), 50–67.

Pratt, S.C., Sumpter, D.J., Mallon, E.B., and Franks, N.R. (2005). An Agent-Based Model of Collective Nest Choice by the Ant Temnothorax Albipennis. *Animal Behaviour*, *70*(5), 1023–36.

Ramseyer, J.M. (1994). The Puzzling (In)Dependence of Courts: A Comparative Approach. *The Journal of Legal Studies*, *23*(2), 721–47.

Roithmayr, D. (2004). Locked in Segregation. *Virginia Journal of Social Policy & Law*, *12*(2), 197–259.

Rouchier, J., and Tubaro, P. (2011). Can Opinion be Stable in an Open Network with Hierarchy? An Agent-Based Model of the Commercial Court of Paris. *Procedia: Social and Behavioral Sciences*, *10*, 123–31.

Schelling, T.C. (1971). Dynamic Models of Segregation. *Journal of Mathematical Sociology*, *1*(2), 143–86.

Scheutz, M., and Mayer, T. (2016) Combining Agent-Based Modeling with Big Data Methods to Support Architectural and Urban Design. In C. Walloth, E. Gebetsroither-Geringer, F. Atun, and L. Werner (eds), *Understanding Complex Urban Systems* (pp. 15–1). New York: Springer.

Schwartz, A. (2019a) An Agent-Based Model of Judicial Power. *The Journal of Law*, *9*(1), 21–53.

Schwartz, A. (2019b) NetLogo Judicial Review Model. Accessed 23 June 2020 at http://modelingcommons.org/browse/one_model/6039#model_tabs_browse_info.

Squazzoni, F. (2010). The Impact of Agent-Based Models in the Social Sciences after 15 Years of Incursions. *History of Economic Ideas*, *18*(2), 197–233.

Stephenson, M.C. (2003). "When the Devil turns . . .": The Political Foundations of Independent Judicial Review. *The Journal of Legal Studies*, *32*(1), 59–89.

Wilensky, U., and Rand, W. (2015). *An Introduction to Agent-Based Modeling: Modeling Natural, Social, and Engineered Complex Systems with NetLogo.* Cambridge, MA: MIT Press.

15. Analyzing high volumes of German court decisions in an interdisciplinary class of law and computer science students*

Janis Beckedorf, Dirk Hartung and Phillip Sittig

1. INTRODUCTION

Empirical legal research is an area of growing scientific interest. This thriving field aims to provide a more realistic view on law, its effects and options to improve it. The shift to more empirical research is entangled with opening legal studies up to new methods, for example, from sociology, psychology, economics and political science (Boom et al. 2018). As the importance of empirical legal research increases (Leeuw and Schmeets 2016), it becomes more and more important to develop approaches for academic training. On the business side this meets the current transformation of the market for legal services through digitization. So, both from a scientific as well as a practical perspective we concluded that there is a growing want for increased collaboration between computer science and law students in joint projects. Especially as any fruitful collaboration requires a thorough understanding of interdisciplinary methods and tangible expertise in working with members of other professions. Although the idea of empirical legal research was introduced several decades ago, teaching empirical research at law schools is a rather new topic (Cane and Kritzer 2010).

Coding classes in law schools and even extensive non-degree technology programs can merely build a fundamental understanding of technology and

* We would like to thank Chris Biemann, Tjorben Gschwander, Lennart Rönneburg and Tobias Killing for their valuable contribution in particular during the first phase of the project. We would also like to thank Eugen Ruppert for help and guidance throughout the entire project and Evgenia Chabanova, Corinna Coupette, Lauritz Gerlach, Malte Persike, Philipp Sahrmann and Alexander Ulmer for additional support.

code. Without a formal education or several years of practical experience, law students are either incapable of or at least very slow at developing actual applications for practical use cases. As is often experienced in introductory classes on legal technology, many students lack sufficient technological knowledge to even identify possible use cases, let alone to actually conceptualize and build them. They might, we suspected, still be very productive members of interdisciplinary teams if they are capable of communicating their domain-specific needs to software developers. This is all the more relevant as advances in computing led to significant improvement of predictive analytics in recent years. The legal field experiences a rise of quantitative prediction. This offers new opportunities for data literate lawyers to more efficiently and effectively work in the legal field (Katz 2014).

Computer science, on the other hand, is – in particular in the first and second year of studies – heavily loaded with theoretical knowledge. For future software developers, then, this class provides a welcome opportunity to train for real-world scenarios with law students as mock clients. Computer science students are sensitized to differences between their mental models and the ones of their clients. In addition, they encounter future lawyers as enablers and understand the societal function of law better. This helps dismantle barriers and fears of contact with regard to legal issues. From a scientific perspective empirical legal research has the potential to enrich doctrinal research by providing proof of the effects of legal rules and similar concepts (Boom et al. 2018, p. 5–6).

In the beginning, we noticed several drawbacks of the concept of "a legal hackathon". Most of the events we had attended or read about lacked sufficiently capable software developers and very little was built during the actual event. We hoped, however, that – given more time and preparation – a team of junior computer scientists and lawyers could create a useful application. After three weeks of intense work and roughly 150 hours of subsequent refinement, we were not disappointed. The application built by these student teams provides a reliable statistical description of a corpus of roughly 60,000 cases from the Federal Court of Justice (Bundesgerichtshof – BGH), their outcomes, and some factors influencing the latter, including the deciding bodies, previous instances, and judges.[1] In order to enable students to build this application, we had to provide sufficient legal data[2] and develop a course structure[3] that would unlock the students' creative and technical potential.

---

[1] For details see below section 4.
[2] For details see below section 2.
[3] For details see below section 3.

2.   LEGAL DATA IN GERMANY

Sufficient data is a necessary precondition for quantitative analysis of court decisions. However, in Germany, most court decisions are never published. Theoretically, legal data, in particular court decisions, should be widely available. The BGH reaffirmed in 2017 (Bundesgerichtshof, IV AR(VZ) 2/16, 5 April 2017) that German courts are under an obligation to publish their decisions under constitutional law (Bundesverfassungsgericht, 1 BvR 857/15, 14 September 2015) as well as the procedural law principle of transparency pursuant to Articles 169 and 173 of the Courts Constitution Act (Gerichtsverfassungsgesetz; Bundesverwaltungsgericht, 6 C 3/96, 26 February 1997).

In practice, the required anonymization of the decision constitutes a major obstacle to extensive publication, as it is currently done manually. As a consequence, most lower court decisions are only available on demand and on a case-by-case basis. Both the code of criminal and civil procedure contain provisions which aim to provide access to case files or court decisions for third parties. However, all of these require a substantial interest. Merely commercial interests usually do not satisfy this criterion. Courts and parties to a legal procedure still can (and frequently do) provide legal publishers with decisions on a voluntary basis, often in exchange for money. This has led to a number of commercial and non-commercial databases for court decisions.

The most comprehensive databases of German court decisions are Juris[4] and Beck-Online,[5] both proprietary offerings. A majority stake in the former is held by the Federal Republic of Germany, with minority shareholders Éditions Lefebvre Sarrut (ELS), the state Saarland, the Federal Bar Association and various other organizations. The latter is wholly owned by the private publisher Verlag C.H. Beck. They jointly contain slightly more than 2 million ordinary (i.e. civil and criminal) court decisions for the entire German judicial history. However, in 2017 alone, the ordinary courts decided 2,082,867 cases overall.[6] Free sources are even more limited, but only these provide unrestricted access for independent statistical analysis. The most notable free databases

---

[4]   https://www.juris.de.

[5]   https://beck-online.beck.de.

[6]   BGH: http://www.bundesgerichtshof.de/DE/Service/Statistik/statistik_node. html (last accessed 29 May 2020); Lower Courts: https://www.destatis.de/DE/ Themen/Staat/Justiz-Rechtspflege/Tabellen/gerichtsverfahren.html (last accessed 29 May 2020).

are a joint portal for the highest federal courts[7] and the website of the BGH.[8]

The available databases of court decisions, including those of the BGH, have several major drawbacks when used for statistical analysis (Coupette and Fleckner 2018). First, the databases contain only a selection of decisions. Most commonly, decisions are filtered by "relevance". This selection makes a statistical analysis of decisions problematic, since detailed standards of the selection process are not published. Furthermore, it is most likely that these standards vary depending on the database and even within a database. An example of the low availability ratio is given in a study regarding the XI senate of the BGH: it estimates that the ratio of published decisions in Juris of the years 2006 until 2016 varied between 9.4 percent and 31.2 percent (Coupette and Fleckner 2018).

Second, those free databases which can be used for own statistical analyses often cover only recent decisions. The website of the BGH, for example, contains only judgments rendered after 1 January 2000. A similar limitation applies to the joint portal for the highest federal courts, which only covers decisions since 2010.

However, some developments give hope that more decisions might become available in the future. On 5 July 2017, the German parliament passed a law that introduced digital court files.[9] Digital court files will not necessarily lead to a higher rate of published decisions. However, they may lower the effort needed to publish decisions and thereby improve the chances of more decisions being published. In addition, one of the authors is part of a multidisciplinary research group, consisting of three industry partners, Bucerius Law School, and the University of Hamburg, which is currently preparing a three year research project to address data protection law issues and explore distributed human-in-the-loop training of machine learning models to be used for anonymization.

---

[7]　https://www.rechtsprechung-im-internet.de.

[8]　https://www.bundesgerichtshof.de.

[9]　BGBl. I 2017, 2208–29, http://www.bgbl.de/xaver/bgbl/start.xav?startbk=Bundesanzeiger_BGBl&jumpTo=bgbl117s2208.pdf (last accessed 29 May 2020).

3. A CONCEPT FOR THE COLLABORATION BETWEEN COMPUTER SCIENCE AND LAW STUDENTS

Bucerius Law School in Hamburg, Germany provides a number of interdisciplinary classes with a focus on technology, computer science, and statistics, the completion of which leads to a technology certificate. These classes and the certificate are offered as part of the Bachelor of Laws program (undergraduate).[10] As a part of this curriculum, Bucerius Law School and the University of Hamburg offer a joint class for students in computer science and law to gain practical experience in interdisciplinary collaboration. For the computer science students, the class is embedded in a software development project necessary for their Bachelor of Science in Informatics.[11] The class is part of a greater collaboration between both institutions, which includes research projects and interdisciplinary master theses.

During the second iteration of the class in 2017, 12 students – 6 of each discipline – participated. This number has risen to 14 in 2018, reflecting the general growth of the collaboration and rise in student interest. The law students' professional education varied from participants in their first trimester of law school up to students about to take the bar exam,[12] with a slight tendency towards attracting more advanced students. Computer science students can take the class either in their second or third year. At this point in time, they will have undergone substantial theoretical training, but have had little exposure to practical application development. A majority of them, however, has already had practical programming experience – either as part of their side jobs, or as a hobby interest. It is important to note that typically neither group of students has been exposed extensively to members of the other domain in their professional education. Students may have taken an introductory class, but never actually collaborated with lawyers or software developers.

The class runs for a total of three weeks, at the end of which the students should have completed a functioning web application of practical use. On the first day, law students, who – at this point in time – have spent about one month discussing ideas on a weekly basis, pitch their ideas to their computer science peers. If the latter are interested and select the

---

[10]   https://www.law-school.de/studium/jurastudium/ueber-das-studium/zusatz zertifikate#c20150 (last accessed 29 May 2020).

[11]   https://www.inf.uni-hamburg.de/en/studies/bachelor/inf.html (29 May 2020).

[12]   This term refers to the German "*Staatsexamen*" (first state exam), which concludes German law degrees and qualifies for professional training.

project, they instantly start working in their groups, loosely supervised by PhD students or postdocs of both fields. The following three weeks are spent writing code and attending daily or twice daily SCRUM meetings to discuss project progress and possible issues. Weekly presentations are an opportunity to share useful resources and findings among all groups. Apart from these mandatory meetings, students are free in their time management. Typically, computer science students start with a meeting in the morning, spend the rest of the morning coding, and meet with some of their law counterparts over lunch. There they discuss any functional issues or questions concerning legal mechanisms. One or two of the law students, typically those with the most advanced interest or even programming skills, spend the afternoon on the computer science campus and discuss their input with the development team and – depending on their technical expertise – clean data, annotate training materials for machine learning models, or even search for possible technology solutions on the web, mainly in popular technology communities like http://www.github.com or https://stackoverflow.com/.

A rather unique or law-specific challenge – the reasons for which we have described above – is the availability of data in a suitable form for analysis. As data architecture decisions typically have to be made early on, students need to find reliable and legally usable data sources within the first days. In both instances of the class so far, students decided to use the online archive of the BGH.[13] This is due to it being available under a suitable license and, while there is no feature for bulk downloads, it is possible to scrape the website, offering a good coding exercise to get started.

Intensive user experience testing and feedback starts in week two at the latest. For this purpose, law students test parts of the applications and provide specific feedback, which is implemented on a tight schedule. A new version is tested on the spot, introducing students to actual rapid application development (Martin 1991). While performing tests, however, students tend to find more than just design glitches or functionality problems: law students adopt the rather systematic test methodology and often discover inconsistencies in the legal data or the way legal knowledge is handled, for example, cases are formatted or parties are addressed. At the same time, computer science students learn that law is far less formalized than they often believe and start to think about ways to handle law-specific irregularities in their applications.

At the end of the three-week collaboration, students present their

---

[13]   It is available under https://www.bundesgerichtshof.de/DE/Entscheidungen/entscheidungen_node.html (last accessed 29 May 2020).

learnings regarding both the computer science and legal domain and give a live demonstration for their peers. In particular the law students are invited to ask critical questions, and a joint discussion of possible further developments follows. Students write a report explaining their application with an emphasis on the technology stack and the exchange with the other discipline in the weeks after. While the class is graded on a scale of 1.00 to 6.00 (with 1.0 being the best grade) for computer science students, law students can either pass or fail.

The research purpose of this project class is to determine whether computer science and law students could develop a joint language and actually build usable software in a short time frame. In both iterations of the class, students were able to build usable web applications, which performed useful legal tasks such as guiding through an application for legal aid, extracting valuable information from legal texts as well as analyzing and visualizing data from court decisions. To create a better understanding of the results of this class, one of its projects – LawStatsInAction (LSIA) – is described in detail below.

4.   LAWSTATSINACTION – LSIA

4.1   Aims

LSIA was one of the 2018 projects. While we have described the general class design above,[14] this section contains the details of the development process of LSIA. The initial approach was to extract information from all cases of the BGH, which are published on the court's website. This information could then be used to give an overview of the published decisions and conduct statistical analysis. Therefore, extracted named entities such as the judges, the deciding judicial body at the BGH (which are called senates) and previous instances, as well as docket numbers and dates were extracted. These were extended by a classification of whether the appeal to the BGH was successful. The final step was to present a description of the analyzed data and search for notable statistical properties.

4.2   Methodology

The development took place in two phases. The first phase – which spanned the duration of the three-week class – was spent developing the

---

[14]   For details see above section 3.

original idea and building a prototype. The second phase of about 150 hours was spent after the official class to refine the methodology, extensively test the approach, mass scale to the entire data set and compile the actual statistics. The technical details of phase one have been published in a separate paper (Ruppert et al. 2018). The details for phase two follow below.

Students chose to work with the BGH data set, which contained roughly 60,000 decisions in PDF format at this point. After an initial discussion about the desired functionality, students quickly moved to developing a data model, which could fulfill all requirements. This determined the information to be extracted: judges, docket numbers, previous instances, decision dates, the deciding senate at the BGH and the ultimate result, that is, whether or not the lower court decision was reversed (i.e. the appeal was successful) or upheld (i.e. the appeal was unsuccessful).

Next, the corpus was downloaded using a Python web scraper. The data needed substantial cleaning and reformatting to be fit for annotation, for which we used preliminary works from the first iteration of the class.[15] Law students then annotated 200 decisions, before realizing that the process had to be improved if a sufficiently high amount of decisions was to be annotated at the end of the two-week annotation period. Pre-annotations based on regular expressions and dictionaries proved to be the most efficient way to reduce the time spent per decision. Expert input was still indispensable as the pre-annotations led to false positives, annotating irrelevant docket numbers, courts and dates. In addition, the task of manually annotating several hundred decisions had another educational benefit for law students. Once confronted with their own inaccuracies and the fatigue from uniform, repetitive tasks, the students seemed observably more sensitive to humans as the source of errors in data handling. Moreover, as students realized the vast amount of data they were working with, they started to develop an initial understanding for key concepts of quantitative methods such as representativeness and bias.

At the end of the first phase, we concluded that the result of a court decision could reliably and on scale be determined using machine learning techniques (Ruppert et al. 2018). Due to time constraints some obvious improvements could not be made during the class. We decided to eliminate these constraints and continue the development among the authors. As the focus was on iterative, methodical improvement, we gave up any front-end development. In addition, we eliminated the machine learning component

---

[15] In 2017 one team focused on an efficient pipeline for data processing, see https://github.com/bigabig/lawnet (last accessed 29 May 2020).

Table 15.1   Evaluation of appeal outcome classification

Class	Precision	Recall	F1
Success	0.87	0.95	0.91
Failure	0.92	0.92	0.92
Miscellaneous	0.62	0.36	0.46

Table 15.2   Confusion matrix of appeal outcome classification

	Success	Failure	Miscellaneous
Success	78	4	0
Failure	4	109	5
Miscellaneous	8	6	8

for the information extraction and relied on rule-based approaches, while the result qualification remained machine learning-based. Given the limited scope of the task and its educational benefit, we developed a tailored information extraction engine with minimal dependencies in Java.[16] This allowed us to take into account the position of individual entities within the document. As German court decisions adhere to – albeit a limited extent of – layout guidelines, this opened a new dimension of information. While dictionary-based extraction, for example, finds all courts mentioned and their decisions referenced in a judgment, only the ones in the section containing the actual decision are relevant. As these sections can be identified due to formal requirements, a combination of these two rules allows a high rate of accurately identified entities.

We trained the model with 1769 annotated decisions and evaluated it with a blind set of 222 decisions. Table 15.1 indicates the overall performance of the machine learning model on the blind set. Table 15.2 contains a confusion matrix for the classifier, demonstrating that successes and failures are equally likely to be erroneously classified as miscellaneous. As we therefore found no evidence that the classifier overly skews the results, we used this model to classify the entire corpus and performed a statistical analysis of the results.

---

[16]   Source code is available under a permissive license at https://github.com/LawStats/LawStatsInAction (last accessed 29 May 2020).

4.3   Statistical Description of the Corpus

After the description of the class design and the technical methodology, one might wonder whether the transformation of unstructured text data for 56,288 court decisions into a structured form in a database is actually useful. To prove that developing and adapting this tool is a worthwhile endeavor, we subsequently provide a short statistical description and point to some interesting findings. Before we go into detail, it is important to issue a caveat: the decisions analyzed for this chapter have been selected on the sole ground of their being available. As explained above, the BGH database is neither complete nor demonstrably representative. While we stand by our findings with the limitations set forth, they cannot be generalized without further research. For the purposes of this chapter (which are to illustrate research methods and to call for action with regard to access to information), this means no harm. However, our findings should not be used as the basis of policy decisions at this point in time.

4.3.1   The population
From a total of 56,288 decisions we were able to extract docket numbers in 56,011 cases. As we rely upon docket numbers – which are explicit and specific to a judicial body – to determine the area of law, we excluded cases without docket numbers. From a total of 56,011 decisions, we were able to determine the decision outcome in 53,573 cases. In total, 24,658 or 46.03 percent of the appeals to the BGH were successful, leaving 28,915 or 53.97 percent unsuccessful appeals. The difference of 14.56 percentage points between civil law cases with 40.99 percent of successful appeals and criminal law cases with 55.55 percent points to factors beyond coincidence (e.g. different procedural laws and so on) influencing the outcome.

4.3.2   Temporal analysis
Decisions are not equally distributed among the days of the week with civil courts favoring Thursdays (38.12 percent) and criminal courts Tuesdays (35.16 percent) while a total of 88.13 percent of the decisions are handed down between these days. Data shows that also within the respective area of law, the day of the week varies substantially depending on the deciding senate.

If grouped by weekday, the data shows interesting patterns as for civil law matters success rates vary between 52.27 percent on Fridays and 29.20 percent on Mondays. For criminal law matters, success rates vary between 58.13 percent on Thursdays and 46.25 percent on Mondays.[17]

---

[17]   Disregarding the rates for the weekend as the total numbers of decisions

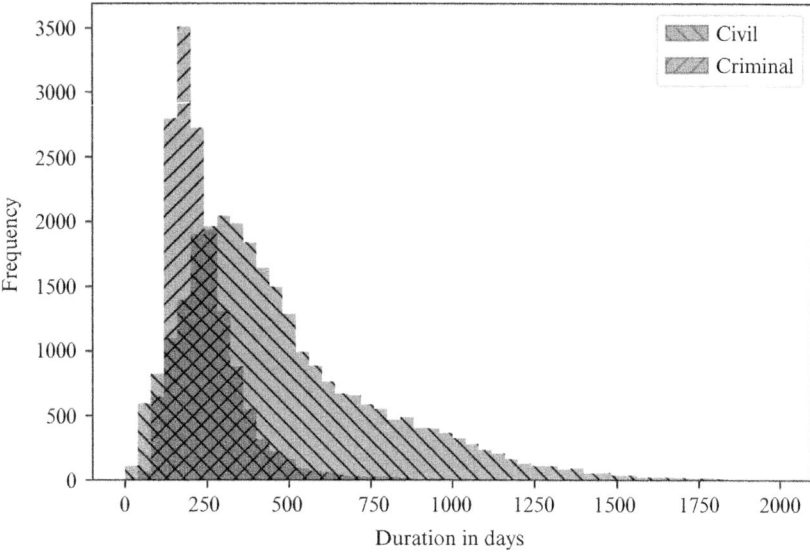

Figure 15.1   Comparison of duration of proceedings between civil and criminal law matters

However, as success rates also vary depending on the senate[18] in civil matters between as little as 27.03 percent up to 57.52 percent and in criminal matters between 42.62 percent and 64.55 percent, it is questionable whether the day of the week actually influences the success rate. Still, the majority of senates tests negative for independence between appeal success and weekday so that either the day of week or external factors affect the success rate.

An exploration of the duration of proceedings before the BGH yields an interesting observation. As shown in Figure 15.1, criminal law cases are handled faster and their duration varies less (193.79 days standard deviation) than for civil law matters (359.07 days standard deviation). Median duration for civil procedures of 400 days is substantially higher than 211 days for criminal procedures.

---

handed down on these days is too low (0.05 percent of the decisions) and thereby prone to measurement errors or coincidence.

[18] A senate is the deciding body of a court. Another term in the context of lower courts would be a chamber.

4.3.3 Previous instance

Success rates also vary in a similar way depending on the lower court that the case is appealed from. Among the 24 Higher Regional Court (Oberlandesgericht) districts between 37.13 percent and 50.65 percent of civil law decisions are overturned by the BGH in our dataset.[19] The unweighted average of all Higher Regional Courts is 43.50 percent with a standard deviation of 4.01 percentage points in civil law matters. In criminal law, the 318 detected previous instance courts show an even wider variation. However, the total number of decisions by the individual court can become very low, so that this might be caused by coincidence.

We wondered whether due to authority and custom, Higher Regional Courts geographically closer to the BGH were more in line with its judicial reasoning and, therefore, their decisions were less likely to be reversed. When looking at appeal success rates grouped by Higher Regional Court, the table is led by courts further away from Karlsruhe,[20] while the bottom is made up of courts in geographic proximity. This can be tested with a simple linear regression analysis. Figure 15.2 shows that the success rate increases by 0.01 percentage points per kilometer from the BGH with an intercept of 0.39 percent and a standard error of 3.30 percentage points. The coefficient of determination of $r^2 = 0.35$ indicates a moderate correlation between distance of the Higher Regional Court from the BGH and appeal success in civil law matters.[21]

4.3.4 Judges

On the level of individual judges participating in the decision, success rates vary between 74.69 percent and 17.07 percent for civil law decisions between 74.88 percent and 32.89 percent if only judges with at least 100 detected appeal outcomes are taken into account and special senates[22] are disregarded. In the next step, we wondered whether individual judges have an impact on their senates' decisions. We therefore tested whether the number of successful and unsuccessful decisions of the respective senate

---

[19]   Due to a particularity in criminal procedure law (*"Sprungrevision"*), most BGH decisions in criminal law deal with lower regional court judgments so that there is only a small number of Higher Regional Court (Oberlandesgericht) decisions on appeal.

[20]   Karlsruhe in the state of Baden-Wurtemberg is the seat of all but one senate of the BGH – for that senate we calculated distances to its seat in Leipzig.

[21]   Again, criminal procedural law (see footnote 19) leads to so few decisions from the Higher Regional Court (385 in total or 2.08 percent) that a regression analysis would not yield any meaningful insights.

[22]   These are deciding bodies with a different structure and lay judges such as senates for agricultural or professional law, which we excluded from further analysis.

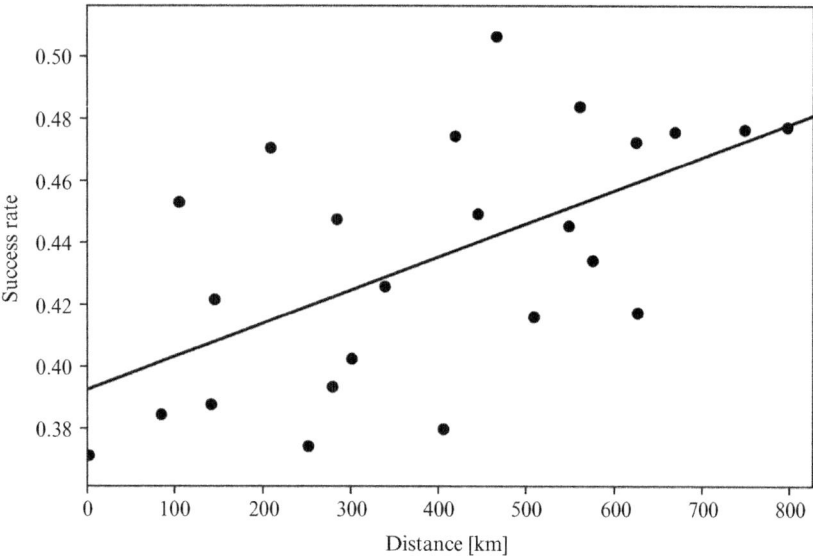

Figure 15.2   Linear regression analysis of success/distance

is independent from the number of successful and unsuccessful decisions of the individual judge. To fulfill the χ^2 test requirement of independent samples, we compare each judge's decisions only to those decisions of the respective senate without his or her participation. Applying an α-level of 0.01 and examining only judges, who decided enough cases for a chi square test, the data indicates for 35 judges that their participation significantly influences their senates' rate of successful appeals with an effect size of at least 0.1, the maximum Cramer's V being 0.24. Eighteen of them produce higher, 17 lower rates of successful appeals.

Claims that judges in senates with a higher case load are more likely to reject an appeal are falsified by our findings. At least in our dataset, caseload and appeal success show no significant correlation for either civil or criminal law cases on senate level.

5.   CONCLUSION

It is tempting to either confirm or rebuff presumed truisms about the quality of certain lower courts or the attitudes and decision patterns of BGH senates or judges. Yet, as mentioned above, the current dataset does not permit scientifically sound statements to this end. What our chapter demonstrates incontrovertibly, however, is that computational legal studies are easy to both understand and teach and can generate reliable and important insights into current jurisprudence. To date, little has been done to incorporate these approaches into legal curricula. While this needs to change, it also provides astounding opportunities for scientific discovery, as vast parts of the legal domain are uncharted territory in these regards. Most importantly, a broader availability of legal data, structured and unstructured, will likely spur extensive further research and unlock valuable knowledge about the law.

The data set as well as the Python notebook containing the statistical analysis can be found in the repository,[23] and an up-to-date version can be produced from the BGH website using our fully functional pipeline. This allows for a study of the corpus over time, potentially on a yearly or bi-yearly basis. Further research could also focus on improving the classifier and information extraction. A more detailed error analysis and adjustment for information extraction would probably lead to significant improvements.[24] Another possible way forward would be the construction of subsets in the data, to which different classifiers/extraction methods could be applied.[25] While exceeding the scope of this chapter, the rule-based nature of the extraction should be easily adaptable. On the machine learning side, unsurprisingly, an increase in training data in general and a refinement of the categories of "miscellaneous" in particular would likely yield better results.

One further approach for future statistical research into the corpus could use binomial testing, in which any given subset of decisions with a certain criterion (e.g. from a particular senate, judge or in a given time frame) would be compared against a multitude of artificially drawn samples from the population without said criterion. This could potentially allow statements on the influence of these factors, provided that success and failure could generally be treated as equally likely.

For the statistical description we have repeatedly used research community standard levels of significance of $\alpha = 0.01$ or $\alpha = 0.05$ to account for measurement errors and coincidence (e.g. for the χ^2-test above), which makes our results understandable. We do, however, know at least an

---

[23] See https://github.com/LawStats/LawStatsInAction (last accessed 29 May 2020).

[24] One such improvement could come from named entity disambiguation, for example of judge's names like "Fischer", all three of whom are currently counted as one.

[25] An exploratory test using only those decisions, for which we could extract a full set of information, has shown significant improvement in the classification results.

approximation for the measurement error concerning the classification from the evaluation of the machine learning model.[26] It could therefore be argued that the influence of a measurement error is known and does not equal 0.01 or 0.05. This raises the question whether the accepted levels of significance can at all be used and, if not, which better value to use for α. The influence of measurement errors on statistical tests is non-trivial, which was shown for linear regression analyses (Bloch 1978). While beyond the scope of this chapter, the problem of known measurement errors from machine learning models and their influence on subsequent statistical analysis can be generalized and should be examined in more detail.

Given its nature as a first approach to the topic in Germany, this chapter focused only on a small selection of extracted information. Hence, further research may involve the extraction and statistical analysis of other entities. As the cost and duration of litigation typically concern parties, further research could focus on temporal and financial influences on the success of appeals. While this chapter mainly deals with the outcome of cases before the BGH, it might be fruitful to look for relationships between the area of law, the geographic and temporal origin of the case, the amount in dispute, and its duration.

While the above might prove useful to illustrate possible application of statistical analysis of legal corpora this chapter also provides an interesting perspective on training future legal data scientists from educational backgrounds in both law and computer science. A hands-on and project-oriented elaboration of concepts at the intersection of law and computer science can provide valuable skills to participating students. In this regard it differs from shorter projects like legal hackathons and is more suitable for a higher education setting.

We conceptualized this chapter as a hybrid between a description of the pedagogical approach and a proof of concept for statistical description and analysis of results provided by machine learning classification. We intend to continue our interdisciplinary cooperation to provide more in-depth analyses in the future.

REFERENCES

Bloch, Farell E. 1978. "Measurement Error and Statistical Significance of an Independent Variable". *The American Statistician* 32 (1), 26–7, http://dx.doi.org /10.1080/00031305.1978.10479239.

---

[26]   For details regarding errors see above Table 15.2.

Boom, Willem H. van, Pieter Desmet and Peter Mascini. 2018. *Empirical Legal Research in Action.* Cheltenham, UK and Northampton, MA, USA: Edward Elgar Publishing, https://doi.org/10.4337/9781785362750.

Bundesgerichtshof, IV AR(VZ) 2/16.

Bundesverfassungsgericht, 1 BvR 857/15.

Bundesverwaltungsgericht, 6 C 3/96.

Cane, Peter, and Herbert M. Kritzer. 2010. "Introduction". In Peter Cane and Herbert M. Kritzer (eds), *The Oxford Handbook of Empirical Legal Research* (pp. 1–7). New York: Oxford University Press.

Coupette, Corinna, and Andreas M. Fleckner. 2018. "Quantitative Rechtswissenschaft – Sammlung, Analyse Und Kommunikation Juristischer Daten". *JuristenZeitung (JZ)* 73 (8): 379–89. http://dx.doi.org/10.1628/jz-2018-0020.

Katz, D. 2014. "The MIT School of Law: A Perspective on Legal Education in the 21st Century. *University of Illinois Law Review* 2014 (5), 1431–72.

Leeuw, Franciscus L., and Hans Schmeets. 2016. *Empirical Legal Research: A Guidance Book for Lawyers, Legislators and Regulators.* Cheltenham, UK and Northampton, MA, USA: Edward Elgar Publishing.

Martin, James. 1991. *Rapid Application Development,* New York: Macmillan.

Ruppert, Eugen, Dirk Hartung, Phillip Sittig, Tjorben Gschwander, Lennart Rönneburg, Tobias Killing and Chris Biemann. 2018. "LawStats: Large-Scale German Court Decision Evaluation Using Web Service Classifiers". Paper presented at Second Ifip Tc 5, Tc 8/Wg 8.4, 8.9, Tc 12/Wg 12.9 International Cross-Domain Conference, Cd-Make 2018, Hamburg, Germany, 27–30 August 2018, https://dx.doi.org/10.1007/978-3-319-99740-7_14.

Index

academic articles 67, 70, 71, 73
academic evaluation system 138
academic fraud 21
accountability 184, 261
accounting for legal values 6, 190–213
    artificial intelligence (AI) and law
        models of reasoning 196–8
    jurisprudential models of reasoning
        193–5, 197–8
    model-comparison or ablation
        studies 192, 197–8
    see also value judgment-based
        argumentative prediction
        (VJAP) program
accuracy metric 222
adjustable parameter 317–18, 323
administrative law 128, 130, 131, 232
agent-based modeling (ABM) of
    judicial review 7–8, 312–25
    adjustable parameter 317–18, 323
    avoider decision rule 318–19, 320–23
    bottom-up simulations 312, 324–5
    court curbing 321–2, 323–4
    default decision rule 318, 320–22
    definition and uses 312–17
    how it works 317–20
    individual strategic choices 316
    model extension 322–4
    parameter sweep 321
    procedures 312, 314
    systemic effects or patterns 312
    things to notice 320–22
    time series (or steps) 313
Alexander, C.S. 4, 95–121
Alexy, R. 195, 196, 206
algorithms
    Diff 15
    hierarchical clustering 24
    Hyperlink-Induced Topic Search
        (HITS) 272, 286, 287, 288
    law 154

    selection 286
    suspense 39, 45
    see also community detection
        algorithms
Alibaba (China) 124, 129–30, 141
AlphaZero program 248
Alschner, W. 3, 9–26, 30
"always-on" big data systems 154,
    155–6, 161
Amazon 129
American Association of Law
    Libraries 97
analogical reasoning 194–5
analogy-warranting rule (AWR) 191,
    195
anonymization 330–31
Ant Financial (China) 129
Application Programming Interface
    (API) 101, 271
Area under the Curve (AUC) metric
    222
artificial intelligence (AI) 3, 6
    accounting for legal values 190, 192,
        195, 213
    automated classification of modes
        or moral reasoning in judicial
        decisions 89
    China 124, 129, 130–33
    and law models of reasoning 196–8
    legal analytics and court data access
        107
    legal cognition 218, 233–4
    rule by rules 238, 240, 242, 248,
        260
    surveillance chill measurement
        impacts at scale 146–7, 150,
        154
Artificial Intelligence and Law journal
    243
artificial neural networks (ANN) 152,
    240, 248, 249, 250–60